T0258160

Advanced Concepts and Applications
of Fuzzy Logic

Advanced Concepts and Applications of Fuzzy Logic

Edited by **Frank West**

New York

Published by NY Research Press,
23 West, 55th Street, Suite 816,
New York, NY 10019, USA
www.nyresearchpress.com

Advanced Concepts and Applications of Fuzzy Logic
Edited by Frank West

International Standard Book Number: 978-1-63238-010-4 (Hardback)

Printed in the United States of America.

Contents

Preface

The advanced concepts and applications of fuzzy logic are elucidated in this comprehensive book. This book presents novel perceptions and ideas of Fuzzy Logic Control for their implementation in growth of robotics and intelligent devices. This book discusses three important aspects; Robotics and Electrical Machines, Intelligent Control Systems with various applications, and New Fuzzy Logic Concepts and Theories. It will be handy to practitioners, engineers and students who are keen to gain knowledge about this subject.

Various studies have approached the subject by analyzing it with a single perspective, but the present book provides diverse methodologies and techniques to address this field. This book contains theories and applications needed for understanding the subject from different perspectives. The aim is to keep the readers informed about the progresses in the field; therefore, the contributions were carefully examined to compile novel researches by specialists from across the globe.

Indeed, the job of the editor is the most crucial and challenging in compiling all chapters into a single book. In the end, I would extend my sincere thanks to the chapter authors for their profound work. I am also thankful for the support provided by my family and colleagues during the compilation of this book.

Editor

Part 1

Robotics and Electrical Machines

Fuzzy Control System Design and Analysis for Completely Restrained Cable-Driven Manipulators

Bin Zi[1,2]
[1]School of Mechanical and Electrical Engineering,
China University of Mining and Technology, Xuzhou, Jiangsu,
[2]The State Key Laboratory of Fluid Power and Mechatronic Systems,
Zhejiang University, Hangzhou, Zhejiang
China

1. Introduction

Cable-driven manipulators, referred to as the overhead crane and rotary crane are widely used in the manufacturing and construction industries in order to move heavy objects as illustrated in Fig. 1. Cable-driven manipulators are relatively simple form, with multiple cables attached to a mobile platform or end-effector. The end-effector may be equipped with various attachments, including hooks, cameras, robotic grippers and so on. Cable-driven manipulators have several advantages over rigid-link mechanisms, including the following: 1) remote location of motors and controls; 2) rapid deployability; 3) potentially large workspaces; 4) high load capacity; 5) reliability (Borgstrom et al., 2009; Zi et al., 2008). For the preceding reasons, cable-driven manipulators have received attention and have been recently studied since 1980s (Behzadipour & Khajepour, 2005; Ghasemi et al., 2008; Motoji, 2004; Oh & Agrawal, 2005; Pham et al., 2006).

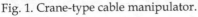

Fig. 1. Crane-type cable manipulator.

Cable-driven manipulators can be classified as either incompletely restrained or completely restrained (Bosscher & Ebert-Uphoff, 2006). Cable-driven manipulators are underconstrained if it relies on gravity to determine the pose (position and orientation) of the end-effector, while they are completely restrained if the pose of the end-effector is completely determined by the lengths of the cables. As you know, dynamics is a huge field of study devoted to studying the forces required to cause motion. In order to accelerate the robot from rest, glide at a constant end-effector velocity, and finally decelerate to a stop, a complex set of torque functions must be applied by the joint actuators (Craig, 2005). The motivation for this paper comes directly from the design, mechanics analysis, and control of completely restrained cable-driven manipulators (CRCM) with 3 Degrees of Freedom (DOF). As demonstrated in (Anupoju et al., 2005), servomechanism dynamics constitute an important component of the complete robotic dynamics. Therefore, the dynamics of the servomotors and its gears must be modeled for further control design. However, the literature on the CRCM system including the actuator dynamics is sparse.

CRCM systems are multivariable in nature. The control of the multivariable systems is a complicated problem due to the coupling that exists between the control inputs and the outputs, and the multivariable systems are nonlinear and uncertain, therefore, their control problem becomes more challenging (Chien, 2008; Yousef et al., 2009). In order to achieve a high-precision performance, the controller of the CRCM must effectively and accurately manipulate the motion trajectory. It is well known that up until now, a conventional proportional-integral-derivative (PID) controller has been widely used in industry due to its simple control structure, ease of design, and inexpensive cost (Reznik et al., 2000; Visioli, 2001). However, the CRCM is a multivariable nonlinear coupling dynamic system which suffers from structured and unstructured uncertainties such as payload variation, external disturbances, etc. As a result, the PID controller cannot yield a good control performance for this type of control system. For dealing with nonlinear effects, various control algorithms have been proposed. Among them, adaptive control and fuzzy logic system algorithm draw much attention due to the applicability for typically highly nonlinear systems (Chang, 2000; Soyguder & Alli, 2010; Su & Stepanenko, 1994). The idea of fuzzy set and fuzzy control is introduced by Zadeh in an attempt to control systems that are structurally difficult to model (Feng, 2006; Zadeh, 1965). Fuzzy controllers have been well accepted in control engineering practice. The major advantages in all these fuzzy-based control schemes are that the developed controllers can be employed to deal with increasingly complex systems to implement the controller without any precise knowledge of the structure of entire dynamic model. As a knowledge-based approach, the fuzzy controller usually depends on linguistics-based reasoning in design. However, even though a system is well defined mathematically, the fuzzy controller is still preferred by control engineers since it is relatively more understandable whereas expert knowledge can be incorporated conveniently. Recently, the fuzzy controller of nonlinear systems was studied by many authors and has also been extensively adopted in adaptive control of robot manipulators (Chen et al., 1996; Labiod et al., 2005; Purwar et al., 2005; Yoo & Ham, 1998). It has been proven that adaptive fuzzy control is a powerful technique and being increasingly applied in the discipline of systems control, especially when the controlled system has uncertainties and highly nonlinearities (Yu et al., 2011).

This chapter is organized as follows. First, the mechanical system is designed in Section 2. Then, modeling and analysis of the cable-driven manipulator are described in Section 3. Section 4 presents the developed systematic approach for the adaptive fuzzy controller design. Results and discussions are presented in Section 5. Finally, concluding remarks are provided in Section 6.

2. Mechanical design

The CRCM suspends an end-effector (clog) by four cables and restrains all motion degrees of freedom for the object using the cables and gravitational force when the end-effector moves within the workspace. In the design, of each cable in the CRCM, one end is connected to the end-effector, the other end rolls through a pulley fixed on the top of the relative pillar and then is fed into a servo mechanism, with which cable length can be altered. The design of CRCM follows a built-up modular system, as illustrated in Fig.2. The system comprises several components: servo motor, belt pulley drive mechanism, speed reducer, girder, windlass, cable pillar, cable, end-effector, and so on.

Reliability, long-distance transmission, high speed and precision are paramount for the CRCM design. The structure of the CRCM is shown in Fig.3, and the end-effector is driven by four sets of servomechanism. Belts are looped over pulleys. In a two pulley system, the belt can either drive the pulleys in the same direction. As a source of motion, a conveyor belt is one application where the belt is adapted to continually carry a load between two distant points. Typically, gears and elastic drive belts are applied to transmit motion.

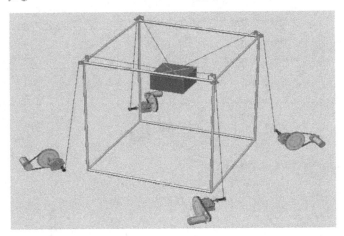

Fig. 2. Model of the CRCM.

3. Modeling and analysis

A simple schematic of the CRCM representing the coordinate systems is shown in Fig. 4. With the bottom of the pillar corresponding to the point B_3 as the origin, a Cartesian coordinate system is established. The end-effector is predigested as a particle whose location coordinates are $A(x,y,z)$, and the distance between each pulley center whose coordinates are $B_i(x_i,y_i,z_i)$ and the end-effector is $l_i(i=1,2,3,4)$. Four pillars have the same height and are arrayed in a rectangular on the ground, whose deformation in movement is ignored. In order to simplify the calculation, the cable is treated as a kind of massless rigid body, which has no deformation, and can only sustain tension.

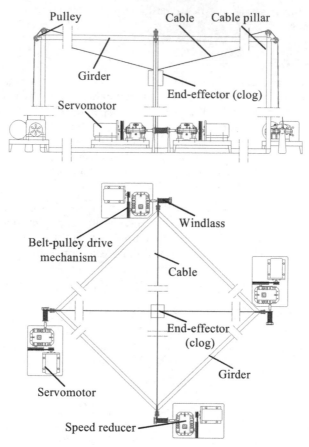

Fig. 3. Mechanical structure of the CRCM

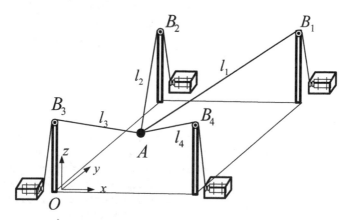

Fig. 4. Structure model of the CRCM

The relationship between the cable length l_i and the end-effector location $A(x,y,z)$, can be easily obtained as follows:

$$\begin{cases} l_1 = \sqrt{(x-x_1)^2 + (y-y_1)^2 + (z-z_1)^2} \\ l_2 = \sqrt{(x-x_2)^2 + (y-y_2)^2 + (z-z_2)^2} \\ l_3 = \sqrt{(x-x_3)^2 + (y-y_3)^2 + (z-z_3)^2} \\ l_4 = \sqrt{(x-x_4)^2 + (y-y_4)^2 + (z-z_4)^2} \end{cases} \tag{1}$$

The forward kinematic equations can be found by solving (1) for (x,y,z), which results in the following:

$$\begin{cases} x = (l_1^2 - l_2^2 + x_2^2 - x_1^2)/2(x_2 - x_1) \\ y = (l_2^2 - l_3^2 + y_3^2 - y_2^2)/2(y_3 - y_2) \\ z = -\sqrt{l_i^2 - (x-x_i)^2 - (y-y_i)^2} + z_i \end{cases} \tag{2}$$

As the pillars are arrayed in a rectangular on the base, according to the geometric relationship, the geometric constraint of the cable length is calculated as

$$l_4^2 + l_2^2 = l_1^2 + l_3^2 \tag{3}$$

The general dynamic equations of motion can be derived from the Lagrangian method. In the model, the end-effector is assumed to act as a point mass and the cable is treated as a kind of massless rigid body. As a result, the kinetic energy, K, and the potential energy, P, of the end-effector can be written in Cartesian coordinates as

$$K = \frac{1}{2}m(\dot{x}^2 + \dot{y}^2 + \dot{z}^2) \tag{4}$$

$$P = mgz \tag{5}$$

where m is mass of end-effector, g is acceleration of gravity.

The cable lengths, l_1, l_2, l_3 and l_4, are directly controlled by rotating the winch to reel the cable in or let it out, therefore, it is desirable to regard the cable lengths as the variables. By substituting the forward kinematic equations (2) into the kinetic energy and potential energy shown in Eqs. (4) and (5), respectively, the Lagrange's Equation can be written in the following form

$$\frac{d}{dt}(\frac{\partial K}{\partial \dot{q}_i}) - \frac{\partial K}{\partial q_i} + \frac{\partial P}{\partial q_i} = Q_i \tag{6}$$

where and the variables, q_i (for $i = 1,2,3,4$), the generalized forces, Q_i, respectively, can be expressed as

$$q_i = \begin{bmatrix} l_1 & l_2 & l_3 & l_4 \end{bmatrix}^T \tag{7}$$

$$Q_i = \begin{bmatrix} -\tau_1/r_1 & -\tau_2/r_2 & -\tau_3/r_3 & -\tau_4/r_4 \end{bmatrix}^T \tag{8}$$

The windlass torques, τ_1, τ_2, τ_3 and τ_4, are the control inputs r_1, r_2, r_3 and r_4, is the radius of the windlass.

Given the equations of motion shown above, using the assumptions along with various substitutions and algebraic manipulations of the CRCM derived, the dynamic equation of the CRCM can be expressed as

$$D(q)\ddot{q} + C(q,\dot{q}) + \tau_d = \tau \tag{9}$$

where $D(q) \in \mathbb{R}^{4\times4}$ is the inertia matrix which is symmetric positive define, $C(q,\dot{q}) \in \mathbb{R}^4$ is a nonlinear Coriolis/centripetal/gravity vector terms, $\tau_d \in \mathbb{R}^4$ represents the disturbance which is bounded, and $\tau \in \mathbb{R}^4$ is the input torque vector with $\tau = \begin{bmatrix} \tau_1 & \tau_2 & \tau_3 & \tau_4 \end{bmatrix}^T$. The 4x4 matrix $D(q)$ and the 4x1 vector $C(q,\dot{q})$ will be referred to as D and C respectively. The details of these expressions will be omitted for the sake of brevity.

The dynamic model is presented in two parts: one is directed to the structural model (CRCM) above and the other is related to the actuator dynamics (servo mechanism). We have already developed mechanics equations of the drive transmission system (Zi et al., 2009), and briefly outline here. The extendable actuator of each subsystem of the CRCM system is comprised of an alternating current (AC) servomotor & drive unit, belt pulley drive mechanism, two-level cycloid-gear speed reducer, and windlass. To simplify matters, here without regard to the belt pulley drive mechanism, the next step servomechanism model is developed. Without going into details, the servomechanism dynamic model is briefly described by the following formulation,

$$\begin{cases} K_U U_C = J_{mi} \dfrac{d^2\theta_{mi}}{dt^2} + K_\omega \dfrac{d\theta_{mi}}{dt} \\ \tau_{bi} = n_i (K_U U_C - K_\omega \dfrac{d\theta_{mi}}{dt} - J_{ni} \dfrac{d^2\theta_{mi}}{dt^2}) \end{cases} \tag{10}$$

where τ_{bi} (for $i = 1,2,3,4$) is the torque of the windlass; n_i is the gear ratio; U_C is control voltage ; U_C and K_w are positive constant, respectively; J_{mi} denotes the moment of inertia of the motor; J_{ni} is the equivalent moment of inertia including motor, speed reducer, flywheel and windlass, and θ_{mi} is the rotor angular position.

The driving force of cable T_i (for $i = 1,2,3,4$) can be expressed as

$$\begin{cases} K_U U_C = J_{mi} \dfrac{d^2\theta_{mi}}{dt^2} + K_\omega \dfrac{d\theta_{mi}}{dt} \\ T_i = \dfrac{\tau_{bi}}{r_i} = \dfrac{n_i}{r_i}(K_U U_C - K_\omega \dfrac{d\theta_{mi}}{dt} - J_{ni} \dfrac{d^2\theta_{mi}}{dt^2}) \end{cases} \tag{11}$$

In which, $T = [T_1\ T_2\ T_3\ T_4]^T$; r_i is the radius of the windlass, (for $i = 1,2,3,4$). For more details on the specification of the drive transmission system, refer to (Zi et al., 2009).

The nominal model of CRCM including servomechanism dynamics is described by the following formulation

$$
\begin{cases}
K_U U_C = J_{mi} \dfrac{d^2\theta_{mi}}{dt^2} + K_\omega \dfrac{d\theta_{mi}}{dt} \\[2mm]
\tau_{bi} = n_i (K_U U_C - K_\omega \dfrac{d\theta_{mi}}{dt} - J_{ni} \dfrac{d^2\theta_{mi}}{dt^2}) \\[2mm]
D(q)\ddot{q} + C(q,\dot{q}) + \tau_d = \tau_{bi}
\end{cases}
\tag{12}
$$

It is also well known that there is a dual relation between externally applied wrench on the end-effector and the cable tensions required to keep the system in equilibrium. The above dynamic model is valid only for $T_i > 0$, i.e., the cables are in tension. Clearly, the equation (12) is a non-homogeneous linear quaternary equations. The solution of the equations will be multiple. For the sake of this, the suitable solution is found through MATLAB software based on the pseudo-inverse method.

4. Adaptive fuzzy control

In general, a fuzzy logic system consists of four parts: the knowledge base, the fuzzifier, the fuzzy inference engine, and the defuzzifier. There are many different choices for the design of fuzzy system if the mapping is static. In this study, we consider a MIMO fuzzy logic system (Liu, 2008; Yoo & Ham, 2000). Supposing the fuzzy logic system performs a mapping from fuzzy sets in $U \subseteq R^n$ to fuzzy sets in $V \subseteq R^m$, where $U = U_1 \times ... \times U_n \subseteq R^n$, $U_i \in R$ (for $i = 1,2,...,n$), $V = V_1 \times ... \times V_m \subseteq R^m$, $V_j \in R$ (for $j = 1,2,...,m$). For a MIMO system, the fuzzy knowledge base consists of a collection of fuzzy IF–THEN rules in the following form

$$R^{(l)} : \text{IF } x_1 \text{ is } F_1^l \text{ and...and } x_n \text{ is } F_n^l$$

$$\text{THEN } y_1 \text{ is } C_1^l \text{ and...and } y_m \text{ is } C_m^l \tag{13}$$

where $x = [x_1,...,x_n]^T \in U$ and $y = [y_1,...,y_m]^T \in V$ are the input and output vectors of the fuzzy system, respectively, F_i^l and C_j^l (for $l = 1,2,...,M$) are linguistic variables, and M is the number of fuzzy rules. Based on the fuzzy inference engine working on fuzzy rules, the defuzzifier maps fuzzy sets in U to a crisp point in V.

The output of the fuzzy control system with singleton fuzzifier, product inference engine, center average defuzzifier is in the following form (Yoo & Ham, 2000)

$$
y_j = \frac{\displaystyle\sum_{l=1}^{M} \bar{y}_j^l \left(\prod_{i=1}^{n} \mu_{F_i^l}(x_i) \right)}{\displaystyle\sum_{l=1}^{M} \left(\prod_{i=1}^{n} \mu_{F_i^l}(x_i) \right)}
\tag{14}
$$

where $\bar{y}_j^l \in R$ (for $j = 1, 2, \dots, m$) is a criop value at which the membership function μ_{C^l} for output fuzzy set reaches its maximum , and $\mu_{F_i^l}(x_i)$ is the membership function of the linguistic variable x_i, defined as

$$\mu_{F_i^l}(x_i) = \exp\left[-\frac{(x_i - \bar{x}_i^l)^2}{\sigma^2}\right] \tag{15}$$

where $\bar{x}_i^l$ and σ are respectively, the mean and the deviation of the Gaussian membership function. The fuzzy control system inputs are composed of the five linguistic terms: NB (Negative Big), NO (Negative Medium), SS (Zero), PO (Positive Medium), and PB (Positive Big).

As the fixed nonlinear mapping in the hidden layer, $\varepsilon(x)$ is defined as

$$\varepsilon_l(x) = \frac{\prod\limits_{i=1}^{n} \mu_{F_i^l}(x_i)}{\sum\limits_{l=1}^{M}\left(\prod\limits_{i=1}^{n} \mu_{F_i^l}(x_i)\right)} \tag{16}$$

In order to maintain the consistent performance of the fuzzy control system in situations where there is uncertainty variation, the fuzzy control system should be adaptive. Therefore, (14) can be rewritten as

$$y_j = \Theta_j^T \varepsilon(x) \tag{17}$$

where $\varepsilon(x) = [\varepsilon_1(x), \dots, \varepsilon_M(x)]^T \in R^M$ is the fuzzy antecedent function vector, and $\Theta_j = \left[\bar{y}_j^{-1}, \dots, \bar{y}_j^{-M}\right]^T \in R^M$ is the center of the fuzzy subset C_j.

In the following analysis, it will be assumed that the dynamic model of the robot manipulator to be controlled is well known, and all the state variables can be measurable. The control system requirements for the CRCM are similar to those of almost all manipulators. In order to follow the desired continuously differentiable and uniformly bounded trajectory q_d and keep the tracking error $e(t) = q - q_d$ approach zero, a sliding surface, s, is defined in the stable state space (Liu, 2008). The most common sliding surface is chosen as follows

$$s = \dot{e} + \lambda e \tag{18}$$

where λ is a positive definite design parameter matrix.

Now introduce the variable q_r, and define

$$\dot{q}_r(t) = \dot{q}_d(t) - \lambda e(t) \tag{19}$$

Then Eq. (18) can be rewritten as

$$s = \dot{q} - \dot{q}_r \tag{20}$$

Let us consider the Lyapunov function candidate

$$V(t) = \frac{1}{2}\left(s^T D s + \sum_{i=1}^{n} \tilde{\Theta}_i^T \Gamma_i \tilde{\Theta}_i\right) \tag{21}$$

where $\tilde{\Theta}_i = \Theta_i^* - \Theta_i$, Θ_i (for i=1, 2, 3, 4) is the parameter vector, Θ_i^* is the ideal parameter, and Γ_i is a positive definite diagonal matrix.

To prove the negative definition of $\dot{V}(t)$, the time derivative of (21) is given as follows

$$\dot{V}(t) = -s^T\left(D\ddot{q}_r + C + \tau_d - \tau\right) + \sum_{i=1}^{4} \tilde{\Theta}_i^T \Gamma_i \dot{\tilde{\Theta}}_i \tag{22}$$

where τ_d is nonlinear function. Since the disturbance is related to the position and velocity signal, τ_d can be written in the form of $F(q,\dot{q})$. Hence, Eq. (22) can be rewritten as

$$\dot{V}(t) = -s^T\left(D\ddot{q}_r + C + F - \tau\right) + \sum_{i=1}^{4} \tilde{\Theta}_i^T \Gamma_i \dot{\tilde{\Theta}}_i \tag{23}$$

It is considered that the fuzzy logic compensation control is to approach just for the external disturbance, and the fuzzy logic system $F\left(q,\dot{q}|\tilde{\Theta}\right)$ for the CRCM system is defined as

$$\hat{F}\left(q,\dot{q}|\tilde{\Theta}\right) = \Theta_i^T \varepsilon\left(q,\dot{q}\right) \tag{24}$$

where $\varepsilon\left(q,\dot{q}\right)$ is fuzzy basis function (for i=1,2,3,4).

From the previous results, the control law is given as follows

$$\tau = D(q)\ddot{q} + C(q,\dot{q})\hat{F}_i\left(q,\dot{q}|\tilde{\Theta}\right) - K_D s \tag{25}$$

where $K_D = diag(K_i)$, $K_i > 0$ (for $i = 1,2,3,4$), and $\hat{F}\left(q,\dot{q}|\tilde{\Theta}\right)$ can be written as

$$\hat{F}\left(q,\dot{q}|\tilde{\Theta}\right) = \begin{bmatrix} \hat{F}_1\left(q,\dot{q}|\tilde{\Theta}\right) \\ \hat{F}_2\left(q,\dot{q}|\tilde{\Theta}\right) \\ \hat{F}_3\left(q,\dot{q}|\tilde{\Theta}\right) \\ \hat{F}_4\left(q,\dot{q}|\tilde{\Theta}\right) \end{bmatrix} = \begin{bmatrix} \Theta_1^T \varepsilon\left(q,\dot{q}\right) \\ \Theta_2^T \varepsilon\left(q,\dot{q}\right) \\ \Theta_3^T \varepsilon\left(q,\dot{q}\right) \\ \Theta_4^T \varepsilon\left(q,\dot{q}\right) \end{bmatrix} \tag{26}$$

The fuzzy approximation error is defined as

$$w = F(q,\dot{q}) - \hat{F}(q,\dot{q}|\hat{\Theta})$$ (27)

Substituting Eqs. (25)-(27) into Eq. (23), the following equation can be derived

$$
\begin{aligned}
\dot{V}(t) &= -s^T\left(D\ddot{q}_r + C + F - \tau\right) + \sum_{i=1}^{4}\tilde{\Theta}_i^T\Gamma_i\dot{\tilde{\Theta}}_i \\
&= -s^T\left(\Theta_i^T\varepsilon(q,\dot{q}) + w + K_D s\right) + \sum_{i=1}^{4}\tilde{\Theta}_i^T\Gamma_i\dot{\tilde{\Theta}}_i \\
&= -s^T K_D s - s^T w + \sum_{i=1}^{4}\left(\tilde{\Theta}_i^T\Gamma_i\dot{\tilde{\Theta}}_i - s_i\Theta_i^T\varepsilon(q,\dot{q})\right)
\end{aligned}
$$ (28)

Then, the adaptive law is defined as

$$\dot{\Theta}_i = -\Gamma_i^{-1}s_i\varepsilon(q,\dot{q})$$ (29)

Since the minimum approximation error, w, can be sufficiently small through designing the fuzzzy logic system with enough rules, and satisfying $\sum_{i=1}^{4}\left(\tilde{\Theta}_i^T\Gamma_i\dot{\tilde{\Theta}}_i - s_i\Theta_i^T\varepsilon(q,\dot{q})\right) = 0$. In addition, $K_D > 0$. Consequently, we get

$$\dot{V}(t) - s^T K_D s - s^T w < 0$$ (30)

Based on Lyapunov stability theory, and the result of Eq. (30), it is shown that the closed-loop system is asymptotically stable, and the scheduled control object can be realized.

5. Results and analysis

In order to justify the dynamic modeling the CRCM, we performed a series of simulations. This section presents two motion cases of the end-effector for dynamic simulation. A simulation for the dynamic model of the CRCM was carried out by Matlab 7.0 software. Some parameters of the CRCM are given as follows: the height of the pillar is 2 m, Pillars $B_1 \sim B_4$ are distributed evenly on the vertices of a square, with the side length of 2 m, and the quality of the end-effector is 5 kg. The acceleration of gravity g is 9.8 m/s^2.

The spatial circle trajectory can be expressed as

$$
\begin{cases}
x = 1 + 0.3 \times \cos(0.2\pi t) \\
y = 1.5 + 0.3 \times \sin(0.2\pi t) \\
z = 1
\end{cases}
$$ (31)

And the spatial helical trajectory is as follows

$$\begin{cases} x = 0.5 + 0.3\cos(0.1\pi t) \\ y = 0.5 + 0.3\sin(0.1\pi t) \\ z = 0.2 + 0.05t \end{cases} \tag{32}$$

Fig. 5 displays the workspace of the end-effector of the CRCM. The spatial helical following trajectory and the spatial circle following trajectory of the end-effector are shown in Fig. 6 and Fig. 9, respectively.

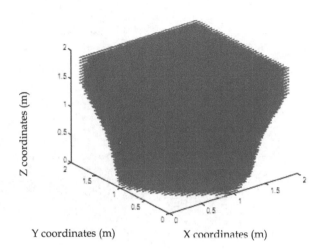

Fig. 5. Workspace of the end-effector.

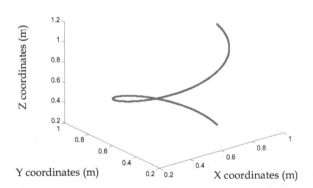

Fig. 6. Following trajectory of the end-effector.

Fig. 7, Fig. 8, Fig. 10 and Fig. 11 show the changes in length and the tension of the cables in the two different trajectories tracking, respectively. As can be seen in Figs. 6-11, the above formulation tracks the planned trajectory relatively well. From the above simulation results, it can be concluded that the dynamic modeling is justified.

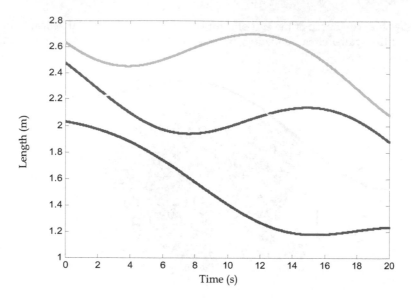

Fig. 7. Changes in length of cable for the helical motion.

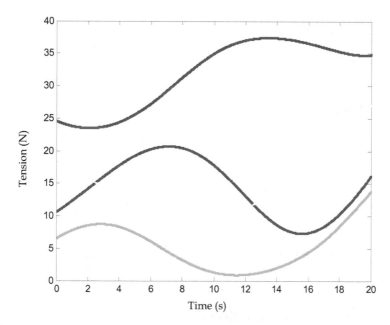

Fig. 8. Changes in tension of cable for the helical motion.

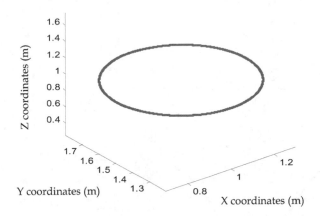

Fig. 9. Following trajectory of the end-effector.

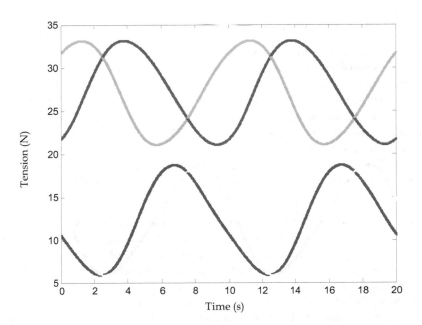

Fig. 10. Changes in tension of cable for the circle motion

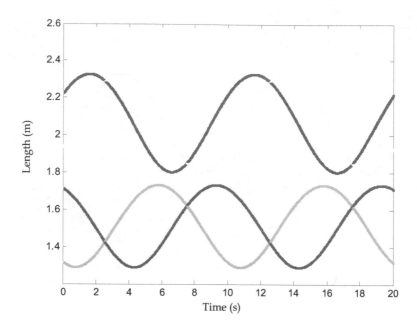

Fig. 11. Changes in length of cable for the circle motion.

In order to assess the performance of the adaptive fuzzy control system of the CRCM, simulations in spatial circle trajectory motion have been performed. The initial length configuration of the cables of the CRCM is given as $q(0) = [1.32\ 1.71\ 2.22\ 1.93]^T$, and the other consequent parameters areinitialized to zero. The nonlinearity $F(q,\dot{q})$ is estimated by using five Gaussian fuzzy sets for q and $\dot{q}$, which is constructed, as shown in Fig 12. The disturbance vector is $\tau_d = [15\sin(20t)\ 10\sin(20t)\ 10\sin(20t)\ 15\sin(20t)]^T$. The design parameters of the controller are determined as $\lambda = 10$, $\Gamma = 0.001$, $K_D = 250I$, and I is a 4×4 matrix. The resulting fuzzy set must be converted to a signal that can be sent to the process as a control input. Based on S-Function, the Simulink model of the CRCM is shown in Fig 13.

Figs. 14 and 15 display the trajectory tracking of the end-effector of the CRCM, respectively. From Fig. 14, the above formulation tracks the planned trajectory relatively well. Figs. 16 and 17 illustrate the position trajectory and the position errors of the end-effector in x, y, z directions, respectively. The changes in length and the length trajectory tracking errors of the cables l_1, l_2, l_3, l_4 are shown in Fig. 18 and Fig. 19, respectively. In Figs. 16 and 18, the desired trajectory is indicated in a red solid line, and the actual output is in a blue dash line, and from Fig. 16 and Fig. 18, it can be seen that the actual and desired trajectories almost overlap each other.

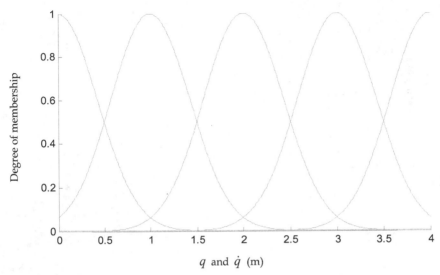

q and $\dot{q}$ (m)

Fig. 12. Membership function of input variables.

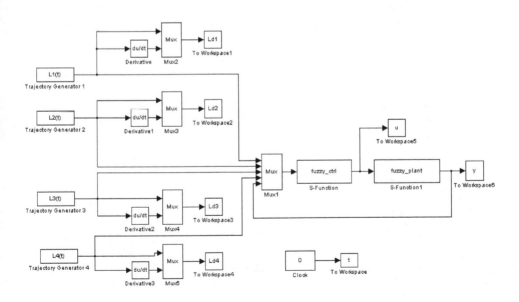

Fig. 13. Simulink model of the CRCM.

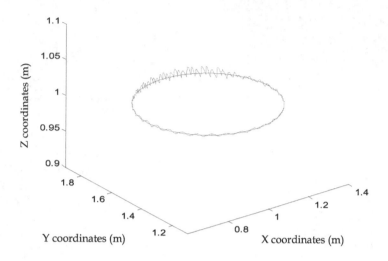

Fig. 14. Following trajectory of the end-effector.

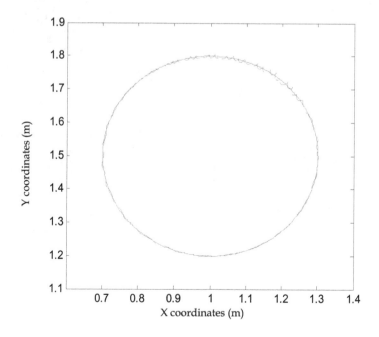

Fig. 15. Following trajectory of the end-effector

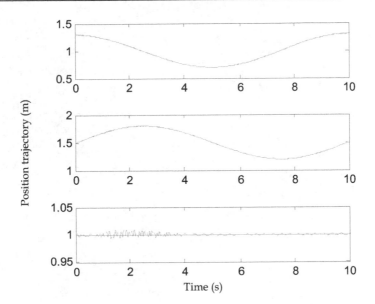

Fig. 16. Position trajectory of the end-effector in x, y and z directions

Fig. 20 displays the disturbance τ_d and its compensator, and the control input torques of the windlass are shown in Fig. 21. From the simulation results, it may be concluded that the adaptive fuzzy control strategy can achieve a favourable control performance and has high robustness.

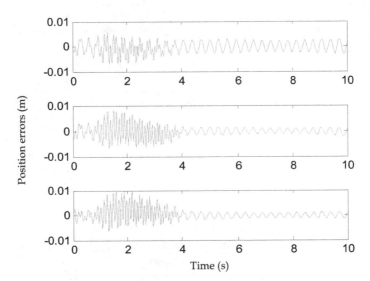

Fig. 17. Position errors of the end-effector in x, y and z directions.

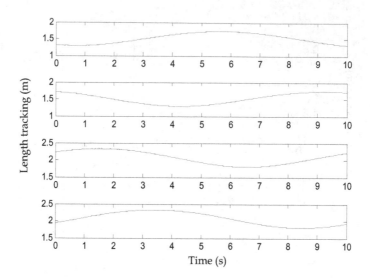

Fig. 18. Length tracking of the cables l_1, l_2, l_3, l_4

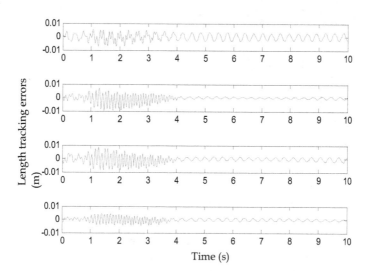

Fig. 19. Length tracking errors of the cables l_1, l_2, l_3, l_4

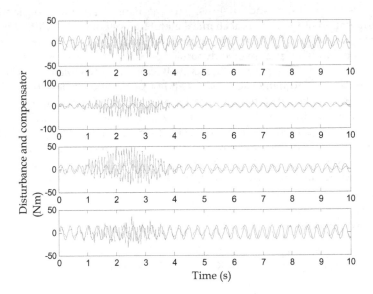

Fig. 20. The disturbance τ_d and its compensator.

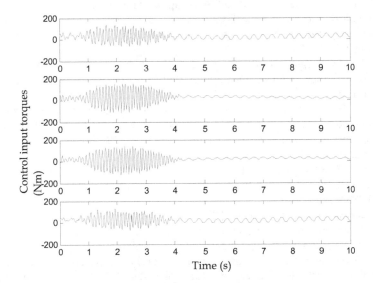

Fig. 21. The control input torques of the windlass $\tau_1, \tau_2, \tau_3, \tau_4$

6. Conclusion

Cable parallel manipulators are a class of robotic mechanisms whose simplicity of design, light weight and ability to support large loads make them useful in many industrial and military settings. This chapter presented in detail a 3-DOF, 4-cable CRCM for its adaptive fuzzy control system design and analysis. The mechanical system is designed, and the dynamic formulation of the electromechanical coupling system for the CRCM is studied on the basis of the Lagrange's Equation and equivalent circuit of the servo mechanism, and the inverse kinematic problem and inverse dynamics problem of the CRCM system is resolved on condition that operation path of the end-effector has been planned. Computational examples are provided to demonstrate the validity of the model developed. In addition, according to the established dynamic equation of the CRCM, an adaptive fuzzy control system is designed to track a given trajectory. Based on Lyapunov stability analysis, we have proved that the end-effector motion tracking errors converge asymptotically to zero. Simulation results are presented to show the satisfactory performance of the adaptive fuzzy control system. This will make the CRCM used in the more precision production field such as part assembly. Future work will be devoted to the experimental validation of the control system.

7. Acknowledgements

This work was supported by the National Natural Science Foundation of China (50905179) and the Visiting Scholar Foundation of Key Lab in University (GZKF-201112).

8. References

Anupoju, C. M.; Su, C. Y. & Oya, M. (2005). Adaptive Motion Tracking Control of Uncertain Nonholonomic Mechanical Systems Including Actuator Dynamics. *IEEE Proceedings Control Theory and Applications*, Vol.152, No.5, (September 2005), pp. 575-580, ISSN 1350-2379

Borgstrom, P. H.; Borgstrom, N. P.; Stealey, M. J. & Jordan, B. (2009). Design and Implementation of NIMS3D, a 3-D Cabled Robot for Actuated Sensing Applications. *IEEE Transaction on Robotics*, Vol.25, No.2, (April 2009), pp. 325-339, ISSN 1552-3098

Bosscher, P. & Ebert-Uphoff, I. (2006). Disturbance robustness measures for underconstrained cable-driven robots. *Proceedings of the IEEE International Conference on Robotics and Automation*, pp. 4205-4212, ISBN 0-7803-9505-0, Orlando, Florida, USA, May 15-19, 2006.

Behzadipour, S. & Khajepour, A. (2005). A New Cable-Based Parallel Robot with Three Degrees of Freedom. *Multibody System Dynamics*, Vol. 13, No.4, (May 2005), pp. 371-383, ISSN 1384-5640

Chen, B. S.; Lee, C. H. & Chang, Y. C. (1996). H∞ Tracking Design of Uncertain Nonlinear SISO Systems: Adaptive Fuzzy Approach. *IEEE Transaction on Fuzzy Systems*, Vol. 4, No.1, (February 1996), pp. 32-43, ISSN 1063-6706

Chien, C. J. (2008). A Combined Adaptive Law for Fuzzy Iterative Learning Control of Nonlinear Systems With Varying Control Tasks. *IEEE Transaction on Fuzzy Systems*, Vol. 16, No. 1, (February 2008), pp. 40-51, ISSN 1063-6706

Craig, J. J. (2005). *Introduction to robotics, mechanics and control*, China Machine Press, ISBN 7-111-11577-5, Beijing, China

Chang, Y. C. (2000). Robust Tracking Control for Nonlinear MIMO Systems via Fuzzy Approaches. *Automatica*, vol. 36, No. 10, (February 2000), pp. 1535-1545, ISSN 0005-1098

Feng, G. (2006). A Survey on Analysis and Design of Model-based Fuzzy Control Systems, *IEEE Transaction on Fuzzy Systems*, Vol. 14, No. 5, (October 2006), pp. 676–697, ISSN 1063-6706

Ghasemi, A.; Eghtesad, M. & Farid, M. (2008). Workspace analysis of planar and spatial redundant cable robots. *American Control Conference*, pp. 2389-2394, ISBN 978-1-4244-2078-0, Seattle, Washington, USA, June 11-13, 2008.

Labiod, S.; Boucherit, M. S. & Guerra, T. M. (2005). Adaptive Fuzzy Control of A Class of MIMO Nonlinear Systems. *Fuzzy Sets and Systems*, Vol. 151, No. 1, (April 2005), pp. 59-77, ISSN 0165-0114

Liu, J. K. (2008). *Design of Robot Control System and Matlab Simulation*. Tsinghua University Press, ISBN 7-302-09658-9, Beijing, China.

Motoji, Y.; Noritaka Y. & Akira M. (2004). Trajectory Control of Incompletely Restrained Parallel Wire-Suspended Mechanism Based on Inverse Dynamics. *IEEE Transaction on Robotics*, Vol.20, No.5, (October 2004), pp. 840-850, ISSN 1052-3098

Oh, S. R. & Agrawal, S. K. (2005). Cable Suspended Planar Robots with Redundant Cables: Controllers with Positive Tensions. *IEEE Transaction on Robotics*, Vol.21, No.3, (June 2005), pp. 457-465, ISSN 1052-3098

Purwar, S.; Kar, I. N. & Jha, A. N. (2005). Adaptive Control of Robot Manipulators Using Fuzzy Logic Systems Under Actuator Constraints. *Fuzzy Sets and Systems*, (June 2005), Vol. 152, No. 3, pp. 651-664, ISSN 0165-0114

Pham, C. B.; Yeo, S. H.; Yang, G.; Kurbanhusen, M. S. & Chen, I. M. (2006). Force-Closure Workspace Analysis of Cable-Driven Parallel Mechanisms. *Mechanism and Machine Theory*, Vol.41, No.1, (January 2006), pp. 53–69, ISSN 0094-114X

Reznik, L.; Ghanayem, O. & Bourmistrov, A. (2000). PID Plus Fuzzy Controller Structures as Design Base for Industrial Applications. *Engineering Application of Artificial Intelligence*, (August 2000), vol.13, No. 4, pp. 419-430, ISSN 0952-1976

Soyguder, S. & Alli, H. (2010). Fuzzy Adaptive Control for the Actuators Position Control and Modeling of An Expert System. *Expert Systems with Applications*, Vol. 37, No. 3, (March 2010), pp. 2072 – 2080, ISSN 0957-4174

Su, C. Y. & Stepanenko, Y. (1994). Adaptive Control of a Class of Nonlinear Systems with Fuzzy Logic. *IEEE Transaction on Fuzzy Systems*, Vol. 2, No. 4, (November 1994), pp. 285-294, ISSN 1063-6706

Visioli, A. (2001). Tuning of PID Controllers With Fuzzy Logic. *IEEE Proceedings Control Theory and Application*, Vol.148, No.1, (January 2001), pp. 1-8, ISSN 1350-2379

Yu, J. P.; Chen, B.; Yu, H. S. & Gao, J. W. (2011). Adaptive Fuzzy Tracking Control for The Chaotic Permanent Magnet Synchronous Motor Drive System via Backstepping. *Nonlinear Analysis: Real World Applications*, Vol. 12, No. 1, (February 2011) pp. 671–681, ISSN 1468-1218

Yoo, B. K. & Ham, W. C. (2000). Adaptive Control of Robot Manipulator Using Fuzzy Compensator. *IEEE Transaction on Fuzzy Systems*, (April 2000), Vol. 8, No. 2, pp. 186-199, ISSN 1063-6706

Yoo, B. K. & Ham, W. C. (1998). Adaptive Fuzzy Sliding Mode Control of Nonlinear System. *IEEE Transaction on Fuzzy Systems*, Vol. 6, No.2, (May 1998), pp. 315-321, ISSN 1063-6706

Yousef, H.; Hamdy, M.; El-Madbouly, E. & Eteim, D. (2009). Adaptive Fuzzy Decentralized
       Control for Interconnected MIMO Nonlinear Subsystems. *Automatica*, Vol. 45, No.
       2, (February 2009), pp. 456-462, ISSN 0005-1098

Zi, B.; Duan, B.Y.; Du, J. L. & Bao H. (2008). Dynamic Analysis and Active Control of A
       Cable-Suspended Parallel Robot. *Mechatronics*, Vol.18, No.1, (February 2008), pp. 1-
       12, ISSN 0957-4158

Zi, B.; Zhu, Z. C. & Wei, M. S. (2009). Dynamic Modeling and Control on AC
       Servomechanism. *China Mechanical Engineering*, Vol.20, No.8, (August 2009),
       pp.920-927, ISSN 1004-132X

Zadeh, L. A. (1965). Fuzzy Sets. *Information and Control*, Vol.148, No.1, (January 1965), pp.
       338-353, ISSN 1349-4198

2

Control and Estimation of Asynchronous Machines Using Fuzzy Logic

José Antonio Cortajarena, Julián De Marcos,
Fco. Javier Vicandi, Pedro Alvarez and Patxi Alkorta
University of the Basque Country (EUITI Eibar),
Spain

1. Introduction

In the conventional design of controllers, the first step is to obtain the model of the plant. With the plant model, the controller is designed considering aspects such as stability, dynamic response behaviour, performance against disturbances, etc. This type of controller design is called model-based design.

An asynchronous machine is normally controlled using traditional PI or PID controllers. In practice these conventional controllers are often developed via crude system models that satisfy basic and necessary assumptions before being tuned by using established methods.

These techniques are traditionally solved using a mathematical model of the machine with fixed parameters. However, in a real machine, the stator and rotor resistances are altered by temperature and the inductances are altered by the magnetizing current values that change for example when the machine is running in the flux weakening region or by an improper detuning between the flux and torque producing currents. For these reasons, the induction machine shows properties of nonlinear and time-varying systems. Parameter variations degrade the system performance over the full range of motor operation and in extreme conditions this can lead to instability (Vas, 1999). To solve this problem the controller parameters have to be continuously adapted. This adaptation can be achieved using different techniques such as MRAC or model reference adaptive control (Zhen & Xu, 1998), sliding mode (Won & Bose, 1992), or self tuning PIDs (Astrom & Hagglung, 1996). For some of these techniques the motor parameters and load inertia must be calculated in real time, so there is a high processing requirement for the used processors.

In the model-based controller design process, heuristics also enters into the implementation and tuning of the final design. Consequently, successful controller design can in part be attributable to the clever heuristic tuning of a control engineer. An advantage of fuzzy control is that it provides a method of manipulating and implementing a human's heuristic knowledge to control such a system (Zadeh, 1965).

Because the fuzzy logic approach is based on linguistic rules, the controller design does not need to use any machine parameters to make a controller adjustment, so the controller robustness is high (Li, 1998).

This chapter is composed of 5 sections. Section 2 begins with a mathematical description of the asynchronous machine. These equations are used to get the appropriate expressions and then use the adequate reference system to realize a good regulation of both asynchronous machines. Section 3 explains the used hybrid fuzzy controller. This hybrid controller will be used in all the applications and can be converted in a fuzzy controller cancelling the proportional term.

Section 4, explains the fuzzy control of the squirrel-cage motor using the indirect vector control strategy. Also, speed estimation for a sensorless control is implemented.

Section 5, explains the control strategy to control a double fed induction generator used mainly in wind turbines. Fuzzy control is implemented and tested in a real system.

Section 6, explains the fuzzy control robustness when the squirrel-cage motor is replaced for a new one with different parameters and when there is noise in the stator current measurement.

2. Induction machine model

The following equations describe the behaviour of the asynchronous machine in an arbitrary rotating reference frame.

$$\overline{v}_{s,dq} = R_s \overline{i}_{s,dq} + \frac{d\overline{\psi}_{s,dq}}{dt} + j\omega_e \overline{\psi}_{s,dq} \tag{1}$$

$$\overline{v}_{r,dq} = R_r \overline{i}_{r,dq} + \frac{d\overline{\psi}_{r,dq}}{dt} + j(\omega_e - \omega_r)\overline{\psi}_{r,dq} \tag{2}$$

$$\overline{\psi}_{s,dq} = L_s \overline{i}_{s,dq} + L_m \overline{i}_{r,dq} \quad \text{and} \quad L_s = L_m + L_{ls} \tag{3}$$

$$\overline{\psi}_{r,dq} = L_r \overline{i}_{r,dq} + L_m \overline{i}_{s,dq} \quad \text{and} \quad L_r = L_m + L_{lr} \tag{4}$$

$$T_e = \frac{3}{2} P \frac{L_m}{L_r} \left(\psi_{rd} i_{sq} - \psi_{rq} i_{sd} \right) \tag{5}$$

$$T_e - T_L = J \frac{d\omega_m}{dt} + B\omega_m \tag{6}$$

Where dq are the axis of the arbitrary reference system. $\overline{v}_{s,dq}$, $\overline{i}_{s,dq}$ and $\overline{\psi}_{s,dq}$ are the stator voltage, current and flux vectors. $\overline{v}_{r,dq}$, $\overline{i}_{r,dq}$ and $\overline{\psi}_{r,dq}$ are the rotor voltage, current and flux vectors. ω_r, ω_e and ω_m are the rotor electrical speed, arbitrary reference system speed, and rotor mechanical speed. L_m, L_s and L_r are the mutual, stator and rotor inductances. L_{ls} and L_{lr} are the stator and rotor leakage inductances. R_s and R_r are the stator and rotor resistances. T_e and T_L are the motor and load torque. J and B are the inertia of the system and friction coefficient. $\sigma = 1 - \left(L^2_m / L_r L_s \right)$ is the total leakage coefficient. P is the machine pole pares and $\omega_{sl} = \omega_e - \omega_r$ is the slip speed.

3. Fuzzy controller

The proposed controller is a hybrid controller with a fuzzy proportional-integral controller and a proportional term (FPI+P). The full controller structure is shown in figure 1.

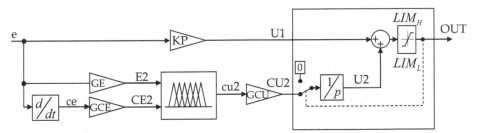

Fig. 1. Hybrid fuzzy controller structure

The proportional gain KP makes the fast corrections when a sudden change occurs in the input e. To eliminate the stationary error an integral action is necessary, so a fuzzy PI is included in the controller. If the error is large and the controller tries to obtain a larger output value than the limits, the integral action will remain in pause until the correction level drops below the saturation level. So, as the error becomes smaller the integral action gains in importance as does the proportional action of the fuzzy PI controller. This second proportional action is used for fine tuning and to correct the response to sudden reference changes, helping to the proportional controller.

E_2, CE_2 and cu_2 are defined according to figure 1 as,

$$E_2 = GE \cdot e, \quad CE_2 = GCE \cdot ce, \quad CU_2 = GCU \cdot cu_2 \qquad (7)$$

Where, GE, GCE and GCU are the scaling factors of the error, change of error and output, used to tuning the response of the controller (Patel, 2005). E_2 (error) and CE_2 (change of error) are the inputs of the fuzzy controller, an cu_2 (control action) is its output. Because the inputs of the fuzzy controller are the error and change of error it is useful to configure it as an incremental controller. This incremental controller adds a change to the current control signal of $\Delta U2_n$.

$$U2_n = U2_{n-1} + \Delta U2_n \qquad (8)$$

And the $\Delta U2_n$ value in a PI controller would be,

$$\Delta U2_n = Kp \cdot \left(e_n - e_{n-1} + \frac{Ts}{Ti} e_n \right) \qquad (9)$$

Where, Kp is the proportional gain and Ts and Ti the sample or control period and the integral time.

It is an advantage that the controller output $CU2_n$ is driven directly from an integrator, as it is then is easier to deal with windup and noise (Jantzen, 1998). The fuzzy PI controller output, $U2$, is called the change in output, and $U2_n$ is defined by,

$$U2_n = \sum_i \left(cu2_i \cdot GCU \cdot Ts \right) \tag{10}$$

The integrator will add only if $LIM_L < OUT_n < LIM_H$ and $cu2_i \neq 0$. The value of $cu2$ according to the inputs is,

$$cu2_n = f\left(GE \cdot e_n, GCE \cdot ce_n \right) \tag{11}$$

The function f is the fuzzy input-output map of the fuzzy controller. If it were possible to take the function f as a linear approximation, considering equations (8-11), the gains related to the conventional PI would be,

$$Kp = GCE \cdot GCU \tag{12}$$

$$\frac{1}{Ti} = \frac{GE}{GCE} \tag{13}$$

These relations had shown the importance of the scaling factors. High values of GE produce a short rise time when a step reference is introduced but also a high overshot and a long settling time could arise. The system may become oscillatory and even unstable. If GE is low the overshot will decrease or disappear and the settling time increases. High values of GCE have the same effect as small values of GE and vice versa.

High values of GCU originate a short rise time and overshot when a step reference is introduced. If GCU is small the system gain is small and the rise time increases.

The global output value of the hybrid fuzzy controller is,

$$OUT_n = LIM_H \quad \textbf{if} \quad U1_n + U2_n > LIM_H$$
$$OUT_n = LIM_L \quad \textbf{if} \quad U1_n + U2_n < LIM_L \tag{14}$$
$$OUT_n = KP \cdot e_n + \sum_i^n \left(f\left(GE \cdot e_n, GCE \cdot ce_n \right) \cdot GCU \cdot Ts \right) \quad \textbf{if} \quad LIM_L < U1_n + U2_n < LIM_H$$

The output of the controller is limited according to the maximum value of the hybrid fuzzy controller, for example for a speed controller the limit will be the maximum admissible torque and for the current controllers the limit will be the maximum admissible voltage of the machine.

For a practical implementation of the fuzzy controllers on a DSP the fuzzy membership functions of the antecedents and consequents are triangular and trapezoidal types because the calculus complexity is lower than the calculus complexity when are used Gaussian or Bell membership functions.

With the information of the plant model, the fuzzy sets and their linguistic variables are defined for the antecedents and consequents. The control strategy has to be implemented based on the engineer experience and if it is possible using simulation tools. The control strategy is stored in the rule-base in the form If-Then and an inference strategy will be chosen.

Then the system is ready to be tested to see if the closed-loop specifications are met. First simulations will be carried analyzing the dynamic behaviour and the stability of the plant and finally the adjustment will be tested and adjusted again in the real machine control platform.

To get the rule-base of the controller the reference and feedback values are compared and the control action is determined to correct the deviation between reference and feedback. As an example, in the speed loop a positive increase of the speed error because the real speed is lower than the reference, must force to the controller to increase their output or torque reference, Te, to increase the machine speed as detailed in equation 6. Something similar happens with the change of error; if the change of error is positive big, that means that the machine is decelerating, then the controller has to increase the torque to reduce the effect, so the controller has to produce a positive big output to increase the electromagnetic torque.

For another error and change of error combinations, the base-rule of table 1 applied to the fuzzy controller shows a phase trajectory reducing the error as shown in figure 2. This is valid for the speed, flux and current loops. The base-rule of table 1 characterizes the control objectives and it is shown as a matrix with the phase trajectory superimposed. The dynamic behaviour of the controller to make zero the error will depend on the antecedents and consequents position, on the selected inference strategy, on the used defuzzification method and on the scaling factors.

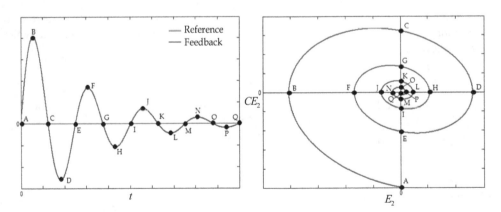

Fig. 2. Fuzzy controller phase diagram when used table 1

The meaning of the linguistic terms used in table I are: NB, negative big; NM, negative medium; NS, negative small; ZE, zero; PS, positive small; PM, positive medium and PB, positive big.

Table 1 indicates the use of 49 rules. The first is read as,

If E_2 is Negative Big and CE_2 is Negative Big Then cu_2 is Negative Big

CE_2 \ E_2	NB	NM	NS	ZE	PS	PM	PB
NB	NB	NB	NB	NB A	NM	NS	ZE
NM	NB	NB	NB	NM E	NS	ZE	PS
NS	NB	NB	NM	NS I	ZE	PS	PM
ZE	NB B	NM F	NS J	ZE	PS H	PM D	PB
PS	NM	NS	ZE	PS G	PM	PB	PB
PM	NS	ZE	PS	PM	PB	PB	PB
PB	ZE	PS	PM	PB	PB	PB	PB

Table 1. Rule-base of the fuzzy controller and phase diagram

To adjust the scaling factors and the membership functions a first approximation is to make the controller as close as possible to a conventional PI controller (Jantzen, 1998). Then, the scaling factors and the position of the antecedents and consequents are adjusted making multiples simulations with Matlab/Simulink©.

The linguistic variable error and their linguistic terms position, figure 3, is the same for all fuzzy controllers. The error value is normalized for every controller, as an example when the speed error is 1000 rpm, their normalized value is 1.

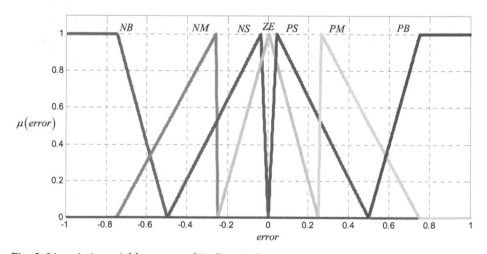

Fig. 3. Linguistic variable error and its linguistic terms

The linguistic variable change of error and their linguistic terms position, figure 4, is also the same for all fuzzy controllers. The change of error value is normalized for every controller.

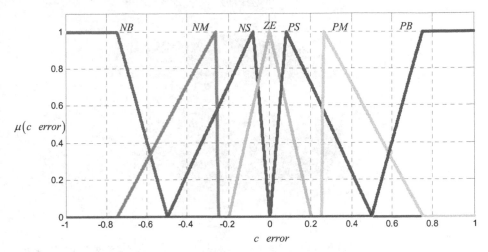

Fig. 4. Linguistic variable change of error and its linguistic terms

The linguistic variable of the control action or consequent and the position of its linguistic terms are shown in figure 5. The values are normalized, where a value of 20 in the real control action is normalized to 1.

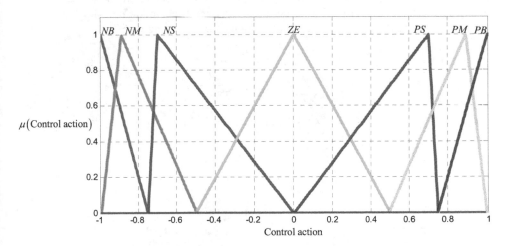

Fig. 5. Control action linguistic terms

In figure 6, the fuzzy controller surface can be seen. The used implication method is the AND method or min (minimum), which truncates the output fuzzy set and as aggregation the S-norm max (maximum) has been used. The used defuzzification method is the centroid or center of gravity, equation 15.

$$y_o = \frac{\sum y \mu_T(y)}{\sum \mu_T(y)} \qquad (15)$$

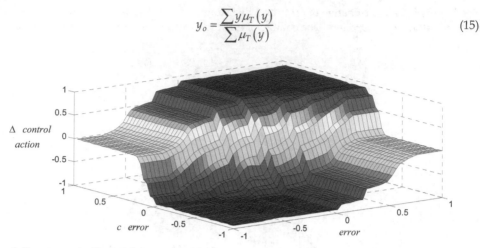

Fig. 6. Fuzzy controller surface

As it can be seen in figure 3 and 4, the linguistic variables are joined close to zero, showing a higher sensibility in this area. For this reason the slope of the surface in figure 6 is high in a surrounding area around the point (0,0,0).

4. Squirrel-cage machine control

A schematic diagram of the induction motor indirect vector control with the fuzzy PI + P controllers is shown in figure 7. The scheme is obtained after operating with the machine equations and using the rotor flux reference system as shown in figure 8.

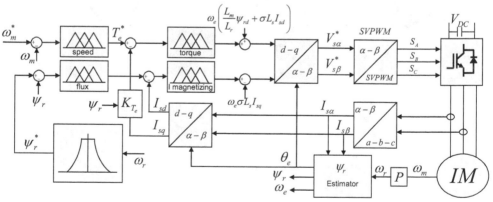

Fig. 7. Squirrel cage control structure

The rotor flux reference system makes possible the control of the AC machine as a DC machine, allowing the control of the machine torque with the stator current q component and the flux with the d component of the same current as can be deducted from equations 2 to 6. A scheme showing these equations is shown in figure 9.

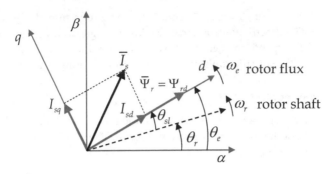

Fig. 8. Rotor flux reference system

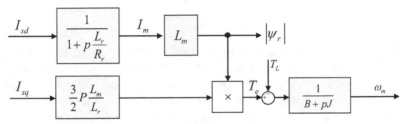

Fig. 9. Torque, flux and speed control structure in the rotor flux reference system

The speed error is the input of a hybrid fuzzy controller and the output of FPI+P controller will generate the torque producing stator current component command Isq. The flux controller generates the flux producing stator current component Isd according to the flux-speed profile. Both currents are the input of two controllers to produce the stator voltages in the synchronous reference and then transformed to the stationary reference system to generate in the inverter the voltage vector for the motor.

The real platform to test the asynchronous motor and its main characteristics used also for the simulation purpose are shown in figure 10.

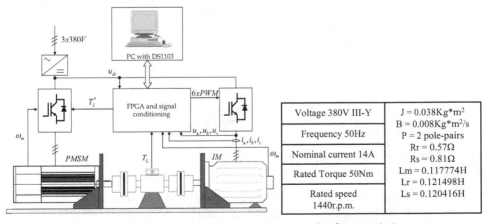

Fig. 10. Induction motor rig test and asynchronous motor main characteristics

The real system is based on a DS1103 board and is programmed using the software Matlab/Simulink©. The board controls the IM inverter generating the SVPWM pulses (dSPACE©, 2005). The speed is measured with a 4096 impulse encoder via a FPGA connected to the DS1103 using the multiple period method (Cortajarena et al., 2006).

4.1 Torque or current control

As mentioned and shown in figure 9, the torque of the machine is controlled with the stator current q component and the flux with the d component. The relation between the torque Te and the stator current q component is,

$$T_e = \underbrace{\frac{3}{2} P \frac{L_m}{L_r} \psi_r}_{K_{T_e}} I_{sq} \qquad (16)$$

So first, torque and current magnetizing controllers will be adjusted. In a classical PI controller the proportional term for a bandwidth of 2500 rad/s and a phase margin of 80° with the machine parameters given in figure 10 is 0.05. For the adjustment of the hybrid fuzzy controller KP will be 0.025, half of the proportional term in the PI. The scaling factors adjusted after simulations for the current controllers are $GE = 150$, $GCE = 0.03$ and $GCU = 8$. The regulators maximum and minimum limits are ±310V, the maximum motor phase voltage.

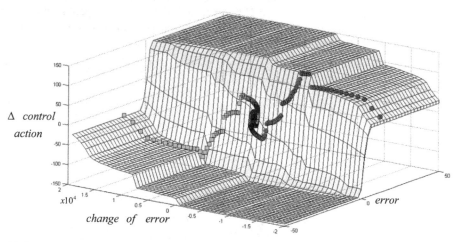

Fig. 11. Stator current q component controller fuzzy surface and trajectory after current step of figure 12

Figure 11 shows the hybrid fuzzy stator q current controller surface and the trajectory when a step reference of -20 amperes is produced, and after 200 ms another step of 20 amperes as shown in figure 12 is applied to the torque controller.

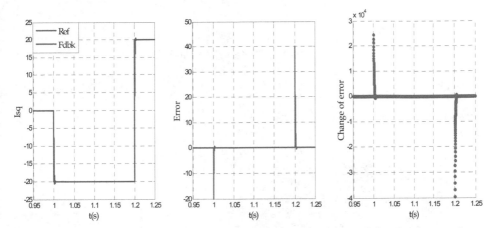

Fig. 12. Stator current q component step reference and feedback, error for the step, and change of error

When the step reference is -20 amperes the feedback or real stator q current reaches the real value quickly, it takes 2 ms. The trajectory on the fuzzy surface for this step is the green line in the surface showing how the change of error and the error are decreasing to zero in about 2 ms. When the step reference goes from -20 to 20 amperes the feedback or real stator q current reaches the real value in 3 ms. The trajectory on the fuzzy surface for this step is the red line in the surface showing how the change of error and the error are decreasing to zero due to the value of the control action.

4.2 Speed and rotor flux control

Once the current loops have been adjusted, the speed and flux loops will be adjusted. As mentioned and shown in figure 9, the machine speed is regulated adjusting the torque command and the flux adjusting the stator current d component.

In a classical speed PI controller the proportional term for a bandwidth of 750 rad/s and a phase margin of 80° with the machine parameters given in figure 10 is 0.5. For the adjustment of the hybrid fuzzy controller KP will be 0.4, a little bit smaller than the proportional term in the PI. The scaling factors adjusted after simulations for the speed controllers are $GE = 2$, $GCE = 0.01$ and $GCU = 300$. The regulators maximum and minimum limits are ±50 Nm, the maximum motor torque or a stator current q component of 20 amperes.

Figure 13 shows the hybrid fuzzy speed controller surface and the trajectory when a step reference from -1000 rpm to 1000 rpm and again to -1000 rpm as shown in figure 14 is applied to the speed controller.

When the step goes from -1000 to 1000 rpm the trajectory on the fuzzy surface for this step is the green line, showing how the change of error and the error are decreasing to zero in about 180 ms. When the step reference goes from 1000 to -1000 rpm the feedback or real speed reaches the real value in 180 ms. The trajectory on the fuzzy surface for this step is the red line, showing how the change of error and the error are decreasing to zero due to the value of the control action.

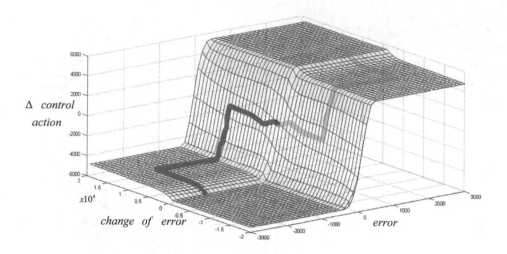

Fig. 13. Speed controller fuzzy surface and trajectory after speed step of figure 14

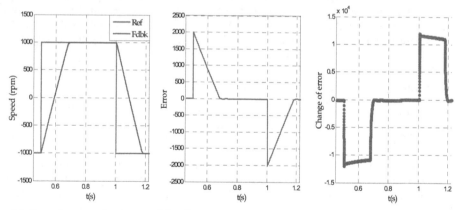

Fig. 14. Speed step reference and feedback, error for the step, and change of error

When the change of error is high, the controller output is at its maximum limit, and when the change of error decreases the control action also decreases close to zero as it can be seen in the trajectory of figure 13. The error and change of error trajectory of the surface in figure 13 correspond to the values represented in figure 14. The control action contribution can be obtained from the fuzzy controller surface.

Figure 15 shows the response of the real asynchronous motor of figure 10 when a speed step is applied to the machine and later a load torque of 40 Nm after 0.3 s. Three classes of speed controllers are tested to see the response and compare them. A classical PI controller with a 750 rad/s and a phase margin of 80°, the adjusted hybrid Fuzzy PI + P controller and a Fuzzy controller without the KP term and $GE = 2$, $GCE = 0.06$ and $GCU = 300$.

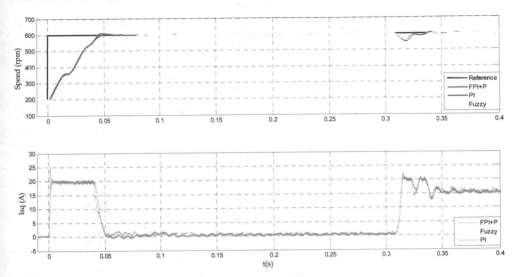

Fig. 15. Top, speed step and response when PI, Fuzzy and Fuzzy PI + P controllers are used. Bottom, torque current controllers output

To compare the controllers, table 2 shows time domain specifications and performance criteria, integrated absolute error (IAE), the integral of time-weighted absolute error (ITAE), the integral of the square of the error, ISE, and the integral of time multiply squared error (ITSE).

	Delay time	Rise time	Settling time	% Overshoot	IAE	ITAE	ISE	ITSE
PI	1.4ms	42ms	56ms	3	97470	6754	2.23e7	3.29e5
Fuzzy	3.2ms	77ms	80ms	0	1.28e5	7579	2.86e7	4.8e5
FPI+P	1.4ms	42ms	47ms	0	96270	6000	2.23e7	3.01e5

Table 2. Time domain specifications and performance criteria for three classes of controllers

Very similar results are obtained with the PI and FPI+P controllers, although according to the performance criteria the hybrid fuzzy controller is slightly better. The worst controller is the fuzzy controller as it is shown in table 2 and figure 15.

To check the control of the machine with the hybrid fuzzy controller the machine will be forced to run at a speed higher than the nominal value. In such conditions the machine rotor flux has to decrease because the inverter DC voltage can't be higher, so the torque and stator current q component relation is changing as shown in equation 16 and figure 9. This change should be taken in consideration in a classical PI regulator. In the hybrid fuzzy controller the adjustment done with the linguistic variables and the scaling factors shows that the control works properly. In figure 16, the left signals correspond to the real signals obtained whit the machine of the test rig and the right side signals are the simulated in the same conditions than the real case. Because the speed is higher than nominal value, the flux decreases below the nominal value, to do this the stator current d component decreases and increases when the flux is increasing to the nominal value. The q component of the stator current related with the torque increases when the machine is accelerating and decreases when the machine decelerates.

The speed regulation in the flux weakening region is good, and real platform signals and simulations corroborate the hybrid fuzzy good performance.

The flux hybrid fuzzy controller scaling factors are $GE = 200$, $GCE = 20$ and $GCU = 100$. To evaluate the flux regulation, the rotor flux reference and feedback values could be compared in the flux weakening shown in figure 16. Both are very similar showing a very good flux regulation and the flux controller output corresponds with the stator current d component shown in the same figure.

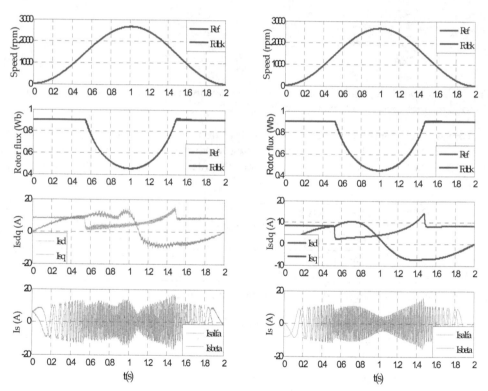

Fig. 16. Left, real machine signals, speed, flux and stator currents. Right, simulated signals

4.3 Speed estimation

There are in literature many techniques of sensorless control. The first group is based on the fundamental mathematical model of the machine, that is, the flux density distribution in the air gap is sinusoidal. All these models depend on the machine parameters so the accuracy of the estimators will depend on different manner of the precision of these parameters. It is not possible with these techniques to achieve a stable and precise operation at very low speed.

The second group of techniques is based on the anisotropic properties of the machine. Techniques like rotor slot ripple or main inductance saturation are used in this group.

From equations 2 and 4, considering rotor voltage zero, and after Laplace transformation of the respective space vectors the rotor flux will be,

$$\overline{\psi}_{r,dq}(p) = \frac{L_m}{1 + \dfrac{L_r}{R_r}p + j\left(\omega_e - \omega_r\right)\dfrac{L_r}{R_r}} \overline{i}_{s,dq}(p) \tag{17}$$

Operating with equations 1 to 4 the next equation is obtained,

$$\sigma L_s \frac{d\overline{i}_{s,dq}}{dt} = \overline{v}_{s,dq} - \left[R_s + \left(\frac{L_m}{L_r}\right)^2 R_r + j\omega_e \right]\overline{i}_{s,dq} + \underbrace{\frac{L_m}{L_r}\left(\frac{R_r}{L_r} - j\omega_r\right)\overline{\psi}_{r,dq}}_{\overline{v}r_{s,dq}} \tag{18}$$

It can be seen the induced voltage from the rotor into the stator as $\overline{v}_{r_{s,dq}}$.

As the feeding voltage vector of the stator approaches zero frequency, the rotor speed approaches zero. If the equation 18 is observed in the stationary reference frame, $\omega_e = 0$, and using equation 17, $\overline{v}_{r_{s,dq}}$ is calculated when p→0,

$$\overline{v}r_{s,\alpha\beta}\Big|_{\omega_r \to 0} = \lim_{p \to 0}\overline{v}r_{s,\alpha\beta} = \frac{L_m^2 R_r}{L_r^2}\overline{i}_{s,\alpha\beta} \tag{19}$$

The equation 19 is independent of ω_r when stator frequency is close to zero, so the variations of rotor speed have no influence on the stator equation 18 and this makes impossible to detect a speed variation on the stator current. So the mechanical speed of the rotor becomes not observable. Instead of this, when the magnitude of the induced voltage from the rotor into the stator is substantial, its value can be determined and the rotor state variables are then observable. So, there will be a limitation for very low speed operation due to the dc offset components in the measured stator currents and voltages.

The minimum stator frequency must be superior to zero to have an appropriate relation between induced voltage from the rotor into the stator and also to reduce the noise and parameters mismatch influence (Holtz, 1996).

The rotor speed estimator used, figure 17, is based on the fundamental mathematical model of the machine. The rotor speed is obtained with the derivative of the rotor flux angle minus the slip speed, see figure 8. The precision of the estimator has a great dependence on motor parameters and at low speeds a small error (offset for example) in the stator voltage can suppose an estimation error.

The rotor flux estimator contains two models, the open loop current model, which is supposed to produce an accurate estimation at low speed range, and an adaptive voltage model for a medium high speed range of operation. The transition between both models is adjusted by two hybrid fuzzy controllers, reducing the problems due to stator resistance and pure integrators at low speed.

The stator flux in the fixed reference frame related to the rotor flux and the stator current is,

$$\overline{\psi}^i_{s,\alpha\beta} = \frac{L_m}{L_r}\overline{\psi}^i_{r,\alpha\beta} + \frac{L_sL_r - L^2_m}{L_r}\overline{i}_{s,\alpha\beta} \tag{20}$$

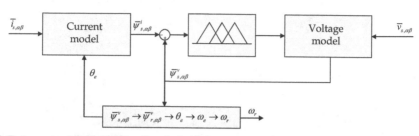

Fig. 17. Rotor speed estimation using hybrid fuzzy controllers

The stator flux using the voltage model is corrected by a compensation term, generated by two hybrid fuzzy controllers,

$$\overline{\psi}^v_{s,\alpha\beta} = \int\left(\overline{v}_{s,\alpha\beta} - R_s\overline{i}_{s,\alpha\beta} - \overline{v}_{comp}\right) \tag{21}$$

And,

$$\overline{v}_{comp_n} = KP\cdot\left(\overline{\psi}^v_{s,\alpha\beta} - \overline{\psi}^i_{s,\alpha\beta}\right) + \sum_i^n\left(f\left(GE\cdot\left(\overline{\psi}^v_{s,\alpha\beta} - \overline{\psi}^i_{s,\alpha\beta}\right)_n, GCE\cdot c\left(\overline{\psi}^v_{s,\alpha\beta} - \overline{\psi}^i_{s,\alpha\beta}\right)_n\right)\cdot GCU\cdot Ts\right) \tag{22}$$

With the obtained stator flux, the rotor flux and angle according to the voltage model are determined,

$$\overline{\psi}^v_{r,\alpha\beta} = \frac{L_r}{L_m}\overline{\psi}^v_{s,\alpha\beta} + \frac{L_sL_r - L^2_m}{L_m}\overline{i}_{s,\alpha\beta} \tag{23}$$

And,

$$\theta_e = \theta_{\psi_r} = \tan^{-1}\frac{\psi^v_{r\beta}}{\psi^v_{r\alpha}} \tag{24}$$

Finally the rotor speed is obtained,

$$\omega_r = \omega_{\psi r} - \omega_{sl} = \frac{d\theta_{\psi r}}{dt} - \frac{L_m R_r}{L_r\left(\psi^2_{r\alpha} + \psi^2_{r\beta}\right)}\left(\psi_{r\alpha}i_{s\beta} + \psi_{r\beta}i_{s\alpha}\right) \tag{25}$$

The scaling factors adjusted after simulations for the hybrid fuzzy controllers are, $KP = 245$, $GE = 105$, $GCE = 1$ and $GCU = 11$.

With the adjusted hybrid fuzzy controllers some estimated speed profiles in the real machine are presented.

Figure 18 shows three speed references when the machine is unloaded. The speed reference of the left figure is a square signal from -1000 to 1000 rpm. The estimated speed is used as feedback signal and for check purposes the measured or real speed is also shown. As can be seen the real and estimated speeds are very similar. The speed reference of the middle figure is sinusoidal and the reference, estimated and real signals are very similar, showing a good regulation and speed estimation. The right figure shows a random speed reference crossing during 2 seconds at a speed close to zero rpm, where the speed is poorly observable. The reference, estimated and real signals are very similar even at zero speed for a short time.

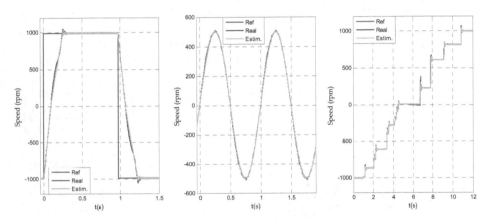

Fig. 18. Sensorless control for different speed references when the load torque is cero

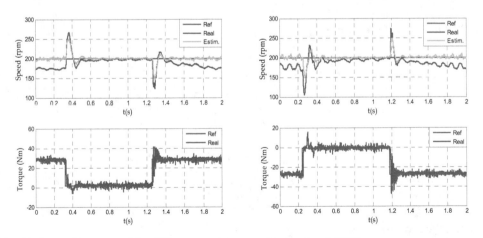

Fig. 19. Sensorless control for 200 rpm and torque step loads of ±30Nm

Figure 19 shows the speed estimation when a load perturbation of ±30 Nm is applied to the machine. There is an error between the real speed and the estimated speed when the machine is loaded due to parameters mismatch.

5. Doubly fed induction generator control

A doubly fed induction generator (DFIG) vector control with the fuzzy PI + P controllers is shown in figure 20. The scheme is obtained after operating with the machine equations and using the stator flux reference system shown in figure 21.

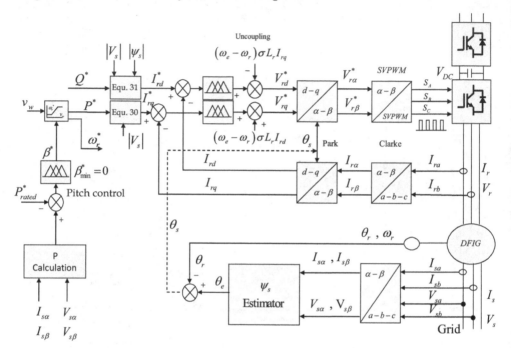

Fig. 20. DFIG control structure

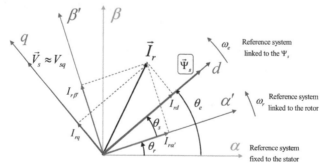

Fig. 21. DFIG control reference systems

The converter Back to Back configuration provides to the DFIG the ability of reactive power control. Using the appropriate reference system it is possible to decouple the active and reactive power control by the independent control of the rotor excitation current. Due to the bi-directional power converter in the rotor side, the DFIG is able to work as a generator in the sub-synchronous (slip speed is positive, s>0) and super-synchronous (slip speed is negative, s<0) operating area (Hansen et al., 2007).

When the reference system is linked to the stator flux, as it can be seen in figure 21, the stator flux q component is zero, and when operating with equation 3 the next two equations are obtained,

$$i_{sd} = \frac{|\bar{\psi}_s|}{L_s} - \frac{L_m}{L_s} i_{rd}$$ (26)

$$i_{sq} = -\frac{L_m}{L_s} i_{rq}$$ (27)

This means that the stator current can be controlled with the rotor current. Taking into account that the stator resistance is small, the stator flux can be considered constant and its value is,

$$|\bar{\psi}_s| \approx \frac{|\bar{V}_s|}{\omega_e}$$ (28)

The stator voltage d component is almost zero because the reference system is oriented along the stator flux, so considering that the stator active and reactive power is,

$$P_s = \frac{3}{2}\left(v_{sd}i_{sd} + v_{sq}i_{sq}\right) \quad \text{and} \quad Q_s = \frac{3}{2}\left(v_{sq}i_{sd} - v_{sd}i_{sq}\right)$$ (29)

It can be obtained that,

$$P_s \approx -\frac{3}{2}\omega_e \Psi_s \frac{L_m}{L_s} i_{rq}$$ (30)

And,

$$Q_s \approx \frac{3}{2}|V_s|\left[\frac{|V_s|}{\omega_e L_s} - \frac{L_m}{L_s} i_{rd}\right]$$ (31)

Equations 30 and 31 showed that the stator active power is controlled with the q component of the rotor current and the stator reactive power with the rotor current d component. In figure 20 can be seen both hybrid fuzzy controllers to regulate the d and q rotor current components.

The real platform to test the double feed induction generator and its main characteristics used also for the simulation purpose are shown in figure 22.

The real system is based on a DS1103 board and is programmed using the software Matlab/Simulink©. The board controls the inverters in a Back to Back configuration generating the SVPWM pulses (dSPACE©, 2005). The grid connected inverter, is regulated keeping the DC bus voltage constant. The speed of the DFIG is measured with a 4096 impulse encoder connected to the DS1103 using the frequency method (Cortajarena et al., 2006).

First, the inner current loops are adjusted. The used hybrid fuzzy controller is the same as have been used in the squirrel cage machine. The scaling factors have been adapted after realizing multiple simulations and finally adjusted in the DFIG test rig.

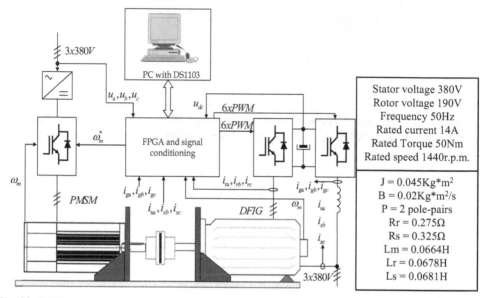

Fig. 22. DFIG rig test and its main characteristics

To test the performance of the hybrid fuzzy controller it will be compared to a conventional PI controller. In a classical PI controller the proportional term for a bandwidth of 3000 rad/s and a phase margin of 80° with the machine parameters given in figure 22 is 0.015. For both current controllers, the proportional term KP will be 0.015 and the scaling factors are $GE = 300$, $GCE = 0.025$ and $GCU = 0.2$. The regulators maximum and minimum limits are ±1, equivalent to ±310 V per phase in the rotor.

Figure 23 shows the hybrid fuzzy rotor q current controller surface and the trajectory when a step reference from 10 to 20 amperes is produced. The feedback or real rotor q current reaches the real value quickly, it takes around 3 ms.

The trajectory on the fuzzy surface for this step shows how the error is moving around the high slope where the error is close to zero. In table 3, the performances of two controllers are summarized. The hybrid fuzzy and the conventional PI have similar dynamic response, showing the fuzzy controller a better performance when IAE, ITAE, ISE and ITSE indexes are used to evaluate the performance.

In a DFIG control there are two operating regions depending on the wind speed. Below the machine rated power, the blade pitch angle is set to zero degrees to get the maximum power. When the wind speed is sufficiently fast to get power from the wind higher than the rated power, enters into the second region. In this region the blade pitch angle controller regulates the output power modifying the pitch angle to get the rated power from the generator without damage it.

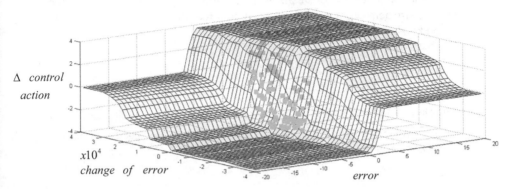

Fig. 23. Rotor current q component controller fuzzy surface and trajectory after current step of figure 24

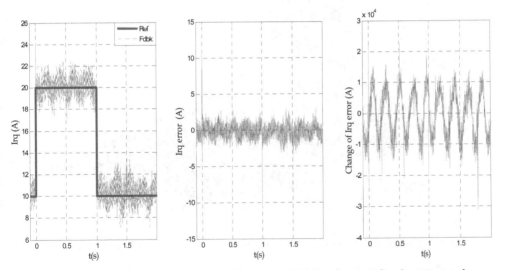

Fig. 24. Rotor current q component step reference and feedback, error for the step, and change of error

	Delay time	Rise Time	Settling time	% Overshoot	IAE	ITAE	ISE	ITSE
PI	1.2ms	1.2ms	4ms	20	8413	4110	11576	5105
FPI+P	1ms	1ms	3.5ms	20	7925	3880	10200	4510

Table 3. Time domain specifications and performance criteria for two classes of controllers

The power transmitted to the hub of a wind turbine can be expressed as,

$$P_{turb} = \frac{1}{2} C_p(\lambda, \beta) \rho_{air} \pi R^2 v_w^3 \tag{32}$$

Where ρ_{air}, is the mass density of the air, R is the radius of the propeller, Cp is the power performance coe4fficient, v_w is the wind speed, β is the pitch angle and λ is the blade tip speed ratio and is defined as,

$$\lambda = \frac{R \cdot \omega_{pr}}{v_w} \tag{33}$$

and ω_{pr} is the angular velocity of the propeller.

The power performance coefficient Cp, used according to the tip speed ratio and the pitch angle for the DFIG is shown in figure 25.

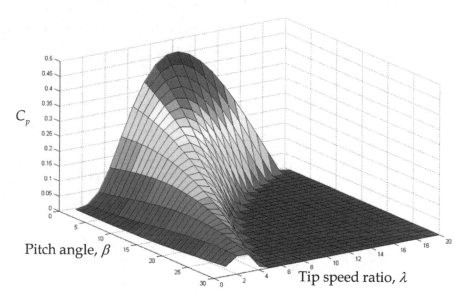

Fig. 25. Power performance coefficient depending on tip speed ratio and pitch angle

Figure 26 shows for a pitch angle of 0° the obtained power from the wind according to the propeller speed. The black line indicates the maximum power and the propeller speed to get this power from every wind speed. When the obtained power reaches the machine rated power, the wind energy is wasted changing the pitch angle and getting the rated power.

For a known wind speed and using figure 26, the propeller optimum speed and the power are obtained. Then, with equation 30 the rotor q component is determined as reference.

The inertia of the blades turned by the drive is large and a real pitch actuator has thus limited capabilities. Its dynamics are non-linear with saturation limits on pitch angle (usually from 0 to 30°) and pitching speed rate around 10°/s.

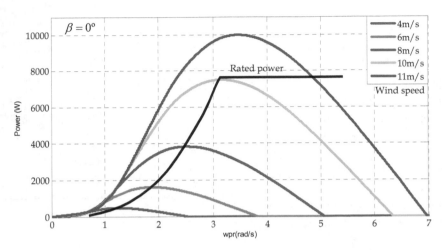

Fig. 26. Obtained wind power for a pitch angle of 0°, depending on wind speed and propeller speed

The actuator is modelled in closed loop with saturation of the pitch angle and a pitch rate limitation. This closed loop configuration with integrator, gives similar result as a first order transfer function but with limitation of the pitch rate (Bindner, 1999). If the pitch reference angle is outside the lower and higher limits, the integrator output is prevented from growing indefinitely.

The pitch control diagram is shown in figure 27, where P is the DFIG real power, Pmax DFIG is the maximum admissible power for the DFIG and P* is the active power reference.

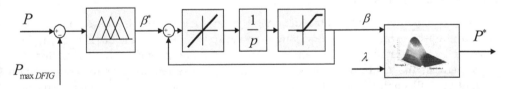

Fig. 27. Pitch control diagram

The pitching speed rate is fixed to 10°/s, the pitch angle is limited from 0 to 30°, the KP value and the scaling factors adjusted after simulations ensuring stability for the pitch controller are $KP = 0.003$, $GE = 400$, $GCE = 0.24$ and $GCU = 0.1$. The hybrid fuzzy regulator maximum and minimum limits are 0 to 30° as pitch angle reference limit.

Figure 28 left, shows the response of the pitch control when a wind speed step from 9m/s to 13m/s is produced. The obtained total power from the wind at 9m/s is 3800w and when the wind speed power is higher than the fixed 7000w, the pitch angle starts the regulation to limit the total power. The figure to the right shows the same signals for a random speed profile. When the wind speed is lower than 10m/s the pitch angle is zero, and all wind power is converted in electric power, but when the speed is higher, the pitch angle is regulated limiting the maximum power returned to the grid.

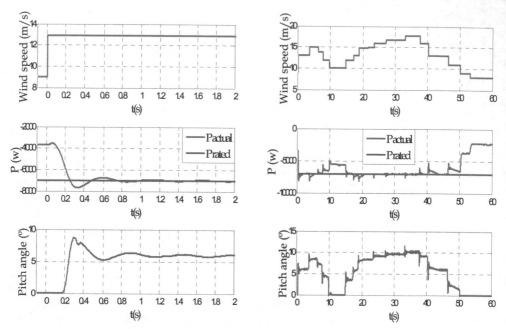

Fig. 28. Fuzzy pitch control performance when a step of wind speed and a random wind speed profile are produced

6. Parameter variations

As it was commented into the introduction, the fuzzy logic approach is based on linguistic rules, and the controller robustness is high. To verify the above, the squirrel-cage motor is replaced by a different one. The motor parameters change and without realizing any adjustment in the controllers the speed regulation is tested in a motor control with conventional PI controllers and with the proposed hybrid fuzzy controllers. The new motor parameters are: Rr=1.2 Ω, Rs=1.5 Ω, Lm=0.108 H, Lr=0.12 H, Ls=0.12 H, J=0.038 Kg*m².

Figure 29 shows the speed of the machine when there is a big noise in the stator alfa and beta components; in fact the noise is very high. The speed reference is 1000 rpm and a load step of 40 Nm is applied to the new machine, without readjusting the controllers, at 0.5s. The left figure shows the response of the machine controlled with PI controllers. The performance of the system becomes wrong when the load changes after 0.5s, the system becomes instable. Instead, in the right figure the motor is controlled with the hybrid fuzzy controllers adjusted in section 4. When the load torque is applied to the machine the speed regulation after that moment is correct. This is an example of the robustness of the fuzzy controller compared with the conventional PI controllers when there is noise in the measurements, in this case stator current measurement.

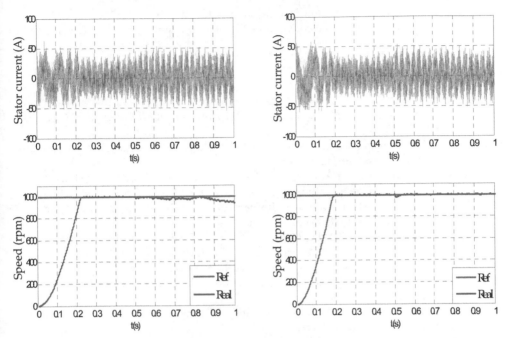

Fig. 29. Speed regulation when there is a big noise in the stator current measurement. A load step of 40Nm is applied to the machine at 0.5s. Left, PI controllers. Right, hybrid fuzzy controllers

7. Conclusions

Control of asynchronous machines can be made relatively simple if the machine is understood as a DC machine. This is obtained making the appropriate transformations of reference systems. The squirrel cage machine has been used as a motor and hybrid fuzzy controllers have been used to control the speed of the machine. The performance has been compared with classical PI and fuzzy controllers, showing a better performance. Also a speed estimator has been implemented using two hybrid fuzzy controllers. The speed sensor has been replaced for the speed estimator to get a sensorless system.

The control of the double feed induction generator used in wind turbines has been studied. First the main control equations are presented and then, the rotor current controllers are implemented with the hybrid fuzzy controllers. The performance is compared to conventional PI controllers, showing a slightly better performance. Also pitch control is realized to limit the maximum power obtained from the wind. The real system shows how the controller limits the maximum power properly.

All the proposed controllers have been simulated and compared to the real system to validate the systems model. With the checked models, the adjustments to guarantee the stability and to get good performance are done. Then, all of simulated hybrid fuzzy controllers have been implemented in the real platforms giving good results.

Also, the robustness of the controlled system with the hybrid fuzzy controllers is demonstrated, compared with the conventional control implemented with conventional PI regulators.

8. References

Astrom, K.J. ; Hagglung, T. (1996). Automatic tuning of PID controllers. *The Control Handbook. A CRC Handbook Published in Cooperation with IEEE Press* 1996 CRC Press, Inc. pp 817-846.

Bindner, H. (1999). Active Control : Wind Turbine Model. *Riso-R-920(EN)*. Riso National Laboratory, Roskilde, Denmark.

Cortajarena, J.A. ; Marcos,J. ; Alkorta, P. ; Vicandi, F.J. ; Alvarez, P. (2006). System to study induction motor speed estimators. *Proceedings of SAAEI06*. Gijón.

dSPACE©, (2005). Real –Time Interface. Implementattion Guide. Experiment Guide. For Realese 5.0. GmbH Paderborn, Germany.

Hansen, A.D. ; Sørensen, P. ; Iov, F. ; Blaabjerg, F. (2007) Overall control strategy of variable speed doubly-fed induction generator wind turbine. *Proc. of Wind Power Nordic Conference*, Chalmers University of Technology, Göteborg, Sweden, pp. 1-7.

Holtz, J. (1996). Methods for Speed Sensorless Control of AC Drives. Sensorless Control of AC Motor Drives. *IEEE Press*,pp21-29.

Jantzen, J. (1998). Tuning of Fuzzy PID Controllers. *Tech. report no 98-H-871 (fpid)*. Technical University of Denmark, Lyngby.

Li, W. (1998). Design of a hybrid fuzzy logic proportional plus conventional integral-derivative controller. *IEEE. Trans. Fuzzy Syst.*, Vol. 6, no. 4, pp 449-463.

Patel, A.V. (2005). Simplest Fuzzy PI Controllers under Various Defuzzification Methods. *International Journal Of Computational Cognition*. Vol. 3, no. 1, pp 21-34.

Vas, P. (1999). *Artificial-Intelligent-Based Elecrical Machines and Drives. Application of Fuzzy, Neural, Fuzzy-Neural, and Genetic-Algorithm-Based Techniques*. Oxford University Press, Inc., ISBN 0 19 859397 X, New York.

Won, C.Y. ; Bose, B.K. (1992). An Induction Motor Servo System with Improved Sliding Mode Control. *IEEE Conf. Proceedings of IECON'92*, pp. 60-66.

Zadeh, L.A. (1965). Fuzzy sets. *Information and Control*, Vol. 8 pp 338-353.

Zhen, L. ; Xu, L. (1998). Sensorless Field Oriented Control of Induction Machines Based on a Mutual MRAS Scheme. *IEEE Trans. on Indust. Electonics*. Vol 45. no.5. pp 824-830.

3

Humanoid Robot: Design and Fuzzy Logic Control Technique for Its Intelligent Behaviors

Elmer P. Dadios, Jazper Jan C. Biliran,
Ron-Ron G. Garcia, D. Johnson, and Adranne Rachel B. Valencia
*De La Salle University, Manila,
Philippines*

1. Introduction

A humanoid robot is a robot with its overall appearance based on that of the human body [1]. In general humanoid robots have a torso with a head, two arms and two legs, although some forms of humanoid robots may model only part of the body, for example, the upper torso. Some humanoid robots may also have a face with eyes and mouth equip with facial interfaces [2, 3, 4, 5]. A humanoid robot is autonomous because it can adapt to changes in its environment or itself and continue to reach its goal [6]. This is the main difference between humanoids and other kinds of robots, like industrial robots, which are used to performing tasks in highly structured environments.

Humanoid robots are created to imitate some of the same physical and mental tasks that humans undergo daily [7]. Scientists and specialists from many different fields including engineering, cognitive science, and linguistics combine their efforts to create a robot as human-like as possible [8, 9]. Their creators' goal for the robot is that for it to both understand human intelligence, reason and act like humans [7]. If humanoids are able to do so, they could eventually work alongside with humans.

There are many issues involves in developing a humanoid robot [1, 10, 11]. But the most difficult is balancing the robot while it does its motion. Babies take several months before they learn to walk; one reason is the gravity affecting our body weight. Like humans, robots also have gravitational force affecting on it. This is the reason why conducting research in this field is still very challenging and exciting [14.15].

The next section of this chapter is organized as follows: section 2 discusses the physical design of the robot. This involves the design and development of mechanical structure of the robot. Section 3 presents the sensors that are use for gathering environment information. The inputs from these sensors are used for robot perception and intelligence. Section 4 discusses the power needed to fully operate the humanoid robot. Section 5 discusses the microcontroller used that does the control execution and operation of the robot. Section 6 discusses the fuzzy logic algorithm developed for the total intelligence and control of the robot. Section 7 present the experiment results conducted in this research. Discussions and analysis of these results are also presented in this section. Finally, section 8 presents the conclusion and recommendations for future work.

2. The humanoid robot mechanical design

The physical structure of the robot developed in this research is shown in figure 1. It has 17 degrees of freedom. Hence, it utilizes 17 servomotors as its actuators to perform its dynamic motions. There are 10 motors employed for the legs, 6 motors for the arms, and 1 motor for the head. The servo motor used in this research requires 3-5 Volts peak-to-peak square wave pulse. Pulse duration is from 0.9ms to 2.1ms with 1.5 ms as center. The pulse refreshes at 50 Hz (20ms). It is operated with a 4.8-6.0 Volts.

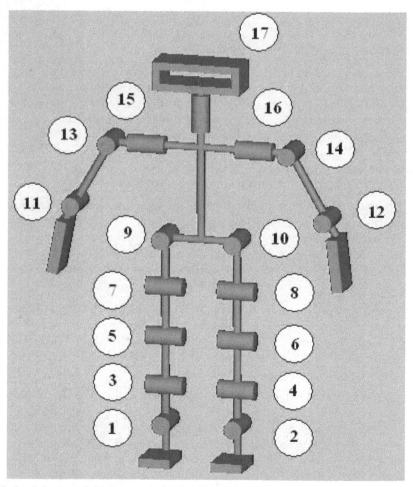

Fig. 1. Skeletal design of the humanoid robot with 17 degrees of freedom.

The arrangement or position of the motors is crucial for the movement of the robot. The motors are connected to each other using aluminum brackets. Design for the aluminum brackets for the arm and legs follow the movements set for the motor. Each bracket is capable of tilting to the left and right for the rotational span allowed by the servo motor. Each aluminum bracket has multiple holes for connecting plates and brackets to one another. The brackets also act as the shield that protects the servo motor and robust enough to avoid damage when it falls. Despite of its rigidity, the bracket material should be lighter and can carry the servo motors as well as the total load of the robot including its circuitry.

The body of the robot is made of a durable acrylic plastic case and is used to protect the control board and circuitry from damage. Several factors were considered in the design of the body casing. The dimensions of the casing were designed to accommodate the IC power battery and the microcontroller. It is also important for the body case to be proportional to the dimensions of the legs and the arms of the robot.

3. The sensors used for the humanoid robot intelligence

The sensors are needed by the robot to gather information about the conditions of the environment to allow the robot to make necessary decisions about its position or certain actions that the situation requires. In this research, four types of sensors are utilized: infrared and ultrasonic sensors for obstacle detection, tilt sensor for robot balancing, and color sensor for ball recognition. Details of the position of these sensors are shown in figure 2.

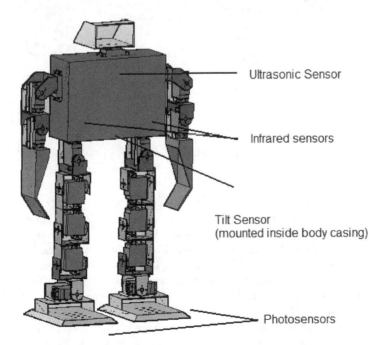

Fig. 2. The Humanoid Robot with sensors locations.

Figure3 shows the reflective infrared sensor used to detect objects in proximity. The basic circuit involves an IR LED and an IR photodiode. The IR LED will emit light and the photodiode will measure the amount of light reflected back. When an object is in proximity, more light will be reflected to the IR photodiode. The Ultrasonic Sensor SRF04 is used also in this research to avoid obstacles. This is an Ultrasonic Range Finder Designed and manufactured by Devantech and is capable of non-contact distance measurements from 3 cm to 3 m. The SRF04 is also easy to connect to the microcontroller as it only needs two I/O pins. It requires a 10uS minimum TTL level pulse input trigger. The echo pulse is a positive TTL level signal (100 uS – 18 mS), with its width proportional to the range. If no object is detected, the width of the echo is approximately 36 mS.

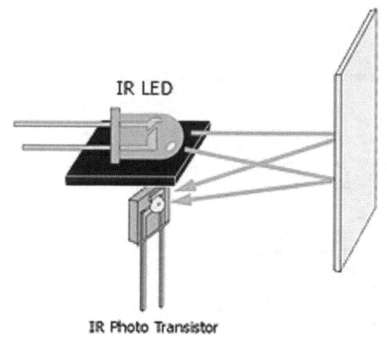

IR LED

IR Photo Transistor

Fig. 3. Basic Reflective IR Proximity Sensor.

The tilt sensor ADXL202 is used in this research to determine the inclination of the robot which is then used by the controller developed to stabilize and balance the robot. It measures the tilting in two axes of a reference plane. Full motion uses at least three axes and additional sensors. One way to measure tilt angle with reference to the earth's ground is to use the accelerometer. The ADXL202 is a low-cost, low power 2-axis accelerometer which can measure both dynamic acceleration and static acceleration. This accelerometer is small, requires small amount of voltage, and outputs an analog voltage that could readily be used by the main controller. A Photo Sensor is used to identify the yellow ball which the robot has to kick. The circuit of this sensor is basically a voltage divider a simple linear circuit that generates an output voltage that is a fraction of its input voltage. Voltage division refers to the partitioning of a voltage among the components of the divider.

The Photo Sensor circuit component is a photoresistor or an LDR (Light Dependent Resistor) in series with a fixed resistor. The LDR must be a part of a voltage divider circuit in order to give an output voltage which varies with illumination. The super bright light emitting diode will provide the light to the LDR. When an object is placed in front of the LDR and LED at about 10-20mm away, some of the light will reflect back to the LDR, depending on the material. A material with a bright color will reflect more light to the LDR. A black material will absorb all the light and nothing will be reflected. In this project, the robot needs to detect a yellow ball for it to kick. The disadvantage with the circuit presented is that it will also detect a material brighter than yellow. However, the scope of this project is only to detect the yellow ball, and not to differentiate it from other colors.

4. Power management and power source

Power management is an essential part of the humanoid robot. This part functions to ensure that the proper voltage is supplied to the servos as well as the sensors and the microcontroller. There are circumstances where in the power supplied to the motors exceeds the power required. In cases like this, probable damage could occur. That is why it is essential to have the voltage regulated.

For voltage regulation, the LM338k transistor was used as the primary part of the regulator circuit. The primary choice would have been the LM7805, which is the most widely used transistor. It supplies 5 volts and is capable of generating 1 to 1.5 A of current. However, with the number of motors used in this project, the current rating of the LM7805 would be insufficient. Hence, the LM338k was opted due to its higher current rating at about 1 to 5 Amperes, ensuring that ample amount of current is supplied to the motors.

There are six outputs in the circuit for the servo motors. Four voltage regulators were used to accommodate 24 motors. Only 17 motors were used but additional outputs were added to accommodate the sensors and other additions. The output voltage can be solved using the formula

$$Vo = V_{ref} + (1 + R2/R1) + I_{adj}R2 \qquad (1)$$

An output of 5.9 volts is desired so R2 is set at 450 ohms, and R1, which is constant, is 120 ohms. Vref = 1.25 and Iadj = 50uA.

Substituting,

$$Vo = 1.25(1+450/120) + 50uA(340) \qquad (2)$$

the value of Vo is obtained.

$$Vo = 5.95 \text{ V} \qquad (3)$$

This research utilizes packed 7.2 volt Lithium Ion Batteries as the power source of the robot. It would then be regulated to approximately 5.9 volts. Lithium Ion batteries are light weight which is a big factor for this project considering the size and the movements needed to be performed by the robot. NiMH batteries (Nickel Metal Hydrite) were also an option but to be able to supply the required voltage needed by the robot, the battery has to be customized, which made the batteries bulky and heavy. Litihium Ion Batteries were also readily available.

5. The microcontroller: Robot brain

The Atmega128 microcontroller used in this research serves as the main controller of the entire system. It is in-charge for processing all the input data and output data needed by the robot. Input data refers to the information taken from all the sensors and control switches. Output data are the signals needed by the servo motors in order to provide proper results in different situations for robot actions. Being the only microcontroller in the system, information from all modules is all carried in and out from this single controller. These modules are: the power management unit, the sensor information unit, the servo motor control unit, the artificial intelligence unit, and the central control unit.

The power management unit is the one responsible for distributing and monitoring the power to the entire system supplied by the batteries. If one of these batteries reaches critical level, the power management unit updates the microcontroller about the situation so that the microcontroller will be able to decide if the robot should continue its task or should stop.

The sensor information unit is responsible for all the system inputs of the robot. All of these inputs are fed into the microcontroller and then processed to provide the robot appropriate action for every situation.

The servo motor control unit is responsible for providing signals for each servo motor of the robot. Timing is considered an important factor in this module unlike all other modules where timing is not as important. One problem encountered in this research was that it would be difficult to control all motors from the output port pins of the microcontroller. Because of this problem, several approaches were considered. Using a separate microcontroller was first considered for controlling all the 17 servo motors. But using another microcontroller just for controlling the servo motors will defeat the purpose of using just one microcontroller for the whole system and will only pose new problems for the whole system like the communication and synchronization of the two microcontrollers. The solution was to make use of the Atmega128's timer/counter and connect the 17 servo motors to two 4017 decade counters.

The central control unit is responsible for the main controls of the robot. This module is a switch panel consists of a power supply switch, a reset switch, and 8 action switches. All batteries are connected to the power supply switch which turns the robot on and off. The reset switch is a normally open tact switch that is connected to the active low reset pin of the microcontroller and ground. The action switches determine what action the robot will be performing. These switches are connected to the 8 external interrupt pins of the microcontroller which are configured as level triggered, meaning the interrupt will trigger once the switch is held low. Also, these external interrupts INT0-INT7 have priority levels. INT0 being the most prioritized and INT7 as least prioritized interrupt.

6. The robot intelligence: Fuzzy logic system

The Fuzzy Logic System module is used for the artificial intelligence control algorithm of the robot. This module is responsible for the stability and balancing of the robot while it is performing actions such as walking and kicking. Implementation of fuzzy logic is inside the microcontroller software which is modifiable and adjustable. Since the implementation is in software, this procedure is processed inside the microcontroller in which the input values are taken from the tilt sensor and the output values provide the servo motors correct positions.

Fuzzy logic is a problem-solving control system methodology that mimics how humans derive a conclusion based on vague, ambiguous, imprecise, noisy or missing input information [12, 13]. The general idea about fuzzy logic is that it takes the inputs from the sensors which is a crisp value and transforms it into membership values ranging from 0 to 1. It then undergoes fuzzy reasoning process using the obtained membership values with the set of rules created. From the previous process, the system obtains a fuzzy set that will be transformed back to crisp values which controls the servo motors [12, 13]. Fuzzy logic systems are capable of processing inexact data and produce acceptable outputs. In addition, there is no need for very complex mathematical computations to control the robot. Also, the physical design of the robot does not need to be very exact and complicated as the fuzzy logic system can compensate for these flaws. Since the fuzzy logic is implemented using software, adjustments in the system is easier, cheaper and additional space is not needed which will only mean additional weight to the robot.

Two fuzzy logic system (FLS) controllers are developed in this research for the robot's balancing and stability. One FLS controls the left and right tilt and the other FLS controls the forward and backward tilt. Tilt angle in the first fuzzy logic system, which is for the left and right tilt, is taken and processed. Then the second fuzzy logic system will do the same with the forward and backward tilt angle. The idea is to operate the two fuzzy logic systems independently. This approach is more advantageous in terms of software implementation and complexity of the entire fuzzy logic system.

The Mamdani's method was used for implementing the fuzzy logic systems because of its simple yet great composition of 'min-max' operations [16]. Sample membership functions are shown in figures 4 to 9. Tables 1 and 2 shows the fuzzy associative memory matrix of the 2 fuzzy logic systems with the corresponding rules. Tables 3 and 4 show the final output on deciding what motors to activate. The idea is all the affected motors are going to increase or decrease their current angle until the system becomes stable. The amount of the angle shift will depend on the position of the motor in the robot. Observably, change in the angle of the motors located near the ground will have greater effect to the whole body than motors located less near the ground.

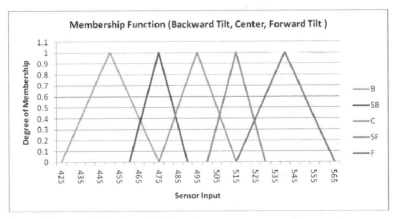

Fig. 4. Backward-Forward Membership Function

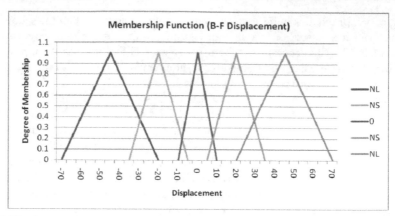

Fig. 5. B-F Displacement

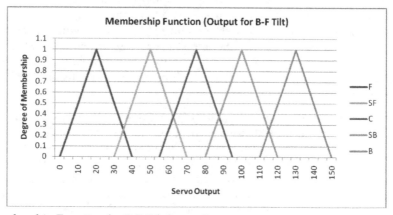

Fig. 6. Membership Function for B-F Tilt Servo Output

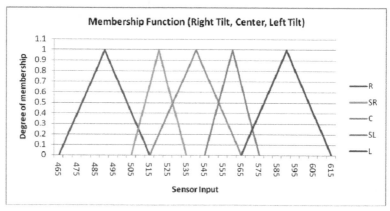

Fig. 7. Right-Left Membership Function

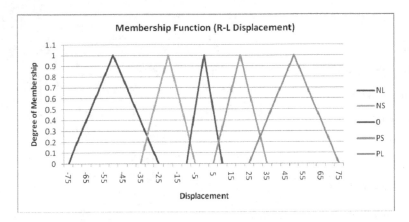

Fig. 8. R-L Displacement

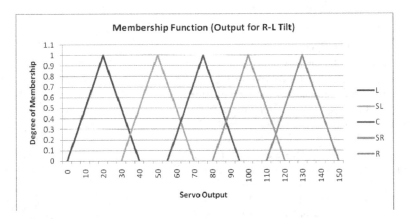

Fig. 9. Membership Function for R-L Tilt Servo Output

FLC 1		Displacement				
		NL	NS	0	PS	PL
B-F Tilt	B			F	F	F
	SB			SF	SF	F
	C	C	C	C	C	C
	SF	B	SB	SB		
	F	B	B	B		

Table 1. Fuzzy Logic Controller (FLC) 1 FAM

B – backward

F – forward

R - right

L - left

C - center

SB - slightly backward

SF - slightly forward

SR - slightly right

SL - slightly left

NL - negative large

NS - negative small

0 (zero) - negligible

PS - positive small

PL - positive large

RULES for (FLC) 1

1. if tilt is B and delta x is 0 (zero) then output is F.
2. if tilt is B and delta x is PS then output is F.
3. if tilt is B and delta x is PL then output is F.
4. if tilt is SB and delta x is 0 (zero) then output is SF.
5. if tilt is SB and delta x is PS then output is SF.
6. if tilt is SB and delta x is PL then output is F.
7. if tilt is C and delta x is NL then output is C.
8. if tilt is C and delta x is NS then output is C.
9. if tilt is C and delta x is 0 (zero) then output is C.
10. if tilt is C and delta x is PS then output is C.
11. if tilt is C and delta x is PL then output is C.
12. if tilt is SF and delta x is NL then output is B.
13. if tilt is SF and delta x is NS then output is SB.
14. if tilt is SF and delta x is 0 (zero) then output is SB.
15. if tilt is F and delta x is NL then output is B.
16. if tilt is F and delta x is NS then output is B.
17. if tilt is F and delta x is 0 (zero) then output is B.

FLC 2		Displacement				
		NL	NS	0	PS	PL
R-L Tilt	R			L	L	L
	SR			SL	SL	L
	C	C	C	C	C	C
	SL	R	SR	SR		
	L	R	R	R		

Table 2. Fuzzy Logic Controller (FLC) 2 FAM

RULES for (FLC) 2

1. if tilt is R and delta x is 0 (zero) then output is L.
2. if tilt is R and delta x is PS then output is L.
3. if tilt is R and delta x is PL then output is L.
4. if tilt is SR and delta x is 0 (zero) then output is SL.
5. if tilt is SR and delta x is PS then output is SL.
6. if tilt is SR and delta x is PL then output is L.
7. if tilt is C and delta x is NL then output is C.
8. if tilt is C and delta x is NS then output is C.
9. if tilt is C and delta x is 0 (zero) then output is C.
10. if tilt is C and delta x is PS then output is C.
11. if tilt is C and delta x is PL then output is C.
12. if tilt is SL and delta x is NL then output is R.
13. if tilt is SL and delta x is NS then output is SR.
14. if tilt is SL and delta x is 0 (zero) then output is SR.
15. if tilt is L and delta x is NL then output is R.
16. if tilt is L and delta x is NS then output is R.
17. if tilt is L and delta x is 0 (zero) then output is R.

Having established these two fuzzy logic systems, the balancing task will entirely depend on these. Failure to one of these systems would mean failure to the entire balancing task of the robot.

Output	Affected Motor
L	1,2,3,4,5,6,7,8
SL	1,2,3,4,5,6,7,8
C	None
SR	1,2,3,4,5,6,7,8
R	1,2,3,4,5,6,7,8

Table 3. Fuzzy Logic System R-L Output

Output	Affected Motor
F	3,4,7,8
SF	3,4,7,8
C	None
SB	3,4,7,8
B	3,4,7,8

Table 4. Fuzzy Logic System B-F Output

7. Experiment results

7.1 Inclined steel plate balancing experiments

In this experiment, a steel plate platform was used to measure the balancing capability of the robot. One end of the platform was gradually elevated so that the robot is standing on an inclined plane and the maximum angle the robot can stay on standing position is recorded. Figures 10-13 shows the sample results of the real and physical experiments conducted. It can be seen in this figure that the robot uses its left foot to maintain its balance that compensate the angle taken on the inclined plane.

There were 4 tests of experiments conducted based on actual position of the robot relative to the inclined plane. The first test was the robot facing right of elevated steel plate as shown in figure 7. The second test was the robot facing left of the inclined steel plate as shown in figure 8. The third was the robot facing front of the inclined steel plate as shown in figure 9. And the fourth was the robot facing back of the inclined steel plate as shown in figure 10. It can be seen from these pictures that the robot uses its foot and body to maintain its stability. Figures 14a and 14b shows the results of these experiments with a comparison of the performance of the fuzzy logic controller against the conventional controller. Clearly from these results we can see the superiority of the fuzzy logic controller developed.

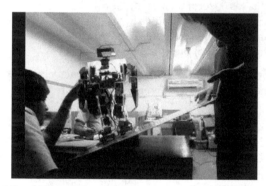

Fig. 10. Robot Inclined Steel Plate Balancing Experiment. Right position. Note that the hand of the person is not touching the robot. This is just in preparation to catch the robot when it falls.

Fig. 11. Robot Inclined Steel Plate Balancing Experiment. Left position. Note that the hand of the person is not touching the robot. This is just in preparation to catch the robot when it falls.

Fig. 12. Robot Inclined Steel Plate Balancing Experiment. Back position. Note that the hand of the person is not touching the robot. This is just in preparation to catch the robot when it falls.

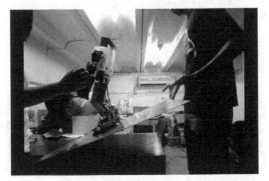

Fig. 13. Robot Inclined Steel Plate Balancing Experiment. Front position. Note that the hand of the person is not touching the robot. This is just in preparation to catch the robot when it falls.

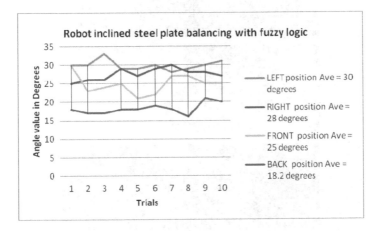

Fig. 14a. Humanoid robot steel plate balancing performance with fuzzy logic controller

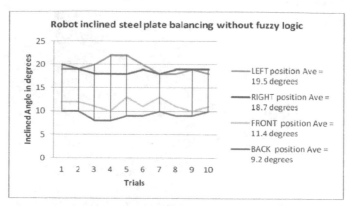

Fig. 14b. Humanoid robot steel plate balancing performance without fuzzy logic controller

7.2 Ball kicking experiments

The humanoid robot developed in this research can identify and kick a yellow tennis ball. A photo sensor is installed on the foot of the robot. Once the sensor found the ball the robot position itself to do the kicking. Complete animation of this task is shown in figure 15.

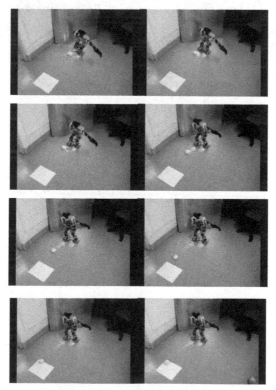

Fig. 15. Ball kicking experiment results

The robot uses its arm to balance itself in addition to its body alignment. Figure 16 shows the statistics of the robot performance in kicking the ball. The average distance the ball travel after kicking is 14.6 inches. Clearly from this figures the robot is very stable and reliable in performing this motions.

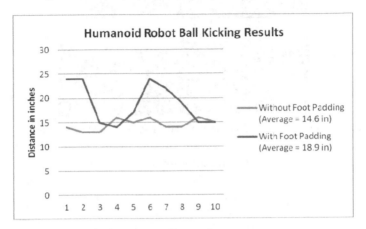

Fig. 16. Humanoid robot ball kicking controller performance.

7.3 Obstacle avoidance experiments

The robot uses ultrasonic and infra red sensors to detect the obstacles on its path. The positions of these sensors are evenly distributed on the robot's body. It is at the right, left, and center positions. When only the right sensor detects the obstacle the robot will do left side step motions until no obstacle is found. When only the left sensor detects the obstacle the robot will do right side steps motions until no obstacle is found. When all three ultrasonic sensors detect obstacle the robot will stop. If there are no more obstacles found the robot will walk forward right away. Figure 17 shows the animated motions of the robot in performing this task. The obstacle is on the right side of the robot hence the robot did left side step motion until the obstacle is not found. Figure 18 shows the distance accuracy of the robot in detecting obstacles. In all obstacle avoidance experiments conducted the robot shows very accurate, reliable, and robust behavior.

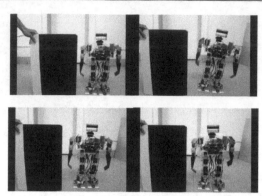

Fig. 17. Humanoid robot obstacle Avoidance - side step and forward motion.

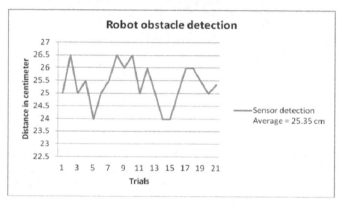

Fig. 18. Robot accuracy in detecting obstacles

7.4 Robot dancing experiments

The humanoid robot developed in this research has the capability to entertain people by dancing. In this experiment, the beat of the music is synchronized to the robot body, arm, head, and leg motions. Figure 19 shows the sample robot dancing motions with the music beats.

Fig. 19. Humanoid robot dancing results

8. Conclusions and recommendation

The paper showed a working prototype of a humanoid robot with artificial intelligence that has the ability to walk on two legs, kick a tennis ball, balance in an inclined steel plate, avoid obstacles, and dance with the beat of the music. Harmony between the parts of the robot namely mechanical, electrical and software is a must. The mechanical design deals with the overall physical architecture of the robot. It considers everything about the robot's whole skeletal system. The degrees of freedom for the robot are determined in this part. Proportion between the parts of the robot is very important as it would help in its stability thus making it easier to control.

The software design tackles all the decision making of the robot. This acts as the main brain of the robot. Fuzzy logic is implemented in order for the robot to maintain its balance and stability. The controller developed using fuzzy logic in this research exhibits very accurate, reliable, and robust behavior as shown in the defferent experiments conducted in section seven.

Electrical design deals with connecting the mechanical and software parts of the robot to translate into actual robot movement. Tilt sensor, infrared and ultrasonic is provided with ample voltage supply to work efficiently. An analog to digital converter is not needed anymore as Atmega128 has its built in capability. Power sources were designed to output sufficient amounts of energy that would run the motors and sensors efficiently. A double sided PCB is used to implement the circuit main board. The result of using a big and dual sided PCB was a harder time troubleshooting when problems occurred as well as aligning the two sides correctly.

All of these parts are needed to be done meticulously with the aim of making it very reliable. A design plan should always be followed as well as coordination between all of its parts. A conflict was experienced on whether to use rubber padding or not for the feet. Balancing in an inclined plane would require rubber padding. Without rubber padding, the robot slips down the plane. However, with the rubber padding on, the robot's walking is compromised even with slightly slippery rubber padding. The authors decided not to use the rubber padding as the robot's walking has a higher priority. For future works, it will be good to put an internal vision system on this robot in order for it to recognize and know the environment better.

9. References

[1] Kazuo Hirai, *"Current and future perspective of honda humanoid robot"*, In Proc. IEEE/RSJ Int. Conf. Intell. Robot. & Sys. (IROS), pages 500-508, 1997.

[2] B. Robins, K. Dautenhahn, R. Te Boekhorst, A. Billard,*"Robotic assistants in therapy and education of children with autism: can a small humanoid robot help encourage social interaction skills?"* ,pages 105-120 Published online: 8 July 2005, Springer-Verlag 2005

[3] Sproull, L., Subramani, M., Kiesler, S., Walker, J.H. and et al. *"When the interface is a face. Human-Computer Interaction"*, 11 (2). 97-124.

[4] Takeuchi, A. and Nagao, K., *"Communicative Facial Displays as A New Conversational Modality"*,. In Proceedings of INTERCHI 93, (Amsterdam, the Netherlands, 1993), ACM Press: New York, 187-193.

[5] Takeuchi, A. and Naito, T., *"Situated Facial displays: Towards Social interaction"*, In Proceedings of Human Factors in Computing Systems 95, (1995), ACM Press: New York, 450-455.

[6] S. Kagami, F. Kanehiro, Y. Tamiya, M. Inaba, and H. Inoue, *"AutoBalancer: An Online Dynamic Balance Compensation Scheme for Humanoid Robots"*, In Proc. Int. Workshop Alg. Found. Robot.(WAFR), 2000.

[7] A. Bruce, I. Nourbakhsh, and R. Simmons, *"The Role of Expressiveness and Attention in Human-Robot Interaction"*, In Proceedings, AAAI Fall Symposium. (2001).

[8] C. Breazeal, J. Velasquez, *"Toward Teaching a Robot Infant" using Emotive Communication Acts"*, In Proceedings of Simulation of Adaptive Behavior, workshop on Socially Situated Intelligence 98, (Zurich, Switzerland, 1998), 25-40.

[9] C. Breazeal, J. Velasquez, *"Robot in Society: Friend or Appliance?"*, In Proceedings of Agents 99 Workshop on emotion-based agent architectures, (Seattle, WA, 1999), 18-26.

[10] K. Nagasaka, M. Inaba, and H. Inoue, *" Walking pattern generation for a humanoid robot based on optimal gradient method"*, In Proc. IEEE Int. Conf. Sys. Man. & Cyber., 1999.

[11] J. Yamaguchi, S. Inoue, D. Nishino, and A. Takanishi, *" Development of a bipedal humanoid robot having antagonistic driven joints and three dof trunk"*, In Proc. IEEE/RSJ Int. Conf. Intell. Robot. & Sys. (IROS), pages 96{101, 1998.

[12] E.P. Dadios, et. al, *"Hybrid Fuzzy Logic Strategy for Soccer Robot Game"*, *Journal of Advanced Computational Intelligence and Intelligent Informatics*, Vol 8 No. 1, pp 65-71, FUJI Technology Press, January 2004.

[13] E.P. Dadios, et. al, *"Fuzzy Logic Controller for Micro Robot Soccer Game"*, *Proceedings of the 27th Annual Conference of the IEEE Industrial Electronics Society (IECON'01)*, Hyatt Regency Tech Center, Denver, Colorado, USA, pp. 2154-2159, Nov. 29 – Dec. 2, 2001.

[14] G. Oriolo, L. Sciavicco, B. Siciliano, and L. Villani, *"Robotics: modelling, planning and control."*, Springer Verlag, London 2010.

[15] B. Siciliano, and O. Khatib, Springer Handbook of Robotics. (ISBN 978-3-540-30301-5), Springer Verlag, Berlin Heidelberg, 2008.

[16] E.H. Mamdani, *"Application Of Fuzzy Algorithm for the Control of a dynamic plant"*, IEEE Proc., Vol. 121, pages 1585-1588, 1974.

4

Application of Fuzzy Logic in Mobile Robot Navigation

Tang Sai Hong, Danial Nakhaeinia and Babak Karasfi
Universiti Putra Malaysia
Malaysia

1. Introduction

An autonomous robot is a programmable and multi-functional machine, able to extract information from its surrounding using different kinds of sensors to plan and execute collision free motions within its environment without human intervention. Navigation is a crucial issue for robots that claim to be mobile. A navigation system can be divided into two layers: High level global planning and Low-level reactive control. In high-level planning, a prior knowledge of environment is available and the robot workspace is completely or partially known. Using the world model, the global planner can determine the robot motion direction and generates minimum-cost paths towards the target in the presence of complex obstacles. However, since it is not capable of changing the motion direction in presence of unforeseen or moving obstacles, it fails to reach target. In contrast, in low-level reactive control, the robot work space is unknown and dynamic. It generates control commands based on perception-action configuration, which the robot uses current sensory information to take appropriate actions without planning process. Thus, it has a quick response in reacting to unforeseen obstacles and uncertainties with changing the motion direction.

Several Artificial intelligence techniques such as reinforcement learning, neural networks, fuzzy logic and genetic algorithms, can be applied for the reactive navigation of mobile robots to improve their performance. Amongst the techniques ability of fuzzy logic to represent linguistic terms and reliable decision making in spite of uncertainty and imprecise information makes it a useful tool in control systems.

Fuzzy control systems are rule-based or knowledge-based systems containing a collection of fuzzy IF-THEN rules based on the domain knowledge or human experts. The simplicity of fuzzy rule-based systems, capability to perform a wide variety tasks without explicit computations and measurements make it extensively popular among the scientists and researcher. This book chapter presents the significance and effectiveness of fuzzy logic in solving the navigation problem. The chapter is organized as follows:

After the introduction of fuzzy logic importance in mobile robot navigation, **Section 2** reviews methodology of previous works on navigation of mobile robots using fuzzy logic design. **Section 3,** first gives a brief description about the design of a Fuzzy Controller, then a case study shows how the fuzzy control system is used in mobile robots navigation.

Results from real systems address the fuzzy control influence and effectiveness to solve some of the navigation difficulties and to reduce their navigation costs. Closing this book chapter, **Section 4** concludes the chapter with few comments and summarizes the advantages and limitations of using fuzzy logic in mobile robot navigation. The chapter can be interesting for students, researchers and different scientific communities in the areas of robotics, artificial intelligence, intelligent transportation systems, and fuzzy control.

2. Review of fuzzy logic applications for mobile robot navigation

Robust and reliable navigation in dynamic or unknown environment relies on ability of the robots in moving among unknown obstacles without collision and fast reaction to uncertainties. It is highly desirable to develop these tasks using a technique which utilize human reasoning and decision making. Fuzzy logic provides a means to capture the human mind's expertise. It utilizes this heuristic knowledge for representing and accomplishment of a methodology to develop perception-action based strategies for mobile robots navigation. Furthermore, the methodology of the FLC is very helpful dealing with uncertainties in real world and accurate model of the environment is not absolutely required for navigation. Therefore, based on a simple design, easy implementation and robustness properties of FLC, many approaches were developed to solve mobile robot navigation problem in target tracking, path tracking, obstacle avoidance, behaviour coordination, environment modelling, and layer integration (Saffiotti, 1997). This section reviews the proposed fuzzy control methods which used fuzzy sets for velocity control, rotation control and command fusion with focusing on the three most popular categories of: Path tracking, Obstacle avoidance and Behavior coordination.

2.1 Fuzzy logic for path tracking

Path tracking is a crucial function for autonomous mobile robots to navigate along a desired path. This task includes tracking of previously computed paths using a path planner, a defined path by human operator, tracking of walls, road edges, and other natural features in the robot workspace (Chee et al., 1996). It involves real-time perception of the environment to determine the position and orientation of the robot with respect to the desired path. For example in Figure 1, if the robot is misplaced, the controller task is to steer it back on course and minimize the orientation error ($\Delta\varphi$) and the position error (Δx) (Moustris & Tzafestas, 2005). Path tracking difficulties in dealing with imprecise or incomplete perception of environment, representation of inaccuracy in measurements, sensor fusion and compliance with the kinematic limits of the vehicle motivated many researchers to use fuzzy control techniques for path tracking.

Ollero et al. (1994) developed a new fuzzy path-tracking method by combining fuzzy logic with the geometric pure-pursuit and the generalized predictive control techniques. Fuzzy logic is applied to supervise path trackers. Input of the fuzzy is the current state of the robot to the path to generate the appropriate steering angle. A new approach proposed by Braunstingl et al. (1995) to solve the wall following of mobile robots based on the concept of general perception. To construct a general perception of the surroundings from the measuring data provided by all the sensors and representing, a perception vector is assigned to each ultrasonic sensor. All these vectors adding together then combine into a single vector of general perception. A fuzzy controller then uses the perception information to guide the robot along arbitrary walls and obstacles. Sanchez et al. (1999) proposed a fuzzy control system for path tracking of an autonomous vehicle in outdoor environment. The fuzzy controller is used to generate steering and velocity required to track the path using the data collected from experiments of driving the vehicle by a human. Bento et al. (2002) implemented a path-tracking method by means of fuzzy logic for a Wheeled Mobile Robot. Input variables of the fuzzy controller are position and orientation of the robot with respect to the path. Output variables are linear velocity and angular velocity. Hajjaji and Bentalba (2003) have designed a fuzzy controller for path tracking control of vehicles using its nonlinear dynamics model. A Takagi–Sugeno (T–S) fuzzy model presents the nonlinear model of the vehicle. Then a model-based fuzzy controller is developed based on the T–S fuzzy model. A wall-following robot presented by Peri & Simon (2005) which the robot's motion is controlled by a fuzzy controller to drive it along a predefined path. Antonelli et al. (2007) address a path tracking approach based on a fuzzy-logic set of rules which emulates the human driving behavior. The fuzzy system input is represented by approximate information concerning the knowledge of the curvature of the desired path ahead the vehicle and the distance between the next bend and the vehicle. The output is the maximum value of the linear velocity needed to attain by the vehicle in order to safely drive on the path. Yu et al. (2009) used Taguchi method to design an optimal fuzzy logic controller for trajectory tracking of a wheeled mobile robot. Recently, Xiong and Qu (2010) developed a method for intelligent vehicles' path tracking with two fuzzy controller combinations which controls vehicle direction and a preview fuzzy control method presented by Liao et al. (2010) for path tracking of intelligent vehicle. The vehicle speed and direction are adjusted by fuzzy control according to future path information and present path information respectively.

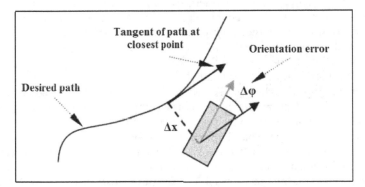

Fig. 1. Typical control input variables for path tracking [9]

2.2 Obstacle avoidance using fuzzy logic

Ability of a robot to avoid collision with unforeseen or dynamic obstacles while it is moving towards a target or tracking a path is a vital task in autonomous navigation. Navigation strategies can be classified to global path planning and local path planning. In global path planning, information about the obstacles and a global model of environment is available which mostly Configuration space, Road map, Voronoi diagram and Potential field techniques are used to plan obstacle-free path towards a target. However, in real world a reliable map of obstacle, accurate model of environment and precise sensory data is unavailable due to uncertainties of the environment. While the computed path may remain valid but to response the unforeseen or dynamic obstacles, it is necessary for the robot to alter its path online. In such situations, Fuzzy logic can provide robust and reliable methodologies dealing with the imprecise input with low computational complexity (Yanik et al., 2010). Different obstacle avoidance approaches were developed during past decades which proposed effective solution to the navigation problems in unknown and dynamic environments.

Chee et al. (1996) presented a two-layer fuzzy inference system in which the first layer fuses the sensor readings. The left and right clearances of the robot were found as outputs of the first-layered fuzzy system. The outputs of the first layer together with the goal direction are used as the inputs of the second-layer. Eventually, the final outputs of the controller are the linear velocity and the turning rate of the robot. The second-stage fuzzy inference system employs the collision avoiding, obstacle following and goal tracking behaviours to achieve robust navigation in unknown environments. Dadios and Maravillas (2002) proposed and implemented a fuzzy control approach for cooperative soccer micro robots. A planner generates a path to the destination and fuzzy logic control the robot's heading direction to avoid obstacles and other robots while the dynamic position of obstacles, ball and robots are considered. Zavlangas et al. (2000) developed a reactive navigation method for omnidirectional mobile robots using fuzzy logic. The fuzzy rule-base generates actuating command to get collision free motions in dynamic environment. The fuzzy logic also provides an adjustable transparent system by a set of learning rules or manually. Seraji and Howard (2002) developed a behavior-based navigation method on challenging terrain using fuzzy logic. The navigation strategy is comprised of three behaviors. Local obstacle avoidance behaviour is consists of a set of fuzzy logic rule statements which generates the robot's speed based on obstacle distance. Parhi (2005) described a control system comprises a fuzzy logic controller and a Petri Net for multi robot navigation. The Fuzzy rules steer the robot according to obstacles distribution or targets position. Since the obstacle's position is not known precisely, to avoid obstacles in a cluttered environment fuzzy logic is a proper technique for this task. Combination of the fuzzy logic controller and a set of collision prevention rules implemented as a Petri Net model embedded in the controller of a mobile robot enable it to avoid obstacles that include other mobile robots. A fuzzy controller designed by Lilly (2007) for obstacle avoidance of an autonomous vehicle using negative fuzzy rules. The negative fuzzy rules define a set of actions to be avoided to direct the vehicle to a target in presence of obstacles. Chao et al. (2009) developed a fuzzy control system for target tracking and obstacle avoidance of a mobile robot. Decision making is handled by the fuzzy control strategy based on the sensed environment using a stereo vision information. A vision- based fuzzy obstacle avoidance proposed for a humanoid robot in (Wong et al., 2011). The nearest obstacle to the robot captured by vision system and the difference angle between goal direction and the robot's heading measured by electronic compass are inputs of the fuzzy system to make a decision for appropriate motion of the robot in unknown environment.

2.3 Fuzzy logic for behaviour coordination

To improve the total performance of a navigation system, complex navigation tasks are broken down into a number of simpler and smaller subsystems (behaviors) which is called behavior-based system. In a behavior-based system, each behavior receives particular sensory information and transforms them into the predefined response. The behaviors include path tracking, obstacle avoidance, target tracking, goal reaching and etc. Finally, based on command output(s) of an active behaviour(s) the robot executes an action (Fig.2) [16].

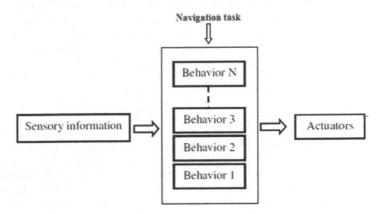

Fig. 2. Behavior- based navigation systems overall architecture

The problems associated with the behavior-based navigation systems is the *behavior coordination* or *action selection*. The multiple behaviors may produce several command outputs simultaneously which may cause the robot move in unintended directions or system fail entirely. Reliable and robust operation of the system relies on the decision about how to integrate high level planning and low level execution behaviors, which behavior should be activated (arbitration) and how output commands should be combined into one command to drive the robot (command fusion). Early solutions were developed based on subsumption architecture (Brooks, 1986) and motor schemas (Arkin, 1989).

The subsumption architecture is composed of several layers of task-achieving behaviors. Coordination of behaviors is based on Priority arbitration (Competitive architecture). In Priority-based arbitration only a behavior with the highest priority is selected to be active when multiple conflicting behaviors are trigged and the other are ignored (Dupre, 2007; Fatmi et al., 2006). The subsumption approach is based on a static arbitration policy which means that the robot actions are predefined and fixed in dealing with certain situations. Since the behavior coordination is competitive and based on a fixed arbitration, it may leads to erratic operation under certain situations (Fatmi et al., 2006). For example in coordination of goal reaching and obstacle avoidance behaviors with rules like:

Obstacle avoidance rules:	Goal reaching rules:
IF Obstacle is left THEN turn right	*IF goal is right THEN turn right*
IF Obstacle is front THEN turn left	*IF goal is left THEN turn left*
.....	....

When an obstacle is detected in front of the robot and the goal is at right, the priority is with Obstacle avoidance behavior and the robot turns left while the goal is at right.

The motor schemas architecture proposed by Arkin (1989) relies on cooperative coordination (command fusion) of behaviors which the multiple behaviors can produce an output concurrently. In this approach output of each behavior is captured based on their particular influence on overall output. The outputs are blended to vote for or against an action. For example in potential fields the outputs are in the vector form. These outputs are combined and the overall response of the system is achieved by the vector summation (Nakhaeinia et al., 2011a). This approach also may lead to conflicting actions or poor performance in certain circumstances. However, fuzzy logic provides a useful mechanism for command fusion coordination and also arbitration fusion coordination. The main fuzzy logic advantages are: i) it can be used for dynamic arbitration which behavior selection is according to the robot's current perceptual state, ii) it allows for easy combination and concurrent execution of various behaviors. A variety of approaches have been developed inspired by the success of fuzzy logic to deal with the behavior coordination limitations.

Leyden (1999) designed a fuzzy logic based navigation system to overcome the subsumption control problem. The proposed system is consists of two behaviors. Output of each behavior is a fuzzy set which are combined using a command fusion process to produce a single fuzzy set. Then, the fuzzy set is defuzzified to make a crisp output. Fatmi et al. (2006) proposed a two layered behavior coordination approach for behavior design and action coordination using fuzzy logic. The first layer is consists of primitive basic behaviors and the second layer is responsible for decision making based on the context about which behavior(s) should be activated and the selected behaviors are blended. In another work presented by (Selekwa, 2005), fuzzy behavior systems proposed for Autonomous navigation of Ground Vehicles in cluttered environment with unknown obstacles. Multivalue reactive fuzzy behaviors are used for arbitrating or fusing of the behaviors which action selection is relied on the available sensor information. In another work by Ramos et al. (2006), a hierarchical fuzzy decision-making algorithm introduced for behaviour coordination of a robot based on arbitration mechanisms. In this method behaviors are not combined and just one behavior with maximum resulting value is selected and executed each time. A Fuzzy action selection approach was developed by Jaafar and McKenzie (2008) for navigation of a virtual agent. The fuzzy controller is comprised of three behaviors. The objective of this work is to solve the behaviour's conflict. The method uses fuzzy α-levels to compute the behavior's weight and the Huwicz criterion is used to select the final action. Wang and Liu (2008) introduced a new behavior-based navigation method called "minimum risk method". This behavior-based method applies the multi-behavior coordination strategy includes the global Goal seeking (GS) and the local Obstacle Avoidance (OA) (or boundary-following) behaviors. The fuzzy logic is applied to design and coordinate the proposed behaviors.

3. Fuzzy control system in mobile robot navigation

In this section, first we show how to design a Fuzzy Controller and then we present a case study to analyze the performance and operation of the fuzzy logic algorithms in the implementation of different behaviors for mobile robot navigation. Most of the proposed methods have applied fuzzy logic algorithm for velocity control, steering control and command fusion in the design of their behaviors. This study evaluates the influence of the design parameters in mobile robots navigation.

3.1 Design of a fuzzy controller

The schematic diagram of the fuzzy controller is shown in Figure 3. The fuzzy controller design steps include: 1) Initialization, 2) Fuzzification, 3) Inference and 4) Difuzzification.

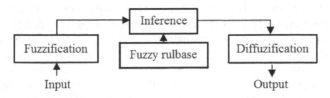

Fig. 3. The fuzzy controller structure

First step is *identifying the linguistic input and output variables and* definition of fuzzy sets (Initialization). *Fuzzification* or *fuzzy classification* is the process of converting a set of crisp data into a set of fuzzy variables using the membership functions (fuzzy sets). For example in Figure 4, the degree of membership for a given crisp is 0.6. Shape of the membership functions depends on the input data can be triangular, piecewise linear, Gaussian, trapezoidal or singleton.

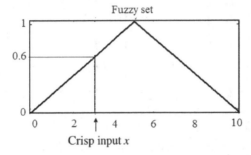

Fig. 4. Membership degree of a crisp input x in the fuzzy set

A rule base is obtained by a set of IF-THEN rules and *inference* evaluates the rules and combines the results of the rules. The final step is *Defuzzification* which is the process of converting fuzzy rules into a crisp output. An example of a simple fuzzy control system is shown in figure 5.

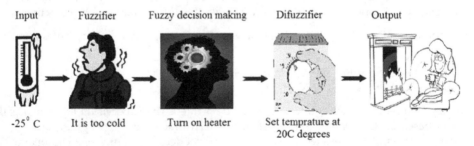

Fig. 5. Example of a fuzzy control system

3.2 A case sudy

The first study shows that how fuzzy logic algorithm can be used for navigation of mobile robots. The selected methodology is a behavior-based approach which fuzzy logic algorithm is used for the design and action coordination of the behaviors (Fatmi et al., 2006). The navigation approach is consists of two layers. The first layer is comprised of primitive basic behaviors include: Goal reaching, Emergency situation, Obstacle avoidance, and Wall following. The second layer is Supervision layer which is responsible for action (behavior) selection based on the context and blending output of the selected ones. All the behaviors are designed using a fuzzy if-then rule base. Fuzzy controller inputs in the first layer are provided by sensory information. The inputs are distance to the goal (D_{rg}) and difference between the goal direction and the robot's current heading (θ_{error}). Fuzzy sets for θ_{error} are: Negative (N), Small Negative (SN), Zero (Z), Small Positive (SP), and Positive (P). Fuzzy sets for D_{rg} are: Near (N), Small (S), and Big (B). Membership functions of the inputs are shown in figure 6.

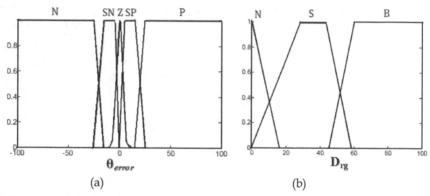

(a)   (b)

Fig. 6. Fuzzy set definition for input variables: (a) θ_{error} and (b) D_{rg}

Each behavior is represented using a set of fuzzy if- then rule base to achieve a set of objectives. The fuzzy rule bases are shown in Table1.

The inputs are defuzzified using the fuzzy interference to convert the fuzzy inputs to an output. Defuzzified outputs for Steering are: Right (R), Right Forward (RF), Forward (F), Left Forward (LF), and Left (L). The fuzzy sets for output variable of Velocity are Zero (Z), Small Positive (SP), and Positive (P). Figure 7 shows the outputs membership functions.

For example the Goal Reaching behaviour is defined using the following rules from the table:

If θerror is P And Drg is Big THEN Velocity is SP
If θerror is P And Drg is Big THEN Steering is L

Next step is to decide which behavior should be activated. The Supervision Layer makes the decision based on the *context blending strategy* which first selects appropriate behavior(s), and then outputs of the selected behaviour(s) are blended to produce one command. The robot is equipped with 15 infrared sensors which are clustered to Right up (RU), Front right (FR), Front Left (FL) and Left up (LU) as shown in Fig. 8. Inputs of the Supervision layer are distances to obstacles which are measured by the IR sensors readings. The behavior selection is based on the following fuzzy rule base:

IF context THEN behavior

For example: *IF RU is F and FR is F and FL is F and LU is F THEN Gaol Reaching.*

Rule	If			Then	
No	θ_{error}	&	D_{rg}	Steering direction	Robot velocity
1	N	&	Near	R	Z
2	SN	&	Small	RF	P
3	Z	&	Big	F	P
4	SP	&	Near	LF	Z
5	P	&	Small	L	SP
6	N	&	Big	R	SP
7	SN	&	Near	RF	Z
8	Z	&	Small	F	P
9	SP	&	Big	LF	P
10	P	&	Near	L	Z
11	N	&	Small	R	SP
12	SN	&	Big	RF	P
13	Z	&	Near	F	Z
14	SP	&	Small	LF	SP
15	P	&	Big	L	SP

Table 1. Fuzzy rules

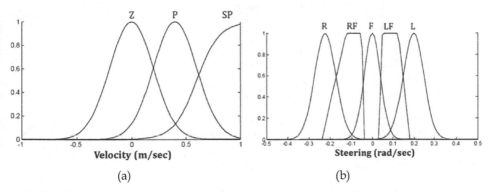

(a)   (b)

Fig. 7. Fuzzy set definition for output variables: (a) Velocity and (b) Steering.

Finally, output of the layer is a crisp control commands in terms of a velocity and an angular velocity according to the selected behavior. Figure 9 shows performance and effectiveness of fuzzy logic in navigation of a mobile robot in crowded and unpredictably changing environment. The obtained result reveals robustness and reliability of the fuzzy logic in association with the design and coordination of the behaviours.

In our previous work (Nankhaeinia et al., 2011b) a behaviour-based motion-planning approach was proposed for autonomous navigation of a mobile robot. This approach lies in the integration of three techniques: fuzzy logic (FL), virtual force field (VFF), and boundary following (BF).

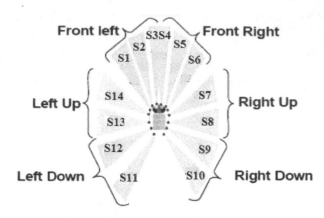

Fig. 8. Infrared sensors arrangement

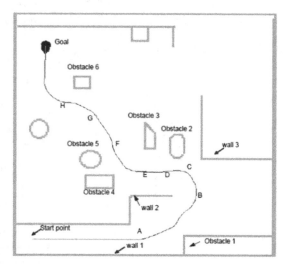

Fig. 9. Navigation of the robot in a sample environment

The robot's translational velocity is controlled by the fuzzy controller to get more safety in dealing with obstacles and to optimize the navigation time. The fuzzy controller inputs are obtained from sensorial data. The inputs are obstacle position and target direction (Fig.10).

For the six-set partitioning of obstacle position (OP) and three-set partitioning of target direction (TD) the fuzzy rule base comprises 18 rules. Table 2 represents the fuzzy rule base. As shown in figure 11, the fuzzy controller has one output. The fuzzy sets for the output variable of Velocity are L (low), C (normal speed), and H (high).

As shown in figure 12, the obtained result shows that the fuzzy controller has a great performance in reducing the navigation time in a sample environment (Fig. 13). However, in this work the fuzzy controller has two inputs and one output which the output is translational velocity. To evaluate influence of the fuzzy logic in the design of a navigation

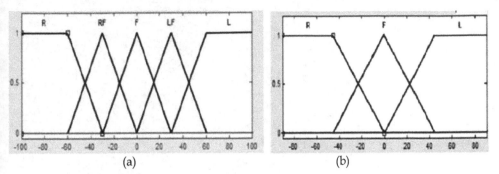

(a)   (b)

Fig. 10. Fuzzy set definition: a) input variable of OP; b) input variable of TD

Rule no.	TD		OP	Robot velocity
				Then
1	L	and	R	H
2	L	and	RF	C
3	L	and	F	C
4	L	and	LF	L
5	L	and	L	L
6	L	and	NO	H
7	F	and	R	C
8	F	and	RF	L
9	F	and	F	L
10	F	and	LF	L
11	F	and	L	H
12	F	and	NO	H
13	R	and	R	L
14	R	and	RF	L
15	R	and	F	C
16	R	and	LF	C
17	R	and	L	H
18	R	and	NO	H

Table 2. The fuzzy rule base

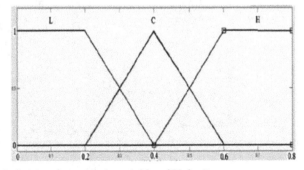

Fig. 11. Fuzzy set definition for output variable of Velocity

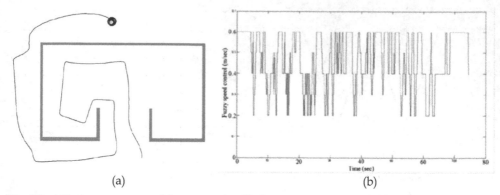

(a)   (b)

Fig. 12. a) Trajectory executed in a recursive U-shape environment and b) Fuzzy speed control.

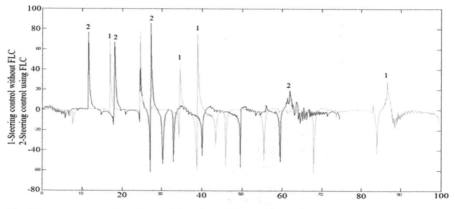

Fig. 13. a) Steering control without (plot 1) and b) with FLC (plot 2)

system more clearly, we designed a fuzzy controller with two inputs and two outputs. Inputs of the proposed controller are obstacle position and obstacle distance. There are three fuzzy sets for obstacle position (Dangerous (D), Uncertain (U) and Safe (S)) and five fuzzy set for obstacle distance (very near (VN), near (N), medium (M), far (F), very far (VF)). The inputs membership functions are shown in figure 14.

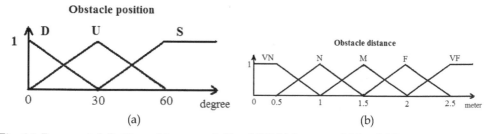

(a)   (b)

Fig. 14. Fuzzy set definition: a) input variable of OP; b) input variable of OD

There are 15 fuzzy rule bases (table 3) for the 3-set partitioning of the obstacle position (OP) and 5-set partitioning of the obstacle distance (**OD**).

If				Then		
Rule no.	OP		OD	Rv		Tv
1	D	&	VN	L	&	S
2	U	&	N	M	&	S
3	S	&	M	S	&	F
4	D	&	F	L	&	M
5	U	&	VF	M	&	F
6	S	&	VN	M	&	M
7	D	&	N	L	&	S
8	U	&	M	M	&	M
9	S	&	F	S	&	F
10	D	&	VF	L	&	M
11	U	&	VN	M	&	S
12	S	&	N	S	&	M
13	D	&	M	L	&	S
14	U	&	F	M	&	M
15	S	&	VF	S	&	F

Table 3. The fuzzy rule base

Outputs of the controller are Rotational Velocity (**Rv**) and Translational Velocity (**Tv**). Membership functions and constants of the **Rv** and **Tv** outputs are shown in figure 15.

The obtained result from navigation of the mobile robot in a sample environment shows influence and effectiveness of the fuzzy controller in reducing the navigation time and increasing safety (Fig. 16). The robot's velocity changes according to the obstacle distance and obstacle position to achieve more safety in dealing with unknown and unforeseen obstacles (Fig. 16(b)). When there is not any obstacle in the robot's path toward the target, it moves with its maximum speed to optimize the navigation time. However, the robot translational speed reduce in the presence of the obstacles and it rotates fast to prevent collision with them. As shown in figure 17 (a), the navigation time was about 90 (ms) which due to using the fuzzy controller it reduces to 48 (ms) (Fig. 17 (b)). In addition, using the fuzzy controller to control the Rotational Velocity resulted in smooth motion of the robot (Fig. 17(b)).

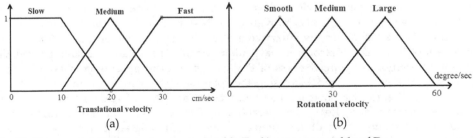

Fig. 15. Fuzzy set definition: a) output variable T_V; b) output variable of R_V

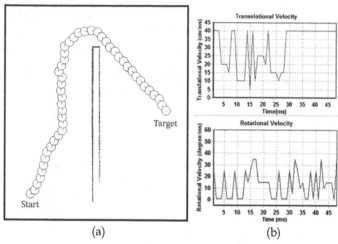

Fig. 16. Robot performance in a sample environment: a) Trajectory; b) Velocity profiles

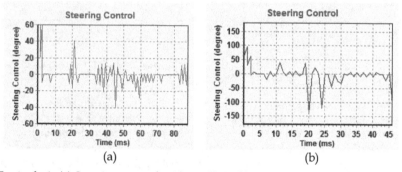

Fig. 17. Example 1: (a) Steering control without FLC; (b) Steering control using FLC

4. Conclusion

Review of different works showed that Fuzzy Logic control is one of the most successful techniques in the design and coordination of behaviors for mobile robots navigation. In this chapter first we performed a study to describe how the fuzzy logic can be applied to design individual behaviors simply and solve complex tasks by the combination of the elementary behaviors. The Fuzzy control addressed a useful mechanism to design various behaviors by the use of linguistic rules. It also provided a robust methodology for combination and arbitration of behaviors. Then, two fuzzy controllers designed to demonstrate influence and robustness of the fuzzy control in a navigation system. The obtained results proved the successful operation and effectiveness of the fuzzy control in generating smooth motion, reducing navigation time and increasing the robot safety. Overall, advantages of fuzzy control in the design of a navigation system are: i) Capability of handling uncertain and imprecise information, ii) Real time operation, iii) Easy combination and coordination of various behaviors, iv) Ability of developing perception-action based strategies, and v) Easy implementation. However, fuzzy navigation methods fail in local minimum situations; they have lakes of self tuning and self-organization and difficulty of rule discovery from expert knowledge. According to the considerable performance of the fuzzy logic control, in future works we will design and evaluate the real time performance of different *types of fuzzy* reasoning and defuzzification methods on the other aspects of robots control.

5. References

Antonelli, G.; Chiaverini, S. & Fusco, G. (2007). A Fuzzy-Logic-Based Approach for Mobile Robot Path Tracking. *IEEE Transactions on Fuzzy Systems*, Vol.15, pp.211-221, *ISSN*1063-6706.

Arkin, R.C. (1989). Motor schema-based mobile robot navigation. *Int. J.Robot Autom*, Vol.8, No.4, pp. 92-112, ISSN: 0826-8185.

Bento, L.C.; Pires, G. & Nunes, U. (2002). A behavior based fuzzy control architecture for path tracking and obstacle avoidance. *Proceedings of the 5th Portuguese Conference on Automatic Control*, pp. 341- 346, Aveiro, Portugal.

Braunstingl, R.; Sanz, P. & Ezkerra, J. M. (1996). Fuzzy logic wall following of a mobile robot based on the concept of general perception, *In 7th International Conference on Advanced Robotics*, PP.367-376, Sant Feliu Guixols,Spain.

Brooks, R. (1986). A robust layered control system for a mobile robot, *IEEE J. Robot Autom*, Vol.2, No. (1), pp. 14-23, ISSN 0882-4967.

Chao, C. H.; Hsueh, B. Y.; Hsiao, M. Y.; Tsai, S. H. & Li, T. H. S. (2009). Fuzzy target tracking and obstacle avoidance of mobile robots with a stereo vision system. *International Journal of Fuzzy Systems*, Vol.11, No.3, pp. 183-191.

Chee, B. Y.; Lang, S.Y.T. & Tse, P.W.T. (1996). Fuzzy mobile robot navigation and sensor integration. *IEEE International Conference on Fuzzy Systems*, Vol.1, pp. 7-12, ISBN 0-7803-3645-3, New Orleans, LA.

Dadios, E. & Maravillas, O. (2002). *Cooperative Mobile Robots with Obstacle and Collision Avoidance Using Fuzzy Logic*. Proc. of IEEE Int. Symposium on Intelligent Control, pp. 75-80, Vancouver, Canada, October 27-30.

Dupre, M.E. (2007). GA optimized fuzzy control of an autonomous mobile robot. Faculty of Graduate Studies, University of Guelph.

El Hajjaji, A. & Bentalba, S. (2003). Fuzzy path tracking control for automatic steering of vehicles, Robotics and Autonomous Systems, Vol. 43, pp. 203–213, ISSN: 0921-8890.

Fatmi, A.; Al Yahmadi, A.; Khriji, L. & Masmoudi, N. (2006). A Fuzzy Logic Based Navigation of a Mobile Robot, *World Academy of Science, Engineering and Technology, Vol. 22*, 169-174, *ISSN*: 1307-6884.

Isik, C. (1987). Identification and fuzzy rule-based control of a mobile robot motion. In Procs. of IEEE Int. Symp. On Intelligent Control, pp. 94-99, Philadelphia.

Jaafar, J. & McKenzie, E. (2008). A Fuzzy Action Selection Method for Virtual Agent Navigation in Unknown Virtual Environments. *Journal of Uncertain Systems*, Vol.2, No.2, pp.144-154, *ISSN* 1752-8909.

Leyden, M.; Toal, D. & Flanagan, C. (1999). A Fuzzy Logic Based Navigation System for a Mobile Robot, Department of Electronic & Computer Engineering, University of Limerick, Ireland.

Liao, Y.; Huang, J. & Zeng, Q. (2010). Preview fuzzy control method for intelligent vehicle path tracking. *IEEE International Conference on Informatics and Computing (PIC)*, pp. 1211-1214, ISBN: 978-1-4244-6788-4, Shanghai, China.

Lilly, J.H. (2007). Evolution of a negative-rule fuzzy obstacle avoidance controller for an autonomous vehicle. IEEE Trans. Fuzzy Systems, Vol.15, pp. 718-728, ISSN1063-6706.

Moustris, G. & Tzafestas, S.G. (2005). A Robust Fuzzy Logic Path Tracker for Non-Holonomic Mobile Robots. *International Journal on Artificial Intelligence Tools*, pp. 935-966, *ISSN* 0218-2130.

Nakhaeinia, D.; Tang, S.H.; Mohd Noor, S.B. & Motlagh, O. (2011). A review of control architectures for autonomous navigation of mobile robots. *International Journal of the Physical Sciences*, Vol. 6, No.2, pp. 169-174, 18, *ISSN* 1992-1950.

Nakhaeinia, D.; Tang, S.H.; karasfi, B.; Motlagh, O. & Ang, C.K (2011). A virtual force field algorithm for a behaviour-based autonomous robot in unknown environments. *Proc. IMechE, Part I: J. Systems and Control Engineering*, Vol.221, No. 1, pp. 51-62, *ISSN*: 0959-6518.

Ollero, A.; García-Cerezo, A. & Martínez, J.L. (1994). Fuzzy supervisory path tracking of mobile reports. *Control Engnnering Practice*, Vol. 2, No.2, pp.313-319, *ISSN*: 0967-0661.

Ollero, A.; García-Cerezo, A.; Martínez, J. L. & Mandow, A. (1997). *Fuzzy Tracking Methods for Mobile Robots*, pp. 347-364, Prentice Hall, ISBN 0133628310.

Parhi, D.R. (2005). Navigation of mobile robots using a fuzzy logic controller. *Journal of intelligent and robotic systems*, Vol.42, No.3, pp. 253–273, *ISSN*: 0921-0296.

Peri, V.M. & Simon, D. (2005). Fuzzy logic control for an autonomous robot. *In: Fuzzy Information Processing Society, Annual Meeting of the North American*, pp. 337 – 342.

Ramos, N.; Lima, P. U. & Sousa, M.J.C. (2006). Robot behavior coordination based on fuzzy decision-making, *In Proceedings of ROBOTICA 2006 - 6th Portuguese Robotics Festival*, Guimarares, Portugal.

Saffiotti, A. (1997). The uses of fuzzy logic in autonomous robot navigation. *Soft Computing*, Vol.1, No.4, pp.180-197, *ISSN* 1433-7479.

Sanchez, O.; Ollero, A. & Heredia, G. (1999). *Hierarchical Fuzzy Path Tracking* and Velocity Control of Autonomous Vehicles. *Integrated Computer-Aided Engineering*, Vol.6, No.4, pp. 289-301, *ISSN* 1069-2509.

Selekwa, M.F.; Dunlap, D.D.; Collins, E.G., Jr. (2005). Implementation of Multi-valued Fuzzy Behavior Control for Robot Navigation in Cluttered Environments. *IEEE International Conference on Robotics and Automation*, pp. 3688 – 3695, ISBN: 0-7803-8914-X.

Seraji, H. & Howard, A. (2002). Behavior-based robot navigation on challenging terrain: A fuzzy logic approach. *IEEE Trans. Robotics and Automation*, Vol. 18, pp. 308-321, *ISSN* 1042-296X.

Wong, C.C.; Hwang, C.L.; Huang, K.H.; Hu, Y.Y & Cheng, C.T. (2011). Design and Implementation of Vision-Based Fuzzy Obstacle Avoidance Method on Humanoid Robot, *International Journal of Fuzzy Systems*, Vol.13, No.1, pp. 45-54.

Xiong, B. & QU, S.R. (2010). Intelligent Vehicle's Path Tracking Based on Fuzzy Control. *Journal of Transportation Systems Engineering and information*, Vol.10, No.2, pp. 70-75, *ISSN*: 1570-6672.

Yu, G.R.; Bai, K.Y. & Chen, M.C. (2009). Applications of Taguchi Method to Fuzzy Control for Path Tracking of a Wheeled Mobile Robot. *Proceedings of the 17th National Conference on Fuzzy Theory and Its Applications*, pp. 857-862.

Yanik, P.; Ford, G. & Howell, B. (2010). *An introduction* and literature review of *fuzzy logic applications for robot motion planning. In Proceedings of ASEE Southeast Section Conference*, pp. 1-10.

Zavlangas, P.G.; Tzafestas, S.G. & Althoefer, K. (2000). *Fuzzy Obstacle Avoidance and Navigation for Omnidirectional Mobile Robots. ESIT 2000*, pp. 375-382, Aachen, Germany.

5

Modular Fuzzy Logic Controller for Motion Control of Two-Wheeled Wheelchair

Salmiah Ahmad[1], N. H. Siddique[2] and M. O. Tokhi[3]
[1]*International Islamic University Malaysia,*
[2]*Ulster University,*
[3]*The University of Sheffield*
[1]*Malaysia*
[2,3]*United Kingdom*

1. Introduction

Most of the wheelchair users are paraplegics, who are not able to move on their own due to permanent injury in their lower extremities. These wheelchairs are four-wheeled and have certain limitations due to design and control mechanism. For example, the wheelchairs cannot move to a higher level, lift the front wheel and stay in an upright position. As a result, wheelchair users cannot reach certain heights to pick and place things on the shelves, and cupboards, etc. without any assistant and also cannot have eye-to-eye conversation with normal people effectively. On the other hand, a two-wheeled wheelchair has a unique characteristic that may help disabled and elderly people who use the wheelchair as the main means of transport and can also use the wheelchair for these added advantages. Now the idea is to transform the standard four-wheeled wheelchair into a two-wheeled upright wheelchair to facilitate such manuoverability. The front wheels (casters) can be lifted up and stabilized as an inverted pendulum, thus increasing the level of height achievable while in the upright position. Similarly, when this upright position is no longer needed it may be transformed back into its normal four-wheeled position. The schematic diagram of the two-wheeled wheelchair is shown in Figure 1. The transformation will result in a highly nonlinear and complex system. Since a human has quite significant mass sitting on the wheelchair, the two-wheeled wheelchair can be modeled with double links that mimic double inverted pendulum scenario that need a clever control strategy.

Most of the classical control design methodologies such as Nyquist, Bode, state-space, optimal control, root locus, H_∞, and μ-analysis are based on assumptions that the process is linear and stationary and hence is represented by a finite dimensional constant coefficient linear model. These methods do not suit complex systems well because few of those represent uncertainty and incompleteness in system knowledge or complexity in design. But the fact is the real world is too complex. As the complexity of a system increases, quantitative analysis and precision become difficult. The increasing complexity of dynamical systems such as this coupled with stringent performance criteria, which are sometimes subject to human satisfaction, necessitates the use of more sophisticated control approaches. However, many processes that are nonlinear, uncertain, incomplete or non-stationary have subtle and interactive exchanges with the operating environment and are controlled by skilled human operators successfully. Rather than mathematically model the process, the human operator models the process in a heuristic or experiential manner. It is evident that human knowledge is becoming more and more important in control systems design. This experiential perspective in controller design requires the acquisition of heuristic and qualitative, rather than quantitative, knowledge or expertise from the human operator. During the past several decades, fuzzy control has emerged as one of the most active and powerful areas for research in the application of such complex and real world systems using fuzzy set theory (Zadeh, 1965).

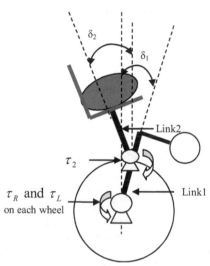

Fig. 1. Schematic diagram of wheelchair with three under actuated joints

Due to many significant advantages of wheelchair usage, this research presents findings of the research carried out on the implementation of new architecture of modular intelligent control strategies on the two-wheeled wheelchair model. The multi-objective control involves lifting and stabilizing of Link1 and Link2 of double-inverted pendulum like two-wheeled wheelchair, wheelchair backward and forward motion control as well as position. It is hoped that the proposed model, mechanisms and control could be of benefit to a wheelchair user, thus enhancing wheelchair technology for paraplegics and elderly.

2. Intelligent control approach

Intelligent control systems have evolved from existing controllers in a natural way competing demanding challenges of the time and are not defined in terms of specific algorithms. They employ techniques that can sense and reason without much *a priori* knowledge about the environment and produce control actions in a flexible, adaptive and robust manner (Harris, 1994). In general, by intelligent control approaches, it is mainly meant the methodologies of fuzzy logic, neural networks, and genetic algorithms. These methodologies have shown to be effective in controlling complex nonlinear systems. The control of complex nonlinear systems has been approached over the last few decades using fuzzy logic techniques due to the fact that fuzziness itself is easy to implement and can be described by expert knowledge, normally possessed by human. A fuzzy logic controller (FLC) has the basic configuration illustrated in Figure 2.

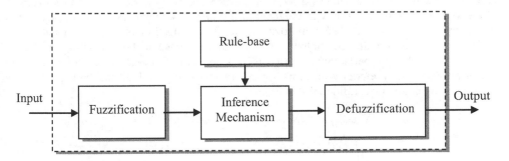

Fig. 2. Fuzzy logic control

Generally, a fuzzy logic controller consists of the following components:

i.   Fuzzification
ii. Inference mechanism
iii. Rule-base
iv. Defuzzification

Fuzzification is a process of transforming an observed input space to fuzzy sets within a universe of discourse. This process consists of associating to each fuzzy set a membership function (MF). These functions can be thought of as maps from the real numbers to the interval $I = [0,1]$. If there are n fuzzy sets associated with a given quantity $x \in R$, such n maps $F_i : R \to I$, $i = 1, \cdots, n$ are defined. They determine to what extent the linguistic label associated with fuzzy set i characterizes the current value of x. There are different kinds of MFs used in designing fuzzy controllers. The most common choices are triangular, trapezoidal, Gaussian and bell shaped MFs. There is no exact method for choosing an MF, and the designer mainly relies upon an expert knowledge or use heuristic rule.

Inference is used to describe the process of formulating a nonlinear mapping from a given input space to an output space. The mapping then provides a basis from which decisions can be taken. The process of fuzzy inference involves the MFs, fuzzy logic operators and rule-base. Generally there are three types of commonly used fuzzy inference. They differ mainly in the consequent part of their fuzzy rules, aggregations and defuzzification procedures. Thus selecting a different fuzzy inference will result in different computational time. The three common fuzzy inferences are: Mamdani fuzzy inference, Sugeno fuzzy inference and Tsukamoto fuzzy inference. The choice of a particular inference mechanism is eventually problem dependent and availability of information about the system in question.

Mamdani type fuzzy modeling was proposed as the first attempt to control a steam engine and boiler by a set of linguistic control rules by (Mamdani 1974). In this type of inference, Max-min is the most common rule of composition used. In this composition rule, the inferred output of each rule is a fuzzy set chosen from the minimum firing strength. On the other hand, in max-product rule of composition the inferred output of each rule is a fuzzy set scaled down by its firing strength via algebraic product.

A fuzzy system is characterized by a set of linguistic statements based on expert knowledge. The expert knowledge is usually in the form of if-then rules, which are easily implemented by fuzzy conditional statements in fuzzy logic. The collection of fuzzy rules that are expressed as fuzzy conditional statements forms the rule base or the rule set of an FLC. A rule consists of two parts, antecedent and consequent. For example, typical rule in Mamdani-type fuzzy model with four-inputs and three-outputs FLC can be expressed by the following linguistic conditional statement.

$$\text{If } (X_1 \text{ is } A_i) \text{ and } (X_2 \text{ is } B_j) \text{ and } (X_3 \text{ is } C_k) \text{ and } (X_4 \text{ is } D_l)$$

$$\text{then } (Y_1 \text{ is } U_p) \text{ and } (Y_2 \text{ is } V_q) \text{ and } (Y_3 \text{ is } W_r)$$

where $\{X_1, X_2, X_3, X_4\}$ are the inputs with linguistic terms $\{A_i, B_j, C_k, D_l\}$ and $\{Y_1, Y_2, Y_3\}$ are the outputs with linguistic terms $\{U_p, V_q, W_r\}$.

Defuzzification is basically a mapping from a space of fuzzy control actions defined over an output universe of discourse into a space of nonfuzzy (crisp) control actions. In a sense this is the inverse of the fuzzification even though mathematically the maps need not be inverses of one another. In general, defuzzification can be viewed as a function $DF: I^n \rightarrow R$, mapping a fuzzy vector x^F with n fuzzy sets to a real number. There are different methods of defuzzification. However, simple methods are available to use depending on the application, among them Centre of Gravity Method (COG), and Weighted Average Method are widely used in Mamdani-type FLC and Sugeno-type FLC. Each method is problem dependent, but the experts should know that these methods are available and should try to see which works best for the application.

The two-wheeled wheelchair model involves lifting and stabilizing the two links (Link1 and Link2) similar to a double-inverted pendulum and hence is a multi-objective control problem. Considering the complexity and non-linearity of the wheelchair, the controller has to be designed in such a way to produce the required torques, namely τ_R, τ_L and τ_2, for acting at three different locations on the wheelchair for lifting the casters/chair and stabilizing the system. The torque τ_R and τ_L represent the input torque to the right and left wheels respectively. τ_2 represents the torque between Link1 and Link2 to cater for the whole weight of the human body. Angular positions of Link1 and Link2, δ_1 and δ_2 respectively, are measured using sensors attached to the wheelchair. This characterizes the system as a highly nonlinear multi-input multi-output (MIMO) system. Fuzzy logic control is therefore very appropriate to use in this case. To achieve upright position for the two links, they need to be lifted and stabilized to zero degree (relative to vertical axis) upright position. This may be realised with a single controller. However, this will lead to a huge fuzzy rule-base. A conventional fuzzy controller with 4 inputs $\{e_{\delta1}, \Delta e_{\delta1}, e_{\delta2}, \Delta e_{\delta2}\}$ and 3 outputs $\{\tau_R, \tau_L, \tau_2\}$ (inputs-outputs are shown in Figure 3) has significant drawback in terms of computational complexity, which increases with the dimension of the system variables; the number of rules increases exponentially as the number of system variables increases. A strategy is sought to simplify the development process and reduce the geometric progression in the number of required rules for general purpose tracking and control situations. Moreover, it should be achieved without compromising the robustness and capability of the complete system.

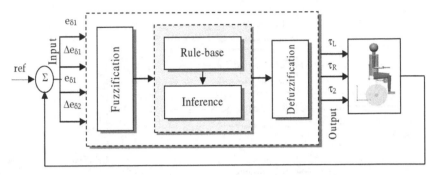

Fig. 3. MIMO FLC for lifting and stabilizing the wheelchair

A generic problem with an FLC is that the number of rules grow exponentially with the number of input-output variables and linguistic terms for each variable. For a complete rule-base with input variables $\{X_i \mid i = 1,...,n\}$ with linguistic terms $\{A_{ij} \mid j = 1,...,m_i\}$ and output variables $\{Y_k \mid k = 1,...,l\}$ with linguistic terms $\{B_{kj} \mid j = 1,...,p_k\}$, the number of rules will be

$$R = \prod_{i=1}^{n} m_i \tag{1}$$

The rules have the form

If $(X_1$ is $A_{11})$ and ... and $(X_n$ is $A_{nm})$ Then $(Y_1$ is $B_{11})$ and ... and $(Y_l$ is $B_{lp})$

This large number of rules complicates the design of an FLC, because for each of the R different premises the expert must provide a combination of term sets for the output variables, which is nearly impossible for a human expert to guess. It is possible to omit a set of rules if it could be guaranteed that a certain combination of input-output variables will never occur during control of the dynamic system. A modular structure of FLCs with minimum number of input-output variables can reduce the number of rules R.

3. Modular fuzzy control

For large scale and complex systems, the reduction in computation and design complexity remains a challenge of intelligent control systems. Hierarchical and modular methodology have gained wide popularity because of its simplicity in design and robustness. There are several approaches in decomposing a system into modules such as decentralized approach, time-scale decomposition, hierarchical system, and workspace decomposition (Siljak, 1991). For control problems with multiple objectives of different priority, sub-controller with a subset of input-output variables can be designed for each objective. Furthermore, each antecedent can be decomposed into single input modules. Each fuzzy module is designed to handle one specific input affiliated with one of the decoupled antecedents $\{X_i \mid i = 1,\ldots,n\}$ and produces a crisp action $\{Y_k \mid k = 1,\ldots,l\}$ where $k = 1,\ldots,l$. Such a generic modular architecture is shown in Figure 4.

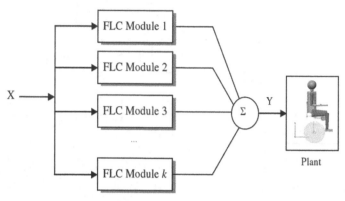

Fig. 4. Modular FLC

A typical fuzzy rule issues an appropriate output action by evaluating the related inputs from the measurement data. In the conventional IF-THEN fuzzy inference formulation, all of the system's input parameters are suggested as antecedents in the fuzzy rule. The total possible number of fuzzy rules that can be generated for the rule base is L^k where k is the number of inputs and L is the number of fuzzy linguistic terms or MFs. As compared to the modular FLC design, each input represents one fuzzy control module. The total number of rules for each module is determined by the number of MFs L. Thus, the total number of fuzzy rules for all k modules is kL. This clearly shows a significant reduction in the number of fuzzy rules from L^k to k as well as savings in computation.

The mathematical model of the two-wheeled wheelchair incorporates three independent actuators; derived from Figure 1, corresponding to control output to be fed into the system. The angular position of Link1 and Link2, denoted as δ_1 and δ_2 respectively, are the controlled variables that will determine the system performance. The control challenge relates to the fact that there is more than one mechanism acted upon with the same actuator. For example, to transform the wheelchair into an upright two-wheeled wheelchair, the torques determined by fuzzy control are located at both right and left wheels. At the same time, if linear motion is considered, the same actuator needs to provide enough torque such that the wheelchair will still move forward or backward while in the upright position. Lifting and stabilizing consist of two system output parameters to be considered, namely angular position of Link1, δ_1 and angular position of Link2, δ_2. Therefore a modular fuzzy logic control (MFC) is adopted to realize this multi-function two-wheeled wheelchair.

The MIMO system with an objective of achieving zero degree upright position is decomposed into small and simpler subsystems: Link1-lifting, Link1-stabilizing, Link2-lifting, and Link2-stabilizing. The structure of the modular FLC for the wheelchair is illustrated in the block diagram in Figure 5. Accordingly, this type of FLC can deal with, for example, N subsystems located at different levels, where each subsystem manages its own control strategy and communicates with the coordinator. The coordinator comprises a pair of switches that gathers information from the subsystems and sends supervisory (threshold condition) instructions back to the subsystems. The supervisor in this case is the condition, (if the angular position error of Link1 and Link2, -5° < e < 5°, then Link1-stabilizing and Link2-stabilizing are activated). In this case, the switches coordinate the condition fulfilment of all the criteria for the activation of actuator to work accordingly. The reference position for lifting and stabilizing of both links is 0 degree at the upright position. The parameters 'a' and 'b' in the figure show the fuzzy input scaling factors (input gain) such that if the stabilizing subsystem of Link1 or Link2 is activated, the sensitivity of the fuzzy inputs is increased by giving higher gain (about 10 times) of a and b. The outputs from the system that are fed back to the controller are the angular position of Link1 (δ_1) and the angular position of Link2 (δ_2). The control approach using this modular strategy is believed to work well with the independently allocated tasks. In the figure, $e_{\delta 1}$ shows the angular position error of Link1, $\Delta e_{\delta 1}$ represents the change of angular position error of Link1. The effect of Link2 onto Link1 is taken into account by using the angular position error of Link2, $e_{\delta 2}$ as the fuzzy input for FLC1 and FLC2. In these two controllers, $e_{\delta 2}$ represents the angular position error of Link2, while $\Delta e_{\delta 2}$ represents the change of angular position error of Link2. Similarly the effect of Link1 onto Link2 is taken into account by using the angular position error of Link1, $e_{\delta 1}$ as the input for FLC3 and FLC4.

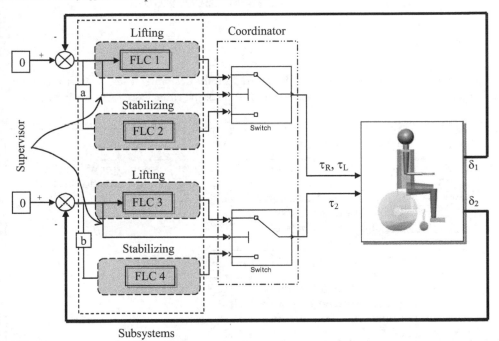

Fig. 5. Modular FLC for Two-wheeled wheelchair.

4. MFC for two-wheeled wheelchair

The MFC is also known as hierarchical fuzzy control (HFC), and the two terms are used interchangeably. It is discussed in detail for two-wheeled application in (Ahmad et al. 2011).

The goal of the controller is to produce the required torques, namely τ_R, τ_L and τ_2, for acting at three different locations on the wheelchair for lifting and stabilizing. The torques τ_R and τ_L represent the input torque to the right and left wheels respectively. On the other hand, τ_2 represents the torque between Link1 and Link2 to be used to cater for the whole weight of the human body. Angular positions of Link1 and Link2, δ_1 and δ_2 respectively, are measured using sensors attached to the wheelchair in Visual Nastran (VN). To achieve upright position of the two links, they need to be lifted and stabilized at zero degree upright position. The goal may be treated as a single objective control that is having Link1 and Link2 at the 0 degree upright position with one controller. This will increase significantly the computational complexity, which increases with the number of system variables; the number of rules increases exponentially as the number of system variables increases.

4.1 Rules reduction strategy for general purpose tracking and control situations

The strategy is sought without compromising the robustness and capability of the system. Such a strategy relies mainly on three concepts, (Ahmad et al. 2011).

- Independence
- Functional Relationship
- Command Manipulation

To assess the effect of coupling in the fuzzy control, the system is tested with two different configurations, which mainly differ at the input side of the controller, as shown in Table 1.

	With coupling effect	Without coupling effect
Link1 (Lifting & Stabilizing)	- Angular position error of Link1, $e_{\delta1}$ - Change of angular position error of Link1, $\Delta e_{\delta1}$ - Angular position error of Link2, $e_{\delta2}$	- Angular position error of Link1, $e_{\delta1}$ - Change of angular position error of Link1, $\Delta e_{\delta1}$
Link2 (Lifting & Stabilizing)	- Angular position error of Link2, $e_{\delta2}$ - Change of angular position error of Link2, $\Delta e_{\delta2}$ - Angular position error of Link1, $e_{\delta1}$	- Angular position error of Link2, $e_{\delta2}$ - Change of angular position error of Link2, $\Delta e_{\delta2}$
Rules of each lifting and stabilizing	$5 \times 5 \times 3 = 75$ rules	$5 \times 5 = 25$ rules

Table 1. Different input configurations of modular fuzzy logic controller

The system was tested with both configurations and the performances, with and without coupling were comparably similar, see Figure 6. Therefore, as seen the second configuration performed well with fewer fuzzy rules fired, and this configuration is used in implementing the motion control for two-wheeled wheelchair.

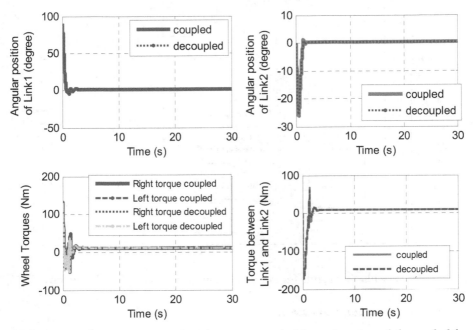

Fig. 6. System performance comparison between coupled fuzzy inputs and decoupled fuzzy inputs in terms of δ_1, δ_2, τ_R, τ_L and τ_2.

The MFC is thus adopted for the two-wheeled wheelchair mechanisms, and the corresponding research objectives are:

- Lifting and stabilizing control
- Linear motion control (forward or backward)
- Steering motion control

The MFC can be divided into two significant categories, primary and secondary (Bessacini and Pinkos 1995). The controller is categorized according to different objectives. The control structure for achieving an upright two-wheeled maneuverable wheelchair is depicted in Figure 7. The general function of MFC is to minimize the errors in system responses considered. The primary goal unit caters for the upright control, which consists of lifting and stabilizing to the upright position and the transformation back to normal four-wheeled position of Link1 and Link2. These controllers are active most of the time even during maneuver. The secondary unit is activated by the coordinator (switch), with certain condition pre-set for output activation. It consists of different unique objectives involving linear motion control, steering control, additional chair height extension control. Each objective in the secondary goal unit is discussed in detail in the following sections.

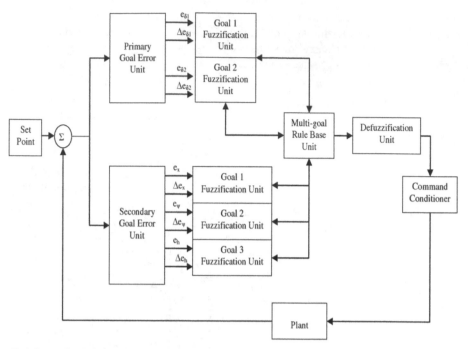

Fig. 7. Adapted modular intercepts fuzzy logic system (Bessacini and Pinkos 1995)

4.2 Simulation based performance analysis

The overall motion control for two-wheeled wheelchair is represented in Figure 8.

a.   FLC for linear motion

The linear motion control generally consists of forward and backward (reverse) motion control. They are both characterized as secondary systems (Bessacini and Pinkos 1995) since the system needs to fulfill the primary target to achieve the upright position for both links. Therefore MFC as discussed in Section 4 is very appropriate to implement.

Similar structure of FLC used for lifting and stabilizing is adopted for linear motion control. The controls differ in terms of input and output scaling factors due to different reference points executed. The control strategy designed in Matlab/Simulink was integrated with wheelchair model, which was developed in VN software environment as a plant. The motion (forward, backward or steering) takes place after lifting and stabilizing has been achieved. Results show that the MFC strategy designed works very well and gives good system performance.

In the current studies of wheelchair mobility, much research has been conducted on wheelchair mobility in large spaces (outdoor mobility) (Vries et al. 1999; Wong et al. 2007). In those researches, the distance and angle are considered at the same time to give output torque of the wheels. On the other hand, note that the two-wheeled wheelchair is designed for use in confined spaces, such that the linear motion and the steering motion are independent.

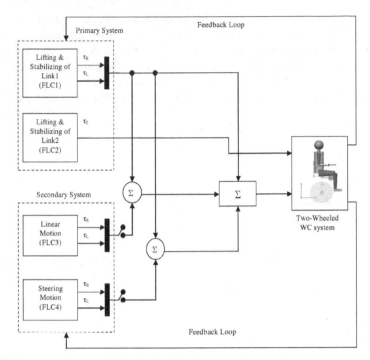

Fig. 8. Block diagram of two-wheeled wheelchair system motion

This confined space is normally found in the domestic environment (home, office and library). Within such environment, linear motion is executed alone before steering is done and vice versa. The block diagram for linear motion control of two-wheeled wheelchair is shown in Figure 9.

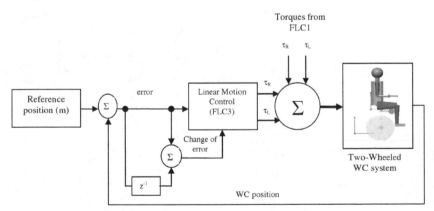

Fig. 9. Block diagram for linear motion control

The FLC for linear motion (FLC3) consists of two inputs and two outputs. The controller inputs are the position error, e and the change of position error, Δe, while the controller outputs are the torques, τ_R and τ_L. The fuzzy inputs are normalized so that they can be generalized and then processed using the fuzzy rules. Moreover, the input normalization is done due to the complexity of predetermining the range of change of position error, Δe. Gaussian (bell shaped) type membership functions with default parameters given by Matlab/Simulink are used for all inputs and outputs. The membership levels for each input and outputs are five in total. These comprise Negative Big (NB), Negative Small (NS), Zero

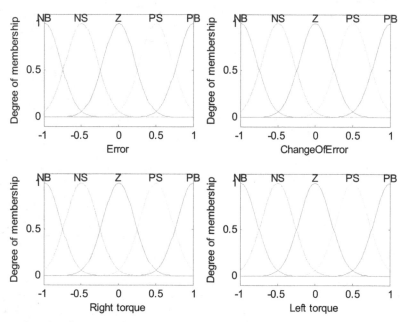

Fig. 10. Membership functions for inputs and outputs for FLC3 of linear motion control

e \ Δe	NB	NS	Z	PS	PB
NB	PB	PB	PB	PS	Z
	PB	PB	PB	PS	Z
NS	PB	PB	PS	Z	NS
	PB	PB	PS	Z	NS
Z	PB	PS	Z	NS	NB
	PB	PS	Z	NS	NB
PS	PS	Z	NS	NB	NB
	PS	Z	NS	NB	NB
PB	Z	NS	NB	NB	NB
	Z	NS	NB	NB	NB

Table 2. Fuzzy rules for linear motion

(Z), Positive Small (PS) and Positive Big (PB). The membership function for inputs and outputs of FLC3 is shown in Figure 10. Table 2 shows the implemented fuzzy rules for FLC3 controller. The two consecutive rows in the output part represent two fuzzy outputs, τ_R (first row) and τ_L (second row). The rules developed are predetermined using expert knowledge available such that all the errors should be brought back to the reference point immediately.

Forward Motion

The system was commanded to move forward after 4s, where at this time the two links had been stabilized at the upright position. Figure 11 shows the final position of forward mechanism execution while Figure 12 to Figure 18 show the results over 15s of simulation time for forward movement of the two-wheeled wheelchair. The wheelchair was set to move 1.5m forward from its initial position. The results show that the FLC approach worked very well with the wheelchair system on two wheels. Figure 11 shows the final wheelchair position when it was set to move forward to 1.5m from the origin. It is noted from Figures 12 and 13 that both links settled after 4s from starting time of linear motion, which can be considered quite good performance for the initial attempts of parameters setting. Link1 tilted with a positive angle from the 0° upright position. This configuration was automatically adjusted to initiate the forward motion. The corresponding wheelchair position is shown in Figure 14. It is noted that as much as 0.1m of the steady state error appeared when it settled. Figure 15 shows the wheel torques (τ_R and τ_L) from the lifting and stabilizing controller of Link1 (FLC1), and the wheel torques from the linear motion control is shown in Figure 16. The torques vary from +40Nm to -40Nm during the forward motion with positive slope during initial phase of travel. The resultant wheel torques contributed by the lifting and stabilizing control as well as the linear motion control are shown in Figure 17. The torque between Link1 and Link2 (τ_2) given by (FLC2) is shown in Figure 18.

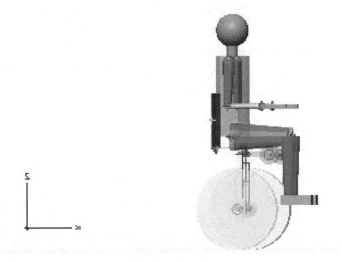

Fig. 11. Final position of 1.5m forward motion

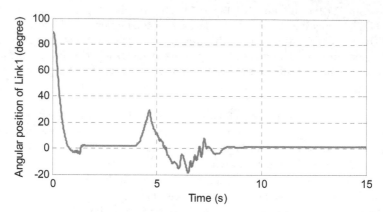

Fig. 12. Angular position of Link1, δ_1 (degree)

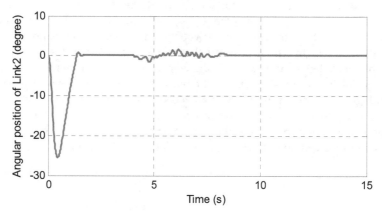

Fig. 13. Angular position of Link2, δ_2 (degree)

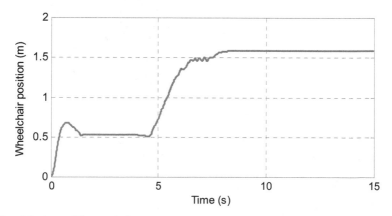

Fig. 14. Wheelchair position, x (m)

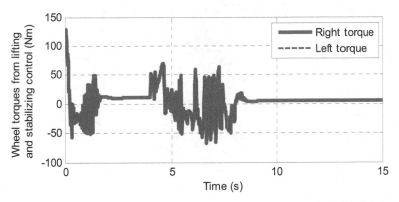

Fig. 15. Wheel torques, τ_R and τ_L due to lifting and stabilizing control, FLC1 (Nm)

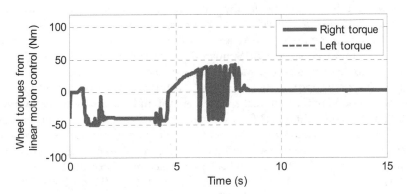

Fig. 16. Wheel torques, τ_R and τ_L due to linear motion control, FLC3 (Nm)

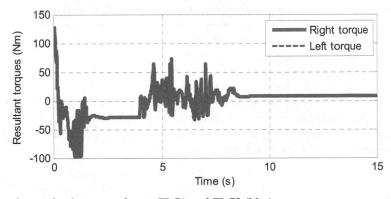

Fig. 17. Resultant wheel torques due to FLC1 and FLC3 (Nm)

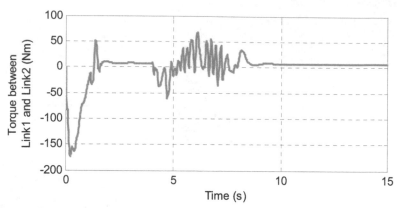

Fig. 18. Torque between Link1 and Link2, τ_2, FLC2 (Nm)

b.   FLC for steering motion

A steering motion is needed when the two-wheeled wheelchair needs to change its direction. The two-wheeled wheelchair can rotate to the right or to the left depending on which direction it is commanded. There are two different approaches where steering could be realized (Tanimoto et al., 2009). Similar direction of wheel rotation with different magnitudes could lead to steering motion (moving both wheels forward with different magnitudes). The first approach causes bigger turning radius as compared to the second approach. The second approach to realize steering motion is by giving different direction of wheel rotation (moving right wheel forward and left backward). The output torques in this work given by the FLC used for steering motion covers both approaches according to the steering error and the change of the steering error. In contrast to normal steering for mobile robots, steering motion for the two-wheeled wheelchair is executed after the upright position has been achieved; Link1 and Link2 at the 0° upright position. Therefore the complexity in this configuration is higher than the steering motion using four wheels, since other motion controls are active at the same time.

A block diagram for steering motion control of two-wheeled wheelchair is shown in Figure 19. As discussed earlier, for reasons of simplicity, the torques applied to the two wheels are the same in magnitudes (one output torque from the controller) so as to move the wheelchair only forward or backward. Then each right and left wheel torque is made independent to realize the steering motion. The weight here represents the human body weight, for which an average 70kg human is used. Sensors are attached at the respective reference bodies for control and measurement. The control signals applied to the wheelchair model comprise the right torque, τ_R (Nm), left torque, τ_L (Nm) and torque between Link1 and Link2, τ_2 (Nm). The measured outputs from the wheelchair system that consist of the angular position of Link1, δ_1, (degree), angular position of Link2, δ_2, (degree) and wheelchair rotation angle about the vertical axis, ψ (degree) are compared with the target references.

The wheelchair system modeled in VN software environment was used as a plant and controlled with the developed FLC in the Matlab/Simulink environment. The steering motion introduced takes place after the lifting and stabilizing mechanism has been achieved.

This new capacity increased the number of DOF of the two-wheeled wheelchair. Thus, it is noticeable challenge to control the two-wheeled wheelchair where limited actuators are available for different functions. Therefore, suitable controllers are needed, and FLC is adopted. Results show that the FLC strategy works well and gives good system performance.

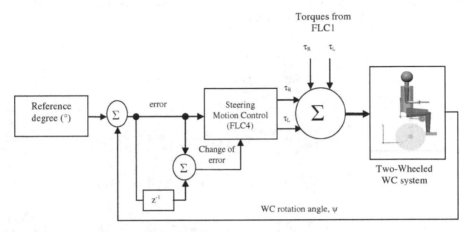

Fig. 19. Block diagram for steering motion control

Two inputs and two outputs FLC is developed to control the steering motion. The membership functions used are shown in Figure 20. The membership levels for each input

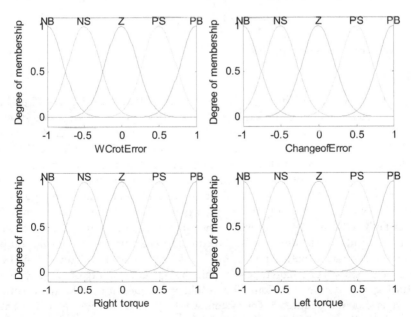

Fig. 20. Membership levels for inputs and outputs of steering control

and output comprise Negative Big (NB), Negative Small (NS), Zero (Z), Positive Small (PS) and Positive Big (PB). The two inputs used were the wheelchair rotation error (e_ψ) and the change of wheelchair rotation error, Δe_ψ. The controller outputs are the right and left wheel torques, τ_R and τ_L. All membership functions of input and output parameters are normalized for ease of control. Table 3 shows the implemented fuzzy rules for steering motion control (FLC4), where the first row relates to right-wheel torque and the second (shaded) row relates to the left-wheel torque.

e_ψ \ Δe_ψ	NB	NS	Z	PS	PB
NB	NB	NB	NB	NS	Z
	PB	PB	PB	PS	Z
NS	NB	NB	NS	Z	PS
	PB	PB	PS	Z	NS
Z	NB	NS	Z	PS	PB
	PB	PS	Z	NS	NB
PS	NS	Z	PS	PB	PB
	PS	Z	NS	NB	NB
PB	Z	PS	PB	PB	PB
	Z	NS	NB	NB	NB

Table 3. Fuzzy rules for steering motion

Steering to 30°

The final position of the wheelchair system can be seen in Figure 21. Figures 22 and Figure 23 show the angular positions of Link1, δ_1 and Link2, δ_2 respectively when the system was set to steer at 30° causing the two-wheeled wheelchair to rotate to the left from its initial position. Both links settled with small steady state error after the steering settlement was achieved. As noted, they settled in less than 4s. As noted in Figure 24, the wheelchair rotated very near to 30°, with < 0.1° of the steady state error. The output torques from each lifting and stabilizing control of Link1 as well as the steering control are shown in Figures 25 and 26 respectively. Note that the output torques from FLC1 had the same magnitude and direction for both right and left wheels. On the other hand, the output torque from FLC4 had the same magnitude but different in direction representing the fuzzy rules output for steering motion. The torque between Link1 and Link2 can be seen in Figure 27. As noted, it changed between +30Nm and -20Nm to maintain the upright stability of Link2 with human payload during the steering motion. The resultant torques for both fuzzy controllers (FLC1+FLC4) is shown in Figure 28. The system was then tested to rotate at a different angle (negative angle leading to rotation to the right).

Fig. 21. Final steering position for 30° reference point

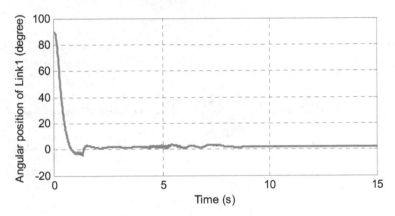

Fig. 22. Angular position of Link1, δ_1 (degree)

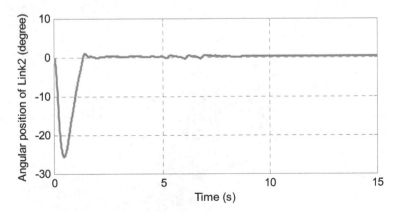

Fig. 23. Angular position of Link2, δ_2 (degree)

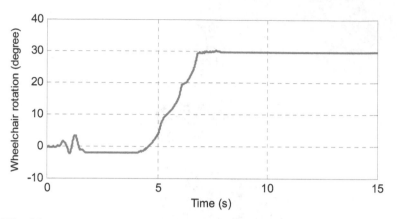

Fig. 24. Wheelchair rotation, ψ (degree)

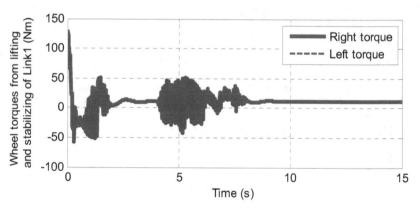

Fig. 25. Wheel torques (τ_R and τ_L) from FLC1 (Nm)

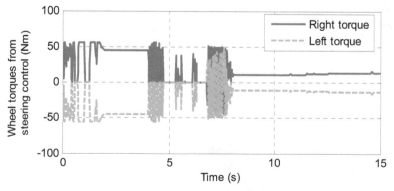

Fig. 26. Wheel torques (τ_R and τ_L) from steering motion control, FLC4 (Nm)

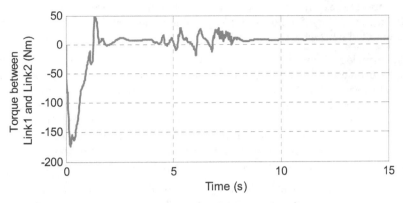

Fig. 27. Torque between Link1 and Link2, τ_2 (Nm)

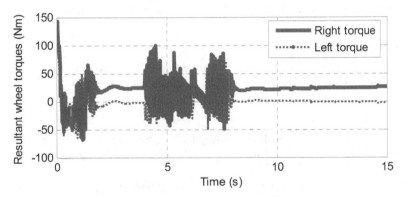

Fig. 28. Resultant wheel torques (Nm)

5. Conclusion

Fuzzy logic is one of the control techniques that is very close to human feelings and expressions. It can be easily understood and implemented although the knowledge about classical or conventional control system is not much identified. Nevertheless the general knowledge of the system involved must be generally known otherwise it is difficult to formulate a fuzzy controller for such system. If the system involved is known to be linear, and simple thus it is more worth to start with conventional Proportional-Integral-Differential (PID) controller. Otherwise if the system is known to be very complex, nonlinear and ill-defined type of system, then it is suggested to use one of the computational approaches such as fuzzy logic. This method was successfully implemented in the two-wheeled wheelchair system where a modular fuzzy control (MFC) was developed and implemented for controlling lifting and stabilizing mechanism, linear and steering motion control. Note that since a wheelchair is a main means of transport for disabled and elderly people, this two-wheeled wheelchair system would allow the user to achieve a higher level of height without assistance and hence independence. The wheelchair has been modeled as a double inverted pendulum. The integrated two-wheeled wheelchair with a human model has been imported as the plant into Matlab/Simulink environment for control and evaluation purposes. Therefore, fuzzy logic techniques have been found suitable for control of the two-wheeled wheelchair.

A Modular Fuzzy logic Control (MFC) approach has been adopted, where the control tasks are divided into primary and secondary tasks (subsystems), and FLC modules have been designed and executed for the various control tasks accordingly. Among the control tasks, lifting and stabilizing in the upright position are considered as the primary control system task. Secondary system tasks include linear motion and steering motion. The MFC strategy developed is based on a hierarchical approach whereby the primary subsystem must be executed followed by selection of secondary subsystems. Both linear and steering motions have been successfully controlled independently using a two-input two-output PD-type FLC.

The proposed MFC has been successfully implemented and tested within simulated exercises for two-wheeled wheelchair application. The results presented proved that the MFC approach works very well in controlling highly nonlinear systems such as a wheelchair on two wheels and significantly reduces the number of rules.

6. Acknowledgment

The authors would like to express their appreciation to the International Islamic University Malaysia (IIUM) for sponsoring the publication of this book chapter.

7. References

Ahmad, S., N. H. Siddique and M. O. Tokhi (2011). A modular fuzzy control approach for two-wheeled wheelchair. *Journal of Intelligent and Robotic Systems* Springer Journal, Vol. 64(3-4), pp. 401-426.

Bessacini, A. F. and R. F. Pinkos (1995). A hierarchical fuzzy controller for intercept guidance with a forbidden zone. Newport, Naval Undersea Warfare Center Division.

Engelbrecht, A. P. (2007). *Computational intelligence: An introduction.* Chichester, England, John Wiley & Sons.

Mamdani, E. H. (1974). Application of fuzzy algorithms for control of a simple dynamic process. *Proceeding of IEEE* 121(12): 1585-1588.

Reznik, L. (1997). *Fuzzy Controllers.* Oxford, Newnes.

Siljak, D. (1991) *Decentralized Control* of *Complex Systems,* Academic Press.

Vries, T. J. A. D., C. V. Heteran and L. Huttenhuis (1999). Modeling and control of a fast moving, highly maneuverable wheelchair. *International Biomechatronics Workshop,* Enschede, Netherlands.

Wong, C.-C., H.-Y. Wang, S.-A. Li and C.-T. Cheng (2007). Fuzzy controller designed by GA for two-wheeled mobile robots. *International Journal of Fuzzy Systems* 9(1).

Zadeh, L. A. (1965). Fuzzy sets. *Information and Control* 8(3): 338 - 353.

6

Application of Fuzzy Logic in Control of Electrical Machines

Abdel Ghani Aissaoui[1] and Ahmed Tahour[2]
[1]Faculty of Science & Technology,
University of Bechar, Bechar,
[2]Faculty of Science & Technology,
University of Mascara, Mascara,
Algeria

1. Introduction

During the past decades, fuzzy logic control (FLC) has been one of the most active and fruitful areas for research in the application of fuzzy set theory. It has has been an active research topic in automation and control theory, since the work of Mamdani proposed in 1974 based on the fuzzy sets theory of Zadeh (1965), to deal with the system control problems which is not easy to be modeled [Mamdani E.H. 1974].

The literature in fuzzy control has been growing rapidly in recent years, making it difficult to present a comprehensive survey of the wide variety of applications that have been made. Fuzzy logic, which is the logic on which fuzzy control is based, is much closer in spirit to human thinking and natural language than the traditional logical systems. Basically, it provides an effective means of capturing the approximate and the inexact nature of the real world. The fuzzy logic controller is a set of linguistic control rules related by the dual concepts of fuzzy implication and the compositional rule of inference. The FLC provides an algorithm which can convert the linguistic control strategy based on expert knowledge into an automatic control strategy.

The concept of FLC is to utilize the qualitative knowledge of a system to design a practical controller. For a process control system, a fuzzy control algorithm embeds the intuition and experience of an operator designer and researcher. The fuzzy control method is suitable for systems with non-specific models, and therefore, it suits well to a process where the model is unknown or ill-defined and particularly to systems with uncertain or complex dynamics [Yu F. M. et al 2003].

The implementation of such control consists of translating the input variables to a language like: positive big, zero, negative small, etc. and to establish control rules so that the decision process can produce the appropriate outputs. Fuzzy control (FC) using linguistic information possesses several advantages such as robustness, model-free, universal approximation theorem and rules-based algorithm [Kim Y.T.& Bien Z. 2000; Lee C.C. 1990; Timothy J. R. 1994].

As an intelligent control technology, fuzzy logic control (FLC) provides a systematic method to incorporate human experience and implement nonlinear algorithms, characterized by a series of linguistic statements, into the controller. In general, a fuzzy control algorithm consists of a set of heuristic decision rules and can be regarded as an adaptive and nonmathematical control algorithm based on a linguistic process, in contrast to a conventional feedback control algorithm [Sousa G.C. D.& Bose B. K. 1994; Yager, R. R. 1997].

The fuzzy control also works as well for complex nonlinear multi-dimensional system, system with parameter variation problem or where the sensor signals are not precise. It is basically nonlinear and adaptive in nature, giving robust performance under parameter variation and load disturbance effect.

In process control applications, recent literature has explored the potentials of fuzzy control for machine drive application [Tang Y. & Xu L. 1994, Heber B. et al 1995]. It has been shown that a properly designed direct fuzzy controller can outperform conventional proportional integral derivative (PID) controllers [Heber B. et al 1995].

This paper presents an application of fuzzy logic to control the speed of a synchronous machine (SM). Based on the analysis of the SM transient response and fuzzy logic, a fuzzy controller is developed. The fuzzy controller generates the variations of the reference current vector of the SM speed control based on the speed error and its change. Digital simulation results shows that the designed fuzzy speed controller realises a good dynamic behaviour of the motor, a perfect speed tracking with no overshoot and a good rejection of impact loads disturbance. The results of applying the fuzzy logic controller to a SM show best performances and high robustness than those obtained by the application of a conventional controller (PI). In this paper, we propose several controllers based on fuzzy logic, to deduce the best one.

The organization of this paper is as follows: in section 2, the fuzzy logic control principle is described and used to design fuzzy logic controllers; in section 3, vector control principle for synchronous motor drive is presented, the proposed controllers are used to control the synchronous motor speed. In section 4, simulation results are given to show the effectiveness of these controllers and finally conclusions are summarized in the last section.

2. Fuzzy logic control

The structure of a complete fuzzy control system consists of the following main parts:

- Fuzzification,
- Knowledge base,
- Inference engine,
- Defuzzification.

Figure (1) shows the internal configuration of a fuzzy logic controller.

2.1 Fuzzy logic principle

The fuzzification module converts the crisp values of the control inputs into fuzzy values. A fuzzy variable has values which are defined by linguistic variables (fuzzy sets or subsets) such as low, Medium, high, big, slow… where each one is defined by a gradually varying

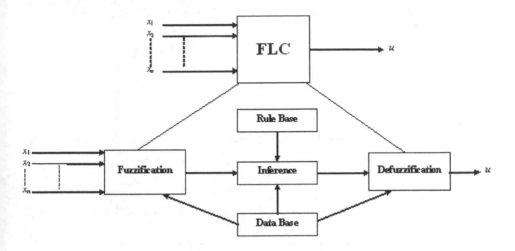

Fig. 1. The internal configuration of a fuzzy logic controller

membership function. In fuzzy set terminology, all the possible values that a variable can assume are named universe of discourse, and the fuzzy sets (characterized by membership functions) cover the whole universe of discourse. The shape of fuzzy sets can be triangular, trapezoïdale, etc [BOSE B. K. 1994; Bühler H. 1994].

A fuzzy control essentially embeds the intuition and experience of a human operator, and sometimes those of a designer and researcher. The data base and the rules form the knowledge base which is used to obtain the inference relation R. The data base contains a description of input and output variables using fuzzy sets. The rule base is essentially the control strategy of the system. It is usually obtained from expert knowledge or heuristics, it contains a collection of fuzzy conditional statements expressed as a set of IF-THEN rules, such as:

$$R^{(i)}: \text{If } x_1 \text{ is } F_1 \text{ and } x_2 \text{ is } F_2 \text{ ...and } x_n \text{ is } F_n \textbf{ THEN } Y \text{ is } G^{(i)}, i=1, ..., M \qquad (1)$$

where : $(x_1, x_2, ..., x_n)$ is the input variables vector, Y is the control variable, M is the number of rules, n is the number of fuzzy variables, $(F_1, F_2, ... F_n)$ are the fuzzy sets.

For the given rule base of a control system, the fuzzy controller determines the rule base to be fired for the specific input signal condition and then computes the effective control action (the output fuzzy variable) [Bose B. K. 1994 ; Spooner J.T. et al 2002].

The composition operation is the method by which such a control output can be generated using the rule base. Several composition methods, such as max-min or sup-min and max-dot have been proposed in the literature.

The mathematical procedure of converting fuzzy values into crisp values is known as 'defuzzification'. A number of defuzzification methods have been suggested. The choice of defuzzification methods usually depends on the application and the available processing power. This operation can be performed by several methods of which center of gravity (or centroïd) and height methods are common [Spooner J.T. et al 2002 ; Rachid A. 1996].

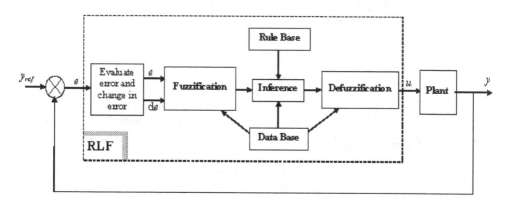

Fig. 2. Basic structure of fuzzy control system

The actual crisp input are approximates to the closer values of the respective universes of discourse. Hence, the fuzzy inputs are described by singleton fuzzy sets.

The elaboration of this controller is based on the phase plan. The control rules are designed to assign a fuzzy set of the control input u for each combination of fuzzy sets of e and Δe [Aissaoui A. G. et al 2007]. The performances of such controller depend on the quality of rules and the choice of the fuzzy sets that describe number of the inputs and the output of the controller.

2.2 Fuzzy control with three fuzzy subsets

Table 1 shows one of possible control rules based on three membership functions [Aissaoui 2007].

	u	de		
		N	Z	P
e	N	N	N	Z
	Z	N	Z	P
	P	Z	P	P

Table 1. Rules Base for speed control

The columns represent the rate of the error change de and the rows represent the error e. Each pair (e, de) determines the output level N to P corresponding to u.

Here N is negative, Z is zero, P is positive, are labels of fuzzy sets and their corresponding membership functions are depicted in figure (3). Figure (4) shows the corresponding output surface.

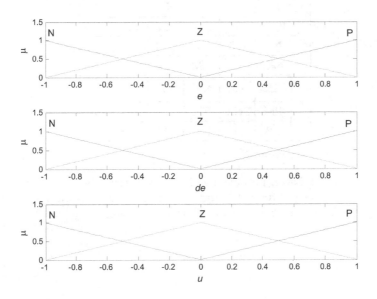

Fig. 3. Membership functions for input e, *de* and *u*

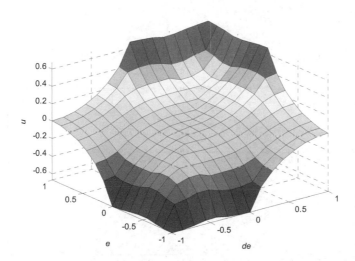

Fig. 4. The output surface of the fuzzy inference system for three fuzzy subsets using the inputs and the output.

2.3 Fuzzy control with five fuzzy subsets

Table 1 shows one of possible control rules based on five membership functions [Aissaoui et al 2007].

		de				
u		NB	NM	ZR	PM	PB
	NB	NB	NB	NM	NM	ZR
	NM	NB	NM	NM	ZR	PM
	ZR	NM	NM	ZR	PM	PM
e	PM	NM	ZR	PM	PM	GP
	PB	ZR	PM	PM	GP	GP

Table 2. Rules Base for speed control

Here NB is negative big, NM is negative medium, ZR is zero, PM is positive medium and PB is positive big, are labels of fuzzy sets and their corresponding membership functions are depicted in figures (5). Figure (6) shows the corresponding output surface.

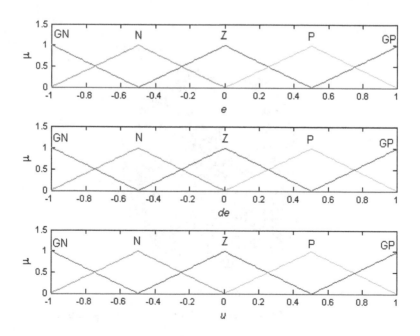

Fig. 5. Membership functions for input e, *de* and *u*

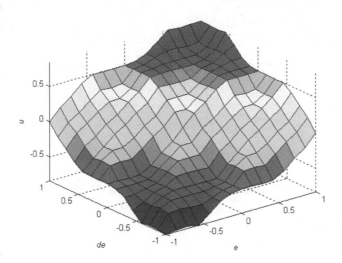

Fig. 6. The output surface of the fuzzy inference system for five fuzzy subsets using the inputs and the output.

2.4 Fuzzy control with seven fuzzy subsets

Table 3 shows one of possible control rules based on seven membership functions [Aissaoui et al 2011].

de \ e — u	NB	NM	NS	Z	PS	PM	PB
NB	NB	NB	NB	NB	NM	NS	Z
NM	NB	NB	NB	NM	NS	Z	PS
NS	NB	NB	NM	NS	Z	PS	PM
Z	NB	NM	NS	Z	PS	PM	PB
PS	NM	NS	Z	PS	PM	PB	PB
PM	NS	Z	PS	PM	PB	PB	PB
PB	Z	PS	PM	PB	PB	PB	PB

Table 3. Rules Base for speed control

Here NS is negative small and PS is positive small. The labels of fuzzy sets and their corresponding membership functions are depicted in figures (7). Figure (8) shows the corresponding output surface.

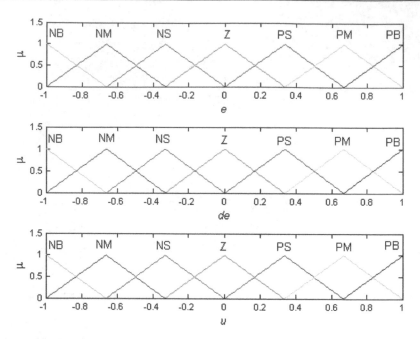

Fig. 7. Membership functions for input e, *de* and *u*

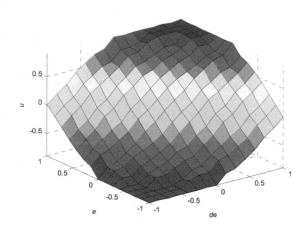

Fig. 8. The output surface of the fuzzy inference system for seven fuzzy subsets using the inputs and the output.

The continuity of input membership functions, reasoning method, and defuzzification method for the continuity of the mapping $u_{fuzzy}(e,\dot{e})$ is necessary. In this paper, the triangular membership function, the max-min reasoning method, and the center of gravity defuzzification method are used, as those methods are most frequently used in many literatures [Bose B. K. 1994; Rachid A. 1996].

2.5 Influence of the choice of Membership Function

The choice of membership functions (MF) is important in the design of fuzzy logic controller. The most MF shapes known and used frequently are: Triangular, Gaussian, Trapezoidal,... Different cases can be subject of our study, following the MF used and their distribution on the universe of discourse.

2.5.1 Symmetrical Gaussian membership functions

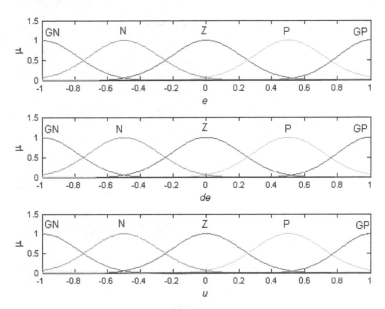

Fig. 9. Membership functions for input e, *de* and *u* arranged in symmetrical Gaussian shape.

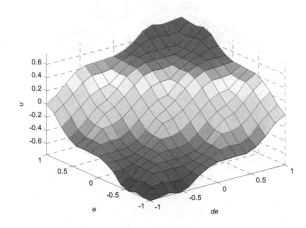

Fig. 10. The output surface of the fuzzy inference system for five fuzzy subsets in symmetrical Gaussian shape.

2.5.2 Asymmetrical triangular membership functions

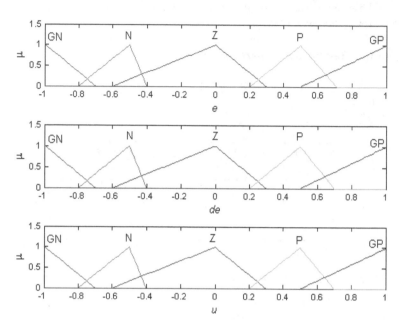

Fig. 11. Membership functions for input e, *de* et *u* arranged in asymmetrical shape.

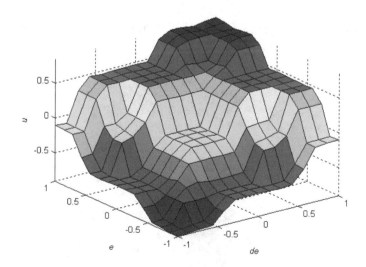

Fig. 12. The output surface of the fuzzy inference system for five fuzzy subsets arranged in asymmetrical shape..

2.5.3 Limit recovery of fuzzy sets

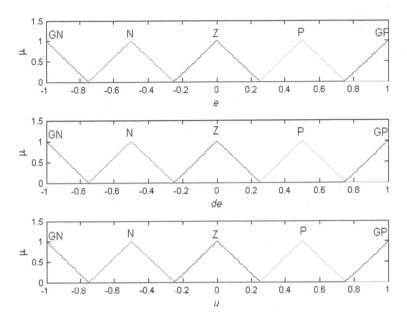

Fig. 13. Membership functions for input e, *de* and *u* arranged in symmetrical triangular shape and with limit recovery of the fuzzy sets

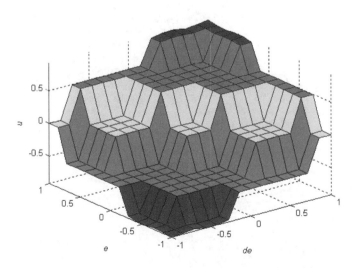

Fig. 14. The output surface of the fuzzy inference system for five fuzzy subsets arranged in symmetrical triangular shape and with limit recovery of the fuzzy sets.

2.5.4 Non recovery of of fuzzy sets

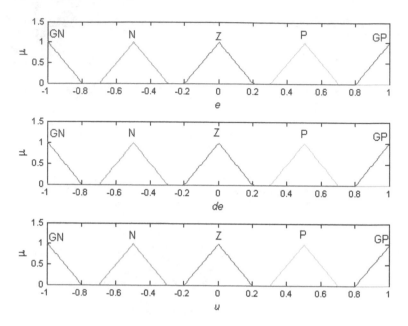

Fig. 15. The output surface of the fuzzy inference system for five fuzzy subsets arranged in symmetrical triangular shape and with non-recovery of the fuzzy sets

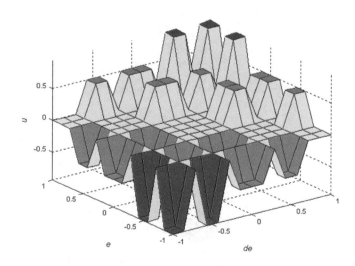

Fig. 16. The output surface of the fuzzy inference system for five fuzzy subsets arranged in symmetrical triangular shape and with non-recovery of the fuzzy sets

2.5.5 Interpretation and discussion

In this section, we have based our study on Triangular MF. It gives same results compared to Gaussian MF as it can see in figures (6) and (10) which represent the output surface of the fuzzy inference system of the inputs (e and de) and the output (u).

The symmetry and the recovery of the fuzzy sets (or MF) are important and they significantly affect the performance of FLC. It appears clearly in the surface of fuzzy inference system (figures 6, 12, 14, 16). It is better to choose the MF with a symmetrical shape and the recovery of two to three fuzzy sets is very interest. This comparison is made using the rules base presented in Table 2.

3. Description of machine drive

The schematic diagram of the speed control system under study is shown in figure (17). The power circuit consists of a continuous voltage supply which can provided by a six rectifier thyristors and a three phase GTO thyristors inverter whose output is connected to the stator of the synchronous machine. The field current i_f of the synchronous machine, which determines the field flux level is controlled by voltage v_f [Aissaoui, A. G. et al 2010; Namuduri, C. & Sen,P. C. 1987].

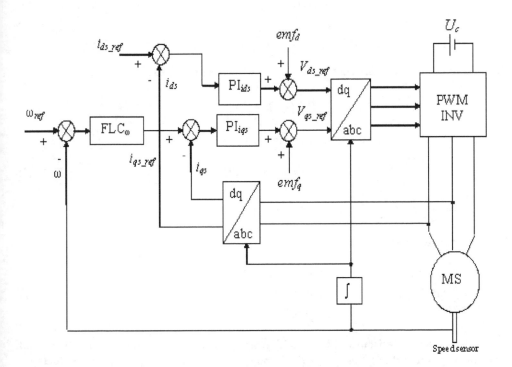

Fig. 17. System Configuration of Field-Oriented Synchronous Motor Control.

The parameters of the synchronous machine are:

Rated output power 3HP, Rated phase voltage 60V, Rated phase current 14 A, Rated field voltage v_f=1.5V, Rated field current i_f =30A, Stator resistance R_s =0.325Ω, Field resistance R_f =0.05Ω, Direct stator inductance L_{ds} =8.4 mH, Quadrature stator inductance L_{qs}=3.5 mH, Field leakage inductance L_f=8.1 mH, Mutual inductance between inductor and armature M_{fd}=7.56mH, The damping coefficient B=0.005 N.m/s, The moment of inertia J=0.05 kg.m2, Pair number of poles p = 2.

Figure (17) shows the schematic diagram of the speed control of synchronous motor using fuzzy logic controller.

3.1 Machine equations

The more comprehensive dynamic performance of a synchronous machine can be studied by synchronously rotating d-q frame model known as Park equations. The dynamic model of synchronous motor in d-q frame can be represented by the following equations [Sturtzer, G. & Smigiel E. 2000; Cambronne, J. P. et al 1996]:

$$v_{ds} = R_s\, i_{ds} + \frac{d}{dt}\phi_{ds} - \omega\,\phi_{qs}$$

$$v_{qs} = R_s i_{qs} + \frac{d}{dt}\phi_{qs} + \omega\,\phi_{ds} \qquad (2)$$

$$v_f = R_f i_f + \frac{d}{dt}\phi_f$$

The mechanical equation of synchronous motor can be represented as:

$$J\frac{d}{dt}\Omega = T_e - T_l - B\Omega \qquad (3)$$

Where the electromagnetic torque is given in d-q frame:

$$T_e = p\left(\phi_{ds}i_{qs} - \phi_{qs}i_{ds}\right) \qquad (4)$$

In which: $\Omega = \frac{d}{dt}\theta$, $\theta = \int \Omega\,dt$, $\omega = \frac{d}{dt}\theta_e = p\Omega$, $\theta_e = p\theta$.

The flux linkage equations are:

$$\phi_{ds} = L_{ds}i_{ds} + M_{fd}i_f$$

$$\phi_{qs} = L_{qs}i_{qs} \qquad (5)$$

$$\phi_f = L_f i_f + M_{fd}i_{ds}$$

Where R_s – stator resistance, R_f – field resistance, L_{ds}, L_{qs} – respectively direct and quadrature stator inductances, L_f – field leakage inductance, M_{fd} – mutual inductance between inductor and armature, ϕ_{ds} and ϕ_{qs} – respectively direct and quadrature flux, ϕ_f –

field flux, T_e – electromagnetic torque, T_l – external load disturbance, p – pair number of poles, B – is the damping coefficient, J – is the moment of inertia, ω – electrical angular speed of motor. Ω – mechanical angular speed of motor, θ – mechanical rotor position, θ_e –electrical rotor position.

3.2 Vector control

The self-control operation of the inverter-fed synchronous machine results in a rotor field oriented control of the torque and flux in the machine. The principle is to maintain the armature flux and the field flux in an orthogonal or decoupled axis. The flux in the machine is controlled independently by the field winding and the torque is affected by the fundamental component of armature current i_{qs}. In order to have an optimal functioning, the direct current i_{ds} is maintained equal to zero [Sturtzer G. & Smigiel E. 2000 ; Cambronne J. P. et al 1996].

Substituting (5) in (4), the electromagnetic torque can be rewritten for $i_f = constant$ and $i_{ds} = 0$ as follow:

$$T_e(t) = \lambda i_{qs}(t) \tag{6}$$

where $\lambda = pM_{fd}i_f$.

In the same conditions, it appears that the v_{ds} and v_{qs} equations are coupled. We have to introduce a decoupling system, by introducing the compensation terms emf_d and emf_q in which

$$\begin{aligned} emf_d &= \omega L_{qs}i_{qs}, \\ emf_q &= -\omega L_{ds}i_{ds} - \omega M_{af}i_f. \end{aligned} \tag{7}$$

4. Simulation results

In order to validate the control strategies as discussed above, digital simulation studies were made on the system described in figure (17). The speed and currents loops of the drive were also designed and simulated respectively with fuzzy control and PI control. The feedback control algorithms were iterated until best simulation results were obtained.

The speed loop was closed, and transient response was tested with both PI current control and fuzzy speed control. We used several types of fuzzy controller based on the cases presented in section (2.2). The simulation of the starting mode without load is done, followed by reversing the speed reference $\omega_{ref} = \pm100\,\text{rad/s}$ at t_3=2s. The load ($T_l = 7\ N.m$) is applied at $t_1 = 1$ s and eliminated at $t_2 = 1.5$ s.

The simulation is realized using the SIMULINK software in MATLAB environment.

Figures (18), (19) and (20) show the performances of the fuzzy controller using respectively Table (1), (2) and (3).

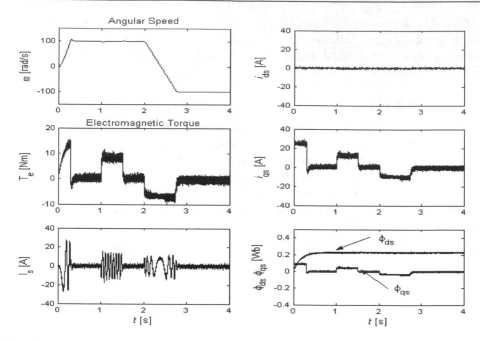

Fig. 18. The response of the system with fuzzy speed controller using Rules base of Table 1.

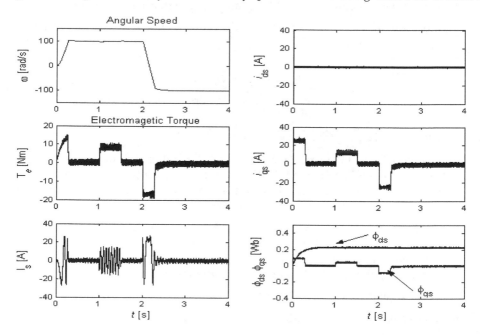

Fig. 19. The response of the system with fuzzy speed controller using Rules base of Table 2.

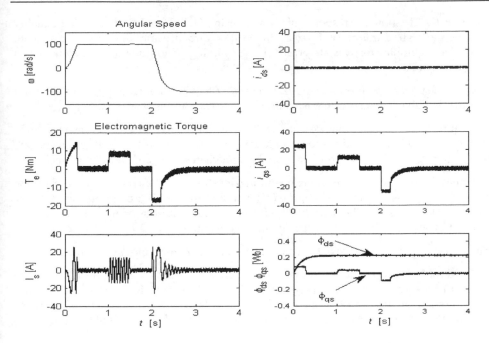

Fig. 20. The response of the system with fuzzy speed controller using Rules base of Table 3.

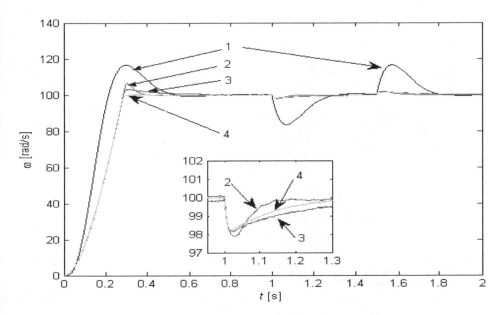

Fig. 21. Comparison of the system response for different controller, 1) PI, 2) 3 Fuzzy subsets
3) 5 Fuzzy subsets, 4) 7 Fuzzy subsets.

The figures (17-21) show the response of SM with using FLC. The FLC presents high quality to achieve the desired trajectory. It rejects the load disturbances rapidly with no overshoot and with a negligible steady state error. The decoupling of torque-flux is maintained in permanent regime.

The reason of superior performance of fuzzy control system is that it is adaptive in nature and the controller is able to realize different control laws for each inputs state (*e* and *de*).

From figure (21), the performances of the FLC can be shown clearly. Compared to PI controller, the FLC give good response to follow the desired trajectory with no overshoot, with a negligible steady state error and with the immediately reject of load disturbances.

The increase of the membership functions in fuzzification and defuzzification improve the quality of the FLC as it is shown in figure (21), however the computation time increase two. It will be better to have a FLC with high performance and with less computation time. The choice of FLC with five Fuzzy-subsets may fulfil these criteria.

Figure (22) shows the influence of the choice of MF on the performance of control.

The choice of MF affects the performances of the FLC, it appears in figure (22) that the triangular or the Gaussian shape doesn't affect the speed control. However, in the presence of asymmetrical distribution the quality of control is bad. The non recovery of fuzzy set gives worst results. It will be better to choose MF with acceptable recovery of fuzzy sets.

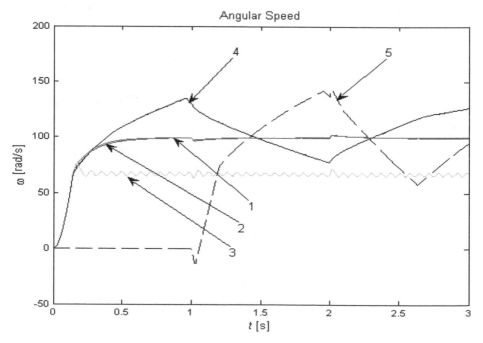

Fig. 22. Comparison of the system response for different MF shape: 1) Triangular, 2)Gaussian, 3) Asymmetrical, 4) limit Recovery, 5) Non recovery.

4.1 Robustness

In order to test the robustness of the used method we have studied the effect of the parameters uncertainties on the performances of the speed control [Aissaoui et al 2007].

To show the effect of the parameters uncertainties, we have simulated the system with different values of the parameter considered and compared to nominal value (real value).

Two cases are considered:

1. The moment of inertia (±50%).
2. The stator and rotor resistances (+50%).

To illustrate the performances of control, we have simulated the starting mode of the motor without load, and the application of the load ($T_l = +7\text{Nm}$) at the instance $t_1 = 2$ s and its elimination at $t_2 = 3$ s; in presence of the variation of parameters considered (the moment of inertia, the stator resistances, the stator inductances) with speed step of +100 rad/s.

Figure (23) shows the tests of robustness realized with the fuzzy controller for different values of the moment of inertia.

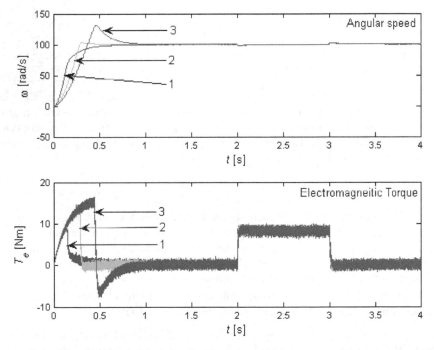

Fig. 23. Test of robustness for different values of the moment of inertia using fuzzy rules of Table 2: 1) – 50%, 2) nominal case, 3) +50%.

Figure (24) shows the tests of robustness realized with the fuzzy control for different values of stator and rotor resistances.

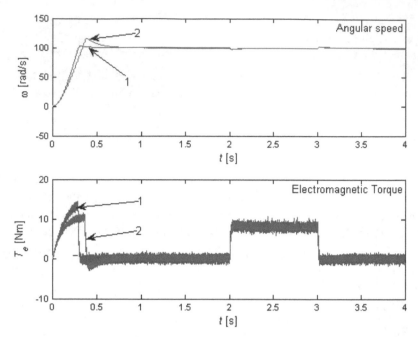

Fig. 24. Test of robustness for different values of stator and rotor resistances using fuzzy rules of Table 2: 1) nominal case, 2) +50%.

For the robustness of control, a decrease or increase of the moment of inertia J or the resistances doesn't have any effects on the performances of the technique used (figures 23 and 24). An increase of the moment of inertia gives best performances, but it presents a slow dynamic response (figure 23). The fuzzy control gives to our controller a great place towards the control of the system with unknown parameters.

5. Conclusion

The study describes an application of fuzzy logic system in control of electrical machines. The fuzzy logic control presents a new approach to robust control. The control methodology is described and used to develop a simple robust controller to deal with uncertain parameters and external disturbances. The design of the FLC depends on the structure adopted in fuzzification, defuzzification and rule base. In choice of FLC structure, we have to reach a compromise between the complexity and the precision of controller. The design of the FLC depends on the shape, symmetry and the recovery of MF.

In this study, a complete fuzzy logic control, based on synchronous motor, has been described. The system was analyzed and designed. The performances were studied extensively by simulation to validate the theoretical concept. To avoid the complexity of the FLC and the decrease of its precision, we have adopted five subsets to describe each inputs and output variables. The simulation results show that the proposed controller is superior to conventional controller in robustness and in tracking precision. The simulation study indicates clearly the superior performance of FLC, because it is adaptive in nature. It appears from the response properties that it has a high performance in presence of the uncertain plant parameters and load disturbances. It is used to control system with unknown model. The control of speed by FLC gives fast dynamic response with no overshoot and negligible steady-state error. The decoupling, stability and convergence to equilibrium point are verified.

This study will be very helpful, to design a new controllers based on FLC. With use of FLC we can reach high quality in control of non linear systems.

6. References

Aissaoui, A. G. 2007. *The use of neural networks and fuzzy logic for control of synchronous machine*, Phd thesis, University Djilali Liabes of Sidi Bel Abbes, Algeria.

Aissaoui, A. G.; Abid, M.; Abid, H. And Tahour A. & Zeblah, A.K. (2007). A Fuzzy Logic Controller For Synchronous Machine", *Journal of ELECTRICAL ENGINEERING*, VOL. 58, NO. 5, 285–290

Aissaoui, A. G.; Abid, M.; Abid, H. And Tahour A.; Megherbi, A. C. (2010). A Fuzzy Logic And Variable Structure Control For Permanent Magnet Synchronous Motors" *International Journal Of Systems Control (Ijsc)*, Vol.1/Iss.1, pp. 13-21.

Aissaoui, A. G.; Abid, M. & Tahour A. (2010). Application Of Fuzzy Sliding Mode Technique In Controller And Observer Of Synchronous Motor, *IEEE International Energy Conference & Exibition, IEEE-Energycon2010*, Manama, Bahrain, December 18-22, 2010.

Aissaoui, A. G.; Tahour, A.; Essenbouli, N.; Nollet, F. ; Abid M. & Chergui, M.I. (2011). A Fuzzy-PI control To Extract An Optimal Power From Wind Turbine, *Global Conference on Renewables and Energy Efficiency for Desert Regions and Exibition : GCREEDER 2011*, Amman-Jordan, April 26th – 28th 2011.

Bose, B. K. (1986). *Power electronics and AC drives*, Prentice Hall, Englewood Cliffs, Newjersey.

Bose, B. K. (1994). Expert System, Fuzzy logic, and neural network Applications in power Electronics and motion control, *Proceedings of the IEEE*, Vol. 82, NO. 8, 1303-1321.

Bühler, H. (1994). *Réglage par logique floue*, Presse Polytechniques et Universitaires romandes, lausanne.

Cambronne, J. P.; Le Moigne Ph. & Hautier J. P. (1996). Synthèse de la commande d'un onduleur de tension. Journal de Physique III, France, 757–778.

Cirstea, M.N.; Dinu, A.; Khor, J.G.; McCormick, M. (2002). *Neural and Fuzzy Logic Control of Drives and Power Systems*, Newnes, Oxford.

Heber, B.; Xu, L. & Tang, Y. (1995). Fuzzy logic enhanced speed control of an indirect field oriented induction machine drive, *IEEE PESC Meet.*, pp. 1288–1294.

Kim, Y.T.; Bien, Z. (2000). Robust self-learning fuzzy controller design for a class of nonlinear MIMO system, *Fuzzy Sets and systems* 111, 117-135.

Lee, C.C. (1990). Fuzzy logic in control system: fuzzy logic controller — Part I/II, *IEEE Trans. systems Man. Cybernet* 20, 404-435.

Mamdani E.H. (1974). Applications of fuzzy algorithms for simple dynamic plants, *Proc. IEE* 121, 1585–1588.

Namuduri, C. & Sen,P. C. (1987). A servo-control system using a self-controlled synchronous motor (SCSM) with sliding mode control. *IEEE Trans. on Industry Application*, vol. IA-23, N°2.

Rachid, A. (1996). *Systèmes de régulation*, Masson, paris.

Sousa, G.C. D.; Bose, B. K. (1994). Fuzzy set theory based control of a phase-controlled converter DC machine drive, *IEEE Transaction on Industry Applications*, Vol. 30, NO. 1, 34-44.

Spooner, J.T.; Maggiore, M.; Ordonez, R; Passino, K. M. (2002). *Stable adaptive control and estimation for nonlinear system, Neural and fuzzy approximator techniques*, Willey-Interscience.

Sturtzer, G. & Smigiel E. (2000). Modélisation et commande des moteurs triphasés. Edition Ellipses.

Tang, Y. & Xu, L. (1994). Fuzzy logic application for intelligent control of a variable speed drive, *IEEE PES Winter Meet*.

Timothy, J. R. (1994). Fuzzy logic with engineering application, McGraw-Hill, New York, 1995.

Yager, R. R. (1997). Fuzzy logics and artificial intelligence. *Fuzzy Sets and Systems* 90, 193-198.

Yu, F. M.; Chung, H. Y.; Chen, S. Y..(2003). Fuzzy sliding mode controller design for uncertain time-delayed systems with nonlinear input. *Fuzzy Sets Syst.*, vol. 140, 359-374.

Part 2

Control Systems

7

Fuzzy Control in Power Electronics Converters for Smart Power Systems

Harold R. Chamorro and Gustavo A. Ramos

Universidad de los Andes, Bogotá,
Colombia

1. Introduction

During the last decade, power systems have experienced continuous challenges due to the increasing of demanded energy and the integration with different Renewable Energy Sources (RES) as a possible reduction option to the pollution around the world, for this reason it is necessary the transition to the new power concept known as "Smart Grid", which has been conceived as the integration of different engineering fields and looks for the application of intelligent controllers with adaptability and interoperability with other systems (Bose, 2010; Momoh, 2009).

Power electronics plays a key role in the interfaces between the Distributed Generation (DG) sources and the power system or users, but it is necessary to add control loops which brings the possibility to give to the power system the flexibility and reconfiguration under disturbances, faults or system requirements (Simoes, 2006; Peng, et al, 2009).

The technology of power electronics converters has evolved dramatically in the last years based on the semiconductors advances, new configuration proposals and important researches in several applications related with the interconnection of Distributed Energy Resources (DER) with the utility grid (Elbuluk & Idris, 2008).

The intelligent control is associated to the emulation of human thought processes and involves some well-known techniques such as expert systems, neural networks and fuzzy logic (Bor-Ren, 1993; Zadeh, 1994; Bose, 2006). The use of these control methods in power electronics has been increased in the last decades, based on its simplicity design, the development of new speed multitasking processors and the necessity to add some controllers which demonstrates robustness in presence of the high nonlinear dynamic characteristics of the power converters.

The primary task of power electronics is the conversion and control of electric power in its two types, Direct Current (DC) and Alternating Current (AC) and its combinations. Fuzzy Logic Control (FLC) has been tested across the whole power converters classification with different objectives. For example in rectifiers, FLC has been used to regulate the output voltage (Cecati et al, 2003 & 2005), in cycloconverters, with the purpose to improve the power quality and regulate the load voltage (Sivakumar & Jickson, 2011). In DC-DC converters, FLC has been applied to the regulation of load voltage in different operation conditions (Bor-Ren, 1993; Mattavelli et al, 1997) or Power Factor Correction (PFC) taking into account the application (Kolokolov, 2004).

In resonant converters and soft self - switching power circuits, the use of FLC has shown significant contributions obtaining the expected results, that with other techniques might not be obtained with the same simplicity design (Corcau & et al, 2010; Chamorro & Trujillo, 2009).

Moreover, FLC has been applied in inverters, specially in Voltage Source Converters (VSC) assuring phase and voltage magnitude (Ayob & et al, 2006) in the power flow control with the utility grid in different operative regions (Diaz & et al, 2007; Chamorro & et al, 2009).

There are plenty of developments of FLC in power electronics in all the voltage scales and power sectors. In Photo Voltaic (PV) applications, FLC has been proposed to optimize the Maximum Power Point (MPP) with outstanding results compared with other methods (Alajmi et al, 2010; Chaouachi et al, 2010; Shireen et al, 2011).

Another important application has been developed in High Voltage Direct Current (HVDC) in both stations (rectifier and inverter) ensuring an adequate performance despite of the system complexity (Liang, 2009).

In the industrial sector as well, FLC has demonstrated a satisfactory use in Adjustable Speed Drivers (ASD) for three phase induction motors under mechanical loads with good results (Chamorro et al, 2009; Chamorro & Toro, 2010).

One important advantage which offers the FLC is the possibility to use it as a hierarchical layer with the ability to supervise and to coordinate other systems such as electric vehicles (Ferreira et al, 2008), Flexible AC Transmission Systems (FACTS) (Sadeghzadeh & Ansarian, 2006) or even Microgrids (MG) and its interaction with power electronic interfaces (Papadimitriou & Vovos, 2010; Chamorro & Ramos, 2011) which is the main point in this chapter.

A basic conceptual representation of a MG is presented in Fig. 1, where it is depicted the physical layer and involves a high penetration of DG (photovoltaic, fuel cell, fly-wheel storage, micro wind turbine) with power electronic interfaces. The MG is connected to the utility distribution system through a static switch and a transformer.

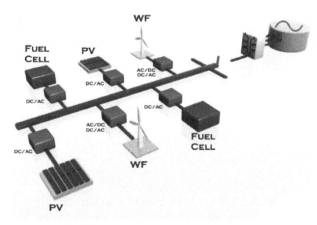

Fig. 1. Microgrid Structure Concept

This chapter gathers together some previous works related with the application of fuzzy logic control in power converters and explain its use in Smart MG. The developments presented in this chapter start from theoretical and mathematical background and are supported in literature and recent contributions in the field exposed. For the rest of this chapter the use of FLC is shown in different power converters as follows: In section II it is presented the application of a FLC in a soft switching converter. In section III it is explained two applications of FLC for a VSC. In section IV it is shown two innovative proposals for MG applying FLC as supervisory/hierarchical control. Finally the obtained conclusions are presented.

2. Takagi Sugeno approach control for a resonant DC link converter

With the advent of the deep penetration of renewable energy sources along the power system, the application of new power electronic techniques are becoming a necessity in order to improve the efficiency and to get the maximum power transfer as long as possible.

Soft switching topologies and resonant power converters are well known by offering a significant reduction in the switching losses and the components size involved, the decreasing of the thermal requirements, and operating at high frequencies (Rashid, 2001).

During the last decades, some important developments have shown the applicability of the soft switching circuits in PV arrays and the interfaces in their power conversion chains as a mean of raising the switch power ratings in the inverters associated (Bellini & et al, 2010; Kasa & et al, 2005).

One of those soft switching topologies is the resonant DC link circuits which are the interfaces between DC power supplies or PV cells and the inverters as it can be seen in Fig. 2. These circuits consist of a front - ended converter to cause the DC link voltage to generate a periodic Zero Voltage Switching (ZVS) condition in which the inverter switches can be turned on or off. However, these kinds of converters require defining previously a timing program for each switch in order to obtain the expected modes and their resonance.

Fig. 2. DC Link Interface

Fuzzy Logic Control (FLC) has been applied in different soft switched inverters in order to provide a standalone way of switching with good results (Shireen & et al, 1996). In a previous work it is demonstrated the applicability of the FLC in a DC link circuit interacting with a VSC (Chamorro & Trujillo, 2009), now it is presented the TS approach, its design and some relevant tests.

2.1 DC link circuit under study

The DC link circuit scheme can be seen in Fig. 3, where is highlighted the tank circuit composed by a L_r inductor and a C_r capacitor and three controllable switches and diodes. It is assumed that a high inductive load represents the inverter as a I_o current source. The states and detail considerations can be seen in (Shireen & et al, 1994).

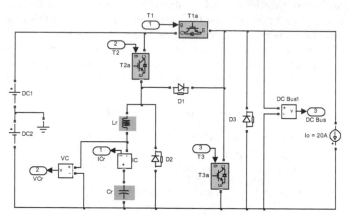

Fig. 3. DC Link Circuit

2.2 Takagi Sugeno design

This approach takes advantage of a previous development originally proposed in (Shireen & et al 1996), where is presented a FLC with the objective to pulsate to zero the DC link, allowing soft switching in an inverter connected and to reduce its switching losses as it is demonstrated in a recent paper (Chamorro & Trujillo, 2009).

The design starting point is the definition and classification of sets according to the voltage and current measurement signals in the capacitor. The definitions of linguistic variables are based on a previous developed knowledge evaluation of the current and voltage waveforms in open loop. These waveforms are presented in Fig. 4

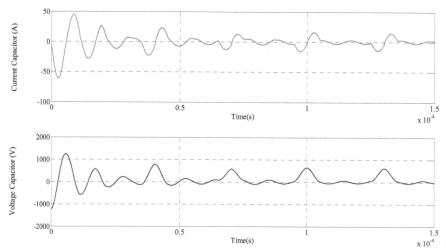

Fig. 4. Current and Voltage Capacitor Waveforms

Some special attention is required, in order to establish the specific boundaries of the regions in each subset, specifically the zero region and the high positive and negative levels, which imply some important details in a real hardware application such as the rated values of the capacitor and inductor and their time response under a fast variability.

According to the waveforms obtained, on the antecedent the input membership functions are conformed as it can be seen in Fig. 5 , where the linguistic labels mean Negative (N), Zero (Z), Positive Small (PS), Positive Large (PL).

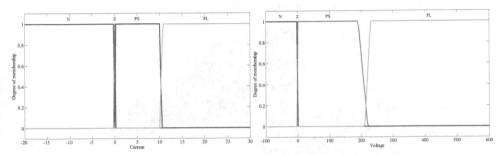

Fig. 5. Input Membership Functions

The Takagi – Sugeno system is employed as inference method, using constants or zero order Sugeno models in the output membership function, which represents the turning off or on action of the switches in the DC link circuit. The positive constants are interpreted as the turning on of the switches and the negative constants like the switches turning off instead, for example to turn on the switch called T_1 the constant associated is 5, or to turn off the switch T_2 the correspondent constant is -10. In order to present these mentioned changes, a graphic of the rule viewer of FIS toolbox of Matlab® are shown displaying the fuzzy inference. The three small plots across the top of the Fig. 6 represent the antecedent and consequent of the rules.

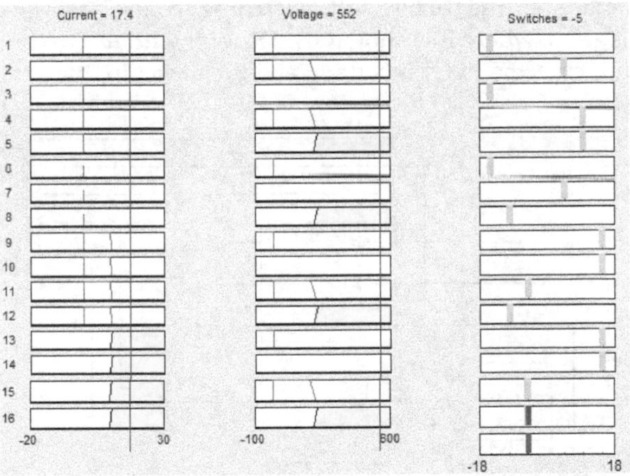

Fig. 6. RuleViewer

The complete rule base determines all the decisions of the switch turning on or off. The decision table is presented next.

v_c/i_c	N	Z	PS	PL
N	NL	NL	PM	PM
Z	NL	PS	PS	NM
PS	PL	PL	NS	NM
PL	PL	PL	NS	NS

Table 1. Decision Table

The surface control associated it is presented in Fig. 7

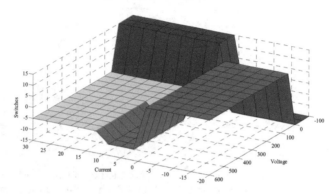

Fig. 7. Surface Control

The final step of the FLC design is the defuzzification process, in this case it is used the common weight average method.

2.3 Simulation results

The proposed structure of the fuzzy soft switching control is presented in the next Simulink(R) block diagram, where it is shown the DC link with its two outputs as the current and voltage measurements, the FLC embedded and the switching pulses generator.

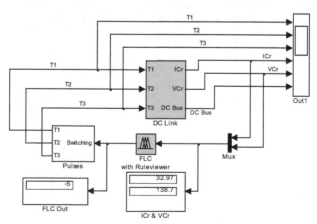

Fig. 8. Closed Loop System

The simulation tests in closed loop with the T-S FLC shows and adequate performance and a similarity with the voltage and current waveforms and the soft switching response, as it can be seen in Fig 9.

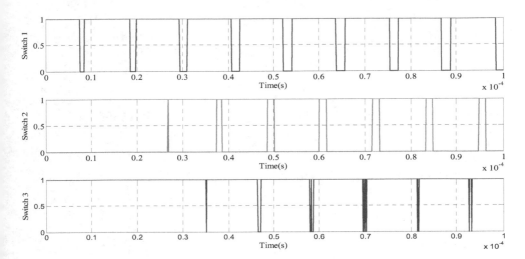

Fig. 9. Self-Switching Pulses

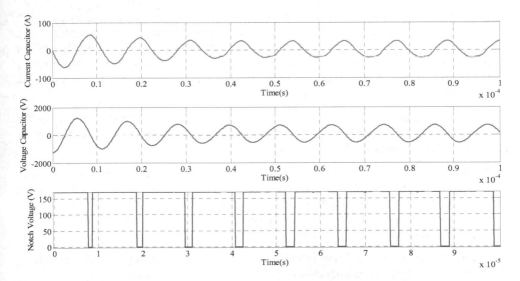

Fig. 10. Obtained Waveforms with FLC

In order to show the adaptability and performance of the DC link circuit and the FLC, another test is done with a current source variation with high and abrupt changes. As it is shown in Fig. 11 the FLC is adaptable even under those several changes and the waveforms conserve their resonant behaviour without instability or not desired transient signals.

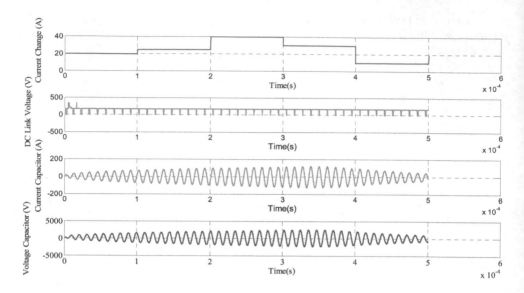

Fig. 11. Current Variability

3. Fuzzy applications in VSC

One of the most significant converters which have played and will play an important role in the power networks, industry and traction systems is the Voltage Source Converter (VSC). This converter has been applied in different applications such as High Voltage Direct Current (HVDC) power transmission, Adjustable Speed Drivers (ASD), Active Power Filters (APF), Uninterruptible Power Supplies (UPS), electric vehicle drives and the connection of RES, mainly with, wind farms and Photo Voltaic (PV) arrays to grid.

Voltage Source Converter (VSC), used in Supergrids (SG) and MG, are able to manage the bidirectional power flow with the grid (Diaz & et al, 2007 & 2008) and other MG through the tie lines involved (Chamorro & Ramos, 2011).

On the other hand, most industries around the world use three phase induction motors due their high durability, low maintenance and cost, however, it is necessary to add an extra controller with the purpose of achieving speed regulation under mechanical loads, hence, the VSC has become an important piece in the industrial processes given its versatility as an ASD (Mokrytzki, 1991).

This section presents two applications using fuzzy logic in their control loops demonstrating the easiness of design and its importance in the smart electrical systems.

3.1 Voltage source converter operation

Fig. 12 depicts the main components of a VSC, where it can be seen a three phase fully controllable of six semiconductors, typically Insulated Gate Bipolar Transistors (IGBT), a DC capacitor on the DC side in order to provide constant DC bus voltage with a minimal ripple.

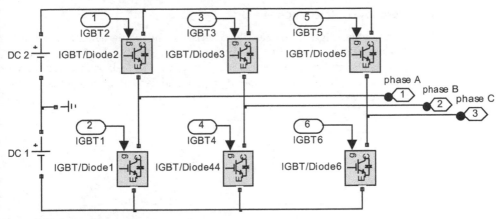

Fig. 12. Voltage Source Converter

One of the simple switching techniques applied to VSC is the conventional method known as Sinusoidal Pulse Width Modulation (SPWM), this method is used to manipulate and control the VSC in both of the cases mentioned above.

3.2 Three phase induction motor speed control

Rotating electrical machines, specifically three phase induction motors are the functional units with more electricity consumption in the industry, due to their widely use in manifold applications as diverse as industrial fans, blowers and pumps and machine tools, keeping in mind its advantages like resistance, easy maintenance, low cost and durability (Xiaodong & Ilochonwu, 2011).

Different techniques and improvements have been used to regulate the speed in induction motors such as sliding control (Chung-Yuen & et al, 1992), scalar control (Bose, 1984), vector control (Matsugae & et al, 1990) or direct torque control (Takahashi & Ohmori, 1989) with notable results, nevertheless these methods require the system model or use indirect measurements in the closed feedback loop control.

With the new developments in power electronics devices and microprocessors, the design and implementation of power converter control circuits based IA it has been made possible and easier than in the past.

In this section it is presented the application of a FLC in order to regulate the speed in a three phase induction motor with the VSC as actuator as it is highlighted in Fig. 13.

Fig. 13. Voltage Source Converter Interface

3.2.1 Induction motor operation in open loop

The induction motors have high nonlinear characteristics and a mathematical complex model associated (Carmona & et al, 2010). Although these electrical machines are quite efficient, they require of a speed regulation algorithm under mechanical loads as it is shown in Fig. 14. The speed rate (1400rpm) is not regulated and is changing insofar as the mechanical load is increased or decreased.

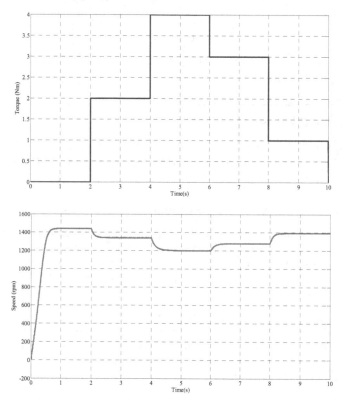

Fig. 14. Speed time response of the induction motor studied in open loop

The three phase voltages are provided by the VSC depending on the SPWM signals and their variation.

Any change in the SPWM signals is reflected in speed changes in the induction motor through the VSC action, hence the frequency and amplitude modulation index are selected to achieve this action properly. The first is the frequency modulation index (m_f), which is the relation between the carrier frequency or triangular signal and the frequency control signal or sinusoidal signal, the latter (m_a) is the amplitude relation of those signals and are expressed as:

$$m_f = \frac{f_{carrier}}{f_{mod\,uler}} \tag{1}$$

$$m_a = \frac{a_{carrier}}{a_{reference}} \qquad (2)$$

A basic scheme of an individual (VSC-Motor) unit it is shown in Fig. 15, where is highlighted the SPWM generation signals block and the main components involved.

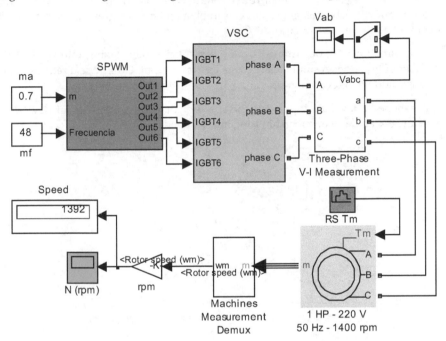

Fig. 15. Open Loop System

3.2.2 Proportional derivative fuzzy speed control

According to the behaviour shown above, it is designed a FLC speed regulation control. FLC design begins from a previous knowledge of the induction motor speed variations where the modulation index (Δm) and frequency (Δf) are changed in the SPWM signals in the VSC, so that the motor model is not required, however it is necessary to keep in mind the rated values of power, torque or speed as limits or condition constraints in the control action, the power and speed are related by the following expression:

$$P = \tau \omega \qquad (3)$$

The control designer should know the speed variability when it is applied a mechanical load and the rated values such as the nominal speed, torque and the rotor and stator resistance and reactance respectively only.

FLC strategy can be developed based on classical architectures design conserving its series or parallel topologies. It is common to use the error as an input as well as the error deviation (PD) or the integral error (PI) even with fuzzy controllers.

When is implemented a FLC, particularly a PD fuzzy control, it is difficult to specify the gain controller effect in the rise time, overshoot and settling time, where the non-linearities are more frequent, therefore it is necessary to determine an adequate tuning procedure of the controller to obtain an optimal and adaptable response.

PD fuzzy control is selected over other fuzzy control types based on its inherent advantages facing significant disturbances and has been implemented with great success in different power converters (Chamorro & Toro, 2010).

Membership functions are determined by the control designer, taking into account that a large number of functions result in a large rule basis per input. Otherwise a reduced number of functions could introduce a non-operative or undesired operation point.

As it is mentioned above, the inputs are the speed error and the speed error deviation. In Fig. 16 it can be seen these membership functions respectively.

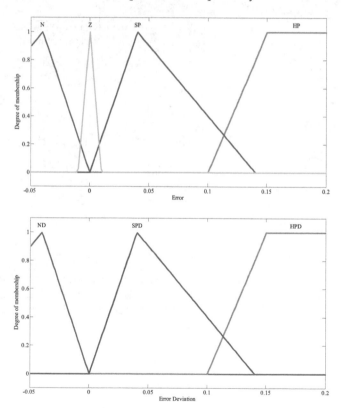

Fig. 16. Antecedent Membership Functions

Speed error is calculated with comparison between reference speed and speed signal feedback. It is established four overlapping fuzzy subsets for speed error, three for speed error deviation and seven for each output. The linguistic labels chosen are: Negative (N), Zero (Z), Small Positive (SP), High Positive (HP), Negative Deviation (ND), Small Positive

Deviation (SPD), High Positive Deviation (HPD), High Decrease (HD), Medium Decrease (MD), Low Decrease (LD), Not change (NC), Low Increase (LI), Medium Increase (MI), High Increase (HI).

The controller outputs are the modulation index deviation (Δm_u) and frequency index deviation (Δm_f) where the membership outputs have the same fuzzy subsets as it can be seen in Table 2 and in Fig. 17 is presented these functions.

Error	Error Deviation	$\Delta m, \Delta f$
HP	BPD	HD
SP	SPD	MD
Z		LD
N	ND	NC
		LI
		MI
		HI

Table 2. Antecedent and Consequent Variables

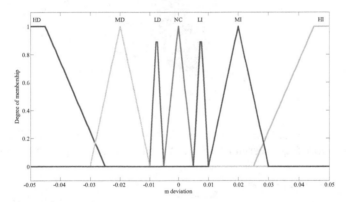

Fig. 17. Consequent Membership Functions

Speed error and speed error deviation are normalised in order to fit out and process adequately the input systems. It is needed an scale factor according to the induction motor rated speed, in this case 1400 rpm, with the aim to guarantee a proper variability.

The fuzzy rules basis is shown in Table 3 with a combinatory option of 12 (3x4) rules:

$\Delta e/e$	N	PN	Z	SP
ND	HD	MD	LD	LD
BPD	LD	LI	LI	MI
SPD	NC	NC	NC	LI

Table 3. Decision Table

The defuzzifier selected is the average of centres as is expressed in (4):

$$y^* = \frac{\sum_{n=1}^{M} y_n w_n}{\sum_{n=1}^{M} w_n} \qquad (4)$$

Where M is the number of fuzzy sets, w are the weights of set defined for its height and y^{-1} is the centre of n-esimal fuzzy set.

The control surface associated is shown in Fig. 18.

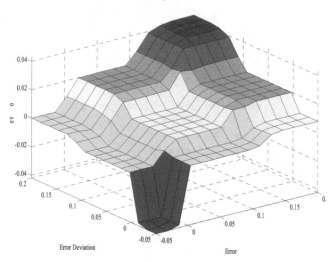

Fig. 18. Control Surface

A detailed design can be seen in previous works (Chamorro & et al, 2009; Chamorro & Toro, 2010), where is exposed the overall performance and the dynamic prefilters used.

3.2.3 Simulation results

With the rules explained above, a variability load is evaluated to confirm the performance of the controller proposed, the control action achieves the rated speed regulation even with an abrupt load decrease as it can be seen in Fig. 19.

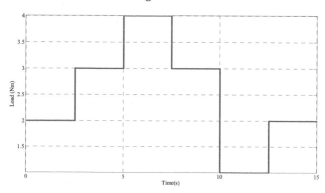

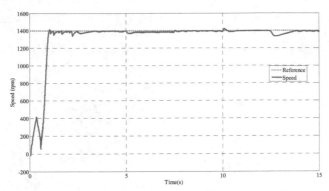

Fig. 19. Speed time response with speed regulation under mechanical load variability

3.3 Power flow control

VSC used as the interface between Renewable Energy Sources (RES) with the utility grid or autonomous systems, has demonstrated the power transfer capability from MG with excess generation to those with power demands. A representation of this application can be seen in Fig. 20.

Fig. 20. VSC Interface

The active and reactive power exchange is possible with the manipulation of the SPWM signals via a small reactor (Guangkai & et al, 2006).

The principle of operation of VSC is subjected to the management of phase shift and modulation index variability signals generated by SPWM. The active and reactive power exchange between the VSC and the AC network or another VSC is expressed as follows in (5) and (6).

$$P = \frac{U_s U_c}{X} \sin \delta \tag{5}$$

$$Q = \frac{U_s(-U_s + U_c \cos \delta)}{X} \tag{6}$$

where,
P: active power
Q: reactive power
U_c: VSC voltage
U_s: bus voltage
δ: phase difference with the voltages
X: coupling reactance reactor

According to these equations, it should be possible a fully control of the active power by δ and the reactive power by U_c deviations respectively (Singh & et al, 2006) and independently (Liu & et al, 2009). The power flow concept is depicted in Fig. 21.

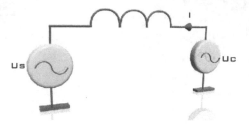

Fig. 21. Power flow equivalent circuit

Fig. 22 represents the four operation regions involved in the MG, which corresponds to the combinations of power imported or exported (Forero & et al, 2009). High non – linearity is experienced when both power references are changed abruptly and the control strategy must adapt to and stabilise the system in order to prevent a critical fault or important damage in any hardware device.

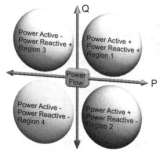

Fig. 22. Division of VSC HVDC Power flow operation zones

A basic MG that consists in one DER, a VSC unit and a low pass LC filter is shown in Fig. 23. A local Fuzzy Logic Control (FLC) which is in charge of the power flow regulation is added too.

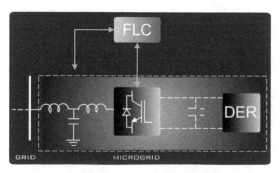

Fig. 23. MG block representation with Fuzzy Logic Controller

3.3.1 Fuzzy logic control VSC-GRID

Fuzzification: in this first step, the crisp inputs are transformed into fuzzy inputs. According to the inputs, error (e) and error deviation (de), the membership functions are assigned.

The output signals are modulation index (m) and shift phase (φ), the variability of these signals implies some changes directly in SWPM, allowing control of the power flow.

The membership functions have five different values to achieve good power reference tracking, big=B, low=L, zero=Z, negative=N, positive=P, change=C, medium=M, decreasing=D and increasing=I respectively. The letter concatenation represents a variable and each variable represents a membership function.

The normalisation signals are achieved with some constants in order to get a specific value with the required accuracy, as it is explained below in detail, and then the crisp data is converted into fuzzy sets to be compatible with the fuzzy set representation, by means of a fuzzifier, which in this case the Mandani implication is used:

$$\phi[\mu_A(x), \mu_A(y)] = \mu_A(x) \wedge \mu_q(y) \qquad (7)$$

Fig. 24 shows the input and output membership functions and the rule basis where the overall combination for Fuzzy Control of active Power (*FCP*) and Fuzzy Control of reactive Power (*FCQ*) can be inferred.

Fig. 24. Membership functions and look – up table

The second step is the fuzzy inference process, in this, the membership functions are combined with the control rules. A possible rule evidenced in this system could be: If the value of error is small but conserves its rate, the SPWM signal requires an increment in the magnitude and angle rigorously.

The linguistic labels are formulated according to the power operation regions and the error and error deviation measurements and limits bordered by the frame system.

In the final step, it is necessary to quantify to get a numerical value, the method of defuzzification used in this section is the Center of gravity (CoG), based on its fast computation and its wide use (Bai & et al, 2006).

3.3.2 Results grid – Connected mode of operation

Fig. 25 shows the MG – VSC – Grid system implemented in Simpower[R]. The green and grey blocks are the (p) and (q) decoupled fuzzy local controllers respectively.

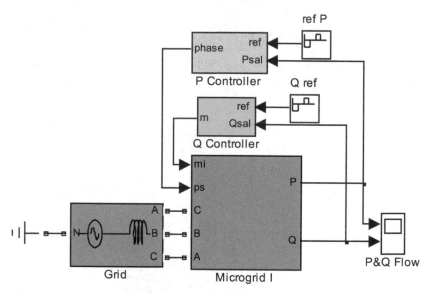

Fig. 25. Block system of three phase grid connected VSC

The time response of the power flow controller is presented in Fig. 26, as it can be seen, the fuzzy control tracks the reference. An important observation is that each reference is generated only when the previous power reference has been reached.

4. Fuzzy hierarchical/supervisory control

The future power networks will require of innovative alternatives and algorithms that can provide some kind of smartness to achieve an effective coordination, self-healing and diagnose and autonomous operation and automation. In this section, the use of fuzzy hierarchical or supervisory frameworks in these systems is considered and it is proposed two applications related.

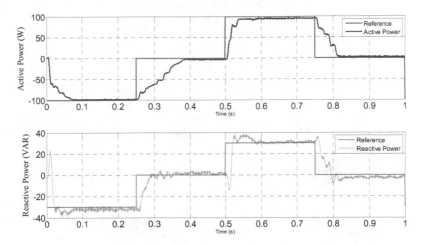

Fig. 26. Active and reactive power controller time response

4.1 Induction motor coordination in industrial environments

The combination of RES and power electronics interfaces in MG requires different control strategies and diverse control layers to obtain multiple objectives and an adequate response avoiding voltage unbalances and power quality disturbances (Lasseter, 2001; Binduhewa & et al, 2008).

Some of the advantages to implement DC MG in industrial environment systems are the reduction of transmission and distribution losses and ensuring power quality in loads. Another advantage of MG is the versatility of connection related with their two operation modes: in grid connected mode, the power supply is shared with the main grid and, in island mode the local RES supply the load system autonomously (Ding et al, 2010).

This approach is oriented to the induction motors coordination in industry, under a fuzzy supervisory frame where there are imprecise and vagueness data, causing loss of synchronism or changes in the different set points.

Fig. 27 depicts a DC MG where are some RES and induction motors. There is a lower control layer that determines the local speed set points and an upper (supervisory) layer that coordinates the whole speed references and synchronise the speed at one if it is necessary.

The upper layer control has a fuzzy structure based on the industrial system knowledge base where it has been experienced several damages and important extra costs associated. In this study is taken as example one type of industry, where has been applied or required the use of induction motors.

The type of industry is concerned with the necessity of the synchronisation of different induction motors at one speed reference like in textile industries, where the speed unification is an important consideration because of a minimal disturbance can cause an unexpected standstill; besides is necessary to consider the fact that not all the motors have the same mechanical load.

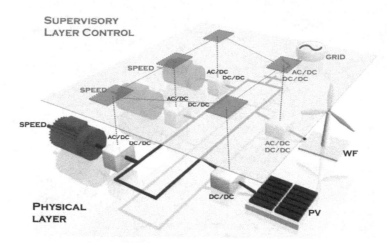

Fig. 27. Supervisory Control in Industrial DC Microgrids

In the study reported in this section are considered conditionals and priority statements to form the decision making actions.

The fuzzy supervisory control specifies the next actions listed as follows:

The first priority is to regulate the speed steady state error in each unit (VSC - Motor) according to the speed set point desired and the operation range involved. This could be expressed like a fuzzy rule as:

if the speed set point is changed in each unit n, then change the m_a and m_f applying the fuzzy local control rules explained above.

The speed error and speed error deviation are given by:

$$e_s = P_o - P_s \tag{8}$$

$$\Delta e_s = e(k) - e(k-1) \tag{9}$$

where,
P_o, is the speed measured
P_s, is the speed required

4.1.1 Simulation results

A desynchronization time is previously defined in order to test the supervisory control layer. In Fig. 27 it is shown the speed response of four units (VSC – three phase induction motors) while it is acting a constant mechanical load of 3 Nm. As it can be seen, immediately the supervisory control starts to apply the weights and two seconds later all the machines reach the rated speed at the same time, it is necessary to do a zoom in the simulation window to see the action mentioned, this effect is shown in Fig. 28 too.

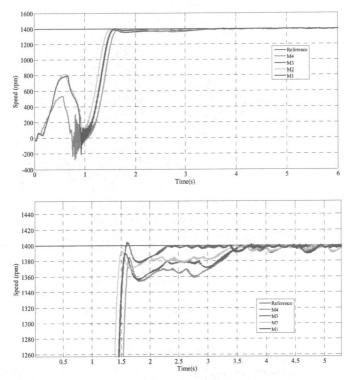

Fig. 28. Supervisory Synchronisation Control Induction Motors in the DC MG and Window Time Zoom In.

4.2 Microgrids power flow hierarchical control

The intentional islanding in MG refers to the condition where it is isolated from the utility grid and operates by itself (Balaguer, 2011), in this situation it is important a hierarchical central control layer to provide power management between the microsources and their loads.

With the integration of a central control in multi – energy generator systems, it is possible to control and to drive the energy to a MG side via the VSC operation. The central control main functions are the synchronization of VSCs in order not to exceed the nominal power limits, to avoid the power flow cancellation and coordinate and decide which VSC is in operation or not, at the same time, for this reason the FLC is chosen as a control method. In Fig. 29 is depicted the overview of the power flow in MG.

The fuzzy control levels specify three actions listed as follows:

1. The decision of power importation and exportation according to the necessity and the coordination of the VSC which is in operation. This could be expressed as a fuzzy rule as:

-   *if* the active and reactive power is required in MG *k*, *then* export them from other MG.

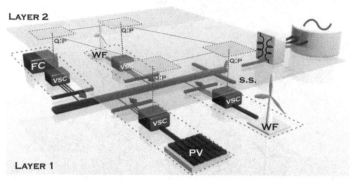

Fig. 29. Hierarchical Fuzzy Control

The power flow control in function of this control architecture following the equations (10) and (11) can be mathematically expressed as:

$$P_{ir} = \frac{U_i U_r}{X} \sin \delta \tag{10}$$

$$Q_{ir} = \frac{U_i(-U_i + U_r \cos \delta)}{X} \tag{11}$$

where,
$r=$ is the VSC unit which requires power,
$i=$ is the VSC unit which exports power,
   with,

$$r = 1,2,.....n \tag{12}$$

$$i = 1,2,.....n \tag{13}$$

N: number of VSC units

and $i \neq r$

1. The power share between VSCs or as a fuzzy rule function:
- *if* a MG k is enabled or disabled, *then* disable or enable the sum or power in the bus.

$$P_{sum} = \sum_{i=1}^{N} P_i \tag{14}$$

$$Q_{sum} = \sum_{i=1}^{N} Q_i \tag{15}$$

1. The regulation of steady – state power error: an important aspect proposed, is the requirement in the coordination of the power reference changes when a MG requires it and involves the primary control level explained above. Based on this desired behaviour, the corresponding fuzzy rule is:

- *if* the power set point is changed in MG *n*, *then* change the power setpoints in the other MG and apply the fuzzy local control rules.

The error and error deviation are given by:

$$e_p = P_o - P_s \tag{16}$$

$$e_q = Q_o - Q_s \tag{17}$$

$$\Delta e_p = e(k) - e(k-1) \quad \wedge \quad \Delta e_q = e(k) - e(k-1) \tag{18}$$

where,

P_o, Q_o are the powers measured

P_s, Q_s are the powers references

The system presented in Fig. 30 shows the power flow control between four VSCs, in this case, one of them requires power (in orange), the fuzzy central control decides to disable one MG and to enable the other two.

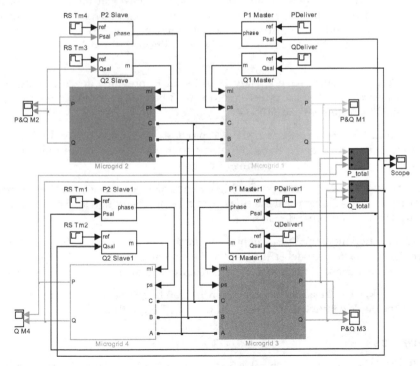

Fig. 30. Power flow control in island MG

The results of the simulations can be seen in Fig.31 for Ps= (-100, -40) W and Qs= (-30, -20) VAr.

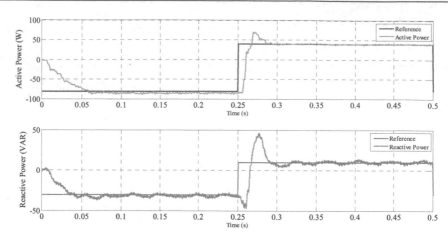

Fig. 31. Power flow control in island MG

5. Conclusion

The smart application schemes studied in this chapter show that the FLC can provide a suitable management for power converters and related developments with RES without an exact mathematical model and just the observed behaviour, due to its important features such as flexibility and adaptability to face high non-linearities and load changes in these kinds of systems.

Due to the local controllers have already been tested in previous developments, the next step in this research is to test the upper layer in an embedded system with the capability of real-time signal management and processing.

The hierarchical fuzzy architecture shown provides the opportunity to increase the autonomous and coordination actions in the converters involved giving a future idea about the low voltage MG to achieve self-healing or diagnose.

The addition of some extra rules in the higher control layer could generate an extensive computational process, however these rules would be necessary in a larger MG system or if it is required to improve other decisions.

If the VSC-Induction motor or VSC-Grid units are increased in large quantities or differ in their characteristics, the system model is increased and the complexity as well. A supervisory fuzzy control is suitable to manage them with the sole requirement to know the entire behaviour.

As a future work, it can be added another coordination targets such as the batteries charging converters, the dc-dc converters involved and the MPPT algorithms.

6. References

Alajmi, B. (2010). Fuzzy Logic Control Approach of a Modified Hill Climbing Method for Maximum Power Point in Microgrid Stand-alone Photovoltaic System. *IEEE Transactions on Power Electronics*, Vol. 26, No. 4, (November 2010), pp. (1022 – 1030), ISSN : 0885-8993

Ayob, S.M., Salam, Z. & Azli, N.A. (2006). Simple PI Fuzzy Logic Controller Applied in DC-AC Converter, *Proceedings of International Power and Energy Conference*, ISBN: 1-4244-0273-5, Putrajaya , Malaysia, November 2006

Bai, Y; Zhuang, H & Wang, D. (2006) Advanced Fuzzy Logic Technologies in Industrial Applications, Series: Advances in Industrial Control. Springer-Verlag 2006

Balaguer, I.J.; Qin, L; Shuitao, Y; Supatti, U. & Fang Z. P. (2011) Control for Grid-Connected and Intentional Islanding Operations of Distributed Power Generation, *IEEE Transactions on Industrial Electronics*, Vol.58, No.1, pp.147-157, Jan. 2011, ISSN: 0278-0046

Bellini, A., Bifaretti, S. & Iacovone, V. (2010). A Zero-Voltage transition full bridge DC-DC converter for photovoltaic applications, *Proceedings of International Symposium on Power Electronics Electrical Drives Automation and Motion*, ISBN: 978-1-4244-4986-6, June 2010

Binduhewa, P.J.; Renfrew, A.C. & Barnes, M. (2008). MicroGrid Power Electronics Interface for Photovoltaics," *Proceedings of IET Conference on Power Electronics, Machines and Drives*, ISSN: 0537-9989, April 2008

Bor-Ren L. & Chihchiang H. (1993). Buck/Boost Converter Control with Fuzzy Logic Approach, *Proceedings of International Conference on Industrial Electronics, Control, and Instrumentation*, ISBN: 0-7803-0891-3, November 1993

Bor-Ren L. & Hoft, R.G. (1993). Power Electronics Converter Control based on Neural Network and Fuzzy Logic Methods, *Proceedings of Power Electronics Specialists Conference*, ISBN: 0-7803-1243-0, June 1993

Bose, A. (2010). Smart Transmission Grid Applications and Their Supporting Infrastructure, *IEEE Transactions on Smart Grid*, Vol.1, No.1, (June 2010), pp.11-19, ISSN: 1949-3053

Bose, B.K. (1984) Scalar Decoupled Control of Induction Motor. *IEEE Transactions on Industry Applications*, Vol.IA-20, No.1, pp.216-225, Jan. 1984, ISSN: 0093-9994

Bose, B.K. (2006). Intelligent Control and Estimation in Power Electronics and Drives, *Proceedings of International Power Electronics Congress*, ISBN: 1-4244-0544-0, October 2006

Carmona-Sánchez, J.; Ruiz-Vega, D. (2010). Review of Static Induction Motor Models, *Proceedings of North American Power Symposium*, ISBN: 978-1-4244-8046-3, September 2010

Cecati, C., Dell'Aquila, A., Liserre, M. & Ometto, A. (2003). A Fuzzy Logic based Controller for Active Rectifier, *IEEE Transactions on Industry Applications*, Vol.39, No.1, January 2003, pp. 105- 112, ISSN: 0093-9994

Cecati, C., Dell'Aquila, A., Lecci, A. & Liserre, M. (2005). Implementation Issues of a Fuzzy Logic based Three-Phase Active Rectifier Employing only Voltage Sensors," *IEEE Transactions on Industrial Electronics*, Vol.52, No.2, April 2005, pp. 378- 385, ISSN: 0278-0046

Corcau, J.I., Coman, A., Dinca, L. & Grigorie, T. (2010). Study of Fuzzy Logic Controller for ZCS Boost Converter, *Proceedings of Electrical Systems for Aircraft, Railway and Ship Propulsion*, ISBN: 978-1-4244-9092-9, October 2010

Chamorro, H. R. & Trujillo, C. L. (2009). Switching Losses Analysis of a DC Link Fuzzy Logic Controller Scheme Applied to a VSC, *Proceedings of North American Power Symposium*, ISBN: 978-1-4244-4428-1, October 2009

Chamorro, H.R. & Toro, B.W. (2010). Simultaneous Fuzzy Logic Control of a Three Phase Induction Motor Speed and Soft Switching DC link, *Proceedings of International Conference on Industry Applications*, ISBN: 978-1-4244-4428-1, Sao Paulo, Brasil, November 2010

Chamorro, H.R., Diaz, N.L., Soriano, J.J. & Espitia, H.E. (2011). Active and Reactive Power Flow Fuzzy Controller for VSC HVDC using DBR and DBR Type 2, *Proceedings of Annual Meeting of the North American Fuzzy Information Processing Society*, ISBN: 978-1-61284-968-3, March 2011

Chamorro, H.R. & Ramos, G. (2011). Microgrid Central Fuzzy Controller for Active and Reactive Power Flow using Instantaneous Power Measurements, *Proceedings of Power and Energy Conference at Illinois*, ISBN: 978-1-4244-8051-7, February 2011

Chamorro, H. R., Toro, B., Trujillo, C; Guarnizo, G. (2009). Simulation and Hardware Verification of a PD Fuzzy Speed Controller for a Three Phase Induction Motor, *Proceedings of Electrical Power & Energy Conference*, ISBN: 978-1-4244-4508-0, October 2009

Chaouachi, A., Kamel, R.M. & Nagasaka, K. (2010). Microgrid Efficiency Enhancement based on Neuro-Fuzzy MPPT control for Photovoltaic Generator, *Proceedings of Photovoltaic Specialists Conference*, ISBN: 978-1-4244-5890-5, June 2010

Chung-Yuen Won, Duek, K, Bose, B.K. (1992). An Induction Motor Servo System with Improved Sliding Mode Control. *Proceedings of Industrial Electronics, Control, Instrumentation, and Automation*, ISBN: 0-7803-0582-5, November 1992

Diaz, N.L., Barbosa, F.H. & Trujillo, C.L. (2007). Analysis and Design of a Nonlinear Fuzzy Controller Applied to a VSC to Control the Active and Reactive Power Flow, *Proceedings of Electronics, Robotics and Automotive Mechanics Conference*, ISBN: 978-0-7695-2974-5, September 2007

Diaz, N.L., Barbosa, F.H. & Trujillo, C.L. (2008). Implementation of Nonlinear Power Flow Controllers to Control a VSC, *Proceedings of Power Electronics and Motion Control Conference*, ISBN: 978-1-4244-1741-4, September 2008

Ding, M.; Zhang, Y.Y.; Mao, M.Q.; Yang, W.; Liu, X. P. (2010). Operation Optimization for Microgrids under Centralized Control. *Proceedings of International Symposium on Power Electronics for Distributed Generation Systems*, ISBN: 978-1-4244-5669-7, June 2010

Elbuluk, M. & Idris, N.R. (2008). The Role Power Electronics in Future Energy Systems and Green Industrialization, *Proceedings of International Power and Energy Conference*, ISBN: 978-1-4244-2404-7, December 2008

Ferreira, A.A., Pomilio, J.A., Spiazzi, G. & de Araujo, L. (2008). Energy Management Fuzzy Logic Supervisory for Electric Vehicle Power Supplies System, *IEEE Transactions on Power Electronics*, Vol.23, No.1, (January 2008), pp.107-115, ISSN: 0885-8993

Forero, F.A.; Molina, A.M.; Guarnizo J.G. & Chamorro, H.R.. (2009). Implementation of Inverse Neural Control to VSC Converter for Active and Reactive Power Flow. *Proceedings of Intelligent System Applications to Power Systems*, ISBN: 978-1-4244-5097-8, November 2009

Guangkai, L; Gengyin, L; Haifeng, L; Chengyong, Z & Ming Yin. (2006). Research on Dynamic Characteristics of VSC-HVDC System. *Proceedings of Power Engineering Society General Meeting*, ISBN: 1-4244-0493-2.

Haifeng, L; Gengyin, L, Ming, Z. & Chengyong, Z., The Implementation of Fuzzy Adaptive PI Controller in VSC-HVDC Systems, *Proceedings of Power Systems Conference and Exposition*, ISBN: 978-1-4244-3810-5, March 2009

Momoh, J.A. (2009). Smart Grid Design for Efficient and Flexible Power Networks Operation and Control, *Proceedings of Power Systems Conference and Exposition*, ISBN: 978-1-4244-3810-5, March 2009

Papadimitriou, C.N. & Vovos, N.A. (2010). A Fuzzy Control Scheme for Integration of DGs into a Microgrid, *Proceedings of Mediterranean Electrotechnical Conference*, ISBN: 978-1-4244-5793-9, April 2010

Kasa, N., Iida, T. & Bhat, A.K. (2005). Zero-Voltage Transition Flyback Inverter for Small Scale Photovoltaic Power System, *Proceedings of Power Electronics Specialists Conference*, ISBN: 0-7803-9033-4, June 2005

Kolokolov, Y., Koschinsky, S.L. & Hamzaoui, A. (2004). Comparative Study of the Dynamics and Overall Performance of Boost converter with Conventional and Fuzzy Control in Application to PFC, *Proceedings of Power Electronics Specialists Conference*, ISBN: 0-7803-8399-0, June 2004

Lasseter, B. (2001). Microgrids [distributed power generation], *Proceedings of Power Engineering Society Winter Meeting*, ISBN: 0-7803-6672-7, Feb 2001

Liu, Z; Shao, W; Song, Q & Liu, W. (2009) A Novel Nonlinear Decoupled Controller For VSC-HVDC System. *Proceedings of Power and Energy Engineering Conference*, ISBN: 978-1-4244-2486-3, March 2009

Mattavelli, P., Rossetto, L., Spiazzi, G. &Tenti, P. (1997). General-Purpose Fuzzy Controller for DC-DC Converters," *IEEE Transactions on Power Electronics*, Vol.12, No.1, January 1997, pp.79-86, ISSN: 0885-8993

Matsugae, H., Hatchisu, Y., Nagao, Y. & Fujita, K. (1990). DSP-based all Digital, Vector Control Induction Motor Drives for Spindle System. *Proceedings of Power Electronics Specialists Conference*, Jun 1990

Mokrytzki, B. (1991) Survey of Adjustable Frequency Technology-1991. *Proceedings of Industry Applications Society Annual Meeting*, ISBN: 0-7803-0453-5, October 1991

Peng, F.Z.; Yun Wei Li; Tolbert, L.M. (2009). Control and Protection of Power Electronics Interfaced Distributed Generation Systems in a Customer-driven Microgrid, *Proceedings of Power & Energy Society General Meeting*, ISBN: 978-1-4244-4241-6, July 2009

Rashid, M. (2001). *Power Electronics Handbook,* Academic Press, ISBN: 012-581650-2, Canada

Sadeghzadeh, S.M. & Ansarian, M., (2006). Transient Stability Improvement with Neuro-Fuzzy Control of FACTS Devices, *Proceedings International Power and Energy Conference*, ISBN: 1-4244-0273-5, November. 2006

Singh, B.; Panigrahi, B.K. & Mohan, D.M. (2006) Voltage Regulation and Power Flow Control of VSC Based HVDC System. *Proceedings of International Conference on Power Electronics, Drives and Energy Systems*, ISBN: 0-7803-9772-X, December 2006

Shireen, W., Misir, D., Malki, H. & Arefeen, M.S. (1996). A Soft Switching Scheme for a PWM Inverter using a Fuzzy Logic Controller. *Proceedings of Telecommunications Energy Conference*, ISBN: 0-7803-3507-4, October 1996

Shireen, W. & Arefeen, M.S. (1994). A DC Voltage Notching Scheme for Zero Voltage Switching (ZVS) of PWM Inverters, *Proceedings of Industry Applications Society Annual Meeting*, ISBN: 0-7803-1993-1, October 1994

Shireen, W. & Patel, S. (2011). Fast converging digital MPPT control for photovoltaic (PV) applications. *Proceedings of Power and Energy Society General Meeting*, ISBN: 978-1-4577-1000-1, July 2011

Simoes, M. (2006). Intelligent based Hierarchical Control Power Electronics for Distributed Generation Systems," *Proceedings of Power Engineering Society General Meeting*, ISBN: 1-4244-0493-2, October 2006

Sivakumar, M., Jickson, C.J. (2011) A Fuzzy based Power Quality Enhancement Strategy for AC-AC Converters, *Proceedings of National Conference on Innovations in Emerging Technology*, ISBN: 978-1-61284-807-5, February 2011

Takahashi, I. & Ohmori, Y. (1989). High-Performance Direct Torque Control of an Induction Motor, *IEEE Transactions on Industry Applications*, Vol.25, No.2, pp.257-264, March 1989, ISSN: 0093-9994

Xiaodong, L & Ilochonwu, O. (2011). Induction Motor Starting in Practical Industrial Applications," *IEEE Transactions on Industry Applications*, Vol.47, No.1, (February 2011) pp.271-280, ISSN: 0093-9994.

Zadeh, L.A. (1994). Fuzzy logic: issues, contentions and perspectives," *Proceedings of International Conference on Acoustics, Speech, and Signal Processing*, ISBN: 0-7803-1775-0, vol.vi, April 1994

8

Synthesis and VHDL Implementation of Fuzzy Logic Controller for Dynamic Voltage and Frequency Scaling (DVFS) Goals in Digital Processors

Hamid Reza Pourshaghaghi,
Juan Diego Echeverri Escobar and José Pineda de Gyvez
Electronic Systems Group,
Eindhoven University of Technology, Eindhoven,
the Netherlands

1. Introduction

The concept of power consumption is becoming the primary concern in modern high performance processors, and in digital circuits and system on chips (SoCs). While CMOS technology has been scaling towards smaller feature sizes, the performance of digital systems has been exponentially increasing as clock frequency increases. Also the computational workload and hence the activity of a digital circuit may change substantially and it exposes a lot of breakthroughs in the exploitation of adaptive low power methodologies. Dynamic voltage and frequency scaling (DVFS) is a popular system level power management technique that dynamically scales the supply voltage and clock frequency level of device (Rabaey, 2010). A DVFS system can be considered as a closed loop control system: contingent on the observed workload, supply voltage and operational speed gets adjusted. Since the changes in supply voltages do not occur instantaneously due to the fact that some delays are involved the large capacitance on the supply rails, the main real challenge in the design of such a system lies in how to measure and predict the workload of processor to change supply voltage accurately. The efficiency of DVFS strongly depends on the accuracy of the workload estimation, and note that misestimating can substantially reduce the effectiveness of such closed loop systems.

Most previous DVFS methods focused on offline profiling to learn the average case execution time or worst case execution time. Different closed loop adaptive controllers have been proposed to deal with time varying workloads. Most of them are based on conventional PID controllers and their variants e.g. PI controller or I controller. These kinds of configurations need offline profiling to tune the coefficients of the controller to be able to track or predict the workload variations. However, for different shapes of workload variations, it is necessary to do the off-line tuning again and determine the coefficients another time. So they are not considered as general solutions for adjusting voltage and frequency. Some other estimation methods e.g. adaptive filters have proposed for predicting workload and controlling the behavior of the power and energy savings. Unfortunately, most of them need offline profiling and/or the applications are limited to some specific periodic workload variations.

In this chapter, we discuss an on-line adaptive fuzzy logic controller for DVFS that is able to accurately and robustly predict and track the workload variations even when those variations are highly nonstationary or soft. Furthermore, we describe comprehensively how one can build the controller in VHDL and use it as the power management controller unit. We propose a new method to use for the defuzzification part of the fuzzy controller that makes the circuit faster. The fuzzy controller can be applicable to different kinds of workload variations with regards to real-time constraints, and can adaptively change the supply voltage and frequency of a processor. The proposed controller can be easily upgraded by adding new rules or adding new features to improve performance. In this chapter, all the practical limitations and real-time constraints for designing the fuzzy logic controller as the DVFS method will be discussed during design procedure.

2. Related works over power management techniques

So far a lot of research has been done to explore different approaches for performing DVFS. Many of the previous works are categorized in task level algorithms that use offline profiling to obtain the average-case execution time (ACET) or worst-case execution time (WCET) as models for the workloads of the given application. For example, one of the earliest works was presented in (Yao et al., 1995) where they assumed that the arrival time, deadline of workloads, and task execution time based on CPU cycle are given to designers as constants. The works proposed in (Im et al., 2006) and (Jejurikar & Gupta, 2006) are two more examples where in (Im et al., 2006) they proposed a technique to reduce the energy consumption based on WCET workload model using buffers; and in (Jejurikar & Gupta, 2006) a dynamic voltage scaling (DVS) method in the presence of task synchronization based on WCET workload model in multiprocessor environment was proposed. This kind of approaches cannot deal with the time-varying workload especially when the workload shows a large variation with nonstationary property. Another category of researches related to DVFS comprise techniques which require either application or compiler support to perform (Azevedo et al., 2002; Yang et al., 2001; Chung et al., 2002). Generality and offline profiling for different workload variations is still a big drawback existing in these classes of works.

Using adaptive approaches for DVFS leads to save more power and energy in comparison to the conventional techniques. Proposing closed loop system architectures started by introducing self-timed adaptive supply-voltage scaling for asynchronous circuits in (Nielsen et al., 1994) where in their architecture, first input-first output (FIFO) buffers are used in both inputs and outputs of the processor. The FIFO-buffers average the computational workload to adjust the supply voltage and frequency. The feedback is based on actual path delays of the circuit. The feedback signal controls the DC-DC converter based on the information derived from the FIFO's. After this architecture, other researchers used a similar configuration to adapt the power supply voltage to lower the power consumption in digital signal processors DSPs (Gutnik & Chandrakasan, 1997). The structure of the proposed system architecture in (Gutnik & Chandrakasan, 1997) is the same as (Nielsen et al., 1994), but they designed a configuration for synchronous designs, and variations in the

Synthesis and VHDL Implementation of Fuzzy Logic Controller for Dynamic Voltage and Frequency
Scaling (DVFS) Goals in Digital Processors

161

computational workload were taken into account as well. Like the self-timed variable voltage system of (Nielsen et al., 1994), input data is buffered into a FIFO type of buffer to enable averaging of the workload. Then, the control loop controls the processing rate to avoid queuing overflow and underflow of the FIFOs. The controller in this methodology consists of a voltage regulator, a ring oscillator, a rate-compare block and a programmable look-up table (LUT). The controller block decides to change the voltage and frequency based on the processing rate and existent LUT. Disadvantage of this configuration is that it comes with extra latency as buffer utilization is only one measure of workload.

An evolution to closed loop control configuration, in the estimation of workload and adaptive control methods become main challenge for design efficient DVFS. These techniques aimed at estimating time varying workload using adaptive filters that most of them were based on a conventional proportional, integral and derivative (PID) controller. One famous PID based approach is presented in (Wei & Horowitz, 2003) where voltage samples are used to control a VCO to change the frequency as feedback signal for the buck converter. The reference signal and feedback signal come into the controller as variable frequency clocks, both feed into counters, and the number of transitions is counted for a fixed period of time. A PID controller, based on the calculated error value between its inputs, decides to change the voltage and frequency of the circuit. Some example of using PID controller to estimate workload variations are proposed in (Hughes and Adve, 2003; Gu & Chakraborty, 2008; Wu et al., 2005; Lu et al., 2002, 2003). In (Hughes and Adve, 2003), the PID controller is used to estimate the frame decoding time in multimedia applications and it was used in (Gu & Chakraborty, 2008) for 3-D games. In (Wu et al., 2005) and (Lu et al., 2003), the PI controller, which is a variant of the PID method, is applied to estimate the buffer occupancy for DVS targeting data buffered systems. In (Lu et al., 2002), an integral controller which is also a variant of PID method is designed and used to estimate workload estimation for performing DVS. Despite the PID controller is an adaptive filter, it suffers from possible overshooting and undershooting, depending on the selected coefficients. Also the PID controller for estimating application is useful when the designer select coefficient for specific workload variations and if the shape of workload changes, the coefficient should be defined again based on new workload variations. Hence, the tuning of coefficients critically determines the prediction accuracy.

Beside PID based controllers, some other estimators and adaptive filters are proposed to forecast workload variations in order to adjust voltage and/or frequency. In (Sinha & Chandrakasan, 2001), an adaptive approach for dynamic voltage scheduling on processors is presented based on workload prediction by filtering a trace history. In this work, they examine some conventional filters and evaluate their accuracy based on power saving amounts. They concluded that adaptive LMS filtering is the most powerful one and can be used to predict workload variations. Also in (Bang et al., 2009), they proposed a Kalman-filter based on-line estimator to predict and track the workload variation that can be applicable to periodic applications with soft real-time constrains.

Compared to previous approaches, the fuzzy logic controller is similar to adaptive filters in the sense of estimating the workload variations. However, the fuzzy logic controller can work as an on-line methodology without updating any parameters during run-time adaptations and also without any other information about the nature of the workload variation. The controller can estimate and track any kind of workload variations accurately and it does not require any coefficient tuning through offline profiling.

3. Principles of Dynamic Voltage and Frequency Scaling (DVFS)

The most important key to save power and energy of a digital circuit or processor is to reduce supply voltage and clock frequency according to the performance requirements. The power consumption of a clocked digital CMOS circuit is given by the well-known formula:

$$Power = \underbrace{\alpha.C.V_{dd}^2.F_{ck}}_{Dynamic\ Power} + \underbrace{I_{leak}.V_{dd}}_{leakage\ power} \tag{1}$$

where $\alpha.C$ is the total switched capacitance, V_{dd} is the supply voltage, F_{ck} is the clock frequency and I_{leak} is the off-state current of the circuit. By reducing the supply voltage and clock frequency, considerable power can be saved while $\alpha.C$ is generally fixed for a specific application. Over the years, researchers have proposed different hardware adaptive power management infrastructures to construct low power system-on-chip (SoC) integrated circuits. Among all the methods, DVFS methods are the most effective ones to save power consumption in processors. Conceptually, online DVFS problem for a digital CMOS circuit e.g. a processor is to scale voltage and frequency based on performance variation demands. The general block diagram of a dynamic supply voltage and frequency scaled system is shown in Fig. 1(Nielsen et al., 1994; Gutnik & Chandrakasan, 1997).

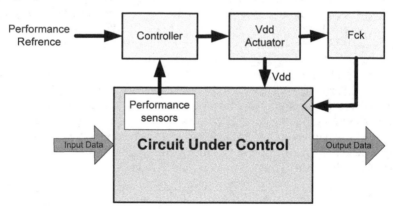

Fig. 1. General block diagram of a DVFS system

In this block diagram, there are three main components. The first component is a performance sensor that monitors the main specification of the processor e.g. average of supply current, temperature and supply voltage variations. The second component is the controller. This controller block works based on an input data received from the sensors by comparing it with the reference performance received from the power management unit or software to decide the change in supply voltage when necessary. The third block is the supply voltage actuator that can be on-chip or off-chip, e.g. a DC-DC converter and clock frequency actuators that can be a PLL. Since reducing the supply voltage causes increasing the delay of circuits, controlling the voltage and frequency of a processor dramatically depends on the accuracy of the controller.

Synthesis and VHDL Implementation of Fuzzy Logic Controller for Dynamic Voltage and Frequency
Scaling (DVFS) Goals in Digital Processors

163

Since there is a strong correlation between the supply current and the workload of a processor (Benini et al., 1999), the controller is designed based on observing and tracking of the average of current variations. The most important purpose is how to predict and track supply current variations of the processor and to drive it to operate at the lowest possible voltage and corresponding minimum frequency, for which a specific application can meet all of its deadlines under specific timing constraints. If the supply current tracking can perform in a proper way, the supply voltage and clock frequency of the processor can be adjusted w.r.t output predicted current signal. Supply voltage variations are same with variations of the predicted supply current signal. For determining clock frequency in each control time, the proper look up table corresponding to the delay-voltage model can be used. The delay of a CMOS gate can be modeled as

$$\tau = \frac{C_{gate}V_{dd}}{K(V_{dd}-V_{th})^\beta} \tag{2}$$

where K and β are technological parameters, and V_{th} is device threshold voltage. The cycle time of a design is modeled as a function of the critical path delay given as $T_C = L_D\tau$ where L_D is the logic depth in number of (equivalent) gates in the critical path. Therefore, the clock frequency for satisfying all timing deadlines of the circuit can be determined as

$$f_{ck}(t) = 1/T_c(t). \tag{3}$$

The relation of the normalized operating frequency versus normalized supply voltage of a sample CMOS digital circuit is shown in Fig. 2. As mentioned before, changing the processor clock frequency can be done by the available PLL in the circuit. PLL can only provide some limited clock frequencies, for instance suppose that a sample PLL can provide six different clock frequencies, like $\{f_{ck1}, f_{ck2}, \ldots, f_{ck6}\}$ shown in Fig. 2.

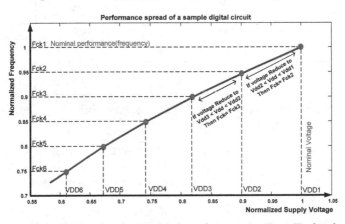

Fig. 2. Performance spread of a sample CMOS digital circuit in 65nm Technology.

Imagine a specific application is running with a constant frequency f_{ck1} at its nominal supply voltage V_{dd1} without any voltage scaling. Now suppose that the supply current is such that there is opportunity to save power by reducing the supply voltage. However, observe that when the supply voltage reduces (e.g. to a point between V_{dd1} and V_{dd2} as shown in Fig. 2), the frequency of operation would reduce as well to f_{ck2}. If the supply voltage goes for a value between V_{dd2} and V_{dd3}, then the frequency can switch to the f_{ck3} value. In this way, adjusting supply voltage to the lowest allowable value together with frequency scaling will ensure that the application is properly executed and the maximum possible power is saved. For switching the supply voltage to different possible values, it is needed to use voltage actuators like on-chip or off-chip DC-DC converters. In most DC-DC converters as voltage regulators, switching between voltage output levels takes a few tens of microseconds. For doing safe voltage and frequency switching, voltage and clock frequency changes may not be done in parallel. While the supply current is going to decrease, the frequency should first be decreased and subsequently the voltage should be lowered to the appropriate value. On the contrary, when the supply current is going to increase, the circuit requires the voltage to be increased first followed by the frequency update. This ensures that the voltage supply to the processor is never lower than the minimum required for the current operating frequency and avoids data corruption due to circuit failure.

4. DVFS based on fuzzy logic controller

The block diagram of the proposed dynamic voltage and frequency scaling configuration is shown in Fig. 3 (Pourshaghaghi & Pineda de Gyvez, 2009).

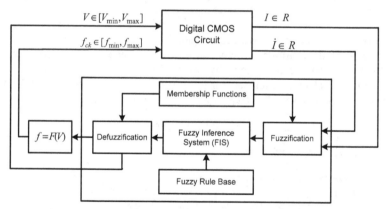

Fig. 3. Dynamic voltage and frequency scaling configuration based on supply-current tracking by fuzzy logic controller.

In this block diagram, the supply current and also the derivative of the supply current are observed as two inputs of the fuzzy logic block. The reason for using the derivative of the supply current is that it helps to predict the variations of the workload. If one can predict variations of the supply current, then it is easier for the actuators to act sooner. Consequently, the amount of saved power can be increased significantly, not to mention finishing the executing task on time. Given a specific value for the supply current, if the derivative is positive, it implies that the supply current is increasing. Otherwise, the supply current is decreasing. Therefore, the fuzzy if-then rules should be defined to follow this concept. It should be taken into account that, for having more precision to predict supply current variations, it is possible to compute the second derivative of the current. Thus, the fuzzy logic block receives two inputs: supply-current and its derivative. Based on these two inputs, the fuzzy logic block, as an expert system, can decide about the voltage and

Synthesis and VHDL Implementation of Fuzzy Logic Controller for Dynamic Voltage and Frequency
Scaling (DVFS) Goals in Digital Processors

165

frequency of the processor. Actually, by this method, the fuzzy logic controller is tracking the supply current to decide upon the new voltage of the digital circuit. Actuators for supply voltage can be an on-chip or off-chip DC-DC converters. The same procedure can be done for determining the frequency of the processor. But for deciding about the final frequency value, it should be taken into account that the frequency obtained by fuzzy logic controller has to be greater than the frequency obtained by worst case execution time. Also the frequency can be defined based on a proper predefined look up table.

Based on performing different experiments, the proposed internal structure of fuzzy controller was resulted to have membership functions and fuzzy rules like ones shown in Fig. 4. In this structure, if N membership functions are defined for the supply current and 3 membership functions are defined for its derivative, then $N \times 3$ rules should define the fuzzy logic rule-base block. The rules should be defined in a way that the supply voltage tracks the variations of the supply current. Therefore, the proposed controller predicts first the supply current variations and then it decides on how to change the voltage and frequency pair. Using fuzzy logic sets, the fuzzy inference system (FIS) formulates the process of getting the output based on the defined input membership functions and the fuzzy if-then rules. Mamdani FIS is the most commonly useful methodology for applying fuzzy logic controllers on practical systems and we recommend using it for DVFS goals (Lee, 1999).

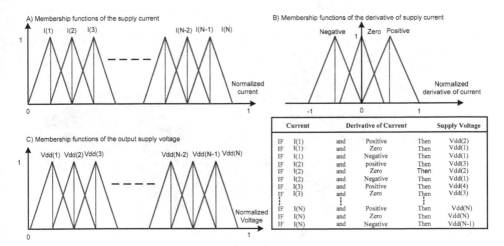

Fig. 4. The defined membership functions of states, A) Supply current as the first input of the fuzzy controller. It has N membership functions named by I(1), I(2),…, I(N) , B) Derivative of supply current as the second input of the fuzzy controller, it has three membership functions named by Negative, Zero, and Positive, C) Supply voltage as the output of the fuzzy controller, it has N membership functions named by Vdd(1), Vdd(2),…, and Vdd(N). Fuzzy if-then rules are defined in the table.

Several experiments have been conducted to evaluate different aspects of the controller. In the first simulation, we designed a controller and implemented it on a sampled supply current of a processor near to reality. This supply current is shown in Fig. (5.a) and its derivative is shown in Fig. (5.b). Based on the internal fuzzy system structure described in Fig. 4, we have considered nine Triangular membership functions for supply current. These functions are defined between $150\mu A$ to $600\mu A$, without losing the generality, with a symmetrical shapes and widths. Each supply current membership function has 50% overlaps with its neighbor membership function (functions). We have considered five Triangular membership functions for derivative of supply current from $-250\,{}^{mA}/_{sec}$ to $250\,{}^{mA}/_{sec}$. Consequently, we defined 27 *if-then* rules based on the rules shown in Fig. 4. Nine symmetrical triangular membership functions for supply voltage have been considered as well. These membership functions have 50% overlap with each other and have same widths too. We used also the centre of area as the defuzzification method. The result of this simulation is shown in Fig. (5.c). As one can see from the supply voltage values, the fuzzy logic can track the variation of supply current very well. The output surface of fuzzy logic controller is shown in Fig. (5.d). In this figure, the entire span of supply voltage based upon the entire span of supply current and its derivative is displayed. It shows pseudo continuity of the output voltage with variations of workload.

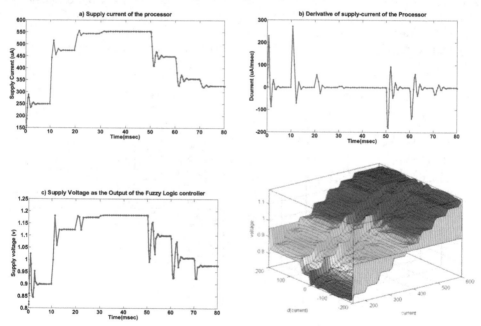

Fig. 5. Simulation results of applying fuzzy Logic controller (FLC) on a sampled supply current. a) Supply current of a sample processor, the variation of current is based on different applications, b) Derivative of the supply current, c) Voltage (output) of the FLC that goes to DC-DC converter, d) Output surface of the controller which shows variations rate of the voltage (output) regarding to input variations.

We simulated a PID controller on another supply current signal and compared the results with the fuzzy controller. Suppose that we have a supply current signal like the one shown in Fig. (6.a). We trained the PID controller with some simulation testing to find out what coefficients are the best for the proportional, integration and derivative part of the

Synthesis and VHDL Implementation of Fuzzy Logic Controller for Dynamic Voltage and Frequency
Scaling (DVFS) Goals in Digital Processors

167

controller. Finally, with a trial and error method we found that with $k_p = 100$, $k_i = 2$ and $k_d = 1$, it can track the supply current very well. The tracking result is shown in Fig. (6.b). But when the shape of the supply current changed, similar to the supply current shown in Fig. (6.c), the PID could not track the variations with the same coefficients and we have to change coefficients again. The output of PID block in the second experiment is shown in Fig. (6.d). It is also important to mention that the fuzzy logic controller works well regardless of the system's inputs, while the PID controller requires the mathematical formulation of the system to adapt its coefficients to be able to work properly. One of the main advantages of the fuzzy logic controller is that the hardware implementation is easy because everything here is digital. Another advantage is that this controller can work on-line to track all workload circumstances with high speed and less error in comparison with other traditional control methods.

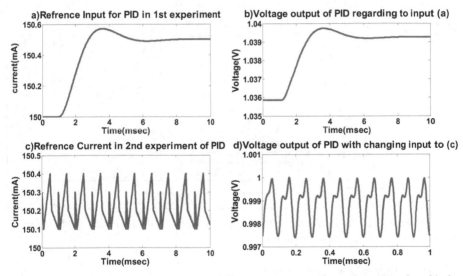

Fig. 6. Simulation of PID controller on two different input supply current signals. a,b) the supply voltage track supply current variations well. c,d) when the current variations changes as c, then supply voltage cannot track the new variations with old PID coefficients.

5. VHDL implementation of the fuzzy logic controller

The general architecture of the fuzzy logic controller to track supply current variations of a processor is shown in Fig. 7 where the information flows from left to right. The fuzzy logic controller is designed based on the Mamdani fuzzy inference system (FIS). The first step to implement the controller as a digital circuit is to convert analogue input values, supply current and its derivative, to digital ones. For this purpose an analogue to digital converter (A/D) is necessary to digitize the input crisp values. The resolution of the selected A/D depends on the desired accuracy for supply current, derivative of supply current and supply voltage data. For example, suppose that the supply current variations of a processors change between 0mA and 100mA and one has selected an 8 bit A/D. In this case, the resolution of the supply current samples is as follows:

$$2^8 = \frac{I_{max} - I_{min}}{res.(I)} \rightarrow res.(I) \cong 0.4mA \qquad (4)$$

Hence if a voltage actuator e.g. a DC-DC converter has been selected to regulate the processor's voltage between 0.7V and 1.2V, the output supply voltage made by the fuzzy logic controller has steps of 1.95 mV for supply voltage. In this section, we design the controller in VHDL based on an 8 bits resolution for digital values, and without loss of generality one can extend the design to other resolutions.

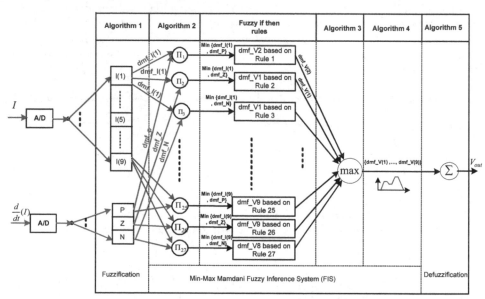

Fig. 7. Architecture of the Mamdani Fuzzy Inference System (FIS) for the supply voltage computation in VHDL implementation

5.1 Implementation of the fuzzification stage

After digitizing the input crisp values, the first step is to define membership functions for the current, derivative of the current and the supply voltage. We consider nine membership functions for the supply current variations, three membership function for its derivative, and nine membership functions for the output supply voltage. The numbers of the membership functions are obtained based on executing different experiments and evaluating the accuracy of the controller with different supply current signatures. These functions are defined in the triangular shapes like the ones presented in Fig. 4 combined with the same corresponding table of fuzzy if-then rules. First we start to design the membership functions (MFs) of the supply current. Since we have used an 8 bits resolution for A/D, the input range of current should map between 0($0) and 255 ($FF). Consider defined MFs of the current as the ones shown in Fig. 8. In this figure, the Y axis shows the degree of membership function as a value between 0 and 1 and the X axis shows the supply current universe of discourse. All these parameters need to be mapped between 0 and 255. Each MF in Fig. 8 is represented by four parameters: point1 (P1), the positive slope value, point2 (P2), and the negative slope value.

Synthesis and VHDL Implementation of Fuzzy Logic Controller for Dynamic Voltage and Frequency
Scaling (DVFS) Goals in Digital Processors

169

For each current value as the input, the degree of membership function (dmf) depends on the location of the current value regarding to these four parameters. The pseudo code to calculate the degree of membership function for a specific input current value is presented in Algorithm 1. In this pseudo code, it is supposed that the slopes of all triangular membership functions have value 8. With this assumption, one can avoid using multipliers in the circuit to calculate the degree of membership functions and increase the speed of the circuit.

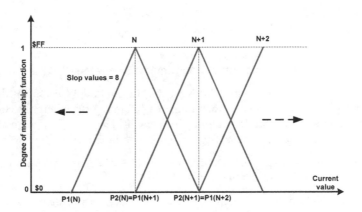

Fig. 8. Triangular membership functions for the supply current variations

To calculate the degree of membership functions of the derivative of supply current, an algorithm similar to Algorithm 1 can be used. The only differences are 1) three MFs are defined (N=3) for the derivative of current, 2) different slopes are defined for the MFs of the derivate of current as slope (MF1) =slope (MF3) =8 and slope (MF2) =16.

Algorithm 1 – Fuzzification : triangular MFs for supply current and calculate dmf

Data(P_1, P_2, slope, I_MFS, dmf_I : std_logic_vector(7 downto 0))

N: Counter for the Number of membership function for supply current variations

$P_1(N)$: Point 1 of the membership function N shown in Fig.8

$P_2(N)$: Point 2 of the membership function N (middle point in each MF)

Slope (N): 8

I_MFS: Number of membership function for supply current variations (here: 9)

dmf_I: Degree of membership functions

I : input supply current

1 **For** N=1 to I_MFS

2   **IF** $I < P_1(N)$

3   dmf_I = 0

4   **Elseif** I < $P_2(N)$

5   dmf_I = (I - $P_1(N)$) * Slope (N)

6   **Elseif** I < $P_2(N + 1)$

7   dmf_I = 255 - (I - $P_1(N)$) * Slope (N)

8   **Else** I > $P_2(N + 1)$

9   dmf_I = 0

10 End

5.2 Rule evaluation: Implementation of fuzzy inference system

Considering Fig. 7 and since there are 9 MFs for the current and 3 MFs for its derivative, 27 fuzzy if-the rules are defined to correspondingly calculate the fuzzy supply voltage output values. The Mamdani FIS is used to evaluate the fuzzy if-then rules. To design Mamdani FIS in VHDL, let's consider the first fuzzy if-the rules defined in Fig. 7:

IF the supply current belongs to I(1) **AND** the derivative of current belongs to P (Positive) **Then** voltage is VDD(2).

For this rule, the AND operator should be applied to obtain one value out of two degree of membership functions (current and its derivative) which represents the result of the antecedent part in rule 1. This value actually represents a weighting factor for this specific rule. In the Mamdani FIS, the AND operator is a fuzzy operator to find the minimum value between two degrees of MFs: current and its derivative. The following minimum function, Algorithm 2, is used to implement the fuzzy AND operator in VHDL. In Fig. 7, this stage is called product layer which is a part of the min-max Mamdani FIS.

Algorithm 2 – Minimum Function

1 Function Minimum(a, b: std_logic_vector(7 downto 0))

2 variable min: std_logic_vector (7 downto 0) := (others => '0');

3   Begin

4   If a < b Then

5   min := a;

6   Else

7   min := b;

8   End If;

9   Return min;

10 End Minimum;

-**Note**: In this function, a represents the dmf_I (degree of membership function of the current) and b represents dmf_di.

Synthesis and VHDL Implementation of Fuzzy Logic Controller for Dynamic Voltage and Frequency
Scaling (DVFS) Goals in Digital Processors

171

The output value of the minimum function is a value that determines the degree of MF for Vdd(2) in rule 1. For all the defined 27 rules, there may exist different degrees of MF values for each fuzzy voltage set. Therefore, one final value for each MF of the supply voltage should be determined. The min-max Mamdani FIS uses the maximum operator to calculate the final degree of the membership function for Vdd(1) to Vdd(9). The fuzzy maximum operator models one fuzzy set with the maximum values returned by the output fuzzy set of each rule. In VHDL, one can use the maximum function presented in Algorithm 3.

Algorithm 3 – Maximum Function

1 Function Maximum(a, b: std_logic_vector(7 downto 0))

2 variable max: std_logic_vector(7 downto 0) := (others => '0');

3   Begin

4   If a > b then

5   max := a;

6   Else

7   max := b;

8   End If;

9   Return max;

10 End Maximum;

-Note: In this function, a and b represent the dmf_V values (degree of membership function of the voltage). This function should be called for each dmf_V(1), …,dmf_v(9) separately.

5.3 Implementation of the defuzzification stage

The last step is to perform the defuzzification process that converts the obtained fuzzy set into a single number as the output supply voltage. The aggregate output fuzzy set consists of a range of voltage output values and has to be defuzzified to determine a single output supply voltage value. For the defuzzification method, the centroid calculation is used to compute the final value. The centroid method computes the center of area under the curve of the fuzzy output set. From the min-max FIS, nine degrees of membership functions for each voltage set is obtained (dmf_V(1), …, dmf_V(9)). For each input value of the current and its derivative, there are a maximum of 3 *dmf* that have a nonzero value. Suppose that the aggregated output fuzzy set is as the one shown in Fig. 9.

To compute the output voltage value, as one can see from eq. (5), the following functions are needed to use: summation, multiplier and divider. Since implementing a divider block results in a circuit that occupies more area, we propose to use a look up table (LUT) stored in the memory of processor. This LUT needs to be filled out by the designer. Under this approach, the data stored in the memory estimates the center of gravity of the output fuzzy set obtained by the min-max Mamdani FIS. Here, we explain the required size of the memory and how to address and access to data in the LUT.

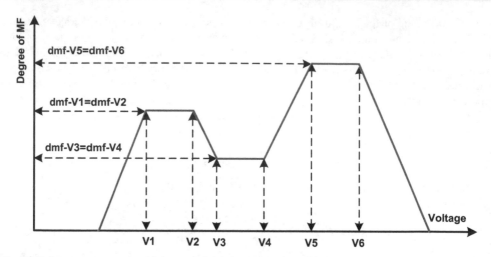

Fig. 9. Defuzzication and calculation of the final supply voltage value

If the centroid method for the defuzzification is applied, the output voltage value is as follows:

$$V = \frac{\sum_{i=1}^{6} Vi * dmf\_Vi}{\sum_{i=1}^{9} dmf\_Vi} \tag{5}$$

To track supply current variations, for each pair of fuzzy inputs (supply current and its derivative) at a specific time, there is a maximum of three adjacent membership functions MFs for the voltage which have degree of membership function *dmf* value distinct from zero. Therefore, one can use Algorithm 4 to first find those involved voltage MFs and then use the LUT to calculate the final voltage value.

Algorithm 4 – Specifying active voltage membership functions in the defuzzification stage

Data:

V_MFS =9: Number of membership function for supply voltage (here: 9)

N[1:9]: Counter for the number of membership functions of supply voltage

dmf_V [0:255]: Degree of MF

rb [0 or1]: a bit to specify which MF is involved in calculating the final voltage value

1   **For** N=1 to V_MFS

2   IF   dmf_V(N) = 0 **Then**

3   rb(N) = 0

4   **Else** rb(N) = 1

5   **End**

6   **End**

Synthesis and VHDL Implementation of Fuzzy Logic Controller for Dynamic Voltage and Frequency
Scaling (DVFS) Goals in Digital Processors

173

To construct the LUT, we only use the first 3 most significant bits (MSB) of each voltage membership function. Since there is a maximum of three membership functions involved in calculating the final crisp voltage value, one needs to consider $2^{3+3+3} = 512$ words of the memory to make the desired LUT. Suppose we want to consider the whole 8 bits of each degree of voltage membership function value, the number of words in the memory changes to 2^{24}. For now, let's assume we have considered 3 MSBs for each degree of MF. Depending on the number of the active voltage membership functions and corresponding degree of membership functions obtained by the Mamdani FIS, one can access the corresponding word in the memory to access the output voltage value stored in it. The VHDL algorithm to access the proper memory address in the defuzzification part of the designed fuzzy controller is shown in Algorithm 5.

Now each address of the memory should be filled out by a proper value to estimate the centre of gravity accordingly. We simulated all the corresponding possible situations for the aggregated fuzzy output voltage sets in MATLAB and estimate the output voltages. Then we stored all the corresponding values into the 512 bytes considered memory.

Algorithm 5 – How to access the data of the memory in the defuzzification stage

Data

address: address of the memory

$N[1:9]$: the number of membership function for supply voltage

$rb [0\ or1]$: a bit to specify which MF is involved in calculating the final voltage value

Vout: output supply voltage value

1 Counter = 0

2 **For** N = 2 to V_MFS

3   Counter = Counter + 1

4   **IF** rb(N) = 1

5   address = concatenate(r(N-1), r(N), r(N+1))

6   break

7   **End IF**

8 **End For**

9 Vout = 32*(Counter - 1) + LUT(address)

5.4 Synthesis results

We have implemented the proposed fuzzy logic controller in a CMOS 90nm technology and synthesized it with Cadence RC compiler to measure its power consumption and area. For benchmarking purposes, the synthesis of the circuit is done with different speeds. Synthesis specifications are mentioned in Table 1.

Synthesis and the Library specifications:
CMOS 90 nm HVT-TSMC
Supply Voltage: 1.2 V
PVT Typical corner
Temperature: 25 degree
Frequencies : {20, 40,60,80,100,200,333} MHz

Table 1. Library specification for synthesizing the fuzzy logic controller

The synthesis results are shown in Fig. 10. Since the fuzzy logic controller is a digital controller, its circuit does not consume much power and it does not occupy much area as shown in Fig. 10.

The main differences between the proposed VHDL implementation of the fuzzy controller and the other already implemented VHDL fuzzy controllers (Vuong et al., 2006; Vasantha et al., 2005; Sakthivel et all., 2010; Daijin, 2000) is about the speed of the controller. In the proposed implementation strategy, there are no multiplier and divider circuits used, and also we have considered a fixed slope value for the membership functions. For these reasons, the circuit naturally works faster. Since we have used the memory to store the defuzzification data, it is worth to mention that the power consumption of the proposed circuit is probably higher than previously reported ones.

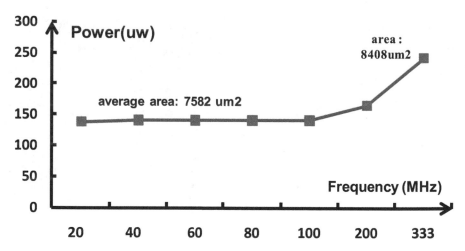

Fig. 10. Synthesis results of the fuzzy logic controller

As way of example, we test the fuzzy logic circuit with the supply current profile of a processor when it executes a MPEG2-decoding application. The output result of the fuzzy logic circuit implemented in VHDL is shown in Fig. 11. The output signal of the fuzzy controller can accurately track the supply current variations. This output signal can be used to scale and adjust the supply voltage of the processor based on current variations for dynamic voltage scaling goals. Also in Fig. 11, the simulation result of the fuzzy controller implemented in Matlab is presented.

Synthesis and VHDL Implementation of Fuzzy Logic Controller for Dynamic Voltage and Frequency
Scaling (DVFS) Goals in Digital Processors

175

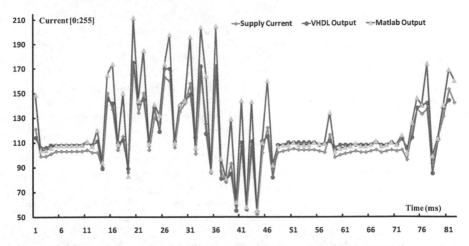

Fig. 11. Comparison between the tracking results of the implemented VHDL fuzzy circuit
and Matlab simulation

6. Conclusion

In this chapter, a dynamic fuzzy logic controller based on supply-current variation tracking
for dynamic voltage and frequency scaling purposes was proposed. In the proposed
method, the fuzzy logic controller decides about changing the supply voltage of the circuit
under control by observing and predicting the supply-current variations. The simulation
results showed the effectiveness of the proposed configuration in comparison to a PID
controller. Furthermore, in this chapter, we described how to implement the proposed
controller in VHDL. Also a new method for implementing the defuzzification stage in
VHDL was proposed. The synthesized results of the implemented fuzzy controller in a
CMOS 90nm technology, using Cadence RC compiler, evaluated in this chapter based on its
power consumption and area.

7. Acknowledgment

This work was supported by the Dutch Technical Science Foundation (STW), under the
agreement 363120-427.

8. References

Azevedo, A.; Issenin, I.; Cornea, R.; Gupta, R.; Dutt, N.; Veidenbaum, A. & Nicolau, A. (2002).
Profile-Based Dynamic Voltage Scheduling Using Program Checkpoints, *Proceedings
of the conference on Design, Automation and Test in Europe (DATE 2002)*, pp. 168-175.
Bang, S.; Bang, K.; Yoon, S. & Chung, E.Y. (2009). Run-time adaptive workload estimation
for dynamic voltage scaling, *IEEE Transactions on Computer-Aided Design of
Integrated Circuits and Systems*, Vol.28, No.9, pp. 1334-1347.
Benini, L.; Bogliolo, A.; Paleologo, G.A. & De Micheli, G. (1999). Policy optimization for
dynamic power management, *IEEE Trans. On Computer-Aided Design of Integrated
Circuits and Systems*, Vol.18, No.6, pp. 813-833.

Chung, E.Y.; De Micheli, G. & Benini, L. (2002). Contents provider-assisted dynamic voltage scaling for low energy multimedia applications, *Proc. of the 2002 international symposium on Low power electronics and design*, Monterey, California, USA, pp. 42-47.

Daijin, K. (2000) An Implementation of Fuzzy Logic Controller on the Reconfigurable FPGA System, *IEEE Transactions on Industrial Electronic*, Vol.47, No.3, pp. 703 – 715.

Gu, Y. & Chakraborty, S., (2008). Control theory-based DVS for interactive 3D games, in *Proc. DAC*, 2008, pp. 740–745.

Gutnik, V. & Chandrakasan, A.P. (1997). Embedded power supply for low-power DSP, *IEEE Trans. On VLSI Syst.*, Vol.5, No.4, pp. 425-435.

Hughes, C.J. & Adve, S.V. (2003). A formal approach to frequent energy adaptations for multimedia applications, in *Proc. Int. Conf. Comput. Des.*, pp. 489–496.

Im, C.; Kim, H. & Ha, S. (2006). Dynamic voltage scheduling technique for low-power multimedia applications using buffers, *Proc. ISLPED*, pp. 34-39.

Jejurikar, R. & Gupta, R. (2006). Energy-aware task scheduling with task synchronization for embedded real-time systems, *IEEE Trans. Comput.- Aided Design Integr. Circuits Syst.*, Vol.25, No.6, pp. 1024–1037.

Lee, C.-C., (1990) Fuzzy Logic in Control Systems: Fuzzy Logic Controller-Parts 1 and 2, *IEEE Trans.on Systems, Man, and Cybernetics*, Vol.20, No.2, pp. 404-435.

Lu, Z.; Hein, J.; Humphrey, M.; Stan, M.; Lach, J. & Skadron, K. (2002). Control-theoretic dynamic frequency and voltage scaling for multimedia workloads, in *Proc. Int. Conf. Compilers, Architecture, Synthesis Embed. Syst.*, pp. 156–163.

Lu, Z.; Lach, J.; Stan, M. & Skadron, K. (2003). Reducing multimedia decode power using feedback control, in *Proc. Int. Conf. Comput. Des.*, pp. 489–496.

Nielsen, L.S.; Nielssen, C.; Sparsø, J. & Van Berkel, K. (1994). Low-power operation using self-timed circuits and adaptive scaling of the supply voltage, *IEEE Trans. VLSI Syst.*, Vol.2, pp. 391–397.

Pourshaghaghi, H.R. & Pineda de Gyvez, J., (2009). Dynamic Voltage Scaling Based on Supply Current Tracking Using Fuzzy Logic Controller, *Proc. of the 16th IEEE Int. Conf. on Electronics, Circuits, and Systems, (ICECS 2009)*, pp. 779-782.

Rabaey J, (2010) *Low Power Design Essentials*. Springer, pp. 249-288.

Sakthivel, G.; Anandhi, T.S. & Natarajan, S.P. (2010) Real time implementation of a fuzzy logic controller on FPGA using VHDL for DC-Motor speed control, *International Journal of Engineering Science and Technology*, Vol.2, No.9, pp. 4511-4519.

Sinha, A. & Chandrakasan, A.P. (2001). Dynamic voltage scheduling using adaptive filtering of workload traces, *Proc. of the 14th International Conference on VLSI Design (VLSID '01)*, pp.221-226.

Vasantha Rani, S.P.J.; Kanagasabapathy, P. & Sathish Kumar, A. (2005). Digital Fuzzy Logic Controller using VHDL, *INDICON2005*, pp. 463-466.

Vuong, P.T.; Madni, A.M. & Vuong, J.B. (2006). VHDL implementation for a fuzzy logic controller, *Automation Congress, 2006. WAC '06. World*, pp. 1-8.

Wei, G. & Horowitz, M. (1999). A fully digital energy-efficient adaptive power supply regulator, *IEEE Journal of solid-state Circuits*, Vol.34, No.4, pp. 520-528.

Wu, Q.; Juang, P.; Martonosi, M. & Clark, D.W. (2005). Formal control techniques for power-performance management, *IEEE Micro*, Vol.25, No.5, pp. 52–62.

Yang, P.; Wong, C.; Marchal, P.; Catthoor, F.; Desmet, D.; Verkest, D. & Lauwereins, R. (2001). Energy-Aware Runtime Scheduling for Embedded-Multiprocessor SOCs, *IEEE Design & Test*, Vol.18, No.5, pp.46-58.

Yao, F.; Demers, A. & Shenker, S. A. (1995). Scheduling model for reduced CPU energy, *Proc. Found. Comput. Sci.*, pp. 374-382.

9

Fuzzy Logic Control for Multiresolutive Adaptive PN Acquisition Scheme in Time-Varying Multipath Ionospheric Channel

Rosa Maria Alsina-Pages, Claudia Mateo Segura,
Joan Claudi Socoró Carrié and Pau Bergada
La Salle - Universitat Ramon Llull
Spain

1. Introduction

Communication with remote places is a challenge often solved using satellites. However, when trying to reach Antarctic stations, this solution suffers from poor visibility range and high operational costs. In such scenarios, skywave ionospheric communication systems represent a good alternative to satellite communications.

The Research Group in Electromagnetism and Communications (GRECO) is designing an HF system for long haul digital communication between the Antarctic Spanish Base in Livingston Island (62.6S, 60.4W) and Observatori de l'Ebre in Spain (40.8N,0.5E) (Vilella et al., 2008). The main interest of Observatori de l'Ebre is the transmission of the data collected from the sensors located at the base, including a geomagnetic sensor, a vertical incidence ionosonde, an oblique incidence ionosonde and a GNSS receiver. The geomagnetic sensor, the vertical incidence ionosonde and the GNSS receiver are commercial solutions from third parties. The oblique incidence ionosonde, used to sound the ionospheric channel between Antarctica and Spain, was developed by the GRECO in the framework of this project.

During the last Antarctic campaign, exhaustive measurements of the HF channel characteristics were performed, which allowed us to determine parameters such as availability, SNR, delay and Doppler spread, etc. In addition to the scientific interest of this sounding, a further objective of the project is the establishment of a backup link for data transmission from the remote sensors in the Antarctica. In this scenario, ionospheric communications appear to be an interesting complementary alternative to geostationary satellite communications since the latter are expensive and not always available from high-latitudes.

Research work in the field of fuzzy logics applied to the estimation of the above mentioned channel was first applied in (Alsina et al., 2005a) for serial search acquisition systems in AWGN channels, afterwards applied to the same channel but in the multiresolutive structure (Alsina et al., 2009a; Morán et al., 2001) in papers (Alsina et al., 2007b; 2009b) achieving good results. In this chapter the application of fuzzy logic control trained for Rayleigh fading channels (Proakis, 1995) with Direct-Sequence Spread-Spectrum (DS-SS) is presented, specifically suited for the ionospheric channel Antarctica-Spain. Stability and reliability of the reception, which are currently being designed, are key factors for the reception.

It is important to note that the fuzzy control design presented in this chapter not only resolves the issue of improving the multiresolutive structure performance presented by (Morán et al., 2001), but also introduces a new option for the control design of many LMS adaptive structures used for PN code acquisition found in the literature. (El-Tarhuni & Sheikh, 1996) presented an LMS-based system to acquire a DS-SS system in Rayleigh channels; years after, (Han et al., 2006) improved the performance of the acquisition system designed by (El-Tarhuni & Sheikh, 1996). And also in other type of channels, LMS filters are used as an acquisition system, even in oceanic transmissions (Stojanovic & Freitag, 2003). Although the fuzzy control system presented in this chapter is compared to the stability control used in (Morán et al., 2001) it also can be used to improve all previous designs performance in terms of stability and robustness. Despite this generalization, the design of every control system should be done according to the requirements of the acquisition system and the specific channel characteristics.

2. Background and system requirements

The design of the transmitter and the receiver, as well as the modulation used to carry out data transmission is severely conditioned to Antarctica constraints. Power restrictions, low bitrate needed and multipath are requirements to be taken into account in the decisions.

2.1 Ionospheric channel and BAE restrictions

One of the major constraints is that, due to power restrictions in the Antarctic Base, the transmission power is strongly limited. Consequently, a very low SNR is usually expected at the receiver. However, when using DS-SS techniques, signal spectrum is spread over a wide bandwidth, becoming robust against narrowband interferences.

Previous research efforts have been focused on using pseudorandom sequences with good autocorrelation characteristics (m-sequences) to evaluate the four-five hops link (12700km length) from Antarctica to Observatori de l'Ebre (Spain). Channel estimation and impairment characteristics have been obtained from these previous experiments (Vilella et al., 2008). DS-SS has also been previously used as a signaling technique (Deumal et al., 2006), for DS-SS modulation (Alsina et al., 2009a) or for OFDM modulation (Bergadà et al., 2009), achieving good results in terms of spectral efficiency although scarcely decreasing the system performance. These outcomes encouraged us to consider DS-SS a proper candidate to modulate the transmitted data. An advantage of DS-SS modulation (Glisic & Vucetic, 1997; Peterson et al., 1995) is that channel estimation is not essential in the demodulation stage, but it can be used to improve its reliability (i.e. using a RAKE receiver).

2.2 Direct-Sequence Spread-Spectrum transmission

Direct-Sequence Spread-Spectrum (Peterson et al., 1995) is a modulation technique that, as well as other spread spectrum technologies, increases the transmitted signal bandwidth and occupies a wider bandwidth (see $x[n]$ in Figure 1) than the information signal (see $b[n]$ in Figure 1) that is being modulated. DS-SS pseudorandomly modulates the wave with a continuous string of pseudonoise (PN) code symbols (see $c[n]$ in Figure 1) called *chips*. Chips are of shorter duration than information bits, hence the wider spectrum and the higher chip rate. So, the chip rate is higher than the information signal bit rate (see Figure 1). DS-SS uses a sequence of chips generated by the transmitter, and also known by the receiver; the receiver can then use the same PN sequence to counteract the effect of the PN sequence used to modulate in the transmitter, in order to reconstruct the information signal.

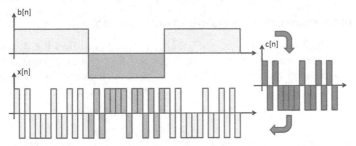

Fig. 1. The DS-SS signal $x[n]$ is generated through multiplication of the information base-band signal $b[n]$ with the (periodic) spreading sequence $c[n]$

One of the main challenges to be solved by DS-SS systems is to achieve a quick and robust acquisition of the pseudonoise sequences (PN sequences). In time-varying environments this fact becomes even more important, because acquisition and tracking performance can heavily degrade communication reliability.

There are several schemes to deal with this problem, such as serial search and parallel algorithms (Sklar, 1988). Serial search algorithms require a low computational load but they are slow to converge. On the other hand, parallel systems are fast converging but require a high computational load. In our system, the low-complexity fast-converging multiresolutive structure that was previously presented in (Morán et al., 2001) is used. Nevertheless, a proper design of the decisional system is a key factor in the overall system performance. This is even more important when dealing with time varying channels with a variable SNR.

Several factors contribute to the performance of the acquisition system (Glisic & Vucetic, 1997): uncertainty about the code phase, channel distortion and variations, noise and interference, and data randomness. Therefore, advanced control systems as fuzzy logic (Zadeh, 1965; 1988) are used to solve this complex acquisition problem. The fuzzy logic estimator used in this chapter was first presented by our research group in (Alsina et al., 2005a) and (Alsina et al., 2008; 2007b; 2009b); in this study, a new control system with a new set of If-Then Rules is presented to cope with the multipath time-variant ionospheric channel (Alsina et al., 2009a).

2.3 Fuzzy logic as an acquisition control

The decision of using fuzzy logic (Zadeh, 1965; 1988) for the acquisition control of the multiresolutive structure (Morán et al., 2001) is based in the high accuracy of fuzzy logic in terms of complex system description. The behavior of the channel is well-known, as a result of several research studies (Vilella et al., 2009; 2008), thus the control performance can be manually adjusted, by means of the acquisition system knowledge.

Fuzzy logic has been widely used to solve engineering problems (Gad & Farouq, 2001). More specifically, (Daffara, 1995) and (Drake & Prasad, 1999) used fuzzy logic to track phase error detectors in synchronization, while (Perez-Neira & Lagunas, 1996) and (Perez-Neira et al., 1997) improved detection results by means of this technique. Finally, (Bas & Perez-Neira, 2003) applied fuzzy logic to interference rejection. These applications are based in the same principles that the one presented in this chapter; the wide knowledge of a system performance by the designer, which fuzzy logic helps to translate to a closed control system.

3. Multiresolutive structure for acquisition and tracking

The aim of the multiresolutive scheme (Morán et al., 2001) is to find the correct acquisition point with low latency and simultaneously requiring low computational cost in a DS-SS transmission. The transmitted signal, the base band continuous signal before spectral shaping is:

$$x(t) = \sum_{i=1}^{I} b_i \cdot c(t - i \cdot T_s) \tag{1}$$

where b_i are the information bits, I is the total number of transmitted bits and T_s is the bit duration in seconds. The received base band signal, after downconversion and filtering is:

$$r(t) = \sum_{j=1}^{L} \gamma_j(t) \cdot x(t - \tau_j(t)) + n(t) \tag{2}$$

where L is the number of multipath components, γ_j is the complex fading coefficient of the jth component, and τ_j is the delay of the jth component. The input signal for the multiresolutive structure is $s[n] = r(n \cdot \frac{T_c}{N})$ (see Figure 2), so it is assumed to be sampled at the frequency of Nf_c, where $f_c = 1/T_c$ is the chip frequency (in number of chips per second) and T_c is the chip duration in seconds. The PN sequence used as reference in the acquisition scheme is also sampled at Nf_c, so is $c[n] = c(n \cdot \frac{T_c}{N})$.

As can be shown in Figure 2, in the acquisition part the signal $s[n]$ is first decimated by a factor N (and then N is the number of samples per chip). Since the acquisition stage can accept uncertainties lower than the chip period, the computational load is reduced by decimating without affecting the performance.

3.1 Acquisition stage

The decimated signal, termed as $s_{dec}[n]$, is fed into the filters of a multiresolutive structure (see Figure 2). There are M different branches that work with decimated versions of the input signal, separated in M disjoint subspaces. Each branch has an adaptive FIR filter of length $H = \left\lceil \frac{PG}{M} \right\rceil$, where PG is the Processing Gain (corresponding to the length of the PN sequence), trained with a decimated version of the PN modulating sequence (c_{dec}), and $\lceil \cdot \rceil$ stands for the ceil operator. FIR filters use the LMS algorithm as adaptive coefficient update procedure and their performance were compared to other adaptive filters; they outstand for being the best in terms of speed of convergence and reliability (Akhter et al., 2010).

LMS filters converge with a steepest descent algorithm (Haykin, 1996), using a convergence parameter μ that has to be adjusted according to the system requirements of stability and time convergence. The steepest descent algorithm is detailed in:

$$w_{k+1} = w_k + \mu e_k s_k^{dec} \tag{3}$$

where w_{k+1} is the tap weight vector at (chip-based) sample time index $k + 1$ and w_k is the tap weight vector at index time k, e_k is the output error at time k and s_k^{dec} is the input signal. μ is the step-size parameter that controls the speed of convergence and the robustness of the filter. It is a parameter that has been carefully designed.

Under ideal conditions, in a non-frequency selective Rayleigh channel with white Gaussian noise, just one of the filters should locally converge to a Dirac delta response like

$$\gamma[k]b_i[n]\delta[k - \tau] \tag{4}$$

where $b_i[n]$ is the information bit, τ represents the chip-based delay between the input signal PN sequence and the reference one and $\gamma[k]$ is the fading coefficient. The algorithm is reseted every symbol period, and a modulus smoothing average algorithm is applied to each LMS filter coefficients solution $W_i[n]$ to remove the data randomness component $b_i[n]$ of Equation 4, obtaining nonnegative averaged impulsional responses $W_i^{av}[n]$.

$$W_{i+1}^{av}[n] = (1 - \beta)W_i^{av}[n] + \beta|W_i[n]| \tag{5}$$

The exponential smoothing filter and the choice of the proper value of the parameter β are fundamental for the good performance of the multiresolutive structure; it is important to note that $|\cdot|$ is the modulus for each coefficient of $W_i[n]$. The design of such components of the multiresolutive structure is optimized in order to stabilize the dynamics of the tap filter coefficients, avoiding impulsive changes due to SNR variations or fast fading.

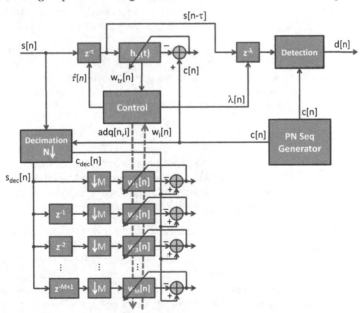

Fig. 2. Multiresolutive structure for acquisition and tracking

A peak detection algorithm is used by the decisional system embedded in the control stage (see Figure 2) which of the acquisition filters has detected the signal (say $W_{con}[n]$), considering $W_{con}[n]$ is the filter coefficients after the convergence. The coarse estimation of the acquisition point is given by the position of the maximum, say n_{max}^i, in the selected filter.

3.2 Tracking stage

Once restored the acquisition point by the decisional system, tracking is solved with another adaptive FIR filter with impulse response $W_{tr}[n]$ (of length H and also using the LMS algorithm as the coefficient update procedure), which expands the search window around the coarse acquisition point n_{max}, using the full bandwidth input signal $s[n]$. The result of the tracking filter is also smoothed using an exponential smoothing as detailed in Section 3.1. Finally, the estimation of the acquisition point is refined by finding the tracking point (see Figure 2, values $\hat{t}$) and the signal can be correctly demodulated.

3.3 Control stage

The control stage of the multiresolutive structure is a key step in this design (Alsina et al., 2009b). The stability and the robustness of the multiresolutive structure are supported by the control system, apart from the quality of the acquisition of the multiresolutive structure. The control system is based on the measurements over the LMS filters used in acquisition and tracking: i) $W_i^{av}[n]$ corresponding to the averaged impulse responses of the tracking filters; ii) $W_{con}^{av}[n]$, referring to the current acquisition filter that gives the current acquisition point; and iii), $W_{tr}^{av}[n]$ as the tracking filter.

Using this information provided by the acquisition and tracking, the decisional system determines if the system is acquired and demodulation can start, or otherwise the acquisition system must remain in the process of acquisition and tracking of a proper point.

In this project the decisional system is based on fuzzy logic (Zadeh, 1988), due to the deep knowledge of the channel behavior acquired in numerous tests involving different kinds of modulations. These tests did not only provide valuable information about the performance of the LMS adaptive filters both in acquisition and tracking, but also how this performance reflects in the *Acquisition* estimation as is shown in Section 4.

4. The acquisition fuzzy control

The acquisition control is designed using information from the impulsional response of the LMS filters of the multiresolutive structure after being smoothed. Their values give information about the probability of being correctly acquired, and this information feeds the fuzzy decisional system designed for the multiresolutive structure.

Previous work started with the design of a fuzzy control for a serial search algorithm based on a CFAR scheme (Glisic, 1991), work presented in (Alsina et al., 2005a). Afterwards, the fuzzy estimator was adapted to the multiresolutive structure (Morán et al., 2001), in order to improve its performance in channels with fast SNR variations. This design and study was presented in (Alsina et al., 2007b) and in (Alsina et al., 2009b). Then, the fuzzy logic estimator was compared with a neural network based control, work presented in (Alsina et al., 2008).

The input variable definition presented in this paper (corresponding to the four ratios $Ratio_1$, $Ratio_2$, $Ratio_3$ and $Ratio_{1trac}$) was initialized in (Alsina et al., 2007b). As the design of a fuzzy logic system is highly dependent on the environment where it works, in this paper it has been specifically redesigned and adapted to a ionospheric Rayleigh channel (Proakis, 1995). The number of membership functions and their position have changed, but not the main basis of the variable definition with respect to previous work where fuzzy logic control was used

(Alsina et al., 2007b). The knowledge of the performance of the multiresolutive structure is a key process for both the first channel (fast SNR variation channel) and for the ionospheric Rayleigh channel currently used.

4.1 Input variables and fuzzy sets

In this Section a detailed explanation of the input variables and their meaning is given. Each input variable is defined and it is chosen according to the information it generates to improve the control performance. Once the four input variables are detailed, they are tested using a family of 10 PN sequences previously designed (Alsina et al., 2005b; 2007a) to improve the multiresolutive structure capabilities. As will be shown (see Section 4.1.2.2), there are substantial differences in the performance of each of the PN sequences in terms of input variables, so a preferred sequence is chosen; the minimization of the values of autocorrelation and crosscorrelation - which contribute to the fitness function of the GA algorithm (Alsina et al., 2007a) - is taken into account. Afterwards, the median and the lower and upper quartiles of the input variables are studied for the preferred sequence; finally the membership functions are defined.

4.1.1 Input variables

Four parameters are defined as inputs in the fuzzy logic control system; three of them refer to the values of the four modulus averaged acquisition LMS filters ($W_i^{av}[n]$), especially the LMS filter adapted and synchronized with the decimated sequence c_{dec} (named $W_{con}^{av}[n]$), and one to the tracking filter ($W_{tr}^{av}[n]$):

- $Ratio_1$: it is computed as the quotient of the peak value of the LMS filter ($W_{con}^{av}[n_{max}^i]$) divided by the mean value of this filter but the maximum (consider n_{max}^i as the LMS maximum equivalent to reconstructed acquisition point, named τ in Figure 2):

$$Ratio_1 = \frac{W_{con}^{av}[n_{max}^i]}{\frac{1}{H}\sum_{\substack{n=1 \\ n \neq n_{max}^i}}^{H} W_{con}^{av}[n]} \tag{6}$$

- $Ratio_2$: it is evaluated as the quotient of the peak value of the LMS filter ($W_{con}^{av}[n_{max}^i]$) divided by the average of the value of the same position in the other three filters ($W_i^{av}[n]$):

$$Ratio_2 = \frac{W_{con}^{av}[n_{max}^i]}{\frac{1}{M-1}\sum_{\substack{i=1 \\ i \neq con}}^{M} W_i^{av}[n_{max}^i]} \tag{7}$$

- $Ratio_3$: it is obtained as the quotient of the peak value of the LMS filter ($W_{con}^{av}[n_{max}^i]$) divided by the mean value of the three other filters ($W_i^{av}[n]$):

$$Ratio_3 = \frac{W_{con}^{av}[n_{max}^i]}{\frac{1}{M-1}\frac{1}{H-1}\sum_{\substack{i=1 \\ i \neq con}}^{M} \sum_{\substack{n=1 \\ n \neq n_{max}^i}}^{H} W_i^{av}[n]} \tag{8}$$

- $Ratio_{1trac}$: it is computed as the quotient of the peak value of the LMS tracking filter ($W_{tr}^{av}[n_{max}]$), being n_{max} the most precise estimation of the correct acquisition point, divided by the mean value of the same filter but the maximum (consider n_{max} as the LMS maximum equivalent to reconstructed tracking point named λ in Figure 2).

$$Ratio_{1trac} = \frac{W_{tr}^{av}[n_{max}]}{\frac{1}{H}\sum_{\substack{n=1 \\ n \neq n_{max}}}^{H} W_{tr}^{av}[n]} \tag{9}$$

$Ratio_1$ gives information about the signal to noise ratio of the channel; in second term it also reflects the mean autocorrelation of the decimated signal used as reference. If the mean values of the tap weights of the converged filter are high, $Ratio_1$ shows a wide dynamic margin to define all membership functions, which means that the autocorrelation for c_{dec} is not negligible. $Ratio_2$ shows information about the SNR and about the delay spread of the channel; if the received data is not spread around the contiguous chips of the detected tracking position $Ratio_2$ obtains good dynamic margin. $Ratio_3$ gives information about the SNR at the receiver, and about the crosscorrelation between the four decimated versions of a PN sequence. If the crosscorrelation is high between subsequences, $Ratio_3$ achieves non-discriminative results and does not help acquisition. Finally, $Ratio_{1trac}$ gives information about the SNR at the receiver in terms of the entire sequence - not the decimated as the three previous ratios - . These parameters have been chosen due to the information they contain about the probability of successful acquisition related to their values; their output dynamic range can be divided into several membership functions referring to their value, in order to help the estimation of the acquisition stage.

4.1.2 Input fuzzy sets

In this Section the input fuzzy sets for each input variable are described. The input fuzzy sets with their membership functions need a ratio value estimation for each input variable. This studio is made for a family of 10 different PN sequences optimized to work with the multiresolutive structure (Alsina et al., 2007a).

A scenario description is firstly described, in order to detail the channel environment in which the tests are made. The channel or simulation settings are defined according to the information given by (Vilella et al., 2009; 2008), using measurements from real transmission campaigns. Lately, the four ratios curves for each scenario are obtained and explained for both acquisition and non-acquisition situations. This information leads us to choose the appropriate preferred PN sequences. Statistical parameters are computed over the performance of the preferred PN sequence, and membership functions are finally defined.

4.1.2.1 Scenario description

In order to train the system to work with real data, four simulation scenarios have been defined in Table 1. They are absolutely based on analysis of real data (Vilella et al., 2009; 2008), except for scenario 0, that is a simpler version of transmissions throughout ionospheric radiolink, considering only the most powerful path in a multipath scenario.

Table 1 is sorted by h_l, that is the hour time - during day or night -. For every hour, three SNR values are shown (-9 dB, -6 dB, -3 dB), measured using a transmission bandwidth $Bw = 3kHz$ around a carrier frequency f_l (expressed in MHz). $Dw_{f,j}$ is the availability of each frequency in %. $\tau(h_l)_{F_k,j}$, where $f_k \in F_k$, is the composite multipath spread in ms, and finally, $v(h_l)_{F_k,j}$, where $f_k \in F_k$, is the Doppler spread in Hertz.

Best availability data from (Vilella et al., 2008) is considered for this research work.

Scenario	h_l	SNR	$Dw(h_l)_{\underline{f},\bar{j}}$	$f_k = \underline{f}$	$\tau(h_l)_{F_k,\bar{j}}, f_k \in F_l$	$v(h_l)_{F_k,\bar{j}}, f_k \in F_k$
Scenario 0 -	-	-	-	-	-	1.2
Scenario 1 01	-9	82%	9	2		1.25
	-6	63%	9	2		1.25
	-3	36%	9	2		1.25
Scenario 2 21	-9	52%	13	1		1.2
	-6	43%	15	0.7		0.9
	-3	36%	15	0.7		0.9
Scenario 3 08	-9	50%	15	0.6		0.8
	-6	36%	15	0.6		0.8
	-3	18%	15	0.6		0.8

Table 1. Ionospheric simulation scenarios (Vilella et al., 2009; 2008)

4.1.2.2 Ratio values for each sequence and scenario

The PN sequence family used to test the four input ratios was designed using evolution strategies (Alsina et al., 2007b; 2005a), in order to satisfy the requirements of the multiresolutive structure (as shown in Figure 2 and in Section 3). This structure uses a decimated PN sequence to estimate the first acquisition point, and therefore it is convenient to obtain good autocorrelation for the decimated sequence, as well as a limited crosscorrelation between the M decimated versions of the PN sequence. These requirements have been used in the evolution strategy design, generating a family of PN sequences that not only minimized the autocorrelation and the crosscorrelation, but also these statistical parameters for the decimated sequences.

In Figures 3, 4, 5 and 6 a four-ratio comparison is made using the four simulation scenarios of Table 1. The four top subfigures plot the ratio values for the acquired situation; the four bottom subfigures plot the ratio values for non-acquired situation. This evaluation is made for each ratio ($Ratio_1$, $Ratio_2$, $Ratio_3$ and $Ratio_{1trac}$) and also for each scenario (scenario 0, scenario 1, scenario 2 and scenario 3) applying at each simulation a different SNR value in order to perform a noise value study.

Figure 3 shows a clear difference between the values for $Ratio_1$ in the case of acquisition and in the case of non-acquisition, especially for scenario 0. Scenario 1, scenario 2 and scenario 3 values for acquisition are not so stable, and neither are the values for the non-acquisition situation. This is a behavior that will be repeated for the four ratios: the first scenario is the one that allows a better discrimination between acquisition and non acquisition in terms of ratios, it is the clearest to detect an acquisition. In the other three scenarios, due to the fact that they produce multipath, the values for the ratios are more ambiguous.

Figure 4 presents very good results for nearly all the PN sequences of the family. These figures show that $Ratio_2$ can be used for performing an stable estimation of the decision to evaluate. Figure 5 shows a noisy $Ratio_3$; but despite its unstable values for the non-acquired situation, values for $Ratio_3$ in acquired scenarios 2 and 3, which are the worst results for the results tests, it exhibits a fairly distinct behavior in acquisition situation with respect to non-acquisition situation. Then $Ratio_3$ information is valuable in the case of severe channel conditions. Finally,

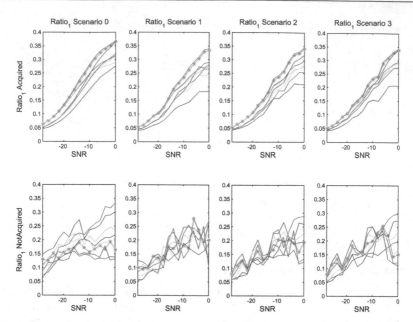

Fig. 3. Performance of the PN sequence ratio values for $Ratio_1$. The four upper figures show $Ratio_1$ values for the four scenarios in the acquired situation. The four lower figures show $Ratio_1$ values for the non-acquired situation.

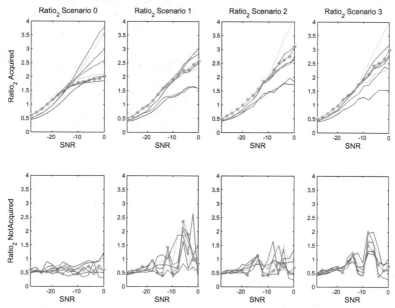

Fig. 4. Performance of the PN sequence ratio values for $Ratio_2$. The four upper figures show $Ratio_2$ values for the four scenarios in the acquired situation. The four lower figures show $Ratio_2$ values for the non-acquired situation.

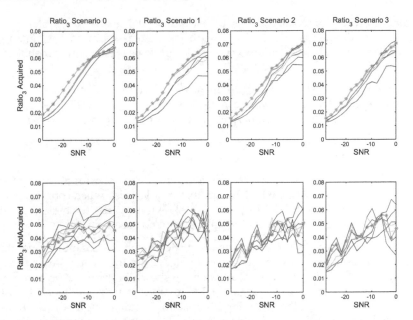

Fig. 5. Performance of the PN sequence ratio values for $Ratio_3$. The four upper figures show $Ratio_3$ values for the four scenarios in the acquired situation. The four lower figures show $Ratio_3$ values for the non-acquired situation.

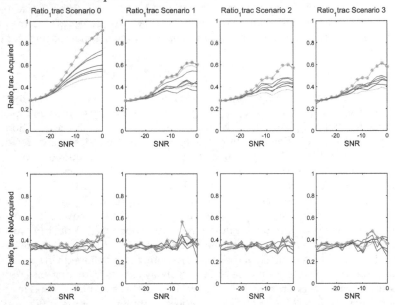

Fig. 6. Performance of the PN sequence ratio values for $Ratio_{1trac}$. The four upper figures show $Ratio_{1trac}$ values for the four scenarios in the acquired situation. The four lower figures show $Ratio_{1trac}$ values for the non-acquired situation.

Figure 6 plots the results for $Ratio_{1trac}$; they are the best results given by the system in the four scenarios and considering the four ratios. Nevertheless there is a drawback for $Ratio_{1trac}$: the system must be acquired for this value to be reliable, otherwise just a noisy amount of output values is shown.

This information is gathered, and one PN sequence is chosen for its good response to the four ratios in the four scenarios. This sequence is the dotted one in the four Figures (3, 4, 5 and 6). It has been chosen due to its minimization of the Euclidean distance with the best sequence at each ratio evaluation.

4.1.2.3 Selected sequence

The selected PN sequence is not the best one for all the ratios and for all the scenarios. It stands for the best global values, which means that is little noisy when comparing with the other sequences. In most of the results previously shown it reaches the best values (i.e. the values that better discriminates between acquisition and non acquisition).

Once chosen the preferred PN sequence, some statistics have to be computed over the ratios obtained using this sequence. The ratios are computed again for a wider group of values of SNR, and the results for the acquisition situation are shown in Figure 7. Over these results median, lower and upper quartiles are computed in order to fix some thresholds to define the membership functions in the fuzzy input variables. Figure 8 shows the boxplots of the values for $Ratio_1$ when acquired, and also performs the boxplots of the values for $Ratio_2$ when acquired. Figure 8 also gives the boxplots of the values for $Ratio_3$ when acquired and the values for $Ratio_{1trac}$ when acquired.

In the last figure, the median values for the four ratios simulated in the four scenarios, and the quartiles for these groups of ratios are also shown. Especially the quartiles over the four ratios when the system is acquired can be considered the key to tune the membership functions for the input variables.

4.1.2.4 Fuzzy membership functions

Finally, the input variables membership functions are defined. Four fuzzy sets have been defined for each variable; two for the acquisition situation and two for the non-acquisition situation; only for $Ratio_{1trac}$ is defined with five fuzzy sets, three for acquisition situation and two for the non-acquisition situation. Only four sets have been considered, because the system needs to give the clear idea of whether the receiver is acquired or not, assuming doubts. The four groups are named (from worse to best performance of the system) **Not Acquired**, **Probably Not Acquired** ($\sim NoAcq$), **Probably Acquired** ($\sim Acq$) and **Acquired**. The division between **Not Acquired** and **Probably Not Acquired** is the median value for the non-acquired situation; and the same for **Probably Acquired** and **Acquired**, the threshold is the median value for the acquired situation. The division between **Probably Not Acquired** and **Probably Acquired** is held assuming that the maximum values for each are the low and high, respectively, quartiles for each of the ratios. All values are obtained with the mean value for the four ratios observed, and in case of doubt, always states the worst case. Some of the thresholds for the membership functions follow the worst case studio rule. Figures for the membership functions for $Ratio_1$, $Ratio_2$ and $Ratio_3$ are shown in Figure 9, Figure 10 and 11, respectively. The only difference in the design is for membership functions of $Ratio_{1trac}$; this ratio gives enough information to affirm that for some very high values (see statistics in Figure 8), not only is acquired, but also is working with only one path, as shown in Figure 12.

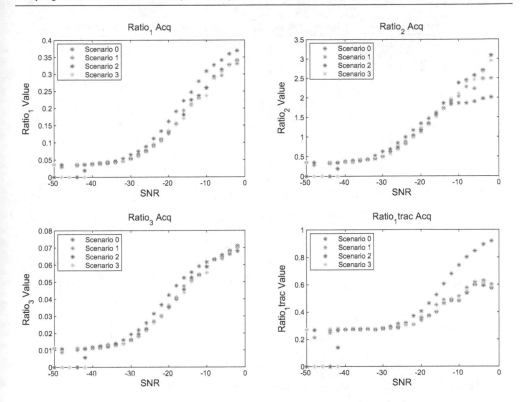

Fig. 7. Values for $Ratio_1$, $Ratio_2$, $Ratio_3$ and $Ratio_{1trac}$ for an Acquired situation

4.2 Output variable and fuzzy sets

The output parameter is *Acquisition*, which gives a value in the range [0,1], being zero when it is **Not Acquired** and one if it is **Acquired**. In between, two other fuzzy sets are defined: **Probably Not Acquired** and **Probably Acquired**.

The parameter *Acquisition* is used to give information to the detection stage about the reliability of the estimation. Notice that the multiresolutive structure gives an estimation of the acquisition point while the *Acquisition* value evaluates the probability of being acquired.

4.2.1 Output fuzzy sets

The critical values of the output variable *Acquisition*, around [0.4, 0.6] are divided into two fuzzy sets, the lower one corresponding to **Probably Not Acquired** and the higher one corresponding to **Probably Acquired**. If the output variable obtains a critical value this is a result of non clear acquisition, so the decisional system does not have certainty about the reliability of the results. An additional period of time for acquisition is needed, and this is the goal of the definition of these two fuzzy sets.

For values over 0.6 and under 0.4 the output variable *Acquisition* is clearly defined, being the first one clearly acquired, and the second one clearly not acquired.

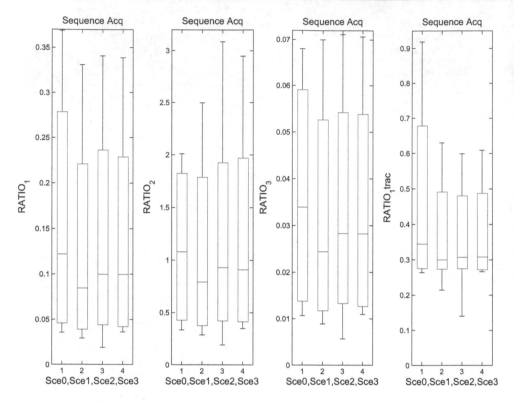

Fig. 8. Median and quartiles for $Ratio_1$, $Ratio_2$, $Ratio_3$ and $Ratio_{1trac}$ for acquisition situation

4.3 If-then rules

If-then rules have been defined to obtain the best performance (in terms of reliability of the output variable *Acquisition* of the fuzzy estimator) along the full range of measured values for each input parameter. Two examples of the dependence between input variables are shown in Figure 14, where dependence among *Acquisition* and $Ratio_1$ and $Ratio_{1trac}$, and also $Ratio_2$ and $Ratio_3$ are depicted.

The most critical estimation for the output variable *Acquisition* is the correspondence to **Probably Not Acquired** and to **Probably Acquired**; this means that the input parameters have no coherent values for **Acquired** or **Not Acquired**. To obtain a precise output value, the fuzzy estimator evaluates the degree of implication of each input parameter to the input variables membership functions and projects this implication to the fuzzy sets of the output variable *Acquisition*, in order to obtain its final value through defuzzyfication.

4.4 Decisional system feedback

Depending on the value of the output variable *Acquisition*, the multiresolutive acquisition block will perform in four different ways:

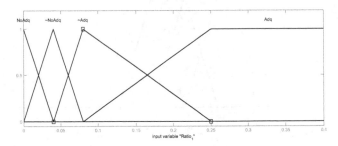

Fig. 9. Membership functions for input variable $Ratio_1$

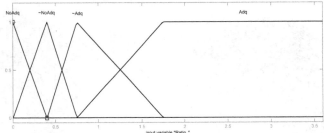

Fig. 10. Membership functions for input variable $Ratio_2$

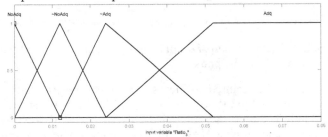

Fig. 11. Membership functions for input variable $Ratio_3$

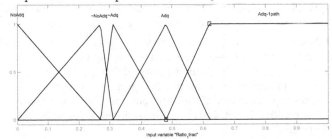

Fig. 12. Membership functions for input variable $Ratio_{1trac}$

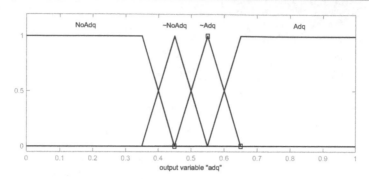

Fig. 13. Membership functions of *Acquisition*

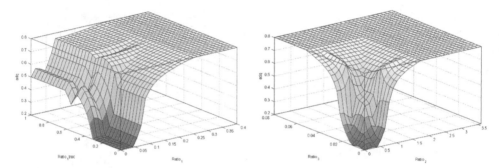

(a) *Acquisition* as a function of $Ratio_1$ and $Ratio_{1trac}$ (b) *Acquisition* as a function of $Ratio_2$ and $Ratio_3$

Fig. 14. Two examples of the variation of output variable *Acquisition* for all the whole range of values of the two ratios, taken by pairs.

- **Acquired**, it maintains the acquired position, saving computational load by stopping some of the adaptive filters used in the acquisition stage. This helps the structure to reduce its computational load. The ratios are computed only for the active filters, and each pause period (fixed to a certain number of symbol periods) ends with a convergence of all the filters, and a recalculation of all the ratios in order to prevent losing acquisition.

- **Probably Acquired**, it keeps the searching procedure to improve acquisition, and of course, evaluations are maintained until the convergence is certain - if this is the case.

- **Probably Not Acquired**, move $\frac{T_s}{4}$ the beginning of the data for the acquisition stage and evaluate improvements; this pointer movement is used to prevent the system from failing in its purpose due to a bad initial pointer position. Not all the initial values are equally convenient for the multiresolutive structure; the optimum situation is when the acquisition point is found in the middle of any of the four adaptive filters, and this approach helps the convergence if the position is not the optimum, despite convergence is possible at any tap of the four LMS filters.

- **Not Acquired**, move $\frac{T_s}{2}$ and evaluate to find changes. The move of $\frac{T_s}{2}$ is larger than in the previous case because if the system is in an *not acquired* situation, it means that the acquisition is far to be detected, so the initial data for the acquisition stage can be found in the worst place - the one that obtains the acquisition point far from the center of the LMS filters -.

These four categories are chosen depending on the *Acquisition* output variable values. This feedback improves the speed of convergence of the acquisition and reduces computational load for the entire structure, by means of stopping the convergence of some of the adaptive filters when convergence is assured.

5. Tests and results

In this Section the results of the performance of the designed fuzzy system are presented. First, an evaluation of the performance of the fuzzy control set designed is shown, evaluating the estimation reliability of the variable *Acquisition* against the true receiver state at every simulation time. The second evaluation devoted to study the whole multiresolutive structure performance. The results for the fuzzy multiresolutive structure are compared with the previously presented multiresolutive structure with a stability control (Morán et al., 2001).

Tests have been made using the four scenarios described in Section 4.1.2.1; in all simulations the same 128 chip PN sequence, obtained using an evolutionary strategy has been used (Alsina et al., 2007a). In each test (for a certain SNR and a certain scenario) 600 symbols length data sequences have been used, and ten repetitions have been simulated using different channel initialization; the presented results are the mean of all these evaluations.

5.1 Evaluation of the control system performance

In the evaluation of the control system performance three variables have been measured. The first is the % of correct acquisition estimations, comparing the *Acquisition* value with the a posteriori measured probability of being acquired. The second is the % of incorrect acquisition estimations, but only for the optimistic ones; this means to evaluate when the fuzzy control system estimates the multiresolutive structure is acquired (assuming this is when *Acquisition* variable value is over 0.5), and the system real estimation of the acquisition position is incorrect. The last one is the % of incorrect acquisition estimation, but only for the pessimistic ones; this means to evaluate when the fuzzy control system estimates the multiresolutive structure is not acquired (assuming this is when *Acquisition* variable is under 0.5), and the system real estimation of the acquisition point is correct.

In Figure 15 these measurements are depicted. As shown in Figure 15.a, the % of correct fuzzy acquisition estimations perform good values, near 100%, except for the range of [-38,-35] dB, where all four scenarios present hit values of around 20%. This is due to a threshold SNR value, where the ratios make confusing evaluations due to the high level of noise. But this fact is temporary, because when the SNR worsens, the ratios evaluated make the fuzzy system converge to the correct evaluation; however, in this case quite a lot of evaluations are for **Not Acquired**.

The error performance evaluations are shown in Figures 15.b and 15.c. These figures outstand that most of the incorrect evaluations are for the system output indicating **Not Acquired** when the system is really **Acquired**. They also show that the *optimistic* incorrect estimations are really better than those related to the *pessimistic* ones. These results are the main indicators of a good system robustness: the system remotely considers *Acquisition* wrongly, so the information detection process works only for the correct *Acquisition* situations. Although this

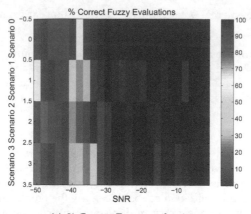

(a) % Correct Fuzzy evaluations

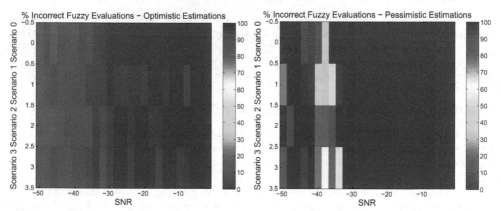

(b) % Incorrect Fuzzy evaluations - *Optimistic* (c) % Incorrect Fuzzy evaluations - *Pessimistic* Errors   Errors

Fig. 15. Performance of the Fuzzy Logic Control. Measurements about the correct and incorrect evaluations.

factor, it must be taken into account that some bad estimations (*pessimistic* ones) prevent the system from obtaining better information ratios in certain ranges of SNR [-38,-35] dB.

5.2 Evaluation of the Fuzzy Multiresolutive Acquisition vs. the Multiresolutive Structure

The evaluation of the Fuzzy Multiresolutive Acquisition structure vs. the Multiresolutive Structure (Morán et al., 2001) is based on the comparison of the *Acquisition* estimation evaluated for both systems, obviously using the same channel conditions for the two systems.

5.2.1 The stability control for the Multiresolutive Structure

The Multiresolutive Structure presented by (Morán et al., 2001) works with a stability control. This control is based on the robustness of the filter convergence, using it as a premise for its design. The stability control gives an output **Acquired** if the adaptive filter structure presents the same results for a certain number of times (in this case, three times). In the work of (Morán et al., 2001) it is shown that the probability of being acquired increases as the acquistion position is more stable, and the stability control is based in this principle. The problems of the performance of this kind of stability control solution are lack of robustness in low SNR environments, interference and fading, and of course, multipath, because it cannot recognize a correct acquisition situation immediately; it was designed for enhance stability, so it keeps a **Not Acquired** output until the acquisition position is stable again.

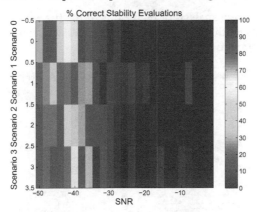

(a) % Correct Stability evaluations

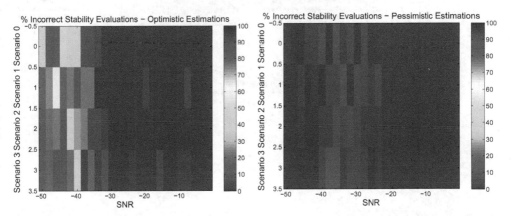

(b) % Incorrect Stability evaluations - *Optimistic* (c) % Incorrect Stability evaluations - *Pessimistic* Errors   Errors

Fig. 16. Performance of the Stability Control. Measurements about the correct and incorrect evaluations.

This lack of robustness is improved with the design of the fuzzy control system, because its estimation uses various instantaneous parameters, so reacquisition is faster; the fact of relying on four different parameters ensures the robustness of the system, despite instantaneous non convergence situations for the LMS filters.

The results for the stability control solution are shown in Figures 16. Figure 16.a shows the correct performance of the stability control, and Figures 16.b and 16.c show the performance for the incorrect stability evaluations, the first for the optimistic errors, and the second one for the pessimistic. Figure 16.b depicts high optimistic error, which deal to the multiresolutive structure to assume acquisition when it is not. This fact globally increases the BER at the receiver in terms of confidence in the demodulation of the information.

5.2.2 Comparison results

In this Section a comparative analysis of the results of the fuzzy and the stability controls is made. Numerical results for the four scenarios are computed, and the mean of these results is taken into account to compare the two control systems.

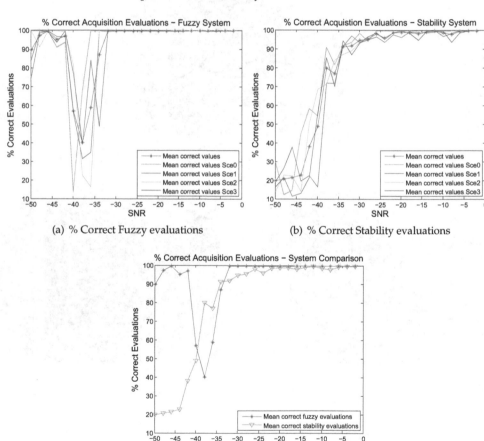

(a) % Correct Fuzzy evaluations

(b) % Correct Stability evaluations

(c) Comparison of the correct evaluations for Fuzzy
and Stability controls

Fig. 17. Comparison of the correct evaluations for both fuzzy and stability controls.

In Figure 17 an analysis of the performance for the correct estimation for both controls is done. In Figure 17.c the comparison for both is made in terms of %. The fuzzy control performs better for each SNR value except for the range [-38,-35] dB, where it performs worse, despite the lowest SNR values back to get into a proper operation. It has to be noticed that the stability control starts performing bad around -37 dB, and does not recover for worse SNR.

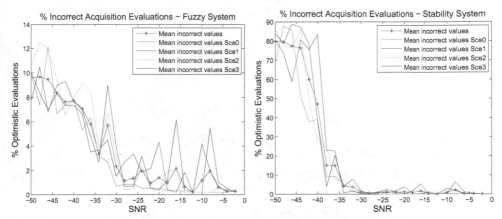

(a) % Incorrect *Optimistic* Fuzzy Control system evaluations

(b) % Incorrect *Optimistic* Stability Control system evaluations

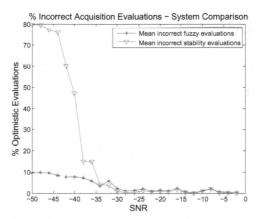

(c) Comparison of the incorrect *Optimistic* evaluations for Fuzzy and Stability Controls

Fig. 18. Comparison of the incorrect evaluations for both fuzzy and stability controls, in case that the error is *optimistic*.

Figure 18 shows the incorrect optimistic evaluations for both fuzzy and stability controls. Optimistic error is very low for fuzzy control at any SNR (see Figure 18.a), and for stability control is just the opposite: it has very high optimistic error, especially for lower SNR (see Figure 18.b, and 18.c for a comparison between the two control systems). Then, the use of the stability control makes the multiresolutive structure be confident in the information demodulation of the system when it is really not correctly acquired, and BER increases in the receiver.

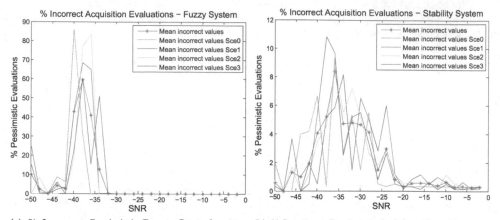

(a) % Incorrect *Pessimistic* Fuzzy Control system evaluations

(b) % Incorrect *Pessimistic* Stability Control system evaluations

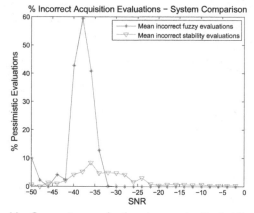

(c) Comparison of the incorrect *Pessimistic* evaluations for Fuzzy and Stability Controls

Fig. 19. Comparison of the incorrect evaluations for both fuzzy and stability controls, in case that the error is *pessimistic*.

In Figure 19 the pessimistic error for both controls is shown. In this case, Figure 19.a depicts a bad performance of the fuzzy control system for values ranging [-38,-35] dB, but its performance becomes better when SNR worsen. Figure 19.b outstands a more constant performance for the stability control in the case of the pessimistic error.

5.3 Multiresolutive structure acquisition feedback

Finally, the possibilities of improving the performance of the multiresolutive structure (Morán et al., 2001) are shown through visualization of the output *Acquisition* behavior for the fuzzy

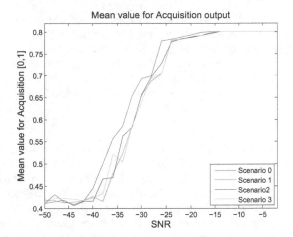

Fig. 20. Mean output *Acquisition* values for the four scenarios

control system. The most important advantage of fuzzy logic vs. a stability control is that the quality of the acquisition can be measured; for high values of *Acquisition*, the performance of the system is better, for lower, the convergence is not guaranteed.

In Figure 20 the mean values of output variable *Acquisition* of the fuzzy control system are shown (each value is computed for a specific scenario and SNR). This figure shows the information that the fuzzy control gives to the decisional system of the multiresolutive structure. At first, it is used to set the convergence (see the details in Section 4.4). If the value of *Acquisition* is higher than 0.75, the convergence is nearly guaranteed, and the system does not need to run all the adaptive filters at each symbol time. If the value of *Acquisition* is between 0.5 and 0.75, the system is **Probably Acquired**, but keeps searching to improve acquisition. But if *Acquisition* is between 0.25 and 0.75, the decisional system moves the data for the acquisition stage by $\frac{T_s}{4}$, and evaluates the improvement of the convergence of the filters. Finally, if the *Acquisition* value is lower than 0.25, the decisional system moves the data for the acquisition stage by $\frac{T_s}{2}$ and evaluates the convergence improvement. In the current simulations, although some of the outputs for *Acquisition* were lower than 0.25, the values of the SNR tested mean *Acquisition* were evaluated over 0.4.

The second advantage of using continuous output values for the *Acquisition* variable is reducing computational load by stopping the search - filters LMS adaptation - during acquisition state. Nearly $\frac{3}{4}$ of the computational load of the LMS filters can be reduced in case of certain acquisition (shown through variable *Acquisition* value over 0.75) for SNR values ranging [-20,0] dB approximately, while this is not possible to be done using a stability control.

5.4 Summary

In this section, the evaluation results have been shown for the performance of the fuzzy logic controller in the multiresolutive acquisition structure. The fuzzy logic control system shows good performance even for low SNR, except for the values in the range [-38,-35]dB; in this range the estimation error increases due to *pessimistic* errors. In comparison with the stability control, the global behavior is improved because the fuzzy control has better results above the critical margin of [-38,-35]dB, and it behaves really well for lower SNR. Another clear advantage of the fuzzy control against the stability control is the wider range of possible output values. This fact allows the multiresolutive structure to decrease its computational load when the system is clearly acquired, and also to change the acquisition pointer in case of a far acquisition estimated point; this information enhances the receiver performance, not only in terms of reliability, but also in terms of computational load.

6. Conclusions

In this chapter a novel fuzzy control system for a multiresolutive acquisition structure (Morán et al., 2001) is detailed. It can be concluded that the four computed ratios used as input values for the control system ($Ratio_1$, $Ratio_2$, $Ratio_3$ and $Ratio_{1trac}$) perform coherently with the results of the multiresolutive structure. Therefore, decisions can be made attending to their values. It can be stated that these ratios stand out for the performance of the whole system, and their values for the four simulated scenarios are found in the same range of values. Therefore, we conclude that they might be useful to describe and optimize the system performance.

The fuzzy logic control gives a more precise output acquisition variable allowing the system to conclude whether it is correctly acquired, probably acquired, probably not acquired, and not acquired; then, the control logic can optimize the computational load of the structure depending on these values. If the system is correctly acquired (depending on the value for *Acquisition*), the decisional system reduces the global computational load by stopping the convergence of some LMS adaptive filters (despite the detailed computational load study is not included in this chapter). So, not only the acquisition estimation is improved, but also the global performance of the structure is optimized. The only SNR range where the fuzzy control system performance can significantly be improved is around [-40,-35] dB, where this performance is poor. It is also important to note that the correct estimation of the acquisition for very low SNR values helps the system in terms of confidence about the demodulated information; in case of the stability control, for values worse than -36 dB the information demodulated is notoriously unreliable; and for fuzzy control, *Acquisition* continuous value gives enough information to know whether the system is out of the correct acquistion area, and hence the system not being confident on the information results. Future research is focused in improving the performance of the fuzzy control in the multiresolutive structure, especially at specific levels of SNR where the results behavior is pessimistic, in order to increase the reliability of the system estimation.

The results shown in this chapter stand out for the application of fuzzy control systems to other acquisition schemes found in the literature, and allow us to state that our work represents an interesting proposal to the future research in this field; the LMS adaptive scheme presented by (El-Tarhuni & Sheikh, 1996), lately improved by (Han et al., 2006), and also the adaptive system for ocean acquisition transmission presented by (Stojanovic & Freitag, 2003). We think that the knowledge of the channel characteristics and the behavior of the LMS filter convergence would be the first data to be taken into account to the design a fuzzy control system conceived with the aim of improving the stability and the robustness of any acquisition receiver for a DS-SS communications system. This aspect is highlighted here, because control systems designed to operate within LMS-based adaptive acquisition schemes found in the literature do not consider other information rather than the stability of the acquisition estimation.

7. Acknowledgments

This work has been funded by the Spanish Government under the projects REN2003-08376-C02-02, CGL2006-12437-C02-01/ANT, CTM2008-03236-E/ANT, CTM2009-13843-C02-02 and CTM2010-21312-C03-03. La Salle thanks the *Comissionat per a Universitats i Recerca del DIUE de la Generalitat de Catalunya* for their support under the grant 2009SGR459. We must also acknowledge the support of the scientists of the Observatory de l'Ebre throughout the research work.

8. References

Akhter, N., Ferdouse, L., Jaigirdar, F. & Nipa, T. (2010). A Performance Analysis of LMS, RLS and Lattice based Algorithms as Applied to the Area of Linear Prediction, *Journal of Global Research in Computer Science* 1: 49–53.

Alsina, R., Bernadó, E. & Morán, J. (2005b). Evolution Strategies for DS-CDMA Pseudonoise Sequence Design, *Frontiers in Artificial Intelligence and Applications - Artificial Intelligence Research and Development* 131: 189 – 196. IOS Press.

Alsina, R. M., Bergadà, P., Socoró, J. C. & Deumal, M. (2009a). Multiresolutive Acquisition Technique for DS-SS Long-Haul HF Data Link, *Proceedings of the 11th Ionospheric Radio Systems and Techniques (IRST)*, IET, Edimburgh (Regne Unit).

Alsina, R. M., Formiga, L., Socoró, J. C. & Bernadó, E. (2007a). Multiobjective Evolution Strategies for DS-CDMA Pseudonoise Sequence Design in a Multiresolutive Acquisition, *Frontiers in Artificial Intelligence and Applications - Artificial Intelligence Research and Development* 163: 384 – 391. IOS Press.

Alsina, R. M., Mateo, C., Socoró, J. C. & Deumal, M. (2008). Neural Network Acquistition Estimator for Multiresolutive Adaptive PN Acquisition Scheme in Multiuser Non Selective Fast SNR Variation Environments, *8th International Conference on Hybrid Intelligent Systems (HIS)*, Barcelona (Espanya).

Alsina, R., Mateo, C. & Socoró, J. (2007b). Multiresolutive Adaptive PN Acquisition Scheme with a Fuzzy Logic Estimator in Non Selective Fast SNR Variation Environments, *Lecture Notes in Computer Science - Springer Verlag* 4507: 367 – 374. International Work-c onference on Artificial Neural Networks (IWANN).

Alsina, R., Mateo, C. & Socoró, J. (2009b). *Artificial Intelligence Enciclopaedia*, IGI Global, (EUA), chapter 'F': Fuzzy Logic Estimator for Variant SNR Environments, pp. 719–728.

Alsina, R., Morán, J. & Socoró, J. (2005a). Sequential PN Acquisition Scheme Based on a Fuzzy Logic Controller, *Lecture Notes in Computer Science - Springer Verlag* 3512: 1238 – 1245. International Work-conference on Artificial Neural Networks (IWANN).

Bas, J. & Perez-Neira, A. (2003). A Fuzzy Logic System for Interference Rejection in Code Division Multiple Access, *IEEE International Conference on Fuzzy Systems* 2: 996–1001.

Bergadà, P., Deumal, M., Alsina, R. & Pijoan, J. (2009). Time Interleaving Study for an OFDM Long-Haul HF Radio Link, *in* T. IET (ed.), *Proceedings of the 11th Ionospheric Radio Systems and Techniques*, Edimburgh (UK).

Daffara, F. (1995). A Fuzzy Rule Based Phase Error Detector, *Proceedings of URSI International Symposium on Signals, Systems, and Electronics*.

Deumal, M., Vilella, C., Socoró, J., Alsina, R. & Pijoan, J. (2006). A DS-SS Signaling Based System Proposal for Low SNR HF Digital Communications, *IEEE International Conference on Ionospheric Radio Systems and Techniques*, IEEE, London, UK.

Drake, J. & Prasad, N. (1999). Current Trends Towards Using Soft Computing Approaches to Phase Shyncrhonization in Communications Systems, *IEEE 42nd Midwest Symposium on Circuits and Systems*.

El-Tarhuni, M. & Sheikh, A. (1996). MSE Tracking Performance of DS-SS Code Tracking Scheme Using an Adaptive Filter, *Electronic Letters* 32: 1543–1545.

Gad, A. & Farouq, M. (2001). Applications of Fuzzy Logic in Engineering Problems, *Proceedings of the Annual Conference of IEEE Industrial Electronics Society*.

Glisic, S. G. (1991). Automatic Decision Threshold Level Control in Direct Sequence Spread Spectrum Systems, *IEEE Transactions on Communications* 39(2): 519–527.

Glisic, S. & Vucetic, B. (1997). *Spread Spectrum CDMA Systems for Wireless Communications*, Artech House Publishers, United States of America.

Han, M., Yu, T., Kang, C. & Hong, D. (2006). A New Adaptive Code-Acquisition Algorithm Using Parallel Subfilter Structure, *IEEE Transactions on Vehicular Technology* 55(6): 1790–1796.

Haykin, S. (1996). *Adaptive Filter Theory*, Prentice Hall International, United States of America.

Morán, J., Socoró, J., Jové, X., Pijoan, J. & Tarrés, F. (2001). Multiresolution Adaptive Structure for acquisition in DS-SS receivers, *International Conference on Acoustics, Speech and Signal Processing* .

Perez-Neira, A. & Lagunas, M. (1996). High Performance DOA Trackers Derived from Parallel Low Resolution Detectors, *IEEE Workshop on SSAP*.

Perez-Neira, A., Lagunas, M. & Bas, J. (1997). Fuzzy Logic for Robust Detection in Wireless Communications, *Proceedings of the 8th IEEE International Symposium on Personal, Indoor and Mobile Radio Communications*.

Peterson, R., Ziemer, R. & Borth, D. (1995). *Introduction to Spread Spectrum Communications*, Prentice Hall, United States of America.

Proakis, J. (1995). *Digital Communications*, McGraw-Hill, Singapore.

Sklar, B. (1988). *Digital Communications, Fundamentals and Applications*, Prentice Hall International, United States of America.

Stojanovic, M. & Freitag, L. (2003). Acquisition of Direct Sequence Spread Spectrum Acoustic Communication Signals, *Oceans* 1: 279 – 286.

Vilella, C., Miralles, D., Altadill, D., Acosta, F., Sole, J., Torta, J. M. & Pijoan, J. (2009). Vertical and Oblique Ionospheric Soundings over a Very Long Multihop HF Radio Link from Polar to Midlatitudes: Results and Relationships, *Radio Science* 44.

Vilella, C., Miralles, D. & Pijoan, J. (2008). An Antarctica-to-Spain HF ionospheric radio link: Sounding results, *Radio Sci.* 43(doi:10.1029/2007RS003812).

Zadeh, L. (1965). Fuzzy Sets, *IEEE Transactions on Information and Control* 8: 338–353.

Zadeh, L. (1988). Fuzzy Logic, *Computer* 21(4): 83–92.

10

Precision Position Control of Servo Systems Using Adaptive Back-Stepping and Recurrent Fuzzy Neural Networks

Jong Shik Kim, Han Me Kim and Seong Ik Han
School of Mechanical Engineering, Pusan National University,
Republic of Korea

1. Introduction

To improve product quality in high-tech industrial fields and in precision product processes, high precision position control systems have been developed. However, high precision position control systems have been faced with a friction problem that exists between the contact surfaces of two materials and produces an obstacle to the precise motion, because the friction is very sensitive to nonlinear time-varying effects such as temperature, lubrication condition, material texture, and contamination degree. Thus, the tracking performance of servo systems can be seriously deteriorated because of the nonlinear friction characteristics.

To overcome the friction problem and to obtain high performance of servo control systems, an appropriate friction model (Olsson, 1998) to describe the nonlinear friction characteristics is required. The LuGre model (Canudas de Wit, 1995) is a representative model. Researchers have used this model because it has a simple structure to be implemented in the design of the controller and can represent most of the friction characteristics except the pre-sliding characteristic.

Model-based control methods for precision position control can be divided into two methods. The first one is the friction feed-forward compensation scheme, which needs the identification of the nonlinear friction phenomena (Olsson, 1998)(Canudas de Wit, 1995). However, it takes a long time and much effort to identify the nonlinear friction. In addition, even with successful completion of the friction identification process, it is difficult to achieve desirable tracking performance due to the nonlinear friction characteristics. Therefore, to achieve desirable tracking performance of servo systems, a robust control scheme should be used simultaneously with the friction feed-forward compensator (Lee, 2004).

The second method is the real time estimation scheme for nonlinear friction coefficients, which is called as the adaptive friction control scheme. This method can actively cope with the variation of the nonlinear friction, which has been proved and studied through experiments (Canudas de Wit, 1997)(Lischinsky, 1999)(Ha, 2000)(Tan, 1999). However, to generate the adaptation rules for the friction coefficients based on the LuGre friction model, a detailed mathematical approach is required. In addition, since the mathematical model of the nonlinear friction may include system uncertainties such as unmodeled dynamics, which can cause an undesirable position tracking error of servo systems.

To compensate these system uncertainties and to improve tracking performance, artificial intelligent algorithms such as fuzzy logic and neural networks have been applied because of their advantages to cope with system uncertainties (Wai, 2003)(Leu, 1997)(Peng, 2007)(Lin, 2006). In general, fuzzy logic and neural network algorithms are effective in inferring ambiguous information because of their logicality such as adaptation for learning ability, capacity for experiences, and parallel process ability (Lin, 1996). The fuzzy neural network(FNN) combining the advantages of fuzzy logic and neural network algorithms was presented (Leu, 1997)(Peng, 2007). However, in real applications, the FNN has a static problem due to its feed-forward network characteristics. Therefore, to overcome this static problem of the FNN, the recurrent fuzzy neural network(RFNN) with robust characteristics due to its feed-back structure was presented (Peng, 2007)(Lin, 2006)(Lin, 2004).

In this paper, an adaptive back-stepping control scheme with the RFNN technique is proposed so that servo systems with nonlinear friction uncertainties can achieve higher precision position tracking performance. A dual adaptive friction observer is also designed to observer the internal states of the nonlinear friction model. The position tracking performance of the proposed control system is evaluated through experiments.

The organization of this paper is as follows: In section 2, the dynamic equations for the position servo system with the LuGre friction model are described. In section 3, to estimate the unknown friction coefficients and to overcome system uncertainties in a position servo system, the adaptive back-stepping controller based on the dual friction observer and the recurrent fuzzy neural networks are designed. In section 4, the experimental results of the tracking performance, the observation of the states, and the estimation of the friction coefficients are shown. Finally, the conclusion is given in section 5.

2. Modeling of a position servo system

The layout of a position servo system consists of mass, linear motion guide, ball-screw, and servo motor as shown in Fig. 1. The dynamic equation for the position servo system can be briefly represented as

$$J\ddot{\theta} = u - T_f - T_d \qquad (1)$$

where J is the moment of inertia of the servo system, $\ddot{\theta}$ is the angular acceleration of the screw, u is the control input torque, T_f is the friction torque, and T_d is the disturbance torque due to system uncertainties.

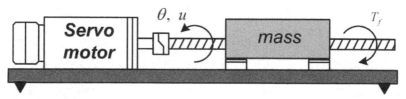

Fig. 1. Layout of the position servo system

The LuGre model is used for modeling the friction in the position servo system. The LuGre model can describe the nonlinear friction characteristics between two contact surfaces in a mechanical system. As shown in Fig. 2, the relative motion between two contact surfaces can be represented by bristles.

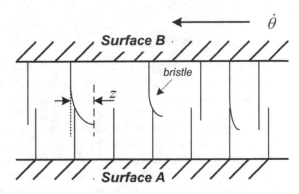

Fig. 2. Friction interfaces with bristles between two surfaces

The stiffness and damping of bristles can be modeled with springs and dampers, respectively. Canudas de Wit represented the average deflection of bristles by a state variable z as follows (Canudas de Wit, 1997) :

$$\dot{z} = \dot{\theta} - \sigma_0 h(\dot{\theta})z, \tag{2}$$

$$h(\dot{\theta}) = \frac{|\dot{\theta}|}{g(\dot{\theta})} \tag{3}$$

where

$$g(\dot{\theta}) = T_c + (T_s - T_c)e^{-(\dot{\theta}/\dot{\theta}_{st})^2}$$

and $\dot{\theta}$ is the generalized velocity, $\dot{\theta}_{st}$ is the Stribeck velocity, σ_0 is the nominal static friction parameter, T_s is the static friction torque, and T_c is the Coulomb friction torque. Also, the friction torque T_f was represented as

$$T_f = \mu_0 z + \mu_1 \dot{z} + \mu_2 \dot{\theta} \tag{4}$$

where μ_0, μ_1, and μ_2 are the bristle stiffness coefficient, bristle damping coefficient, and viscous damping coefficient, respectively. The function $g(\cdot)$ is assumed to be known and to be a positive value, and it depends on some factors such as material properties and temperature. In order to consider the friction torque variations due to the contact condition of the position servo system, the coefficients μ_0, μ_1, and μ_2 are assumed to be independent unknown positive constants.

Substituting Eqs. (2), (3), and (4) into Eq. (1), the dynamic equation for the position servo system with friction can be expressed as

$$J\ddot{\theta} = u - \mu_0 z + \mu_3 h(\dot{\theta})z - \mu_4\dot{\theta} - T_d \tag{5}$$

where

$$\mu_3 = \sigma_0\mu_1, \ \mu_4 = \mu_1 + \mu_2.$$

3. Design of an adaptive control system

System uncertainties such as high nonlinear friction characteristics according to the operation condition should be considered in precise position servo systems. Thus, feedback linearization and robust control schemes can be considered to reject system nonlinearity and have robustness to unmodeled dynamics, respectively. However, the robust control schemes may not be appropriate for precise position control because these schemes require some premises on bounded uncertainties and bounded disturbance. In addition, if the information on system uncertainties is not included in the control scheme, the feedback linearization scheme may not achieve high precision position tracking performance and make servo systems unstabilize. To overcome these problems in position control servo systems, it is desirable to apply an adaptive control scheme.

3.1 Design of back-stepping controller

The back-stepping control(BSC) system can be designed step by step as follows (Krstic, 1995):

Step 1. To achieve the desired tracking performance, the tracking error is defined by the new state y_1 as

$$y_1 = \theta - \theta_r \tag{6}$$

where θ_r is the reference input. The derivative of y_1 is expressed as

$$\dot{y}_1 = \dot{\theta} - \dot{\theta}_r. \tag{7}$$

We define a stabilizing function α_1 as

$$\alpha_1 = \dot{\theta}_r - k_1 y_1 \tag{8}$$

where k_1 is a positive constant. The Lyapunov control function (LCF) V_1 is selected as

$$V_1 = \frac{1}{2}y_1^2 \tag{9}$$

Then, the derivative of V_1 is expressed as

$$\dot{V}_1 = y_1\dot{y}_1 = y_1(\dot{\theta} - \alpha_1 - k_1 y_1) = y_1 y_2 - k_1 y_1^2 \tag{10}$$

where $y_2 = \dot{\theta} - \alpha_1$.

Step 2. The velocity tracking error is defined by the new state y_2 as

$$y_2 = \dot{\theta} - \alpha_1. \tag{11}$$

The derivative of y_2 can be obtained as

$$\dot{y}_2 = \ddot{\theta} - \dot{\alpha}_1 = \frac{1}{J}(u - \mu_0 z + \mu_3 h(\dot{\theta})z - \mu_4 \dot{\theta} - T_d) - \dot{\alpha}_1. \tag{12}$$

From Eq. (12), in order to select a feedback control law that can guarantee system stability, the LCF for Eq. (11) is selected as

$$V_2 = V_1 + \frac{1}{2} y_2^2. \tag{13}$$

The derivative of V_2 can be represented as

$$\dot{V}_2 = \dot{V}_1 + y_2 \dot{y}_2 = -k_1 y_1^2 + y_2 [y_1 + \frac{1}{J}(u - \mu_0 z + \mu_3 h(\dot{\theta})z - \mu_4 \dot{\theta} - T_d) - \dot{\alpha}_1]. \tag{14}$$

If the last term in Eq. (14) is defined as

$$y_1 + \frac{1}{J}(u - \mu_0 z + \mu_3 h(\dot{\theta})z - \mu_4 \dot{\theta} - T_d) - \dot{\alpha}_1 = -k_2 y_2 \tag{15}$$

where $k_2 (> 0)$ is a design parameter, then the BSC law as the feedback control law can be selected as

$$u = J(-y_1 - k_2 y_2 + \dot{\alpha}_1) + \mu_0 z - \mu_3 h(\dot{\theta})z + \mu_4 \dot{\theta} + T_d. \tag{16}$$

However, in Eq. (16), the internal state z of the friction model cannot be measured, and friction parameters and the disturbance torque T_d cannot be known exactly. In addition, if the friction terms in Eq. (16) cannot be exactly considered in position control servo systems, a large steady-state error may occur.

3.2 Design of adaptive back-stepping controller and dual friction observer

In order to select a desired control law, a dual-observer (Tan, 1999) to estimate the unmeasurable internal state z in the friction model is applied as follows:

$$\dot{\hat{z}}_0 = \dot{\theta} - \sigma_0 h(\dot{\theta})\hat{z}_0 + \eta_0, \tag{17}$$

$$\dot{\hat{z}}_1 = \dot{\theta} - \sigma_0 h(\dot{\theta})\hat{z}_1 + \eta_1, \tag{18}$$

where $\hat{z}_0$ and $\hat{z}_1$ are the estimated values of the internal states in the friction model, and η_0 and η_1 are the observer dynamic terms which can be obtained from an adaptive rule. The corresponding observation errors are given by

$$\dot{\tilde{z}}_0 = -\sigma_0 h(\dot{\theta})\tilde{z}_0 - \eta_0, \tag{19}$$

$$\dot{\tilde{z}}_1 = -\sigma_0 h(\dot{\theta})\tilde{z}_1 - \eta_1, \tag{20}$$

where $\tilde{z}_0 = z - \hat{z}_0$ and $\tilde{z}_1 = z - \hat{z}_1$. Equations (19) and (20) will be induced from the adaptive rule.

In order to induce the adaptive rule to guarantee stability against unknown parameters and the observer dynamic terms, the reconstruction error E is defined as

$$E = T_d - \hat{T}_d \tag{21}$$

where $\hat{T}_d$ is the estimated value of T_d and it is assumed that $|E| \leq \overline{E}$, where $\overline{E}$ denotes the bounded value of E.

We now select the 3rd LCF as follows:

$$V_3 = V_2 + \frac{1}{2\rho}(\hat{E} - E)^2 \tag{22}$$

where $\rho(>0)$ is a positive constant and $\hat{E}$ is the estimated value of the reconstruction error. The derivative of V_3 can be represented as

$$\dot{V}_3 = \dot{V}_2 + \frac{1}{\rho}(\hat{E} - E)\dot{\hat{E}} = -k_1 y_1^2 + y_2[y_1 + \frac{1}{J}(u - \mu_0 z + \mu_3 h(\dot{\theta})z - \mu_4\dot{\theta} - T_d) - \dot{\alpha}_1] + \frac{1}{\rho}(\hat{E} - E)\dot{\hat{E}} \tag{23}$$

From Eq. (23), the adaptive back-stepping control(ABSC) law can be selected as

$$u = J(-y_1 - k_2 y_2 + \dot{\alpha}_1) + \hat{\mu}_0 \hat{z}_0 - \hat{\mu}_3 h(\dot{\theta})\hat{z}_1 + \hat{\mu}_4 \dot{\theta} + \hat{T}_d + \hat{E} \tag{24}$$

Substituting Eq. (24) into Eq. (23), then

$$\dot{V}_3 = -k_1 y_1^2 - k_2 y_2^2 + \frac{y_2}{J}[-\mu_0 \tilde{z}_0 - \tilde{\mu}_0 \hat{z}_0 + \mu_3 h(\dot{\theta})\tilde{z}_1 + \tilde{\mu}_3 h(\dot{\theta})\hat{z}_1 - \tilde{\mu}_4 \dot{\theta}) + \hat{T}_d - T_d + \hat{E}] + \frac{1}{\rho}(\hat{E} - E)\dot{\hat{E}} \tag{25}$$

where $\tilde{\mu}_0 = \mu_0 - \hat{\mu}_0$, $\tilde{\mu}_3 = \mu_3 - \hat{\mu}_3$, and $\tilde{\mu}_4 = \mu_4 - \hat{\mu}_4$ are the unknown parameter estimate errors. The 4th LCF V_4 is selected as

$$V_4 = V_3 + \frac{1}{2}\mu_0 \tilde{z}_0^2 + \frac{1}{2}\mu_3 \tilde{z}_1^2 + \frac{1}{2\gamma_0}\tilde{\mu}_0^2 + \frac{1}{2\gamma_3}\tilde{\mu}_3^2 + \frac{1}{2\gamma_4}\tilde{\mu}_4^2. \tag{26}$$

The derivative of V_4 can be obtained as

$$\dot{V}_4 = -k_1 y_1^2 - k_2 y_2^2 - \mu_0 \sigma_0 h(\dot{\theta})\tilde{z}_0^2 - \mu_3 \sigma_0 h(\dot{\theta})\tilde{z}_1^2 + \tilde{\mu}_0(-\frac{y_2}{J}\hat{z}_0 - \frac{1}{\gamma_0}\dot{\hat{\mu}}_0) + \tilde{\mu}_3(\frac{y_2 h(\dot{\theta})}{J}\hat{z}_1 - \frac{1}{\gamma_3}\dot{\hat{\mu}}_3)$$
$$+ \tilde{\mu}_4(-\frac{y_2}{J}\dot{\theta} - \frac{1}{\gamma_4}\dot{\hat{\mu}}_4) + \tilde{z}_0(-\mu_0\frac{y_2}{J} - \mu_0\eta_0) + \tilde{z}_1(\mu_3\frac{y_2}{J}h(\dot{\theta}) - \mu_3\eta_1) + \tilde{E}(\frac{y_2}{J} + \frac{1}{\rho}\dot{\hat{E}}). \tag{27}$$

From Eq. (27), the update laws can be determined as

$$\dot{\hat{\mu}}_0 = -\frac{\gamma_0}{J}y_2\hat{z}_0, \tag{28}$$

$$\dot{\hat{\mu}}_3 = \frac{\gamma_3}{J}y_2 h(\dot{\theta})\hat{z}_1, \tag{29}$$

$$\dot{\hat{\mu}}_4 = -\frac{\gamma_4}{J}y_2\dot{\theta}, \tag{30}$$

and the observer dynamic terms are expressed as

$$\eta_0 = -\frac{y_2}{J}, \tag{31}$$

$$\eta_1 = \frac{y_2}{J}h(\dot{\theta}), \tag{32}$$

$$\dot{\hat{E}} = -\rho\frac{y_2}{J}. \tag{33}$$

Then, Eq. (27) can be represented as

$$\dot{V}_4 = -k_1 y_1^2 - k_2 y_2^2 - \mu_0 \sigma_0 h(\dot{\theta})\tilde{z}_0^2 - \mu_3 \sigma_0 h(\dot{\theta})\tilde{z}_1^2 \le -k_1 y_1^2 - k_2 y_2^2 \le 0. \tag{34}$$

From Eq. (34), we can define $W(y)$ as follows:

$$W(y) = k_1 y_1 + k_2 y_2 \le -\dot{V}(y_1, y_2) \tag{35}$$

Since $\dot{V} \le 0$, V is a non-increasing function. Thus, it has a limit V_∞ as $t \to \infty$. Integrating Eq. (35), then

$$\lim_{t\to\infty}\int_{t_0}^{t}W(y(\tau))d\tau \le -\lim_{t\to\infty}\int_{t_0}^{t}\dot{V}(y_1,y_2)d\tau = \lim_{t\to\infty}\{V(y(t_0),t_0)-V(y(t),t)\} = V(y(t_0),t_0)-V_\infty \quad (36)$$

which means that $\int_{t_0}^{t}W(y(\tau))d\tau$ exists and is finite. Since $W(y)$ is also uniformly continuous, the following result can be obtained from Barbalat lemma (Krstic, 1995)(Slotine, 1991) as

$$\lim_{t\to\infty}W(y)=0. \quad (37)$$

Since y_1 and y_2 are converged to zero as $t\to\infty$, θ and $\dot{\theta}$ approach to θ_r and $\dot{\theta}_r$, respectively, as $t\to\infty$. Therefore, the ABSC system can be asymptotically stable in spite of the variation of system parameters and external disturbance.

3.3 Design of recurrent fuzzy neural networks

To determine the lumped uncertainty T_d, a RFNN observer of a 4-layer structure is proposed, which is shown in Fig. 3. Layer 1 is the input layer with the recurrent loop, which accepts the two input variables. Layer 2 represents the fuzzy rules for calculating the Gaussian membership values. Layer 3 is the rule layer, which represents the preconditions and consequence for the links before and after layer 3, respectively. Layer 4 is the output layer. The interaction and learning algorithms for the layers are given as follows:

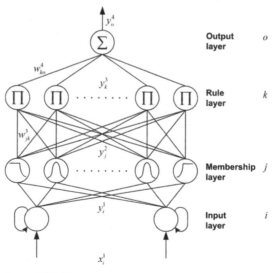

Fig. 3. A general four-layer RFNN

3.3.1 Description of the RFNN

Layer 1, Input layer: For each node i, the net input and output are represented, respectively, as

$$\text{net}_i^1 = x_i^1 + w_i^1 \cdot y_i^1(N-1), \tag{38}$$

$$y_i^1(N) = f_i^1(\text{net}_i^1(N)) = \text{net}_i^1(N), \ i = 1, 2 \tag{39}$$

where $x_1^1 = y_1$, $x_2^1 = \dot{y}$, w_i^1 is the recurrent weights, and N denotes the number of iterations.

Layer 2, Membership layer: For each node, the Gaussian membership values are calculated. For the j th node,

$$\text{net}_j^2(N) = -\frac{(x_i^2 - m_{ij})^2}{(\sigma_{ij})^2} \tag{40}$$

$$y_j^2(N) = f_j^2(\text{net}_j^2(N)) = \exp(\text{net}_j^2(N)), \ j = 1,...,n \tag{41}$$

where m_{ij} and σ_{ij} are the mean and standard deviation of the Gaussian function in the jth term of the ith input linguistic variable x_i^2 to the node of layer 2, respectively. n is the total number of the linguistic variables with respect to the input nodes.

Layer 3, Rule layer: Each node k in this layer is denoted by $\prod$. In addition, the input signals in this layer are multiplied each other and then the result of the product is generated.

$$\text{net}_k^3(N) = \prod_j w_{jk}^3 x_j^3(N), \tag{42}$$

$$y_k^3(N) = f_k^3(\text{net}_k^3(N)) = \text{net}_k^3(N), \ k = 1, ... , l \tag{43}$$

where x_j^3 represents the jth input to the node of layer 3, w_{jk}^3 is the weights between the membership layer and the rule layer. $l = (n/i)^i$ is the number of rules with complete rule connection, if each input node has the same linguistic variables.

Layer 4, Output layer: The single node o in this layer is labeled as Σ, which computes the overall output as the summation of all input signals:

$$\text{net}_o^4(N) = \sum_k w_{ko}^4 x_k^4(N), \tag{44}$$

$$y_o^4(N) = f_o^4(\text{net}_o^4(N)) = \text{net}_o^4(N) \tag{45}$$

where the connecting weight w_{ko}^4 is the output action strength of the oth output associated with the kth rule. x_k^4 represents the kth input to the node of layer 4, and $y_o^4 = \hat{T}_d$.

3.3.2 On-line learning algorithm

In the learning algorithm, it is important to select parameters for the membership functions and weights to decide network performance. In order to train the RFNN effectively, on-line parameter learning is executed by the gradient decent method. There are four adjustable parameters. Our goal is to minimize the error function e represented as

$$e = \frac{1}{2}(\theta_r - \theta)^2 = \frac{1}{2}(y_1)^2.$$

(46)

By using the gradient descent method, the weight in each layer is updated as follows:

Layer 4: The weight is updated by an amount

$$\Delta w_{ko}^4 = -\eta_w \frac{\partial e}{\partial w_{ko}^4} = \left(-\eta_w \frac{\partial e}{\partial u} \frac{\partial u}{\partial net_o^4}\right)\left(\frac{\partial net_o^4}{\partial w_{ko}^4}\right) = \eta_w y_1 x_k^4$$

(47)

where $y_1 = -\dfrac{\partial e}{\partial u}\dfrac{\partial u}{\partial net_o^4}$ and η_w is the learning-rate parameter of the connecting weights of the RFNN.

Layer 3: Since the weights in this layer are unified, the approximated error term needs to be calculated and propagated to calculate the error term of layer 2 as follows:

$$\delta_k^3 = -\frac{\partial e}{\partial net_k^3} = -\frac{\partial e}{\partial u}\frac{\partial u}{\partial net_o^4}\frac{\partial net_o^4}{\partial y_k^3}\frac{\partial y_k^3}{\partial net_k^3} = y_1 w_{ko}^4$$

(48)

Layer 2: The multiplication operation is executed in this layer by using Eq. (46). To update the mean of the Gaussian function, the error term is computed as follows:

$$\delta_j^2 = -\frac{\partial e}{\partial net_j^2} = -\frac{\partial e}{\partial u}\frac{\partial u}{\partial net_o^4}\frac{\partial net_o^4}{\partial y_k^3}\frac{\partial y_k^3}{\partial net_k^3}\frac{\partial net_k^3}{\partial y_j^2}\frac{\partial y_j^2}{\partial net_j^2} = \sum_k \delta_k^3 y_k^3$$

(49)

and then the update law of m_{ij} is

$$\Delta m_{ij} = -\eta_m \frac{\partial e}{\partial m_{ij}} = -\eta_m \frac{\partial e}{\partial y_j^2}\frac{\partial y_j^2}{\partial net_j^2}\frac{\partial net_j^2}{\partial m_{ij}} = \eta_m \delta_j^2 \frac{2(x_i^2 - m_{ij})}{\sigma_{ij}^2}$$

(50)

where η_m is the learning-rate parameter of the mean of the Gaussian functions. The update law of σ_{ij} is

$$\Delta \sigma_{ij} = -\eta_s \frac{\partial e}{\partial \sigma_{ij}} = -\eta_s \frac{\partial e}{\partial y_j^2}\frac{\partial y_j^2}{\partial net_j^2}\frac{\partial net_j^2}{\partial \sigma_{ij}} = \eta_s \delta_j^2 \frac{2(x_i^2 - m_{ij})^2}{\sigma_{ij}^3}$$

(51)

where η_s is the learning-rate parameter of the standard deviation of the Gaussian functions.

The weight, mean, and standard deviation of the hidden layer can be updated by using the following equations:

$$w_{ko}^4(N+1) = w_{ko}^4 + \Delta w_{ko}^4 \tag{52}$$

$$m_{ij}(N+1) = m_{ij}(N) + \Delta m_{ij} \tag{53}$$

$$\sigma_{ij}(N+1) = \sigma_{ij}(N) + \Delta \sigma_{ij} \tag{54}$$

4. Experiment results

Figure 4 shows the servo position tracking control system to evaluate the performance of control schemes. The angular position was measured with an incremental rotary encoder whose counts per encoder was 4 times of 10000 pulses per revolution. A data acquisition board with D/A 12-bit resolution was used to supply the driving voltage to the motor. The sampling rate of the servo system was selected as 500Hz. The control algorithms were programmed with C-language. The parameters of the servo system and friction model for experiment are shown in Table 1. The block diagram of the ABSC system with RFNN is shown in Fig. 5.

Fig. 4. Photograph of the servo position tracking control system

Parameter	Notation	Value
Moment of inertia	J	$2.3 \times 10^{-5}\,\text{kgm}^2$
Bristles stiffness coefficient	σ_0	$0.15\,\text{Nm}$
Stribeck velocity	$\dot{\theta}_{st}$	$0.013\,\text{rad/s}$
Coulomb friction	T_c	$1.97 \times 10^{-3}\,\text{Nm}$
Static friction	T_s	$2.6 \times 10^{-3}\,\text{Nm}$

Table 1. Parameters of the servo and friction model

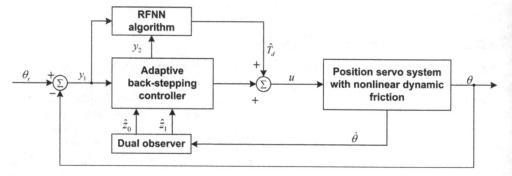

Fig. 5. Block diagram of the ABSC system with RFNN

In order to evaluate the performance of the servo system with the proposed control scheme, two reference inputs were applied as follows:

$$\theta_{r_1} = 0.1\sin(0.4\pi t)\ [\text{rad}],$$

$$\theta_{r_2} = 0.1\sin(0.125\pi t)\sin(0.75\pi t)\ [\text{rad}]$$

To compare the tracking performances of the BSC system, ABSC system, ABSC system with RFNN, the reference input θ_{r_1} was continuously used for experiment as follows: the BSC system was applied during the initial 20 seconds, the ABSC system during the 40 seconds after the application of the BSC system, and the ABSC system with RFNN during the 40 seconds after the application of the ABSC system. The reference input θ_{r_2} was independently experimented for the ABSC system and the ABSC system with RFNN, respectively. In addition, the structure of the RFNN is defined to two neurons at inputs of which each has the recurrent loop, five neurons at the membership layer, five neurons at the rule layer, and one neuron at the output layer. The fuzzy sets at the membership layer, which have the mean (m_{ij}) and standard deviation (σ_{ij}), were determined according to the maximum variation boundaries of y_1 and y_2 of the ABSC system without RFNN. m_{ij} and σ_{ij} vectors applied to experiment are selected as follows:

$$m_{1j} = [-0.002, -0.001, 0.0, 0.001, 0.002] \times \kappa_1,$$

$$m_{2j} = [-0.2, -0.1, 0.0, 0.1, 0.2] \times \kappa_2,$$

$$\sigma_{1j} = [0.003, 0.003, 0.003, 0.003, 0.003] \times \kappa_3,$$

$$\sigma_{2j} = [0.3, 0.3, 0.3, 0.3, 0.3] \times \kappa_4$$

where m_{1j} and σ_{1j} indicate the mean and standard deviation vectors of y_1, respectively, m_{2j} and σ_{2j} indicate the mean and standard deviation vectors of y_2, respectively, and $\kappa_i = 1, (i = 1, 2, 3, 4)$.

Figure 6 shows the error of the BSC system, ABSC system, and ABSC system with RFNN for the reference input θ_{r_1}. The angular displacement rms(root mean square) error of the BSC system is 0.0054. While the ABSC system is operating, its maximum error tends to exponentially decrease and then converge to a steady state value due to $\hat{\sigma}_0$, $\hat{\sigma}_3$, and $\hat{\sigma}_4$ by the update rules which are given by Eqs. (52), (53), and (54). The angular displacement rms error of the ABSC system is 0.0027. In the operating range of the ABSC system with RFNN, the angular displacement error converges to a steady state value after experiencing a transient state for about 1 second because of the switch from the ABSC system to the ABSC system with RFNN. The angular displacement rms error is 0.0005. The tracking performance of the ABSC system compared with it of the BSC system is improved by 2 times and it of the ABSC system with RFNN compared with it of the ABSC system is improved by 5.4 times. The performance improvement of the ABSC system with RFNN implies that the control input of the RFNN including the reconstruction estimation compensates system uncertainties.

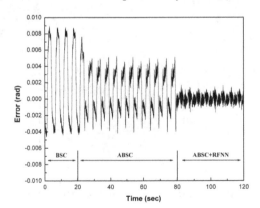

Fig. 6. Error of the BSC system, ABSC system, and ABSC system with RFNN for the reference input θ_{r_1}

Figure 7 shows the estimation and the observation of the BSC system, ABSC system, and ABSC system with RFNN for the reference input θ_{r_1}. The estimations by the update rule are shown in Fig. 7(a). The BSC system estimates the friction parameter to be 0, because the BSC system does not have the update rule for $\hat{\sigma}_0$, $\hat{\sigma}_3$, and $\hat{\sigma}_4$. When the ABSC system is applied to the servo system, the update rules estimates the friction parameters, which converge to some values; this convergence stabilizes the servo position system. When the ABSC system is switched to the ABSC system with RFNN, the estimations of the friction parameters do not vary because the angular displacement error is largely decreased by the RFNN. Therefore, the friction estimation values can maintain steady state in the operating range where the RFNN is used. Figure 7(b) shows the observations of the dual observer. The spike phenomenon of $\hat{z}_0$ among both observation values is occurred to a changing point of velocity, because y_2 corresponds to the velocity error, which directly affects $\hat{z}_0$, as described in Eq. (31). However, in the case of the ABSC system with RFNN, the spike phenomenon of $\hat{z}_0$ is largely removed, which means that the RFNN compensates system uncertainties such as nonlinear friction including Coulomb friction, static friction, Stribeck velocity, and unmodeled dynamics.

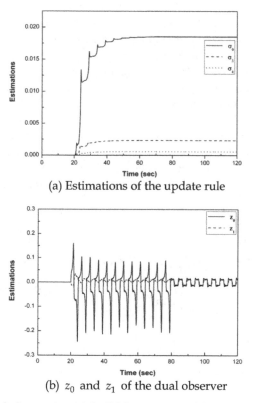

(a) Estimations of the update rule

(b) z_0 and z_1 of the dual observer

Fig. 7. Estimation and observation of the BSC system, ABSC system, and ABSC system with RFNN for the reference input θ_{r_1}

Figure 8 shows the estimated friction torque of the BSC system, ABSC system, and ABSC system with RFNN for the reference input θ_{r_1}. The estimated friction torques of the BSC system, ABSC system, and ABSC system with RFNN reflect the results of Fig. 7. Figure 9 shows the control input of the BSC system, ABSC system, and ABSC system with RFNN for the reference input θ_{r_1}. When the RFNN including reconstruction error estimation is

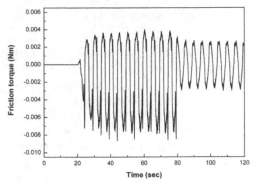

Fig. 8. Estimated friction torque of the BSC system, ABSC system, and ABSC system with RFNN for the reference input θ_{r_1}

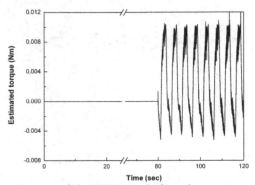

(a) Estimated torque of the RFNN including the reconstruction error

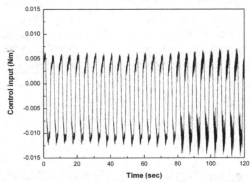

(b) Control input torque applied to the servo system

Fig. 9. Control inputs of the BSC system, ABSC system, and ABSC system with RFNN for the reference input θ_{r_1}

applied to the servo system at 80 seconds as shown in Fig. 9(a), a little more control input than before that is required to compensate system uncertainties as shown in Fig. 9(b). In addition, the deflection of the control input removes the deflection of the error for the BSC and ABSC systems, which is shown in Fig. 6.

Figure 10 shows the errors of the ABSC system and ABSC system with RFNN for the reference input θ_{r_2}. The reference input θ_{r_2} reflects a real situation and includes more system uncertainties because of the time varying amplitude sinusoidal input. In addition, the experiment conditions of the ABSC system and ABSC system with RFNN are all the same. The tracking error rms values of the ABSC system with RFNN and ABSC system are 0.0007 and 0.003, respectively. Therefore, the tracking rms error of the ABSC system with RFNN is four times less than that of the ABSC system, which implies that the RFNN is suitable for compensating system uncertainties.

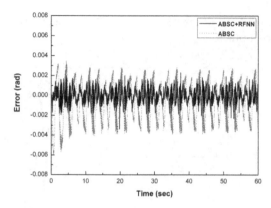

Fig. 10. Errors of the ABSC system, and ABSC system with RFNN for the reference input θ_{r_2}

Figure 11 shows the friction parameter estimations for the ABSC system and ABSC system with RFNN for the reference input θ_{r_2}. The estimations of the friction parameters converge to steady state values in about 20 seconds as shown in Fig. 11(a). The estimation values of the friction parameters for the ABSC system with RFNN are much smaller than those for the ABSC system, as shown in Fig. 11(b), because the RFNN and the reconstruction error estimator rapidly decrease the tracking error by reducing system uncertainties.

Figure 12 shows the estimated friction torques of the ABSC system and ABSC system with RFNN for the reference input θ_{r_2}. The parameters of the ABSC system with RFNN were estimated to be approximately 0, because the RFNN compensated system uncertainties including nonlinear friction. Therefore, the effectiveness of the RFNN was clearly demonstrated from the above results.

Figure 13 shows the control input of the ABSC system and ABSC system with RFNN for the reference input θ_{r_2}. The estimated torque of the RFNN including the reconstruction error and the control input torque applied to the servo motor are shown in Figs. 13(a) and (b), respectively. The ABSC system with RFNN generated a little more control input than the ABSC system due to the estimation result of the RFNN including the reconstruction error, as shown in Fig. 13(a). This implies that the ABSC system with RFNN compensates system uncertainties such as nonlinear friction and unmodeled dynamics, satisfactorily.

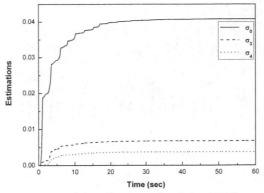

(a) Estimation of the adaptive rule of the ABSC system

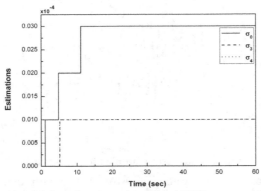

(b) Estimation of the adaptive rule of the ABSC system with RFNN

Fig. 11. Friction parameter estimations of the ABSC system and ABSC system with RFNN for the reference input θ_{r_2}

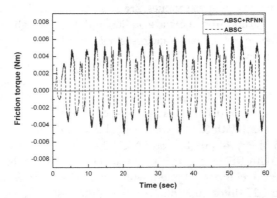

Fig. 12. Estimated friction torques of the ABSC system and ABSC system with RFNN for the reference input θ_{r_2}

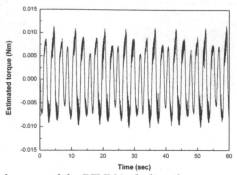

(a) Estimated torque of the RFNN including the reconstruction error

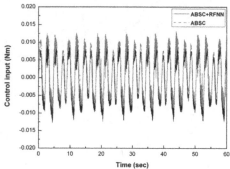

(b) Control input torque applied to the servo system

Fig. 13. Control input of the ABSC system and ABSC system with RFNN for the reference input θ_{r_2}

In order to show an influence of the RFNN parameters on control performance, two main parameters, which are m_{ij} and σ_{ij} of the Gaussian fuzzy membership function in Layer 2, are changed. Initial values of these values are selected by investigating the range and magnitude of y_1 and y_2, and then there are on-line updated through Eqs. (53) and (54). On the other hand, the change in the weight factors is not considered to experimental condition because of using initial random values.

Figure 14 shows the results of the ABSC system with the variation of m_{ij} and σ_{ij} in RFNN for the reference input θ_{r_2}. The changed conditions of the mean and standard deviation are $\kappa_i = 0.5$ and $\kappa_i = 1.5$. For $\kappa_i = 0.5$, the results of the error, estimation, and estimated friction torque of the ABSC system with RFNN are diverged due to the reduction of m_{ij} and σ_{ij} in 7.5 seconds as shown in Fig. 14 (a), (b), and (c). On the other hand, although the error state of the ABSC system with RFNN for $\kappa_i = 1.5$ is stable as shown in Fig. 14(a), the angular displacement rms error of compared system with the ABSC system with RFNN in Fig. 10 is minutely increased to 1.25 times. In addition, although the estimations of the adaptive rule of the ABSC system with RFNN as shown in Fig. 14(b) compared with their estimation values as shown in Fig. 11(b) is increased, their effect for the estimated friction torque is very small as shown in Fig. 14(c) compared with their estimated friction torque of the ABSC system as shown in Fig. 12, which reflects the result of Fig. 14(b). At this time, the ratio of the maximum friction torque in Fig. 12 to it in Fig. 14(c) is approximately 30 times. Thus, we can conclude that m_{ij} and σ_{ij} of the Gaussian membership function in the RFNN depend on the error output of the servo system. Finally, m_{ij} and σ_{ij} of the Gaussian membership function in the RFNN need to be carefully selected.

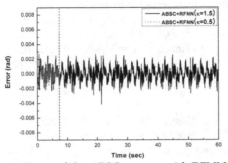

(a) Error of the ABSC system with RFNN

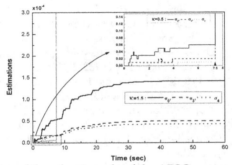

(b) Estimation of the adaptive rule of the ABSC system with RFNN

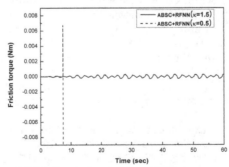

(c) Estimated friction torque of the ABSC system with RFNN

Fig. 14. Results of the ABSC system with the variation of m_{ij} and σ_{ij} in RFNN for the reference input θ_{r_2}

5. Conclunsion

The tracking performance of servo systems is deteriorated by nonlinear friction and system uncertainties, especially in the region where the direction of velocity of servo systems is changed. In order to reduce the effects of the friction and system uncertainties, a robust adaptive precision position control scheme is proposed. Unmeasurable state and parameters of the dynamic friction model are observed and estimated by the dual observer and the adaptive back-stepping controller, respectively. In order to actively cope with system uncertainties, the RFNN scheme is applied to the servo system. Experiments showed that the servo system with the dual observer, adaptive back-stepping controller, and RFNN including the reconstruction error estimator can achieve desired tracking performance and robustness. In addition, the influence of the mean and standard deviation of the RFNN parameters on control performance is shown through experiment.

6. References

C. Canudas de Wit and P. Lischinsky (1997), Adaptive Friction Compensation with Partially Known Dynamic Friction Model, *Int. J. Adaptive Control and Signal Processing*, 11, 65-80.

C. Canudas de Wit, H. Olsson, and P. Lischinsky (1995), A New Model for Control of Systems with Friction. *IEEE Trans. Automatic Control*, 40(3), 419-425.

C. H. Lin (2004), Adaptive Recurrent Fuzzy Neural Network Control for Synchronous Reluctance Motor Servo Drive, *IEE Proc. Electr. Power Appl.*, 151(6), 711-724.

C. T. Lin, and C. S. Greorge (1996), Neural Fuzzy Systems, *Prentice-Hall PTR*, New Jersey, USA.

F. J. Lin, S. L. Yang and P. H. Shen(2006), Self-Constructing Recurrent Fuzzy Neural Network for DSP-Based Permanent-Magnet Linear-Synchronous-Motor Servodrive, *IEE Proc. Electr. Power Appl.*, 153(2), 236-246.

H. Olsson, K. J. Astrom, C. C. Wit, M. Gafvert and P. Lischinsky (1998), Friction Models and Friction Compensation, *Eur. J. Control*, 4(3), 176–185.

J. J. Slotine and W. Li (1991), Applied Nonlinear Control, *Pearson Education*, New Jersey, USA.

J. Z. Peng, Y. N. Wang, W. Sun (2007), Trajectory-Tracking Control for Mobile Robot Using Recurrent Fuzzy Cerebellar Model Articulation Controller, *Neural Inform Process-Letters & Rev*, 11(1), 15-23.

K. J. Lee, H. M. Kim, and J. S. Kim (2004), Design of a Chattering-Free Sliding Mode Controller with a Friction Compensator for Motion Control of a Ball-Screw System, *Proc. ImechE Part-I, Journal of Systems and Control Engineering*, 218 (5), 369-380.

M. Krstic, I. Kanellakopoulos and P. Kokotovic (1995), Nonlinear and Adaptive Control Design, *Wiley Interscience*, New York, USA.

P. Lischinsky, C. Canudas de Wit, and G. Morel (1999), Friction Compensation for an Industrial Hydraulic Robot, *IEEE Contr. Syst. Mag.*, 19, 25-32.

Q. R. Ha, D. C. Rye, and H. F. Durrant-Whyte(2000), Variable Structure Systems Approach to Friction Estimation and Compensation. *Proc. of IEEE, Int. Control on Robot. & Auto*, 3543-3548.

R. J. Wai (2003), Robust Fuzzy Neural Network Control for Nonlinear Motor-Toggle Servomechanism, *Fuzzy Sets and Systems*, 139, 185-208.

Y. G. Leu, T. T. Lee and W. Y. Wang(1997), On-Line Turning of Fuzzy-Neural Networks for Adaptive Control of Nonlinear Dynamic Systems, *IEEE Trans. System Man Cybern*, 27(6), 1034-1043.

Y. Tan, and I. Kanellakopoulos (1999), Adaptive Nonlinear Friction Compensation with Parametric Uncertainties. *Proc. AACC*, 2511-2515.

11

Intelligent Neuro-Fuzzy Application in Semi-Active Suspension System

Seiyed Hamid Zareh, Atabak Sarrafan,
Meisam Abbasi and Amir Ali Akbar Khayyat
Sharif University of Technology, School of Science and Engineering,
Iran

1. Introduction

In the field of artificial intelligence, Neuro-Fuzzy (NF) refers to combinations of artificial neural networks and fuzzy logic and first time introduced in 1990s. Neuro-fuzzy results in a intelligent system that synergizes these two techniques by combining the human-like reasoning style of fuzzy systems with the learning and connectionist structure of neural networks. NF is widely termed as Fuzzy Neural Network (FNN) or Neuro-Fuzzy System (NFS) in the literature. NFS (the more popular term is used henceforth) incorporates the human-like reasoning style of fuzzy systems through the use of fuzzy sets and a linguistic model consisting of a set of IF-THEN fuzzy rules. The main strength of neuro-fuzzy systems is that they are universal approximations with the ability to solicit interpretable IF-THEN rules.

The strength of neuro-fuzzy systems involves two contradictory requirements in fuzzy modeling: interpretability versus accuracy. In practice, one of the two properties prevails. The neuro-fuzzy in fuzzy modeling research field is divided into two areas: linguistic fuzzy modeling that is focused on interpretability, mainly the Mamdani model; and precise fuzzy modeling that is focused on accuracy, mainly the Takagi-Sugeno-Kang (TSK) model.

The previous studies made full use of the advantages of the neural-network and the fuzzy logic controller and solved the different problems in suspension systems. Few researches involved combination of the two techniques to solve the time-delay and the inherent nonlinear nature of the Magneto-Rheological (MR) dampers in semi-active strategy for full car model with high degrees of freedom. In this chapter, four MR dampers are added in a suspension system between body and wheels parallel with passive dampers. For the intelligent system, fuzzy controller which inputs are relative velocities across MR dampers that are excited by road profile for predicting the force of MR damper to receive a desired passenger's displacement is applied. When predicting the displacement and velocity of MR dampers, a four-layer feed forward neural network, trained on-line under the Levenberg–Marquardt (LM) algorithm, is adopted. In order to verify the effectiveness of the proposed neuro-fuzzy control strategy, the uncontrolled system and the clipped optimal controlled suspension system are compared with the neuro-fuzzy controlled system. Through a numerical example under actual road profile excitation, it can be concluded that the control strategy is very important for semi-active control, the neuro-fuzzy control strategy can determine voltage of the MR damper quickly and accurately, and the control effect of the neuro-fuzzy control strategy is better than that of the other control strategies. First have brief reviewed on modelling of a full car model and third section clearly reveals more detailed information about neuro-fuzzy strategy for the full-car model. Finally in sections 4 and 5 the results will be presented and discussed.

2. Full car model

In the full-car model, 11-DOFs is assumed, all wheels and passengers are dependent on each other and on the car's body. It is assumed that each wheel has an effect on the spring and damper of other wheels, and two axles of vehicle are dependent. MR actuator is utilized to damp the effect of road profile on the passengers. Note that MR shock absorber is added between the axel and car's body. In the full-car model, the effects of the rotations of the body around the roll and pitch axes are simulated. The suspension system using a full-car model has 11-DOFs, four of them for the four wheels, three for body displacement and its rotations and the last four for the passengers. Schematic of the full-car model with 11-DOFs and addition of the MR damper is shown in Fig. 1.

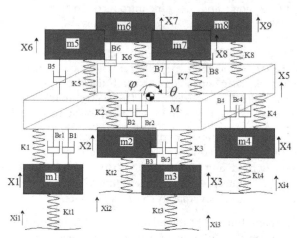

Fig. 1. Full-car model with 11-DOFs

where M_b, m_1, m_2, m_3, m_4, m_5, m_6, m_7 and m_8 stand for the mass of the car's body, mass of four wheels and mass of passengers, respectively. I_1 and I_2 are the moments of inertia of the car's body around two axes. The terms k_1, k_2, k_3, k_4, k_5, k_6, k_7 and k_8 are stiffness of the springs of the suspension system and stiffness of the springs of passengers seat, respectively. The terms k_{t1}, k_{t2}, k_{t3} and k_{t4} are stiffness of the tires. The terms b_1, b_2, b_3, b_4, b_5, b_6, b_7 and b_8 are coefficients of car and passenger's seat dampers. Then, b_{r1}, b_{r2}, b_{r3} and b_{r4} are passive coefficients of the MR dampers, respectively. x_1, x_2, x_3, x_4, x_5, x_6, x_7, x_8, x_9, φ and θ indicate the DOFs of the suspension system model. The terms x_{i1}, x_{i2}, x_{i3} and x_{i4} indicate load profile disturbance, respectively. These parameters are used to clipped optimal strategy which is considered as a desire to train neural network and tuning fuzzy memberships. Here optimal force is depending on all state variables (Zareh et al); therefore model with detail information is necessary.

2.1 Clipped optimal algorithm

The clipped optimal control strategy for an MR damper usually involves two steps. The first step is to assume an ideal actively–controlled device and construct an optimal controller for this active device. In the second step, a secondary controller finally determines the input voltage of the MR damper.

That is, the secondary controller clips the optimal force in a manner consistent with the dissipative nature of the device. The block diagram of the clipped optimal algorithm is shown in Fig. 2.

The clipped optimal control approach is to append a force feedback loop to induce the MR damper to produce approximately a desired control force f_c. The Linear Quadratic Regulator (LQR) algorithm has been employed both for active control and for semi-active control. Using this algorithm, the optimal control force f_c for f, which is force generated by an MR damper. (Zareh et al) utilized clipped optimal algorithm for semi-active full car model.

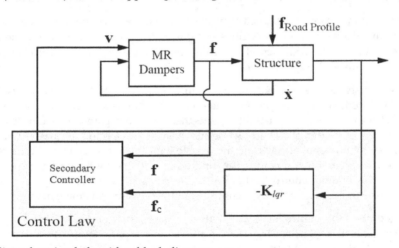

Fig. 2. Clipped optimal algorithm block diagram

3. Neuro-fuzzy strategy using in semi-active vibration control

Unfortunately, due to the inherent nonlinear nature of the MR damper to generate a force, a similar model for its inverse dynamics is difficult to obtain mathematically and also due to the nonlinearity of suspension system, its equations are complicated. Because of these reasons, a neural network with fuzzy logic controller is constructed to copy the inverse dynamics of the MR damper and suspension system.

Neuro-fuzzy controller is an artificial neural network, which is used to aggregate rules and to provide control result for the designed fuzzy logic controller. Application of fuzzy inference systems as a Fuzzy Logic Controller (FLC) has gradually been recognized as the most significant and fruitful application for fuzzy logic and fuzzy set theory. In the past few years, advances in microprocessors and hardware technologies have created an even more diversified application domain for fuzzy logic controllers, which range from consumer electronics to the automobile industry.

Indeed, for complex and/or ill-defined systems that are not easily subjected to conventional automatic control methods, FLCs provide a feasible alternative since they can capture the approximate, qualitative aspects of human reasoning and decision-making processes. However, without adaptive capability, the performance of FLCs relies exclusively on two factors: the availability of human experts, and the knowledge acquisition techniques to convert human expertise into appropriate fuzzy if-then rules and membership functions. These two factors substantially restrict the application domain of FLCs.

Consequently, a neural control design approach can usually be carried over directly to the design of fuzzy controllers, unless the design method depends directly on the specific architecture of the neural networks used. This portability endows us with a number of design methods for fuzzy controllers which can easily take advantage of a priori human information and expertise in the form of fuzzy if-then rules. The result of the above methodology is called Neuro-Fuzzy Control method. Neural and fuzzy logic controllers have been successfully implemented in the control of linear and nonlinear systems.

Unlike conventional controllers, such controllers do not require mathematical model and they can easily deal with the nonlinearities and uncertainties of the controlled systems. Also, a Levenberg-Marquardt (LM) neural controller has been designed for variable geometry suspension systems with MR actuators.

In the present research, an optimal controller Linear Quadratic Regulator (LQR) is designed for control of a semi-active suspension system for a full-model vehicle, using a neuro-fuzzy along with Levenberg-Marquardt learning and the results compared with Linear Quadratic Gaussian (LQG) (Zareh et al). The purpose in a vehicle suspension system is reduction of transmittance of vibrational effects from the road to the vehicle's passengers, hence providing ride comfort. To accomplish this, one can first design a LQR controller for the suspension system, using an optimal control method and use it to train a neuro-fuzzy controller. This controller can be trained using the LQR controller output error on an online manner.

Once trained, the LQR controller is automatically removed from the control loop and the neuro-fuzzy controller takes on. In case of a change in the parameters of the system under control or excitations, the LQR controller enters the control loop again and the neural network gets trained again for the new condition therefore it can ensure the robustness of strategy due to changes in excitations (Sadati et al). An important characteristic of the proposed controller is that no mathematical model is needed for the system components, such as the non-linear actuator, spring, or shock absorbers.

The basic idea of the proposed neuro-fuzzy control strategy is that the forces of the MR dampers are determined by a fuzzy controller, whose inputs are the measured velocity response predicted by a neural network (Zh et al). The architecture of this strategy is shown in Fig. 3, which consists of two parts to perform different tasks. The first part is for the neural network to be trained on-line. The numbers of the sample data pairs are 3500, the training data pairs increase step by step during the entrance disturbance from road profile.

To select the network architecture, it is required to determine the numbers of inputs, outputs, hidden layers, and nodes in the hidden layers; this is usually done by trial and error. Therefore, one hidden layer, with six nodes, was adopted as one of the best suitable topologies for neural network.

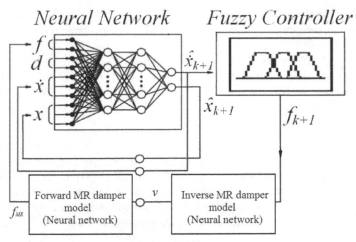

Fig. 3. Architecture of the neuro-fuzzy control strategy

The neural network is trained to generate the one step ahead prediction of the displacement $\hat{x}_{k+1}$ and the velocity $\hat{\dot{x}}_{k+1}$. Inputs to this network are the delayed outputs (x_{k+3}, x_{k+2}, x_{k+1}, x_k, $\dot{x}_{k+3}$, $\dot{x}_{k+2}$, $\dot{x}_{k+1}$, $\dot{x}_k$), the delayed force which is predicted by fuzzy controller (f_{k+1}), and the disturbance input (d_k). At the initial time, the inputs of the network will be assigned the value of zero in accordance with the actual initial circumstance. Before online training, the network is trained off-line so as to obtain the weights that are as near to the desired value as possible (Yildirim et al).

The second part is the fuzzy controller, whose input is the measured relative velocity across MR dampers. The disturbance can be calculated by road profile model. The output of the fuzzy controller is the control force of the MR dampers. The main aim of this part is to determine the control force of the MR dampers quickly in accordance with the input excitation. How to design the fuzzy controller will be explained in the following subsection. In order to reach this aim, it is required to predict the responses of passengers in accordance with the optimal responses.

The third part is the feedforward neural network to be trained on-line to generate the required voltage of MR damper v. In fact, this part is the inverse dynamics model of MR damper.

This block diagram is designed by authors using of combination of advanced works. In this strategy there are three neural networks. First is to mapping of suspension system. Second is inverse model of MR damper and third is forward model of MR damper. The difference between inverse and forward model is their inputs and outputs where the inputs of inverse model is outputs of forward model and vice-versa. All data that are used to training, testing and validating are LQR results because, they are optimal and our desired.

As mentioned, due to the inherent non-linear nature of the MR damper, a model for inverse dynamics of MR damper is difficult to obtain mathematically. Because of this reason, a feedforward back propagation neural network is constructed to copy the inverse dynamics of the MR damper. This neural network model is trained using input-output data generated analytically using the simulated MR model based on clipped algorithm. Using this inverse dynamics of MR damper, the required voltage signal v is calculated based on the desired control force f_c, the velocity of MR dampers $\hat{\dot{x}}_{k+1}$, and the displacement of MR damper x_{k+1}.

The fourth part is the feedforward back propagation neural network to be trained on-line in order to generate the MR damper forces fMR. The inputs of this neural network are voltage signal v, the velocity of MR damper $\hat{\dot{x}}_{k+1}$, and the displacement of MR damper x_{k+1}. The difference between inverse and forward model is in inputs and outputs. The outputs of inverse model are the inputs of forward model.

The third and fourth part of the proposed neuro-fuzzy control strategy which is a three-layer feedforward neural network consists of an input layer with 3 nodes, a hidden layer with 6 nodes, and output layer with one node. Determining the numbers of inputs, outputs, hidden layers, and nodes in hidden layers of these three neural networks is done by trial and error. For all neural parts some of the corresponded results that are obtained by LQR are used as a desire data and some others are used as a testing data.

At the same time, the actual responses will feed back to the neural network and the weights and bias will be revised in real time. In this research, results from the optimal control history analysis method are used to simulate the actual measured responses. The errors between the predicted responses and the actual responses are used to update the weights of the neural network on-line.

3.1 The neural network based on Levenberg-Marquardt (LM) algorithm

The MR damper model discussed earlier in this research estimates the damper forces based on the inputs of the reactive velocity. In such case, it is essential to develop an inverse dynamic model that predicts the corresponding control force which is to be generated by dampers.

Neural network is a simplified model of the biological structure which is found in human brains. This model consists of elementary processing units (also called neurons). It is the large amount of interconnections between these neurons and their capability to learn from data which makes neural network as a strong predicting and classification tool. In this study, a three-layer feed forward neural network, which consists of an input layer, one hidden layer, and an output layer ,as shown in Fig. 4, is selected to predict the responses with MR dampers.

Here the networks are trained by LQR results (as a sample data). For example displacements, velocity and forces that are obtained by LQR are selected as a sample data for training and testing. Also target of networks are LQR results. For example in the second network (Inverse model of MR damper) the targets are voltages that obtained by LQR part of clipped method.

The net input value net_k of the neuron k in some layer and the output value O_k of the same neuron can be calculated by the following equations:

$$net_k = \sum w_{jk} O_j \qquad (1)$$

$$O_k = f(net_k + \theta_k) \qquad (2)$$

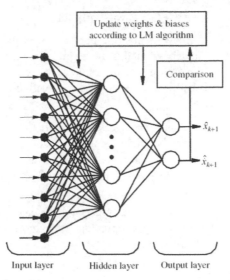

Fig. 4. The neural network architecture

where w_{jk} is the weight between the jth neuron in the previous layer and the kth neuron in the current layer, O_j is the output of the jth neuron in the previous layer, $f(.)$ is the neuron's activation function which can be a linear function, a radial basis function, and a sigmoid function, and y_k is the bias of the kth neuron. Feed forward neural network often has one or more hidden layers of sigmoid neurons followed by an output layer of linear neurons. Multiple layers of neurons with nonlinear transfer functions allow the network to learn nonlinear and linear relationships between input and output vectors. In the neural network architecture as shown in Fig. 4, the logarithmic sigmoid transfer function is chosen as the activation function of the hidden layer.

$$O_k = f(net_k + \theta_k) = 1/(1 + e^{-(net_k + \theta_k)}) \tag{3}$$

The linear transfer function is chosen as the activation function of the output layer.

$$O_k = f(net_k + \theta_k) = net_k + \theta_k \tag{4}$$

We note that neural network needs to be trained before it can predict any responses. As the inputs are applied to the neural network, the network outputs ($\hat{\ }$) are compared with the targets (.). The difference or error between both is processed back through the network to update the weights and biases of the neural network so that the network outputs match closer with the targets.

The input and output data are usually represented by vectors called training pairs. The process as mentioned above is repeated for all the training pairs in the data set, until the network error converges to a threshold minimum defined by a corresponding performance function. In this research, the Mean Square Error (MSE) function is adopted (desired MSE is 1e-5). LM algorithm is adapted to train the neural network (Zh et al), which can be written as a following equation:

$$w^{i+1}=w^i-[(\delta^2 E/\delta w^{i\wedge 2})+\mu I]^{-1}(\delta E/\delta w^i) \tag{5}$$

where i is the iteration index, $\delta E/\delta w^i$ is the gradient descent of the performance function E with respect to the parameter matrix w^i, $\mu \geq 0$ is the learning factor, and I is the unity matrix. During the vibration process, the neural network updates the weights and bias of neurons in real time in accordance with sampling pairs till the objective error is satisfied, i.e. the property of the system is acquired.

As we know, the main aim of the neural network is to predict the dynamic responses of the system, and to provide inputs to the fuzzy controller and also data for calculating the control force of MR dampers. Thus outputs of the neural network are predictions of displacement $\hat{x}_{k+1}$ and velocity $\hat{\dot{x}}_{k+1}$. In order to predict the dynamic responses of the system accurately, the most direct and important factors which affect the predicted dynamic responses are considered, i.e. the delayed outputs $(x_{k+3}, x_{k+2}, x_{k+1}, x_k, \dot{x}_{k+3}, \dot{x}_{k+2}, \dot{x}_{k+1}, \dot{x}_k)$, the predicted force (f_{k+1}), and the disturbance input (d_k). LM algorithm is encoded in Neural Networks Toolbox in MATLAB software.

3.2 Design of fuzzy controller

The first step of designing a fuzzy controller is determining the basic domains of inputs and outputs. The desired displacement and velocity responses are chosen as inputs of the fuzzy controller. The output of fuzzy controller is the control force of the MR damper, whose basic domain is -700N – 300N same as the working force of the MR damper calculated using LQR (Zareh et al).

The membership functions are usually chosen in accordance with their characters and design experience.

For simplifying the calculation, triangular or trapezoidal functions are usually adopted as the membership functions. The triangular membership function is more sensitive to inputs than the trapezoidal form (Zh et al), in expectation that the control forces of the MR dampers are sensitive to excitations and responses, but in this case Gaussian and triangular forms are used because they have demonstrated better responses through trial and error. In this research, gaussian and triangular functions are adopted as the membership functions of velocity. The membership function curves of the velocity are shown in Figs. 5-8. (Relative velocity across dampers)

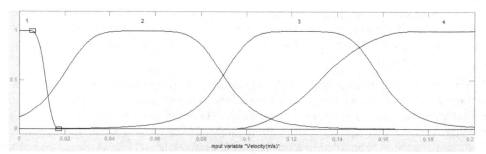

Fig. 5. Membership function of front-left damper velocity

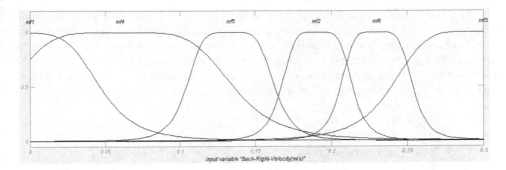

Fig. 6. Membership function of front-right damper velocity

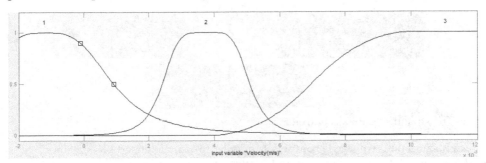

Fig. 7. Membership function of back-left damper velocity

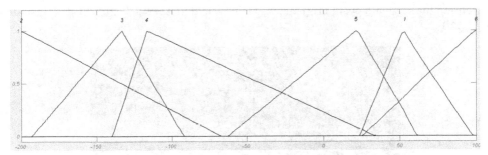

Fig. 8. Membership function of back-right damper velocity

Here, Sugeno inference engine with linear output is used, the main difference between Mamdani and Sugeno is that the Sugeno output membership functions are either linear or constant. It has led to reduction of computational cost because it does not need any defuzzification procedure. A Sugeno fuzzy model is computationally efficient platform that is well suited for implementation of non-linear associations through the construction of many piecewise linear relationships (Yen et al) .A typical rule in a Sugeno fuzzy model has the form:

If X is A1 and Y is B1 then Z = p1*x + q1*y + r1,

If X is A2 and Y is B2 then Z = p2*x + q2*y + r2,

where q1 and q2 are constant. One of the main advantages of Sugeno method is well suited to mathematical analysis and is also computationally efficient, but Mamdani method is well suited to human input and it is intuitive. The basic idea of the fuzzy rules is that the control force increases with the increasing velocity responses. In this research, OR function is MAX, AND function is MIN and the defuzzification method is chosen as the Weighted Average (wtaver) method. The structure of considered fuzzy controller is shown in Fig. 9.

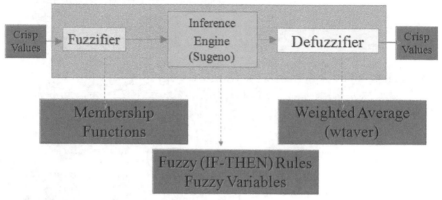

Fig. 9. The structure of fuzzy controller

For defuzzification we apply centre of gravity for singletons (COGS). Since we are implementing a Sugeno type controller, the combined activation, accumulation, and defuzzification operation simplifies to weighted average, with the activation strengths weighting the singleton positions (Jantzen 2007). Weighted Average defuzzifier is illustrated in Fig. 10.

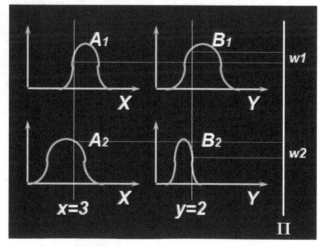

Fig. 10. Sugeno-style rule evaluation

$$z1 = p1*x + q1*y + r1 \tag{6}$$

$$z2 = p2*x + q2*y + r2 \tag{7}$$

$$Z = [w1*z1 + w2*z2] / [w1 + w2] \tag{8}$$

The membership function curves of the force for front-left damper as a fuzzy output (force vs. velocity) is shown in Fig. 11.

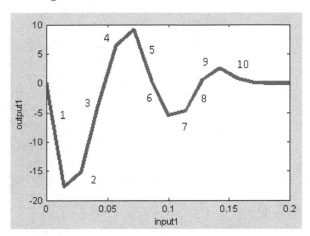

Fig. 11. Membership function of back-right damper velocity (force on vertical axis vs. velocity on horizontal axis)

The rule base used in the semi-active suspension system shown in Table 1 with fuzzy terms derived by the designer's knowledge and experience (because of shortage of space some of them are presented).

Front-left	Front-right	Back-left	Back-right	Force
1	mf$_3$	1	2	1
1	mf$_3$	1	3	1
1	mf$_4$	2	3	6
1	mf$_2$	2	5	4
2	mf$_6$	1	5	6
2	mf$_5$	3	6	6
3	mf$_6$	2	1	8
3	mf$_2$	1	1	10
4	mf$_5$	3	1	1

Table 1. Rule base

4. Results

The full-car model with MR damper and disturbance is modeled by the dynamic equations and state space matrices. One of the desired points of this study is to decrease the amplitude of passenger's displacement, when the suspension system excited from the road profile. Therefore the effect of LQR and LQG controllers and neuro-fuzzy strategy are simulated for road excitation with calculated their amplitude, and then compared with each other. The displacement trajectories for front-right passenger's seat that is excited by bumper under front left wheel are shown in Fig. 12. Notice that, in all graphs, time duration is selected for the best resolution and critical responses are happened when car strikes with bumper.

The trajectories of neuro-fuzzy strategy show that this strategy reduces the amplitude of vibration lower than the passive system and also to some extent as well as optimal controllers; because displacement is predicted by feed forward neural networks.

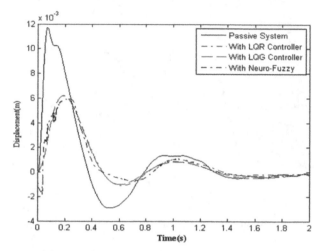

Fig. 12. Displacement of front right seat from front left wheel excite

The primary oscillations are due to the less number of network input to train, on the other hand, there are not strong history in transient, therefore the transient part of response not as well as steady state part. The trajectory for the optimal force which produces the desired displacement is shown in Fig. 13.

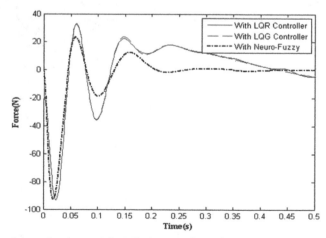

Fig. 13. Generated force by front right MR damper from front left wheel excited

One of the main advantages of using neuro-fuzzy, the control effort of dampers is less than LQR and LQG responses. Forces of neuro-fuzzy cannot follow optimal controller; because, optimal forces depend on twenty two state variables and the forces obtained by fuzzy part of neuro-fuzzy strategy depend on four state variables (relative velocity across MR dampers). The requirement voltage to receive optimal forces is shown in Fig. 14.

The voltages are calculated using of neuro-fuzzy has a less oscillations, therefore it cause of save energy and cost. Performance of the network is shown in Fig. 15.

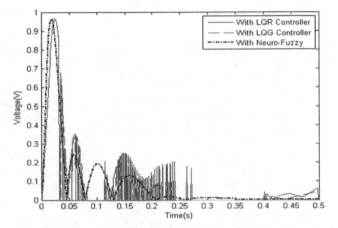

Fig. 14. Requirement voltages to front right MR damper from front left wheel excited

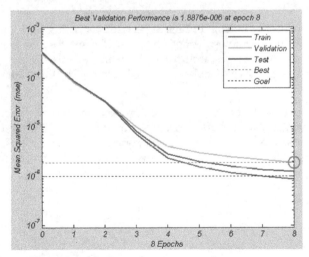

Fig. 15. Performance of the network

5. Conclusion

Usual suspension systems are utilized in the vehicle, and damped the vibration from road profile.Unfortunately, due to the inherent nonlinear nature of the MR damper to generate force and suspension system, a model like that for its inverse dynamics is difficult to obtain mathematically. Because of this reason, a neural network with fuzzy logic controller is constructed to copy the inverse dynamics of the MR damper.

In the proposed control system, a dynamic-feedback neural network has been employed to model non-linear dynamic system and the fuzzy logic controller has been used to determine the control forces of MR dampers. Required voltages and actual forces of MR dampers have been obtained by use of two feedforward neural networks, in which the first neural network and second one have acted as the inverse and forward dynamics models of the MR dampers, respectively.

The most important characteristic of the proposed intelligent control strategy is its inherent robustness and its ability to handle the non-linear behavior of the system. Besides, no mathematical model is needed for calculating forces produced by MR dampers.

The performance of the proposed neuro-fuzzy control system has been compared with that of a traditional semi-active control strategy, i.e., clipped optimal control system with LQR and LQR, through computer simulations, while the uncontrolled system response has been used as the baseline.

According to the graphs that show above, the trajectories of neuro-fuzzy strategy can reduce the amplitude of vibration to some extent as well as optimal controllers with less control effort and oscillation. In addition, the neuro-fuzzy control system is more robust to process/sensing noises.

6. Acknowledgment

Seiyed Hamid Zareh deeply indebted to his Supervisor, Dr. Amir Ali Akbar Khayyat, from the Sharif University of Technology whose help, sincere suggestions and encouragement helped him in all the time of research for and writing of this chapter. His insight and enthusiasm for research have enabled him to accomplish this work and are truly appreciated.

The authors are particularly pleased to thank Dr. Abolghassem Zabihollah, Dr. Kambiz Ghaemi Osgouie, Mr. Atabak Sarrafan, Mr. Meisam Abbasi and Mr. Ali Fellahjahromi for their true friendships, supports, invaluable suggestions, and sharing their knowledge and expertises with us. And our special thanks go to the international campus of Sharif University of Technology for the support provided for this research.

7. References

Atray V. S.; Roschke P. N. (2004). Neuro-Fuzzy Control of Railcar Vibrations Using Semi active Dampers. Computer-Aided Civil and Infrastructure Engineering, Vol.19, pp. 81-92

Biglarbegian M.; Melek W.; Golnaraghi F. (2006). Intelligent control of vehicle semi-active suspension system for improved ride comfort and road handling. IEEE International conference, pp. 19-24

Chang C. C.; Zhou L. (2002). Neural Network Emulation of Inverse Dynamics for a Magnetorheological Damper. Journal of Structural Engineering, vol. 2, pp. 231–239

Jahromi A. F.; Zabihollah A. (2010). Linear Quadratic Regulator and Fuzzy controller Application in Full-car Model of Suspension System with Magnetorheological Shock Absorber. IEEE/ASME International Conference on Mechanical and Embedded Systems and Applications, pp. 522-528

Jang J. R. (1997). Neuro-Fuzzy and Soft Computing: A computational Approach to Learning and Machine Intelligence. Prentice-Hall, ISBN: 0-13-261066-3

Jantzen J. (2007). Foundation of Fuzzy Control. John Wiley & Sons, Ltd. ISBN: 978-0-470-02963-3

Khajekaramodin A.; Hajikazemi H.; Rowhanimanesh A.; Akbarzadeh M. R. (2007).Semi-active Control of Structures Using Neuro-Inverse Model of MR Dampers. First Joint Congress on Fuzzy and Intelligent Systems, Iran, pp. 789-803

Ok S. Y.; Kim D. S.; Park K. S.; Koh H. M. (2007). Semi-active fuzzy control of cable-stayed bridges using magneto-rheological dampers. Engineering Structures, vol. 29, pp. 776–788

Sadati S. H.; Shooredeli M. A.; Panah A. D. (2008) Designing a neuro-fuzzy controller for a vehicle suspension system using feedback error learning. Journal of mechanics and aerospace, Vol.4, No.3, pp. 45-57

Schurter K. C.; Roschke P. N. (2000). Neuro-Fuzzy Modeling of a Magnetorheological Damper Using ANFIS. Proceeding of 9th IEEE International Conference on Fuzzy Systems, San Antonio, TX, pp. 122–127

Shiraishi T.;Nakaya N.; Morishita S. (2001). Vibration Control of Structure Equipped with MR Damper Using Neural Network. Proceeding of Dynamics and Design Conference, vol. 8, pp. 1748–1752

Suhardjo J.; Kareem A. (2001). Feedback-Feedforward Control of Offshore Platforms under Random Waves. Journal of Earthquake Engineering and Structural Dynamics, vol. 30, pp. 213–235

Sun J.; Yang Q. (2008). Modeling and intelligent control of vehicle active suspension system. IEEE International conference on RAM, pp. 239-242

Sung K. G.; Han Y. M., Cho J. W.; Choi S. B. (2007). Vibration control of vehicle ER suspension system using fuzzy moving sliding mode controller. Journal of Sound and Vibration, Vol.311, pp. 1004-1019

Wang H.; Hu H. (2009). The Neuro-Fuzzy Identification of MR Damper. Proceeding of 6th International Conference on Fuzzy Systems and Knowledge Discovery, pp. 464–468

Wang L. X. (1994). Adaptive Fuzzy Systems and Control: Design and Stability Analysis. Prentice-Hall, Englewood Cliffs, New Jersey

Yan G.; Zhou L. L. (2006). Integrated Fuzzy Logic and Genetic Algorithms for Multi-Objective Control of Structures Using MR Dampers. Journal of Sound and Vibration, Vol. 296, pp. 368–392

Yen J.; Langari R. (1999). Fuzzy Logic: Intelligence, Control, and Information. Prentice-Hall, New York, NY

Yildirim S.; Eski I. (2009). Vibration analysis of an experimental suspension system using artificial neural networks. Journal of Scientific & Industrial Research, Vol.68, pp. 522-529

Zareh S. H.; Fellahjahromi A.; Hayeri R.; Khayyat A. A. A.; Zabihollah A. (2011). LQR and Fuzzy Controller Application with Bingham Modified Model in Semi Active

Vibration Control of 11-DOFs Full Car Suspension System. International Journal on Computing, Vol. 1, No. 3, pp. 39-44

Zareh S. H.; Sarrafan A.; Khayyat A. A. A. (2011). Clipped Optimal Control of 11-DOFs of a Passenger Car Using Magnetorheological Damper. IEEE International Conference on Computer Control and Automation , Korea, ISBN: 978-1-4244-9767-6, pp. 162-167

Zareh S. H.; Sarrafan A.; Khayyat A. A. A.; Fellahjahromi A. (2011). Linear Quadratic Gaussian Application and Clipped Optimal Algorithm Using for Semi Active Vibration of Passenger Car. IEEE International Conference on Mechatronics, Turkey, pp. 122-127

Zh. D. X.; Guo Y. Q. (2008). Neuro-Fuzzy control strategy for earthquake-excited nonlinear magnetorheological structures. Soil Dynamics and Earthquake Engineering, Vol.28, pp. 717-727

Zhou L.; Chang C. C.; Wang L. X. (2003). Adaptive Fuzzy Control for Non-Linear Building-Magnetorheological Damper System. Journal of Structural Engineering: Special Issue on Structural Control, Vol. 7, pp. 905–913

12

Operation of Compressor and Electronic Expansion Valve via Different Controllers

Orhan Ekren[1], Savas Sahin[2] and Yalcin Isler[3]
[1]Southern Illinois University,
Mechanical Engineering Department, Edwardsville,
[2]Ege University, Ege Technical College,
Department of Control and Automation, Bornova, Izmir,
[3]Zonguldak Karaelmas University,
Department of Electrical and Electronics Engineering,
Incivez, Zonguldak
[1]USA
[2,3]Turkey

1. Introduction

The most critical problem in the world is to meet the energy demand, because of steadily increasing energy consumption. Refrigeration systems' electricity consumption has big portion in overall consumption. Therefore, considerable attention has been given to refrigeration capacity modulation system in order to decrease electricity consumption of these systems. Capacity modulation is used to meet exact amount of load at partial load and lowered electricity consumption by avoiding over capacity using. Variable speed refrigeration systems are the most common capacity modulation method for commercially and household purposes. Although the vapor compression refrigeration designed to satisfy the maximum load, they work at partial load conditions most of their life cycle and they are generally regulated as on/off controlled. The experimental chiller system contains four main components: compressor, condenser, expansion device, and evaporator in Fig.1 where this study deals with effects of different control methods on variable speed compressor (VSC) and electronic expansion valve (EEV). This chiller system has a scroll type VSC and a stepper motor controlled EEV.

There are electronic parts in the control system: DAQ (data acquisition), Controllers, and Inverter. Data acquisition part reads distinct temperature values of the water outlet (T_{wo}), evaporator input (T_{ei}), and the evaporator output (T_{eo}) points from the evaporator. Controllers drive both expansion valve and compressor, which are named Controller #1 and Controller #2 throughout the paper, respectively. Inverter, which is commanded by controller #1, drives the compressor speed frequency (f) using $f(V)$. Common controllers are on-off, proportional (P), proportional-integral (PI), and PID respectively. "On-off" control method is the most used conventional technique to control refrigeration systems. This method has a big drawback of undesired current peaks during its state transitions (Aprea et al., 2009). PID controller has been found wide usage in industrial applications since it is very simple to design, to implement, and to use (Katsuhiko, 2002; Astrom and Hagglund, 1995). Therefore, it has been widely used in Heating Ventilation Air Conditioning and Refrigeration (HVAC&R) systems (Jiangjiang et al., 2006). Recently, energy consuming is a strict issue in designing new refrigeration system (Aprea and Renno, 2009; Ekren et al., 2010, 2011; Nasutin and Hassan, 2006, Sahin et al., 2010). EEV and VSC have important effect on efficiency of system energy consumption. Hence designing an eligible controller for these parts will improve energy consuming. Conventional controllers cannot deal with nonlinear behaviors including uncertainties in system parameters, time delays and limited operation point of refrigeration systems, which may reduce the energy efficiency. Nonlinear controllers based on Fuzzy Logic (FL) and Artificial Neural Network (ANN) may overcome these issues (Aprea et al., 2006a,b). The most important advantage of these algorithms is to enable solving control problems without any already-known mathematical model (Narendra and Parthasarathy, 1990; Narendra, 1993; Aprea et al., 2004; Ross, 2004).

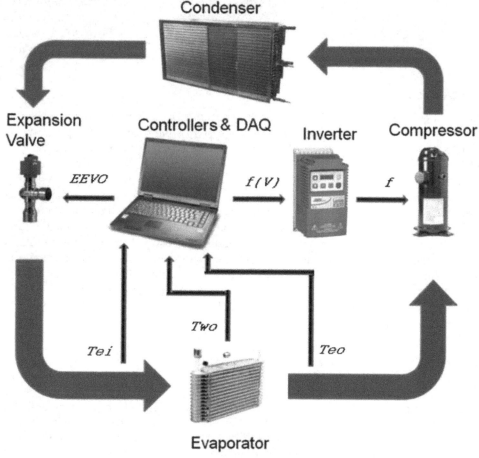

Fig. 1. Schematic of the refrigeration and control system

In this chapter, different control algorithms, based on proportional-integral-derivative (PID), fuzzy logic (FL), artificial neural network (ANN) for compressor speed and opening percentage of electronic expansion valve, were compared by means of achieving their desired output and energy demands.

2. Control methods of the VSRS

There are three parts in a closed-loop control system: error calculation, controller, and plant (Fig. 2). Error calculation part calculates the difference between the desired output, r(k), and the actual output, y(k), of the system. This difference is called error signal, e(k). A controller finds out a control signal, u(k), by considering this error signal. A plant, the system itself under investigation, generates the actual output, y(k), in reply to the u(k). The most important problem is generating the most suitable control signal that derives the plant to minimize the error, which means that the actual output and the desired output are almost equal in the closed-loop control system.

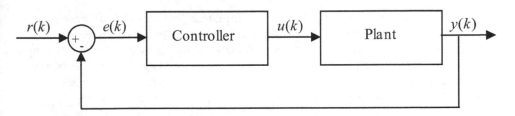

Fig. 2. A general closed-loop control system

In the variable speed refrigeration system (VSRS), which is a typical closed-loop control system, contains VSC and EEV controllable components. The frequency of the compressor and the opening amount of the expansion valve are control parameters in order to drive the water outlet temperature and the degree of superheat respectively to desired values in VSRS (Ekren et al., 2010). By considering controllable parts in the experimental setup, after adapting closed-loop control system into the setup, a detailed block diagram of controllers and system parts for the VSRS are also shown in Fig. 1.

In the following subsections, certain control methods are given in control refrigeration systems. These methods are itemized two main groups: i) linear controller such as PID and ii) nonlinear controllers such as FL and ANN controllers.

2.1 PID control

PID is the most commonly used control technique for industrial applications since it is very simple to design, to implement, and to use (Astrom and Hagglund, 1995). It has also been widely used in Heating Ventilation Air Conditioning and Refrigeration (HVAC&R) systems (Jiangjiang et al., 2006). This controller is tuned by its three variables: proportional (K_p), integral (K_i) and derivative (K_d) parameters. The control action $u(t)$ in time domain can be calculated as

$$u(t) = K_p e(t) + K_i \int_0^t e(t) dt + K_d \dot{e}(t) \tag{6}$$

by means of the error, which is the difference between the desired and the actual output of the plant (e), and the derivative of this error ($\dot{e}$). PID parameters can be determined in using either the step response or the self-oscillation methods from Ziegler-Nichols (Ziegler and Nichols, 1942) are widely used in the literature (Astrom and Hagglund, 1995). In the step response method, if the output response of the plant can be obtained in time domain, PID parameters can be determined. This output response can be approximated as a first-order system

$$H(s) = \frac{K}{Ts+1} e^{-Ls} \tag{7}$$

where T is time constant, L is delay time and K is gain. The T and L give the PID controller design parameters (Katsuhiko, 2002; Astrom and Hagglund, 1995).

The template plot is represented in Fig.3 to find out L and T values. The parameters can be determined from the output plots with respect to step input. The constant gain K indicates the amount of output variation from one steady-state to another, with respect to the input variation. L represents the past time to observe the initial response changes after applying the input. In addition, T denotes the time necessary to reach the output equal to 63.2% of its final value for the first-order systems.

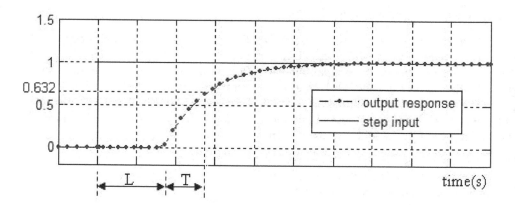

Fig. 3. Output response plots with respect to step function input

In the self-oscillation method, PID controller design parameters are calculated by critical gain and critical period variables. These variables are computed when a stable limit cycle of the closed-loop system is satisfied by using only the proportional gain. This gain is increased slowly, and then the PID parameters are determined. This method possesses very important advantage for the plant because self-oscillation experiment could be in reasonable operating bounds of the plant (Yuksel, 2006; Katsuhiko, 2002; Astrom and Hagglund, 1995).

Although there are some other methods to find out the PID parameters, Ziegler Nichols' methods are still the most used and preferred methods in the literature. In this study, Ziegler Nichols' step response method is used to find out the PID parameters by regarding the plot of the system output.

2.2 Fuzzy logic control

FL controllers consist of certain rules and membership functions. The certain rules is to determine the decision process and the membership functions is to bring up the relation between linguistic and the precise numeric values. These membership functions define input-output variables of any system and formulate control rules. A membership function can be defined by a geometric shape such as triangular, trapezoidal, etc. The selection of the membership functions depends on expert's knowledge about the process (Aprea et al., 2004; Ross, 2004).

The operation procedure of the FL controller can be itemized into three main steps: i) fuzzification, ii) inference, and iii) defuzzification (Zadeh, 1965; Ross, 2004). In the fuzzification step, system inputs-outputs and membership functions are well defined. In the inference step, a rules table is prepared according to the human expertise and these rules calculate the outputs (Ross, 2004). In the last step, defuzzification transforms fuzzy outputs into real world values. A detailed explanation of these steps and their implementation details can be found in the literature (Ross, 2004). In this study, the minimum-maximum method and the center of gravity method were used in the inference and the defuzzification steps, respectively.

EEV is the first controllable equipment in VSRS (Aprea et al., 2006a,b; Lazzarin and Noro, 2008, Ekren et al., 2010, 2011). For this controller, two inputs and one output variable were defined (Ekren et al., 2010) in Fig. 4.

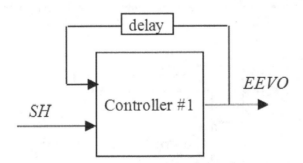

Fig. 4. Inputs and output of the first controller in VSRS.

The first input was the difference between desired and actual superheat (SH) values, of which linguistics were marked as negative high (NH), negative medium (NM), zero (Z), positive medium (PM), positive high (PH). The second one was the previous value of the EEV opening. The output was the value of EEV opening (EEVO). The second input and the output of the system had similar membership functions where linguistics were marked as very closed (VC), closed (C), medium (M), opened (O) and very opened (VO). The membership functions can be seen in Fig. 5.

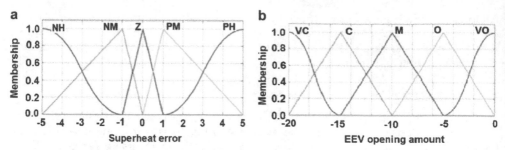

Fig. 5. Membership functions of (a) the superheat error input, (b) the previous opening value of EEV input and the EEV opening amount output.

Fuzzy rules for the EEV control were experimentally verified by using some trials, and it is given in Table 1.

	Previous Opening Value of EEV				
Superheat Error	*VO*	*O*	*M*	*C*	*VC*
NH	*O*	*M*	*C*	*VC*	*VC*
NM	*O*	*M*	*C*	*VC*	*VC*
Z	*VO*	*O*	*M*	*C*	*VC*
PM	*VO*	*VO*	*O*	*M*	*C*
PH	*VO*	*VO*	*O*	*M*	*C*

Table 1. EEV Fuzzy logic control rules

For the second controller, two inputs and one output variable were defined (Ekren et al., 2010) in Fig. 6.

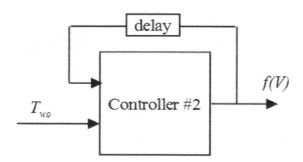

Fig. 6. Inputs and output of the second controller in VSRS.

The first input was the temperature difference between the desired temperature and actual temperature at outlet of the evaporator (T_{wo}), of which linguistics were marked as negative high (NH), negative medium (NM), zero (Z), positive medium (PM), and positive high (PH). The second input was the previous change of frequency value, sent to the inverter by the control unit. The output for this controller was the frequency change of the supply voltage of the compressor electric motor, $f(V)$. The second input and the output of the system had similar membership functions where linguistics were marked as very small (VS), small (S), medium (M), big (B) and very big (VB). The membership functions can be seen in Fig. 7.

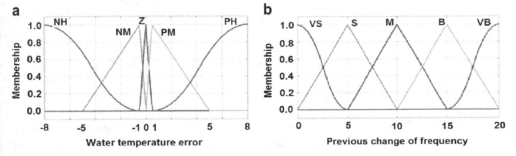

Fig. 7. Membership functions for (a) water temperature error input, (b) for the previous change of frequency input and the frequency change output.

Fuzzy rules for the compressor control were experimentally verified by using some trials, and it is given in Table 2.

Water Temperature Error	Previous Change of Frequency				
	VS	S	M	B	VB
NH	S	M	B	VB	VB
NM	S	M	B	VB	VB
Z	VS	S	M	B	VB
PM	VS	VS	S	M	B
PH	VS	VS	S	M	B

Table 2. Compressor fuzzy logic control rules

2.3 ANN Control

The most important features of the ANN developed by inspiring from biological neural networks are learning, generalizing and making a decision. ANNs are widely used in many industrial applications such as identification, control, data and signal processing area since 1980s. Since ANNs define, in general, a nonlinear algebraic function, they can cope with nonlinearities inherent in control systems possessing complex dynamics. As in the general ANN literature, the mostly widely used ANN model in identification and control is the Multi Layer Perceptron (MLP) due to its function approximation capability and the existence of an efficient learning algorithm (Ahmed, 2000; Lightbody & Irwin, 1995; Meireles et al., 2003; Noriega & Wang, 1998; Omidvar & Elliott, 1997). MLP is a multilayer, algebraic neural network of neurons, called as perceptrons, which are multi-input, single-output functional units taking firstly a weighted sum of their inputs and then pass it through a sigmoidal nonlinearity to produce its output shown in Fig. 8.

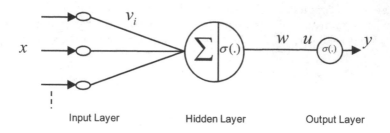

Input Layer   Hidden Layer   Output Layer

Fig. 8. Perceptron as a hidden neuron

Although MLP-ANNs are algebraic models, MLP-ANNs can define nonlinear discrete-time dynamical system due to the fact that its inputs can be connected with delayed outputs. As shown in Fig. 9, a multi-input, multi-output MLP with one hidden layer can be used as a Nonlinear Auto-Regressive-Moving-Array (NARMA) model. Input vector of this NARMA model $x = [y(k-1),...,y(k-n),u(k-1),...,(k-n)]$ where n is the finite value and v and w are weights of the layers.

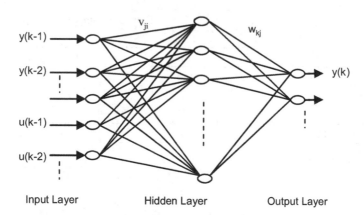

Input Layer   Hidden Layer   Output Layer

Fig. 9. MLP implementing NARMA model

In most industrial cases, an ANN is an adaptive system that changes its internal information in the learning phase. A general feed-forward inverse control system contains two MLP-ANNs such as identification and control structures, which are shown in Fig. 10 (Narendra and Parthasarathy, 1990). In this study, for the identification stage, serial-parallel identification is used for inputs of ANN. These inputs are the actual input with its past values $(u(k) = [u(k-1),...,u(k-15)])$ and the actual output with its past values $(y(k) = [y(k-1),...,y(k-15)])$. The output of ANN identification block is $\hat{y}(k)$. After ANN identification is completed, ANN controller weights are tuned with respect to overall closed-loop error function (Narendra and Parthasarathy,1990).

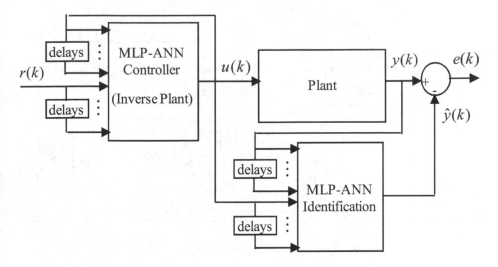

Fig. 10. Feed-forward inverse control system using MLP-ANN.

One of the most important problems in real world applications is the delay time defined the time required before observing the output change after applying a control input. To overcome delay time problem, Smith compensator structure can be used in ANN-based controllers (Ekren et al., 2010; Huang and Lewis, 2003; Lin et al., 2008; Slanvetpan et al., 2003). Inverse system MLP-ANN controller with Smith predictor was used for compensation of the delay time of the plant in Fig. 11. The MLP in both EEV and compressor controllable parts are trained with the gradient algorithm. The number of neurons in the hidden layer of MLP was selected as 20 experimentally. The EEV was controlled using an inverse system ANN controller with Smith compensator. Inputs of the first controller were EEV opening values and SH error with their 15 past values. The output of this controller was EEVO. On the other hand, compressor was controlled using an inverse system ANN controller. Inputs of this controller were compressor frequency and T_{WO} error values with their 15 past values. The output of this controller was the frequency change of the supply voltage of compressor electric motor (f).

3. Applications of the controllers

In this study, the controllers are designed as decoupled ones without interfering loops (Li et al., 2008). In the experimental setup used in this study, there were some limitations of the equipment. EEV opening value is restricted between 0% and 20% since its limits are 15% and 35% to prevent the low pressure alert and to avoid liquid entrance into the compressor. Instantaneous frequency change is restricted between 0 Hz and 20 Hz to prevent system from the vibration and the unsuitable lubrication since the frequency limits are 30 Hz and 50 Hz. By considering these limitations, three different controllers such as PID, FL, and ANN were examined in the VSRS.

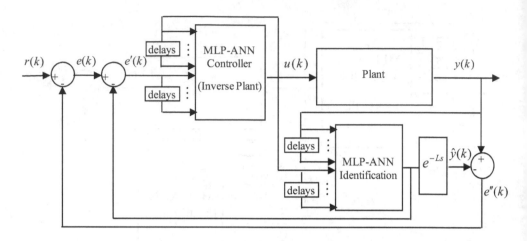

Fig. 11. Smith delay time compensator configuration using MLP-ANN.

Control experiments, conducted during the study, have been classified in three groups. The first was controlling EEV opening, the second one was controlling compressor frequency, and the last one was controlling both together. For the first and second groups, the other controllable part was operated at a constant value. All cases were tested using three different control algorithms of PID, FL and ANN. In addition, the cooling load was decreased 40% of full load to simulate a disturbance input in all cases. This is presumed to be by a change in water flow.

All controller algorithms were implemented using the most famous software of Matlab version 2011a. No ready-made toolbox routines were used throughout the study. The personal computer with a dual-core processor, 2 GB DDR Ram, and a special internal data acquisition board were used to implement controllers and to read system outputs.

3.1 EEV opening control with fixed compressor frequency

EEV opening amount was controlled to drive SH degree to a desired value. Scroll compressor frequency was fixed at 50 Hz and desired SH value was set to 6°C in order to test only EEV control algorithm. Variations of the SH degree at the outlet of the evaporator were compared and visualized in Fig. 12. The vertical dotted line in this figure shows the moment of the disturbance.

3.2 Compressor frequency control with fixed EEV opening

Compressor speed was controlled to drive water temperature at the outlet of the evaporator. EEV opening amount was fixed at 30% to obtain effects of the compressor control algorithm alone. This value was chosen since it gives better COP value for this system (Ekren and Kücüka, 2010). Water temperature variations can be seen in Fig. 13. The vertical dotted line in this figure shows the moment of the disturbance.

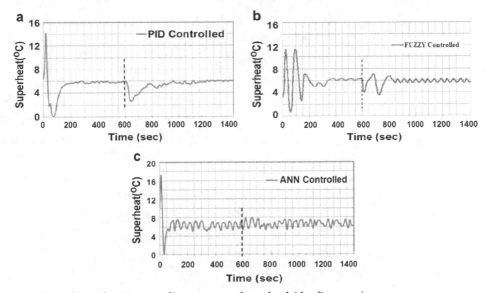

Fig. 12. Superheat change according to control method (the first case).

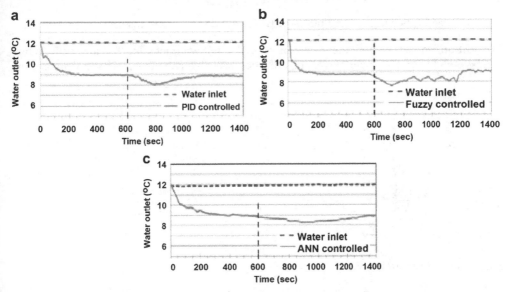

Fig. 13. Water outlet temperature change according to control method.

3.3 Both compressor and EEV control

The system was tested with the set value for SH degree of 7°C and T_{wo} of 9°C using all controller combinations. Results for SH can be seen in Fig. 14. Since the T_{wo} results were similar to results obtained in Fig. 13, T_{wo} graphs were not re-plotted here. The vertical dotted line in the Fig. 14 shows the moment of the disturbance.

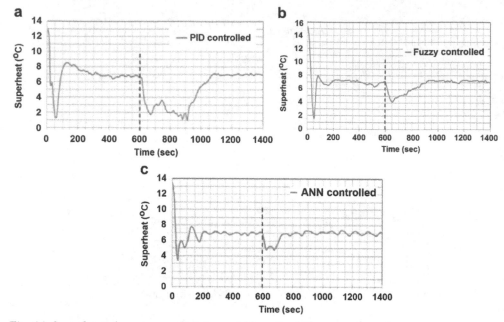

Fig. 14. Superheat change according to control method (the second case).

In addition, power consumptions were measured using wattmeter for the same duty, which can be seen in Fig. 15. Lower power consumption was obtained via ANN control algorithm.

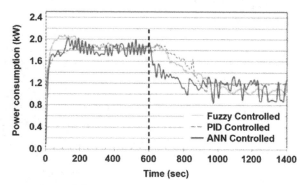

Fig. 15. Power consumptions of the compressor.

4. Conclusion

In this study, effects of different control methods (PID, FL, and ANN) on variable speed compressor (VSC) and electronic expansion valve (EEV) in a VSRS were examined. T_{wo} different procedures were applied to control EEV and VSC: controlling each part individually while the other was set to a constant value and controlling both parts together using the same algorithm. In both cases, the results of the three controllers satisfied for the set values of SH and T_{wo}. PID controller presented reasonable control solution for more stable SH and T_{wo} values in the steady state. ANN controller pair was selected to achieve minimum power consumption and more stable SH and T_{wo} values in the transient behavior and better rising time performance (reach to the desired value rapidly). In the second case, ANN controller showed 8.1 percent and 6.6 percent lower power consumption than both PID and Fuzzy controllers, respectively. In addition, Fuzzy controller showed 1.4 percent lower power consumption than PID controller. While a chiller system is being operated at a lower water flow rate, which means less cooling load, compressor speed decreases. Hence, power consumption of the compressor decreases. It can be seen from Figs. 12-14 that ANN control algorithm gave more robust response to the disturbance effect in the system. On the other hand, other control algorithms needed longer response time to eliminate the disturbance effect. Since most consumer electronics products are under the influence of disturbance effects, control algorithms whose transient response is robust against to the disturbance effect should be used to provide consumer comfort. Although controller design based on ANN is an expensive method in the manner of hardware and software, using such a controller seems necessary if the system has much disturbance.

5. References

Ahmed, M. S., 2000. Neural-Net-Based Direct Adaptive Control for a Class of Nonlinear Plants. *IEEE Transactions on Automatic Control*, 45(1), 119-124.

Aprea, C., Renno, C., 2009. Experimental modelling of variable speed system. Int. J. Energy Res. 33, 29-37.

Aprea, C., Mastrullo, R., Renno, C., 2004. Fuzzy control of the compressor speed in a refrigeration plant. Int. J. Refrigeration 27, 639-648.

Aprea, C., Mastrullo, R., Renno, C., 2006a. Experimental analysis of the scroll compressor performances varying its speed. Appl. Therm. Eng. 26, 983-992.

Aprea, C., Mastrullo, R., Renno, C., 2006b. Performance of thermostatic and electronic expansion valves controlling the compressor. Int. J. Energy Res. 30, 1313-1322.

Aprea, C.,Mastrullo, R.,Renno, C., 2009.Determinationof theoptimal working of compressor. Appl. Therm. Eng. 29, 1991-1997.

Astrom, K., Hagglund, T., 1995. PID Controllers: Theory, Design, and Tuning, second ed. Instrument Society of America.

Ekren, O., Kucuka, S. 2010. Energy saving potential of chiller system with fuzzy logic control. Int. J. Energy Res. 34:897–906.

Ekren, O., Sahin, S., Isler, Y. 2010. Comparison of Different Controllers for Variable Speed Compressor and Electronic Expansion Valve, International Journal of Refrigeration, 33(6), 1161–1168.

Ekren, O., Sahin, S., Isler, Y. 2011. Experimental Development of Transfer Functions for Variable Speed Chiller System, Proceedings of the IMechE Part E: Journal of Process Mechanical Engineering, article in pres, DOI: 10.1177/0954408911414805.

Huang, J.Q., Lewis, F.L., 2003. Neural-network predictive control for nonlinear dynamic systems with time-delay. IEEE Trans. Neural Netw. 2, 377-389.

Jiangjiang, W., Dawei, A., Chengzhi, L., 2006. Application of fuzzy-PID controller in heating ventilating and air-conditioning system. In: Proceedings of the 2006 IEEE International Conference on Mechatronics and Automation, June 25-28, 2006, Luoyang, China.

Katsuhiko, O., 2002. Modern Control Engineering. Prentice Hall, NJ.

Lazzarin, R., Noro, M., 2008. Experimental comparison of electronic and thermostatic expansion valves performance in an air conditioning plant. Int. J. Refrigeration 31, 113-118.

Li, H., Jeong, S.K., Yoon, J.I., You, S.S., 2008. An empirical model for independent control of variable speed refrigeration system. Appl. Therm. Eng. 28, 1918-1924.

Lightbody, G., Irwin, G.W., 1995. Direct Neural Model Reference Adaptive Control. *IEE Proceeding Control Theory Applications*, 142(1), 31-43.

Lin, C.L., Chen, C.H., Shiu, B.M., 2008. A neural net-based timedelay compensation scheme and disturbance rejection for pneumatic systems. J. Intell. Manuf., 19,407-19,419.

Meireles, M.R.G., Almeida, P.E.M., Simoes, M.G., 2003. A comprehensive review for industrial applicability of artificial neural networks. IEEE Trans. Indust. Electron. 3, 585-601.

Narendra, K.S., 1993. Hierarchical neural network models for identification and control. In: Engineering in Medicine and Biology Society Proceedings of the 15th Annual International Conference of the IEEE, vol. 287.

Narendra, K.S., Parthasarathy, K., 1990. Identification and control of dynamical systems using neural networks. IEEE Trans. Neural Netw. 1, 4-27.

Nasutin, H., Hassan, M.N.W., 2006. Potential electricity savings by variable speed control of compressor for air conditioning systems. Clean Technol. Environ. Policy 8, 105-111.

Noriega, J. R., Wang, H., 1998. A Direct Adaptive Neural-Network Control for Unknown Nonlinear Systems and Its Application. *IEEE Transactions on Neural Networks*, 9(1), 27-34.

Omidvar, O. M., Elliott, D. L. 1997. *Neural Systems for Control*. Elsevier Science & Technology Books.

Ross, T.J., 2004. Fuzzy Logic with Engineering Applications. John Wiley and Sons, USA.

Sahin, S., Ekren, O., Isler, Y., Güzeliş, C. 2010. Design and Implementation of Artificial Neural Networks Controller via a Real-Time Simulator for Variable Speed Refrigeration Systems Journal of Engineers and Machinery, 51(603), 8–15.

Slanvetpan, T., Barat, R.B., Stevens, J.G., 2003. Process control of a laboratory combustor using artificial neural networks. Comput. Chem. Eng. 27, 1605-1616.

Yuksel, I. Automatic control, 2006 (Nobel Press, Ankara, Turkiye).

Zadeh, L.A., 1965. Fuzzy sets. Inform. Control 8, 338-353.

Ziegler, J.G., Nichols, N.B., 1942. Optimum setting for automatic controllers. Trans. ASME 1, 759-765.

13

Fuzzy Control Applied to Aluminum Smelting

Vanilson G. Pereira,
Roberto C.L. De Oliveira and Fábio M. Soares
Federal University of Pará,
Brazil

1. Introduction

Aluminum is a modern and new metal, since it has been produced for industry no earlier than 1886, when Hall and Héroult concurrently found out a method to produce free Aluminum through electrolysis (Beck, 2008). In 1900, the Aluminum production worldwide had reached a thousand tons. Nevertheless, at the beginning of the 21st century, global production reached 32 million tons encompassed by 24 million of primary Aluminum and 8 million of recycled material. This fact puts Aluminum at the second place in the list of the most used metals on earth. The world without Aluminum became inacceptable: the businessmen, the tourists, the delivery offices fly over the world in airplanes made of Aluminum, as well as many enterprises and industries are strongly dependent of this metal. Figure 1 shows in a widely perspective where Aluminum is most used.

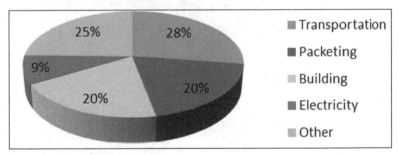

Fig. 1. Fields where Aluminum is most used (source: IAI, 2010)

This metal has contributed to low fuel consumption in cars and trucks, as well as allowing high speeds for trains and ships due to their weight reduction. Since it is a light metal, Aluminum eases the construction of buildings resistant to corrosion and low need for maintenance. Everywhere in the world, the electricity transmission lines for great distances are made of Aluminum, in part or whole. Food quality is preserved by Aluminum packages, reducing waste and giving comfort to users. This metal protects food, cosmetics and pharmaceutical products from ultraviolet rays, bad smells and bacteria. Food waste is avoided 30% when Aluminum packages are used.

Aluminum is a global commodity; its industry employs directly at least one million people, and indirectly more than four million. It is a slight compact industry, provided that around

20 smelters are responsible for 65% or world production. Most companies work only with Aluminum, but 20% of them work with Aluminum with other metals or mines. Half of Aluminum production is done by companies vertically integrated, from bauxite mining to metal recycling (IAI, 2010).

For all these reasons, the Aluminum can be considered a highly important metal, and therefore, its production is a target for many research activities. Researchers all around the world make efforts in making Aluminum production a less costly process, since it spends a lot of energy, and is very complex. In this chapter, we are going to present the whole context, and why and where fuzzy control is important to assist plant operators.

The impact and consequences of this work is the use of rules defined by process operators indirectly through the huge database which provides historic information including control decisions made by them. Since this strategy emulates process operator, it can be said that an expert system can provide this personnel more time to concentrate on other activities. Moreover, this technique will be continually improved by revising its rules and evaluation, provided that fuzzy decisions will also have an impact, and this should be analysed and adjusted.

1.1 Aluminum production process

Aluminum has been produced through the Hall-Héroult process, named after its inventors. So far, this is the only industrial way to produce this metal. Primary Aluminum is produced in a liquid form, through an electrolytic reduction of alumina (Al_2O_3) in a cryolite bath (Na_3AlF_6). This reaction takes place in electrolytic pots, as shown in Figure 2.

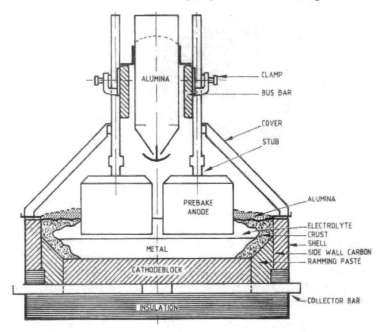

Fig. 2. Sketch of an Alumina reduction pot of prebake type (adapted from Kola & Store, 2009).

Inside these pots, also often called cells, Alumina is fed through silo and it is electrically consumed by the carbon anodes (Solheim, 2005), and as shown in the equation (1), the anode is also consumed during the electrolytic process.

$$\frac{1}{2}Al_2O_3 + 3NaF + \frac{3}{4}C \rightarrow AlF_3 + \frac{3}{4}CO_2 + 3Na^+ + 3e \qquad (1)$$

At the bottom part of the cell, there is a thermal isolated steel covering made of refractory material, named cathode block. The liquid Aluminum is formed above the cathode, and under the anode the electrolytic bath is formed. The cathode, in an electrochemical sense, is an interface between liquid Aluminum and the electrolytic bath, according to equation (2).

$$AlF_3 + 3Na^+ + 3e \rightarrow Al + 3NaF \qquad (2)$$

The full reaction inside the reduction pot is shown in equation (3).

$$\frac{1}{2}Al_2O_3 + \frac{3}{4}C \rightarrow Al + \frac{3}{4}CO_2 \qquad (3)$$

The pure electrolytic bath, i.e. cryolite, has a melting point at 1,011°C. In order to lower this point, called *liquidus* temperature, some additives are added into the bath, from which the main are Aluminum Fluoride (AlF_3) and Calcium Fluoride (CaF_2). The chemical composition of the bath in the reduction pot is 6-13% of AlF_3, 4-6% of CaF_2 and 2-4% of Al_2O_3. With a low liquidus temperature, pot operation is performed with low bath temperature, allowing reducing alumina solubility inside the bath. Therefore a good alumina concentration control system is required. Usually an aluminum reduction pot is operated under temperatures from 940°C to 970°C.

Bath is not consumed during the process, but part of it is lost, during vaporization, constituted of $NaAlF_4$. Moreover, part of bath is lost by drops dragging, by water present in fed alumina and the air aspired from inside the cell to form HF. In order to protect the environment, the gas is collected and cleared by a gas washing system. More than 98% of AlF_3 is retrieved in the gas washing system (Hyland et al, 2001), and recycled back to the pot. Moreover, Sodium Oxide (Na_2O) and Calcium Fluoride (CaF_2) at alumina feeding neutralizes AlF_3. The neutralized amount is also dependent on sodium penetration into the cathode which is, the pot age.

At the cathode sidewall there is a cool layer called ledge, which protects the sidewall from erosion. The ledge is composed of Na_3AlF_6 and CaF_2 (Thonstad & Rolseth, 1983). The ledge thickness is dependent on the heat flux through the cell sides, which is dependent on the bath temperature and liquidus temperature (that difference is called superheat). Once it is established that ledge composition is basically Na_3AlF_6, that means the total cryolite mass varies, while AlF3 and Al2O3 mass do not vary with the ledge thickness. In addition, once the additive concentration is the additive mass divided by the total bath mass, the ledge thickness variation triggers variation in the additives' concentrations. Then, changes in concentrations triggers changes in liquidus temperature, which in turn triggers changes in superheat, affecting ledge thickness. Thus, the challenge is to guarantee a stable pot operation which means a stable protection ledge minimizing energy input and maximizing production.

1.2 Current control systems

Regarding pot control, there are three main variables to be controlled: bath temperature, AlF_3 concentration and Al_2O_3 concentration. For that, there are three control inputs: anode beam moves (controlling energy input, by means of anode-to-cathode distance (ACD), AlF_3 addition and Al_2O_3 addition). The AlF_3 mass reduction dynamic process is slow, the AlF_3 concentration control system should deal with long response times (long delays) to control inputs which in this case are the changes to AlF_3 concentration. On the other hand, the Al_2O_3 mass reduction process is faster, and the Al_2O_3 concentration control system should deal with fast responses to the control inputs which in this case are the Al_2O_3 concentration changes. Usually, the Al_2O_3 concentration control system is considered an isolate problem, decoupled from the other control systems.

Bath temperature is measured manually, once a day or at least once a week. The AlF3 concentration (acidity) is typically measured manually once or twice a week, while Al_2O_3 concentration is not normally measured, except in special situations when process engineers need exceptionally. The only real time measurement is the bath pseudo-resistance (R_b), defined by equation (4),

$$R_b = \frac{U_f - 1,7}{I} \quad (\mu\,\Omega) \tag{4}$$

where U_f is cell voltage in Volts, and I is potline current in KA, these variables are also measured continually. The R_b measurement is used as input for anode-to-cathode distance adjustment, and acts as a control variable along with energy input into the cell.

Due to the fact that there is a strong relation between energy balance and mass balance through the ledge (see, e.g., Drenstig, 1997, Chapter 5), the reduction cell control must be considered as a multivariable non-linear control. A raise in the bath temperature causes acidity decrease and increases bath conductivity (Hives et al, 1993). According to Drenstig (1997, Chapter 5), acidity variation is ruled by bath temperature variation. Likewise, the control system logic should be bath temperature control through the additives (with negative or positive effects), around a setpoint, and Aluminum fluoride (AlF_3) constant addition. While this seems to be obvious and reasonable, there is a long way to go to transform this idea into a viable application in an alumina reduction cell.

1.3 Usage of fuzzy logic in aluminum industry

One easy and cheap method to perform a non-linear control system in an alumina reduction cell is to use fuzzy systems. With a qualitative approach, fuzzy systems offer a methodology to simulate a human expert operational behaviour and allow using available data from these experts' knowledge. Fuzzy expert systems have been largely used in control systems (Benyakhlef&Radouane, 2008; Chiu &Lian, 2009; Yu et al., 2010; Feng, 2010; Wang et al., 2011), since when Mamdani and Assilian developed a fuzzy controller for a boiler (Mamdani&Assilan, 1975).

In Aluminum industry, control strategies involve alumina addition neural control by cell states estimation (Meghlaoui et al., 1997), bath Aluminum fluoride control by mass balance differential equations and algebraic equations that deal with mass balance and thermal balance (Drenstig et al, 1998), the use of LQR (Linear Quadratic Gaussian) to perform cell multivariable control by identifying dynamic models (McFadden et al, 2006); the use of regression models for bath temperature along with IF-THEN rules to add Aluminum fluoride into the cell (Yongbo et al, 2008), and PID (Proportional, Integral and Derivative) control along with a feed-forward loop for Aluminum fluoride addition and a PI (Proportional and Integral) control for bath temperature (Kola & Store, 2009). The use of fuzzy controllers in the cell is also often used (Meghlaoui&Aljabri, 2003; Yan &Taishan, 2006; Shuiping&Jinhong, 2008; Shuiping et al. 2010; Xiaodong et al, 2010; Dan Yang et al., 2011). However these works have not exploited any operational experience stored in process database, and the existing data mining works in the Aluminum Industry (Zhuo et al., 2008) are not addressed to the fluoride addition problem.

1.4 The novelty proposed in this work

In this chapter we propose a data-oriented fuzzy-based strategy applied to one of the Aluminum smelting sub-processes. Aluminum industries usually maintain huge databases which provide historic information regarding the process, including control decisions made by process operators. It can be said that these information contain the system's dynamics and the process team's knowledge. This knowledge can be exploited to develop an expert system, provided that most of process decision makers control the plant based on their own experience in a fuzzy approach. This work shows the whole design of the fuzzy system, their rules formation and fuzzy sets selection, and its results. This work was performed in a Brazilian company whose aim was to develop a fuzzy controller based on an expert system whose rules were generated from the company's process database and interviews with process operators. This work is also fully based on the literature of Gomes et al, 2010. The control system is aimed at adding Aluminum fluoride into alumina reduction cells. The results show more stability on bath temperature and AlF$_3$ concentration.

2. Fuzzy controllers and systems: An overview

The inaccuracy and uncertainty are two aspects that may be part of the information. There are two theories used to deal with inaccuracy and uncertainty: classic sets (crisp) theory and probabilities theory, respectively. However, these theories do not always capture the information content provided by humans in natural language. The classic sets theory cannot deal with the fuzzy aspect of information while the probabilities theory is more suited to handle frequency information than those provided by humans.

The fuzzy sets theory, developed by LoftiZadeh in 1965 (Zadeh, 1965), aimed at dealing with the fuzzy aspect of information, while, in 1978, Zadeh also developed the probabilities theory that deals with information uncertainty (Zadeh, 1978). These theories have been used in systems that use human-provided information. These theories are closely linked with each other. When the fuzzy sets theory is used in a logic context, as knowledge-based systems, it is known as fuzzy logic (term used in this chapter). The fuzzy logic is currently one of the most successful technologies for the development of process control systems, due to low implementation cost, easy maintenance and the fact that complex requirements may be implemented in simple controllers.

In the broad sense, a fuzzy controller is a rule-based fuzzy system, composed of a set of inference rules of the type If <Condition> Then <Action>, that define the control actions according to several ranges the controlled variables in the problem may assume. These ranges (usually poor defined) are modeled by fuzzy sets and named as linguistic terms. In this section, we present all the theoretic aspects for the development of the fuzzy controller.

2.1 Theoretic aspects

2.1.1 Fuzzy sets

Crisp sets have hard defined membership functions (either 0 or 1), while fuzzy set have soft defined membership functions. Given a set A in a universe U, the elements of this universe just belong or not to that set. That is, the element x is true $\left(f_A(x)=1\right)$, or false $\left(f_A(x)=0\right)$. This can be expressed as

$$f_A(x) = \begin{cases} 1 & if \quad x \in A; \\ 0 & if \quad x \notin A \end{cases}$$

(5)

Zadeh(Zadeh, 1965) proposed a more general approach, so the characteristic function could yield float point values in the interval [0,1]. A fuzzy set A in a universe U is defined by a membership function $\mu_A(x) \to [0,1]$, that amounts the element x for the fuzzy set. Fuzzy sets can be defined in continuous or discrete universes. If the universe U is discrete and finite, the fuzzy set A is usually denoted by expression:

$$A = \sum_{i=1}^{m} \frac{\mu_A(x_i)}{x_i}$$

$$A = \frac{\mu_A(x_i)}{x_i} + \cdots + \frac{\mu_A(x_m)}{x_m}$$

(6)

If U is a continuous universe, the fuzzy set A is denoted by expression:

$$A = \int \frac{\mu_A(x)}{x}$$

(7)

Where $\mu_A(x_i)$ is known as membership function which may show how much x belongs to the set A, and U is known as the universe of discourse. In other words, the element x may belong to more than one fuzzy set, but with different membership values.

2.1.2 Linguistic variables

A linguistic variable has its value expressed qualitatively by a linguistic term and quantitatively by a membership function. A linguistic function is characterized by {n,T,X,m(n)} where n is the variable's name, T is the set of linguistic terms of n (Cold, Normal, Hot, Very Hot), X is the domain (Universe of Discourse) of n values which the linguistic term meaning is determined on (the temperature may be between 970° and 975°C) and m(t) is a semantic function that assigns each linguistic term $t \in T$ its meaning, what is a fuzzy set in X (that is, m: T→(X) where (X) is the fuzzy sets space).

2.1.3 Fuzzy sets operation

Given fuzzy sets A and B contained in a universe of μ_A and μ_B, respectively, their operation are defined as sets theoretic operation (union, intersection and complement) as follows:

Equality: If for every $x \in U$, $\mu_A(x) = \mu_B(x)$, then the set A is equal to set B.

Subset: If for every $x \in U$, $\mu_A(x) \leq \mu_B(x)$, then the set B contains set A.

Union: This operation is similar to the union between two classic sets $A \cup B$. The union between fuzzy sets may be written with membership functions of sets A and B, as follows:

$$\mu_{A \cup B}(x) = \max\left[\mu_A(x), \mu_B(x)\right] \tag{8}$$

Intersection: This operation is similar to the intersection between two classic sets $A \cap B$. The intersection between fuzzy sets may be written with membership functions of sets A and B, as follows:

$$\mu_{A \cap B}(x) = \min\left[\mu_A(x), \mu_B(x)\right] \tag{9}$$

Complement: The complement set of A, named as $\overline{A}$, is defined by the membership function:

$$\mu_{\overline{A}}(x) = 1 - \mu_A(x) \tag{10}$$

s-Norms: These are combinations of membership functions of two fuzzy sets A and B, resulting in the union $A \cup B$ of set membership functions:

$$s\left[\mu_A(x), \mu_B(x)\right] = \mu_{A \cup B}(x) \tag{11}$$

The combination s should match these properties:

1. s[1,1]=1,s[a,0]=a
2. s[a,b] = s[b,a]
3. s[a,b] ≤ s[a',b'], if a < a' and b < b'
4. s[s[a,b],c]=s[a,s[b,c]]

t-Norms: These are combinations of membership functions of two fuzzy sets A and B, resulting in the intersection $A \cap B$ of two set membership functions:

$$t\left[\mu_A(x), \mu_B(x)\right] = \mu_{A \cap B}(x) \tag{12}$$

The combination t should match these properties:

1. t[1,1]=1,t[a,0]=a
2. t[a,b] = t[b,a]

3.   t[a,b] ≤ t[a',b'], if a < a' and b < b'
4.   t[t[a,b],c]=t[a,t[b,c]]

2.1.4 Fuzzy relations and compositions

A fuzzy relation describes the presence or absence of an association (or interaction) between two or more sets. Likewise, given two universes U and V, the relation R defined in U x V is a subset of the Cartesian product of the two universes, so that R: U x V →{0,1}. That is, if any $x \in U$ and $y \in V$ are related, R(x,y)=1; otherwise R(x,y)=0. This relation (U,V) can be defined by the following characteristic function.

$$f_A(x) = \begin{cases} 1 & \text{if and only if} (x,y) \in R(U,Y); \\ 0 & otherwise \end{cases} \tag{13}$$

Fuzzy relations represent the association degree between two or more fuzzy sets. The fuzzy operations (union, intersection and complement) are similarly defined. Given two fuzzy relations R(x,y) and S(x,y) defined in one space U x Y, the resulting membership functions are:

$$\mu_{R \cap S}(x,y) = \mu_R(x,y) * \mu_S(x,y)$$

$$\mu_{R \cup S}(x,y) = \mu_R(x,y) \oplus \mu_S(x,y) \tag{14}$$

where * is any t-norm and ⊕ is any t-co-norm.

Given U, V, and W as three universes of discourses, R as a relation on U x V, and S another relation on V x W, in order to obtain the composition R o S, that relates U and W, it is initially extended R and S to U x V x W. Since the relations R and S have now the same domain, then we can determine the relation support between the universes U x W by the following expression:

$$\mu_{ROS}(x,z) = \sup\left[\min\left\{ \mu_R^{ext}(x,y,z), \mu_S^{ext}(x,y,z) \right\} \right] \tag{15}$$

Where

$$\mu_R^{ext}(x,y,z) = \mu_R(x,y)$$

$$\mu_S^{ext}(x,y,z) = \mu_S(x,y) \tag{16}$$

The main difference between the fuzzy relation and the classic relation is that the latter $\mu_R(x,y)$ assumes values 0 or 1, while fuzzy relation may assume infinite values between 0 and 1.

2.1.5 Fuzzy implications

Fuzzy rules are conditional structures that use heuristic methods through linguistic expressions in rule forms, composed by a condition (IF) and a consequence (THEN), forming the following structure

$$IF\{condition\}THEN\{consequence\} \tag{17}$$

where conditions and consequences are fuzzy propositions built by linguistic expressions:

1. x is Low
2. y is NOT Tall
3. x is Low AND y is Tall
4. x is Low OR y is Tall

The rules 1 and 2 define "immediate" propositions, the rules 3 and 4 define combined propositions. These propositions use fuzzy operators NOT, OR and AND, respectively in 2, 3, and 4.

Mamdani (Mamdani & Assilan, 1975) defined the use of fuzzy relations R_{MM} and R_{PM} in U x V as an interpretation for the rule IF <pert$_1$> THEN <pert$_2$>, where R_{MM} and R_{PM} are defined as

$$\mu_{QMM}(x,y) = \min\left[\mu_{pert1}(x), \mu_{pert2}(y)\right] \tag{18}$$

$$\mu_{QPM}(x,y) = \min\left[\mu_{pert1}(x), \mu_{pert2}(y)\right] \tag{19}$$

where $x \in U$ and $y \in V$.

2.2 Fuzzy system structure

Figure 3 shows the structure of a basic model of fuzzy system applied in industrial process. The fuzzy system structure consists of four subsystems: Input Fuzzification, Rule Database, Inference Machine and Defuzzification.

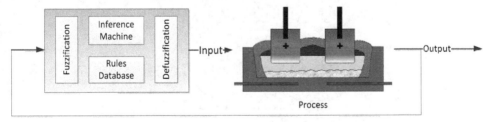

Fig. 3. Fuzzy System Structure

2.2.1 Input fuzzification

In this stage, the input variables (crisp variables) are converted into fuzzy values through a real numbers mapping $x^* \in U \subset R^n$ for a fuzzy set $A' \subset R^n$. The steps for fuzzification are presented:

1. acquire numeric values of input variables (crisp values);
2. map these variables in a universe of discourse U;
3. determine membership functions and linguistic variables.

The variables mapping (crisp) is characterized by membership function $\mu_A(x) \rightarrow [0,1]$. Such functions may be classified in: Triangle-shaped, Trapezoidal, and Gaussian. These functions are shown in Figure 4.

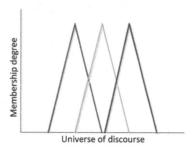

Fig. 4a. Triangle-shaped function

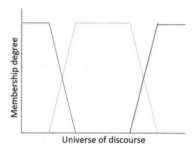

Fig. 4b. Trapezoidal Function

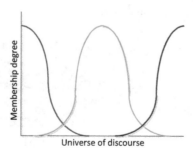

Fig. 4c. Gaussian Function

The Triangle-shaped and Trapezoidal functions use the triangle fuzzificator:

$$
\mu_{A'}(x) = \begin{cases} \left(1 - \dfrac{\left|x_1 - x_1^*\right|}{b_1}\right) \cdots \left(1 - \dfrac{\left|x_n - x_n^*\right|}{b_n}\right) & \text{if} \quad x = \left|x_i - x_i^*\right| \le b_i; \\ 0 & \text{if} \quad x = \left|x_i - x_i^*\right| > b_i \end{cases} \tag{20}
$$

The Gaussian function uses the Gaussian fuzzificator:

$$\mu_{A'}(x) = \exp^{\left(\frac{\left|x_1 - x_1^*\right|}{a_1}\right)^2} \cdots \exp^{\left(\frac{\left|x_n - x_n^*\right|}{a_n}\right)^2} \tag{21}$$

2.2.2 Fuzzy rule database

A fuzzy rule database is a collection of IF-THEN rules that can be expressed as:

$$R^{(l)} : IF \quad x_1 \quad is \quad A_1^l \quad AND \cdots AND \quad x_x \quad is \quad A_n^l \quad THEN \quad y \quad is \quad B^l \tag{22}$$

Where $l = 1, 2, \ldots, M$, A_1^l and B^l are fuzzy sets in $U_i \subset R$ and $U \subset R$ respectively, $x = col(u_1, \ldots, u_n) \in U_1 \times \ldots \times U_n$, and $y \in V$. x and y are linguistic variables. The knowledge of an expert is stored in this rule database, since all decisions taken by an expert can be written as rules. In essence, the rules model the fuzzy system behaviour.

2.2.3 Fuzzy inference machine

The fuzzy inference machine acts on a set of rules, denoted in (22), maps inputs (conditions) into outputs (consequences). In this stage, called inference, the fuzzy operations are performed on these variables. The conditions will trigger some rules then the variables of the triggered rules are combined, performing the implication and summing up the result of all rules. The fuzzy rule database with m rules does:

- Determine the membership value $\mu_{A_1^l \times \ldots \times A_n^l}(x_1, \ldots, x_n)$ for the fuzzy sets triggered for the m rules.

- Perform the fuzzy inference of $A' \subset U$ for $B' \subset V$ based on each rule that compose the fuzzy rule database:

$$\mu_{B^l}^l(y) = \sup_{x \in U} \left[\mu_{A'}(x), \mu_R^l(x, y) \right] \tag{23}$$

The inference machine combines the m fired fuzzy sets, as expressed in:

$$\mu_{B'}(y) = \mu_{B_1}(y) \oplus \ldots \otimes \mu_{B_n}(y) \tag{24}$$

where $\oplus$ denotes the t-norm operator.

There are two main types of inference machine: Product and Minimum.

In the product Inference Machine, we use:

a. inference of rule database individually
b. Mamdani implication (19)
c. Algebraic product for all t-norm operators and maximum for all s-norm operators. This inference machine can be represented as follows:

$$\mu_{B'}(y) = \max_{l=1}^{m} \left[\sup_{x \in u} \left[\mu_{A'}(x) \prod_{i=1}^{n} \mu_{A'}^l(x) \mu_{B^l}(y) \right] \right] \tag{25}$$

In the Minimum Inference machine, we use:

a.   inference of rule database individually
b.   Mamdani implication (19)
c.   Algebric product for all t-norm operators and minimum for all s-norm operators. This
     inference machine can be represented as follows:

$$\mu_{B'}(y) = \max_{l=1}^{m}\left[\sup_{x \in u}\min\left(\mu_{A'}(x), \mu_{A_1^l}, \ldots, \mu_{A_n^l}(x_n), \mu_{B^l}(y)\right)\right]$$ (26)

2.2.4 Defuzzification

In this stage, fuzzy output values are converted back in real values. This conversion is done
through mapping, $B' \subset V$ for a point $y^* \in V$. There are many methods for defuzzification,
namely Centre of Gravity (or Centre of Area), Centre of Maxima, Average of Maxima, to
name a few.

The method Centre of Gravity evaluates the center of area corresponding to the union of
fuzzy sets that contributed to the result. It is mathematically represented by the formula:

$$\bar{y} = \frac{\sum_{i=1}^{N} y_i \mu_B(y_i)}{\sum_{i=1}^{N} \mu_B(y_i)}$$ (27)

where $\bar{y}$ is the resulting center of gravity, y_i is the center of the individual membership
function and $\mu_B(y_i)$ is the area of a membership function modified by the fuzzy inference
result (not null values).

The Centre of Maxima method uses the higher values of membership functions. The not null
values are considered weights and the result is obtained as a support point among them. It
is evaluated by the following equation:

$$\bar{y} = \frac{\sum_{i=1}^{N} y_i \sum_{i=1}^{N} \mu_M(y_i)}{\sum_{i=1}^{N}\sum_{i=1}^{N} \mu_M(y_i)}$$ (28)

where $\mu_M(y_i)$ are the membership functions maximum (height) points.

The Average of Maxima method uses the maximum point of each membership function and
takes the mean value as the defuzzified value. It is represented by the following formula:

$$\bar{y} = \sum_{i=1}^{M} \frac{y_i}{M}$$ (29)

where y_i is the i-th element corresponding to the membership functions maximum and M is the total of elements.

3. Bath chemistry control in aluminum reduction cells

During the Aluminum production process, several chemical additives are used in reduction industries to contro bath chemical and physical composition. These additives' aim to lower the liquidus temperature (Haupin&Kvande, 1993), i.e., to decline the melting point of cryolite (Na_3AlF_6), allowing the solubilisation of alumina (Al_2O_3) and therefore better energy use. There are two strategies for bath chemistry control: Heat Balance and Mass Balance. Any change in the cell's heat balancet results in changes in the bath chemical composition, as well as any change in the bath chemical composition causes changes in the heat balance. It is noted that there is a relationship between cell's heat balance and its current chemical composition, influencing the cells' productivity (Dias, 2002). The current model used for control strategy is based on correlation between bath temperature and fluoride excess (%AlF_3) in the bath. Besides these correlations, there are other variables having some influence in the bath chemistry, which are also used in the control strategy.

The electrolyte used in Aluminium reduction pots is basically composed of melted cryolite (Na_3AlF_6), Aluminum fluoride (AlF_3), calcium fluoride (CaF_2) and alumina (Al_2O_3), and its major concentration is formed by cryolite. The bath components' percentages are directly related to stability. The fluoride percentage has the property of lowering the cryolite melting point from about 1100°C down to. Likewise, the bath is composed of a solid part (non-melted cryolite) and liquid part (melted cryolite) which may vary according to the percentage of fluoride present in the bath. The greater the percentage of fluoride is, the lower the bath melting point is, therefore emphasizing the presence of liquid part in comparison with the solid part (mass balance), leading to a cooling of the cell (heat balance). Similarly, low quantities of fluoride emphasize the solid part regarding the liquid part, causing a heat of the cell (heat balance).

There are many factors contributing to the Aluminum fluoride consumption, which is added in the pot during the Aluminum reduction process. In other to stabilize such situations during the process, a theoretical calculation is defined, considering the following factors:

• Addition due to the absorption by pot lining (Hyland et al, 2001).
• Addition due to the sodium and calcium oxide present in alumina (Al_2O_3), according to the equations 30 and 31:

$$3Na_2O + 2AlF_3 = 6NAF + Al_2O \qquad (30)$$

$$3CaO + 2AlF_3 = 3CaF_2 + Al_2O_3 \qquad (31)$$

Based on these information, the theoretical consumption is determined by the following expression:

$$AlF3[kg] = A*\%Na_2O + B*\%CaO + C*\%AlF_3 \qquad (32)$$

where A, B and C are constants and $\%Na_2O$, $\%CaO$ and $\%AlF_3$ represent respectively the percentages of sodium oxide, calcium oxide and Aluminum fluoride. The electrolyte composition control represents a challenge in Aluminum reduction industries, due to the intrinsic relation between heat and mass balance.

Usually the bath chemistry control is performed daily or weekly, collecting all the information about thermal and mass balance (Bath Temperature, Liquidus Temperature, Super Heat, Fluoride, Bath Composition and so on). With this information, the process team should take decisions on how much should be added into the bath in order to keep temperature and fluoride under control near a setpoint. Figure 5 shows a scheme of this process.

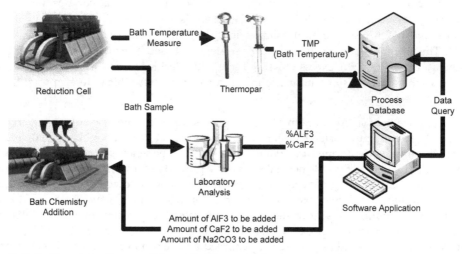

Fig. 5. Bath Chemistry Process Schematic Diagram

Variable	Description
TMP	BathTemperature
%ALF3	Percentage of AluminumFluoride in the bath
%CaF2	Percentage of Calcium Fluoride in the bath
AlF3A	Amount of Aluminum Fluoride to be added
CaF2A	Amount of Calcium Fluoride to be added
Na2CO3A	Amount of Sodium Carbonate to be added
LIFE	Time elasped (in days) since cell startup

Table 1. Variables used in the Bath Chemistry Control Process

3.1 Challenges on this control

The strongest impact of this process in Aluminum smelting is the direct influence on Current Efficiency and on ledge. Because of that, a careful control is required in order to keep both bath temperature and Aluminum fluoride stable. The Current Efficiency means literally how much is produced from the maximum allowed, according to equation 32.

$$Kg_{Al} = \left(\frac{I * 86400}{96485} \right) * 0,009 \qquad (33)$$

where I is the current in Amperes. A hypothetically Current Efficiency of 100% means that production is equal to the theoretical maximum. However, part of the Aluminum formed in the bath is recombined again with carbon gas, as showed in the equation (34).

$$2Al^+ + 3CO_2 \rightarrow Al_2O_3 + 3CO \qquad (34)$$

The optimum point is reached when the variables are stabilized around a setpoint. Each variable is assigned a setpoint, but the cells are subjected to many disturbances that have effect on every controlled variable. This makes the process even harder to control and more complex to model (Prasad, 2000; McFadden et al., 2001; Welch, 2002). Process experts take actions, sometimes predefined, to control the process based on their experience in the process. This means their decisions are usually taken without any model of the system. For that reason, an AI technique approach is useful since it does not need to model analytically the whole process but it can represent it with some accuracy and yield good results. To address the fluoride addition problem, we can build a fuzzy system in which all the process knowledge can be included as rules, and provided that process operators usually refer to variables using linguistic terms, Fuzzy sets can be used to represent these linguistic terms.

4. Fuzzy control applied for fluoride addition in aluminum reduction cells

Fuzzy Controllers have been applied in industrial plants, since many solutions are sold with this technology as part of it(Cao et al, 2010). In Aluminum industry, the Aluminum fluoride addition control is usually performed by parameterized equations, confidentially protected. These are made by data collection and numeric approximation. This model has a poor performance since the plant is very nonlinear and complex and its modeling is very difficult. Very often the process operators must take manual actions to control the process. This decision making process for fluoride addition in reduction cells is a routine for adjusting the bath composition and hence its performance.

In order to maintain performance and stability of electrolytic cells, some action on thermal balance and mass balance is required (Welch, 2000), acting on process variables. These variables are used to determine how much Aluminum fluoride should be added into the bath. Bath chemistry control stands as a great challenge for Aluminum smelters, since it is intrinsic to the thermal balance of electrolytic cells.

4.1 Design procedure

Since human intervention in this process is often required, a fuzzy controller must follow the actions operators usually take when analyzing recent data from the cells. In this sense, a linguistic processing is needed to represent the process data under a fuzzy view. Also, a survey with process engineers responsible for the bath chemistry control is performed in order to find out which data the process operators usually look at before performing a fluoride addition. TThese data can also represent the process dynamic behaviour. In this work they are: Bath Temperature (TMP), Percentage of aluminum fluoride in the bath(ALF), Cell operation time (also known as Pot life) (LIFE). Moreover, the Temperature and Fluoride trend information (TTMP and TALF, respectively)are also viewed by process operators and should be taken into account for fuzzy processing, provided that Bath temperature and Aluminum Fluoride are negatively correlated, which means as one is rising the other is falling. The past fluoride additions are also considered in a separate variable called Accumulated Aluminum Fluoride (ALF3AC), so the information of how much fluoride has been added into the bath in the last three cycles is considered for fuzzy processing. And finally, the output variable for the fuzzy system is Fluoride addition (ALF3A), which is the control variable. It is important to note that the variables TMP, ALF and LIFE are measured, but TTMP, TALF and ALF3AC are calculated from TMP and ALF, as shown in equations.

$$TTMP(t) = TMP(t) - TMP(t-1) \tag{35}$$

$$TALF(t) = ALF(t) - ALF(t-1) \tag{36}$$

$$ALF3AC(t) = \sum_{i}^{3} ALF3A(t-i) \tag{37}$$

After these variables have been chosen, each one is assigned linguistic terms like process operators usually call, as shown in table 2.

Input Variables		Linguistic terms
TMP	Bath Temperature	Very Cold, Cold, Normal, Hot, Very Hot
ALF	Aluminum Fluoride	Very Low, Low, Normal, High, Very High
LIFE	Cell Life	Young, Average, Old
ALF3AC	Accumulated Aluminum Fluoride	Very Low, Low, Normal, High, Very High, Ultra High
TTMP	Bath Temperature Trend	Rise, Fall
TALF	Aluminum Fluoride Trend	Rise, Fall
Output Variable		Linguistic terms
ALF3A	Aluminum Fluoride to be added	No Add, Very Low, Low, Mid-Low, Normal, Mid-High, High, Very High, Super High, Ultra High

Table 2. Fuzzy Variables used in this system and their linguistic terms

4.1.1 Fuzzy sets

The linguistic terms for each process variable are used to form the fuzzy sets, which are characterized by membership functions, as described in 2.1. The membership functions related to each fuzzy set were determined by the dynamic behaviour of each variable as the process evolves. All sets are represented by trapezoidal functions whose limits are based on a qualitative knowledge on the plant. Figures 6a-6g show the fuzzy sets plots for each input variable and for the output variable.

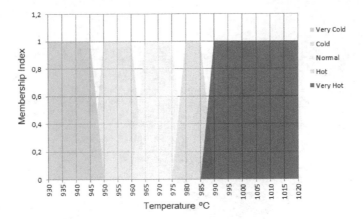

Fig. 6a. Fuzzy sets for the bath temperature

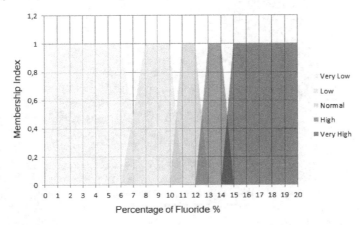

Fig. 6b. Fuzzy sets for Percentage of Aluminum fluoride in the bath

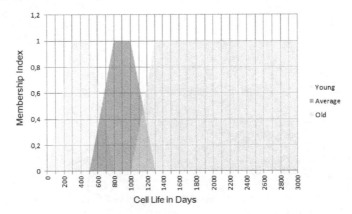

Fig. 6c. Fuzzy sets for Life

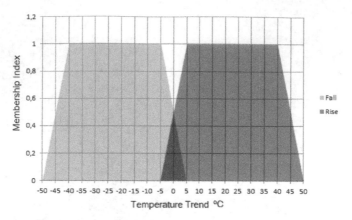

Fig. 6d. Fuzzy sets for Temperature Trend

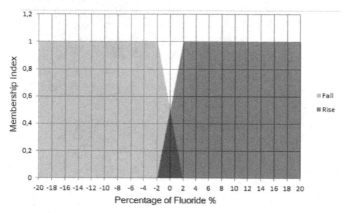

Fig. 6e. Fuzzy sets for Fluoride Trend

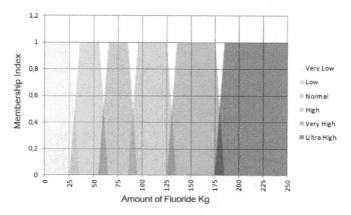

Fig. 6f. Fuzzy sets for Accumulated Aluminum fluoride

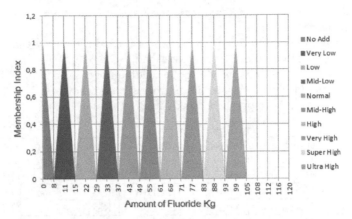

Fig. 6g. Fuzzy sets for Amount of Aluminum fluoride to be added

4.1.2 Fuzzy rules definition

In order to define the fuzzy rules, a database T was built by taking the process variables records from the chosen inputs and outputs. This database encompasses three years of operation and has over 800,000 records. This huge number of records allows querying each combination of variables' fuzzy sets against the database in order to find which output value was chosen in the most of times. This means that the rules definition cannot be performed by interviews as fuzzy system designers usually do, however some adjusts on the rules may be made by process experts. Table 3 shows the number of fuzzy sets for each variable and the number of combinations:

Variable (VAR)	Number of Fuzzy Sets (NVAR)
TMP	5
ALF	5
LIFE	3
TTMP	2
TALF	2
ALF3AC	6
Total of combinations (NTMP x NALF x NLIFE x NTTMP x NTALF x NALF3AC)	1800

Table 3. Combinations of Fuzzy Sets

Through these combinations, one can perform a statistical research in the process database and find which output fuzzy set has more occurrences for every single combination. Table 4 shows how the fuzzy rule database look like, taking into account these combinations. It is assumed for interpretation the connector AND for all rules. Table 5 shows a case for defining an output for a given rule.

The statistical research may fall into three cases:

- **Case 1** - there is only one most frequent set for a condition of a given rule R^l, which is going to be the rule's output.
- **Case 2** – there are two or more frequent set for a condition of a given rule R^l, whose output should be chosen later by a process expert.
- **Case 3** – there are no records matching the condition of a given rule, which means the rule output should be chosen later by a process expert, however it is likely that this situation won't happen, implying no need for adjustment.

#	Conditional Variables						Consequence
	Bath Temp.	Aluminum Fluoride	Cell Life	Accum. Fluoride	Fluoride Trend	Temp. Trend	Fluoride to be added
1	Very Cold	Very Low	Young	Very Low	Fall	Fall	Det. by queries
2	Very Cold	Very Low	Young	Very Low	Fall	Rise	Det. by queries
3	Very Cold	Very Low	Young	Very Low	Rise	Fall	Det. by queries
4	Very Cold	Very Low	Young	Very Low	Rise	Rise	Det. by queries
5	Very Cold	Very Low	Young	Low	Fall	Fall	Det. by queries
...	...	...	...	...	...	...	...
1800	Very Hot	Very High	Old	Ultra High	Rise	Rise	Det. by queries

Table 4. Fuzzy Rule Database Structure

"if **TMP** is *Normal* and **ALF** is *Very Low* and **LIFE** is *Normal* and **ALF3AC** is *Normal* and **TTMP** is *Fall* and **TALF** is *Rise*"	
A query against a database is performed, and the following result is found:	
ALF3A is *Normal*	Twice
ALF3A is *High*	3 Times
ALF3A is *Very High*	6 Times
Thus, as for this rule, the output is chosen as *Very High*, since it is the decision more often.	

Table 5. Fuzzy rule definition upon database research

4.2 Fuzzy operations

Real world (crisp) values are fuzzified by the membership functions defined in figures 6a-6f, which may yield fuzzy values in one or two sets. We used the minimum operator to apply the fuzzy values. Table 6 shows an example of fuzzification and table 7 show an example of the fuzzy minimum operator:

Variable	Crisp Value	Fuzzy Values (with membership indexes)
Bath Temperature (TMP)	962°C	Cold (0.6) and Normal (0.4)
Aluminum Fluoride (ALF)	9.82 %	Low (1)
Cell Life (LIFE)	596 days	Young (0.68) and Normal (0.32)
Accumulated Aluminum Fluoride (ALF3AC)	70 Kg	Normal (1)
Temperature Trend (TTMP)	-13°C	Fall (1)
Fluoride Trend (TALF)	- 3%	Fall (1)

Table 6. Fuzzy Values for a case

Rule	Rule output (Least membership index)
"if **TMP** is *Cold(0.6)* and **ALF** is *Low(1)* and **LIFE** is *Young(0.68)* and **ALF3AC** is *Normal(1)* and **TTMP** is *Fall(1)* and **TALF** is *Fall(1)*"	Mid-High (0.6)
"if **TMP** is *Normal(0.4)* and **ALF** is *Low(1)* and **LIFE** is *Young(0.68)* and **ALF3AC** is *Normal(1)* and **TTMP** is *Fall(1)* and **TALF** is *Fall(1)*"	Very Low (0.4)
"if **TMP** is *Cold(0.6)* and **ALF** is *Low(1)* and **LIFE** is *Normal(0.32)* and **ALF3AC** is *Normal(1)* and **TTMP** is *Fall(1)* and **TALF** is *Fall(1)*"	Mid-High (0.32)
"if TMP is *Normal(0.4)* and ALF is *Low(1)* and LIFE is *Normal(0.32)* and ALF3AC is *Normal(1)* and TTMP is *Fall(1)* and TALF is *Fall(1)*"	High (0.32)

Table 7. Rules triggered for the fuzzy values in the case of table 6

The implication operation chosen in this work is the product method, meaning that every output set is multiplied by the rule's least membership value. And for the aggregation operation, the output sets build the geometric shape by the maximum. The defuzzification method is the centre of area. Figure 7 shows the geometric shape made by the output sets with their least membership index in table 7.

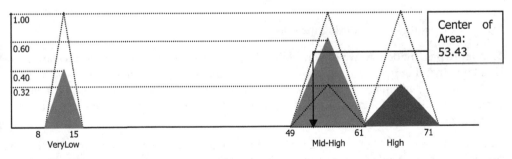

Fig. 7. Implication, Aggregation and Defuzzification operations

4.3 Result and validation

The fuzzy algorithm was directly implemented in an industrial plant of aluminum reduction. Initially 10 pots were chosen from one potline, to which the operators were instructed to intervene only when there is an extreme need. However, it is worth mentioning, that the validation of new fluoride addition logic must be tested for at least seven months. By the time this paper was written, the pots used in these tests were operating for nearly five months with the new logic. The figure 8 show the real result obtained for one pot during the test period.

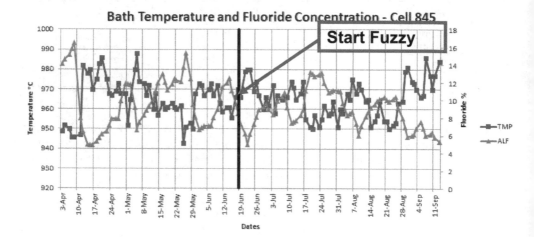

Fig. 8. Real result obtained during the tests

The figure 8 is divided in two regions defined by the date when the fuzzy system started. It is notable that the right (or later) region has less oscillation of the temperature variable (red line) and the percentage fluoride has been decreased. This has been one of the main expected results with the fuzzy logic, being interpreted by the process engineering as a safer operational condition.

Another desired goal was to reduce the human interventions in the process. In the previous control strategy, there was a high oscillation degree, which often required human intervention, by changing the proposed value to a quantity, sometimes, higher than needed, thus destabilizing the process. With the new strategy, the need of an analysis tool arose in order to show the membership values of each set, the activated rules and the corresponding defuzzified output. This tool allows monitoring the decisions made by the fuzzy system, and the historical analysis of past decisions. A screen of this tool is shown in figure 9.

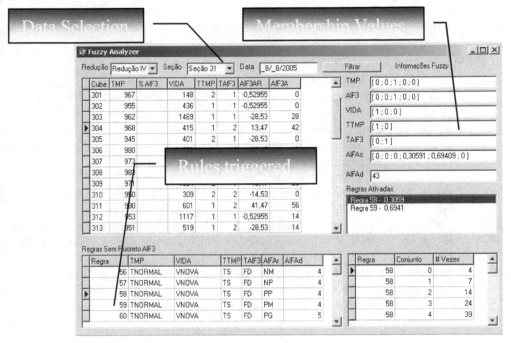

Fig. 9. Fuzzy Analyzer tool

5. Conclusion

There was a need in the Aluminum smelting process for fluoride addition and control using the process experts' knowledge, since the current methodologies does not address well this problem and there are always many human interventions on this process. The results presented by the fuzzy strategy show that it can match the process requirements once it aggregated the interventions or changes made by process technicians to the control variable. This positive result will give technicians more time for other activities, such as process improvements instead of always worried in analyzing, criticizing and change the suggested results by the current system.

The fuzzy strategy not only aggregated human knowledge to the system, but it has also improved the system stability as shown in results and validation, the temperature and fluoride variations declined. However, it is only possible to achieve a trustworthy degree of a new strategy after a period of at least 7 months. Meanwhile, the system is still in the observation state.

The impact of this work can be scaled to a higher level by considering the continual improvement of the rules and the fuzzy system as well, since it will be continually evaluated and adjusted. Thus there will be an efficient control on fluoride addition.

For future works, this methodology can be extended to other decision making process whose decision is taken based on human interpretation or consolidated data. Also we suggest the use of other fuzzy settings such as inference machines, membership functions, and implication and aggregation methods for comparison.

6. References

Beck, T. R. (2008). Electrolytic Production of Aluminum. Electrochemical Technology Corp. May. Download of the http://electrochem.cwru.edu/encycl/, in October/16/2011.

Benyakhlef, M, Radouane, L. (2008) Completely Decentralized Adaptive Fuzzy Control for a Class of Nonlinear Interconnected Systems.. International Journal of Computational Cognition (http://www.ijcc.us), Vol. 6, No. 1, March.

Chiu, C.-S., Lian, K.-Y. (2009) Global Feed-Forward Adaptive Fuzzy Control of Uncertain MIMO Nonlinear Systems.. Frontiers in Adaptive Control, Chapter 6, pp. 97-120, ISBN 978-953-7619-43-5, Edited by: Shuang Cong, InTech, January.

Dan-yang, C., Shui-ping, Z., Jin-hong, L. (2011) Variable universe fuzzy expert system for aluminum electrolysis. TransactionsNonferrousMetalsSocietyof China, 21, 429-436.

Dias, H. P. (2002) Determinação do Teor de AlF3 no Banho Utilizando Temperatura, VIII Seminário Internacional de Tecnologia da Indústria do Alumínio, São Paulo.

Drengstig, T. (1997) On process model representation and AlF3 dynamics of Aluminum electrolysis cells (p. 94). Dr.Ing. thesis, Norwegian University of Science and Technology (NTNU).

Drengstig, T., Ljungquist, D., Foss, B. A. (1998) On the AlF3 and Temperature Control of an Aluminum Electrolysis Cell. Modeling, Identification and Control, Vol. 19, No. 1, 31-59.

Feng G. (2010) Analysis and Synthesis of Fuzzy Control Systems: A Model-Based Approach (Automation and Control Engineering). CRC Press; ISBN: 1420092642, 299 pages, 1 edition (March).

Gomes, V., Soares, F. M., Castro, M., Oliveira, R. C. L. (2010)Usage of Fuzzy Logic as a Strategy for the Aluminum Fluoride Addition in Electrolytic Cells. Light Metals, 247–256.

Haupin, W., Kvande, H. (1993).Mathematical model of fluoride evolution from Hall Heroult cells. *Light Metals*, 257–263.

Hives, J., Thonstad, J., Sterten.,Fellner, F. P. (1993). Electrical conductivity of molten cryolite–based mixtures obtained with a tube-type cell made of pyrolitic boron nitride. Light Metals, 247–256.

Hyland, M. M., Patterson, E. C., Stevens-McFadden, F., Welch, B. J. (2001). Aluminum fluoride consumption and control in smelting cells. Scandinavian Journal of Metallurgy, 30, Issue 6, 404–414.

IAI – International Aluminum Institute (2010) The Aluminum Industry´s Sustainable Development Report, download of the www.world-Aluminum.org/ , in may/20/2011.

Kola, S., Støre, T. (2009) Bath temperature and AlF3 control of naAluminum electrolysis cell. Control Engineering Practice, 17, 1035–1043.

Mamdani, E. H., Assilian, S. (1975) An experiment in linguistic synthesis with a fuzzy logic controller. *Int. J. Man-Machine Studies*, vol. 7, p. 1-13.

McFadden, F.S., Bearne, G. P., Austin, P.C., Welch, B. J. Application of advanced Process Control to Aluminum Reduction Cells – A Review, *TMS Light Metals, Light Metals 2001 – Proceedings of the Technical Sessions, 130rd Technical TMS Annual Meeting, February 11-15, New Orleans, LA, USA, pp.1233-1242*.

McFadden, F. J. S., Welch, B. J., Austin, P. C. (2006) The multivariable model-based control of the non-alumina electrolyte variables in aluminum smelting cells. JOM Journal of the Minerals, Metals and Materials Society, Volume 58, Number 2, 42-47.

Meghlaoui, A., Aljabri, N. A (2003) AluminumFluorideControlStrategyImprovement[C]. Light Metals. Warrendale: Minerals, Metals and Materials Society, 425-429.

Meghlaoui, A., Bui, R. T., Thibault , J., Tikasz L., Santerre, R. (1997) Intelligent Control of the Feeding of Aluminum Electrolytic Cells Using Neural Networks. Metallurgical and Materials Transactions B, Volume 28, Number 2, Pages 215-221.

Prasad, S. (2000) Studies on the Hall-HeroultAluminumelectrowinning Process, *Journal of Brazilian Chemistry Society, May/June, vol. 11, no.3, p.245-251*, ISSN 0103-5053.

Shuiping, Z., Jinhong, L. (2008). Fuzzy Predictive Control System of Cryolite Ratio for Prebake Aluminum Production Cells. Proceedings of the 7th World Congress on Intelligent Control and Automation June 25 - 27, 2008, Chongqing, China.

Shuiping, Z., Jinhong, L., Yuqian, W., Danyang, C. (2010) Calculation and control of equivalent superheat for 300kA prebake aluminum electrolysis. Proceedings of the 8th World Congress on Intelligent Control and Automation, July 6-9, Jinan, China, pp. 4755-4760.

Solheim, A.(2005). Personal communication. Trondheim, June.

Thonstad, J., Rolseth, S. (1983). Equilibrium between bath and side ledge. Light Metals, 415–424.

Wang X., You G., Yang S. (2011) Fuzzy Control Model Study on Precision Irrigation System for Water Stress in Crops.. Journal of Computers, Vol. 6, No. 5, May.

Welch, B. J. Aluminum Fluoride Consumption and Control in Smelting Cells in Proceedings 6th International Conference on Molten Slags, Fluxes and Salts (ISS), Stockholm, June 2002.

Xiaodong, Y., Jiaming, Z., Kangjian, S. (2010) The Pot Technology Development in China. Light Metals 2010; Seattle, Washington; 14-18 February, Pages 349-354.

Yan, Y., Taishan, Z. (2006) Application of Intelligent Integrated Control Technique in Aluminum Electrolysis Process. Control Mini-Micro Systems of Computers, Vol. 27, No. 11, pp. 2172-2176.

Yongbo, H., Jiemin, Z., Xiangdong, Q., Zhiqiang, S. (2008) Electrolyte temperature based control method for aluminum fluoride addition in Hall-Héroult cell. 27th Chinese Control Conference - CCC 2008, 16-18 July, page(s): 99 - 103, Kunming, China.

Yu J., Gao J., Ma Y., Yu H., Pan S. (2010) Robust Adaptive Fuzzy Control of Chaos in the Permanent Magnet Synchronous Motor. Discrete Dynamics in Nature and Society, Volume 2010, 13 pages.

Zadeh, L. A. (1965). Fuzzy sets. *Information and Control, 8*, 338-353.

Zadeh, L.A. *Fuzzy sets as a basis for a theory of possibility* , Fuzzy Sets and Systems, 1:3-28,1978.

Zhuo, C., Bingtu, Y., Yinglong, W., Zefeng, S., (2008) A New Model for the Industrial
    Process Control based on Data Mining. Chinese Control and Decision Conference -
    CCDC 2008; 2-4 July, Yantai, Shandong, China, page(s): 1368 - 1370.

Part 3

Concepts and Theories

14

Rough Controller Synthesis

Carlos Pinheiro, Ulisses Camatta and Angelo Rezek
Federal University of Itajuba,
Brazil

1. Introduction

A new method to design rule-based controllers using concepts about rough sets is proposed. The method provides an efficient alternative for the design of rule-based controllers to compensate complex dynamic systems (nonlinear, with variable parameters, etc.). A systematic methodology to synthesize control rules is proposed. This approach serves to design fuzzy controllers and to define a new class of rule-based controllers, which will be called rough controllers. Numerical examples derived from computer simulations and a real application will be shown.

Rule-based models constitute an important tool in the representation of dynamic systems and controller models that use artificial intelligence techniques (fuzzy logic, neuro-fuzzy system, etc.). In general, the rules encapsulate the relationships between the model variables and provide mechanisms to connect the representations of the same with its computational procedures (Pedrycz & Gomide, 2007). There are two main schemes to construct rule-based models, those based on expert knowledge and those that are data-driven. There are several hybrid schemes that could be somewhere in between. In applications where the extraction of knowledge by experts is difficult due to the amount of data involved, data-driven methods are more efficient.

The Rough Set Theory (Pawlak, 1982) has been successfully applied in various areas such as data mining, decision systems, expert systems and other fields (Pawlak & Skowron, 2007). One of the main advantages of this approach is that it does not need for details in terms of probability distributions, belief intervals or possibilities values (Pawlak, 1991).

Few papers have addressed applications with rough sets related to control systems that use continuous and sampled variables. Most papers deal with mostly pure binary or symbolic variables (Ziarko & Katzberg, 1993; Kusiak & Shah, 2006).

This paper proposes a new approach to design rule-based controllers, aimed at applications in control systems of complex processes that utilize concepts about rough sets.

This chapter is organized as follows: a review of basic concepts about rough sets; the methodology proposed to design rule-based controllers; application examples; and final conclusions.

2. Background

An information system (*IS*) may be defined by $S = (U,A)$, where U is a set of objects or observations (o_i) called universe and A is a set of conditional attributes (a_j). The generic tabular representation of an information systems is illustrated in Table 1, where decision attribute values are defined in the last column of the table for a given decision attribute (d_i) and its corresponding classification $f(o_i, d_i)$. Generally rough sets deal with nominal values. For numerical attributes a discretization process is necessary, converting the values in nominal data. Some approaches may be utilized to minimize eventual effects of data quantization (Skowron and Son, 1995).

	a_1	...	a_j	...	a_n	d
o_1	$f(o_1,a_1)$		$f(o_1,a_j)$		$f(o_1,a_n)$	$f(o_1,d_1)$
:	:		:		:	:
o_i	$f(o_i,a_1)$	...	$f(o_i,a_j)$	...	$f(o_i,a_n)$	$f(o_i,d_i)$
:	:		:		:	:
o_m	$f(o_m,a_1)$	...	$f(o_m,a_j)$	...	$f(o_m,a_n)$	$f(o_m,d_m)$

Table 1. Generic tabular representation of an *IS*

Consider an equivalence relation over U called indiscernibility relation (1). The set of all the equivalence classes determined by $IND(B)$ is represented by the notation $U/IND(B)$.

$$IND(B) = \left\{ (o_i, o_j) \in U^2 \middle| \forall a_k \in B, \ f(o_i, a_k) = f(o_j, a_k) \right\} \tag{1}$$

Consider a set of all the elements from an equivalence class. Given $O \subseteq U$, it is important to know how many elements of O are defined by the elementary sets of S. To achieve this purpose, the lower approximation (*B.*) and the upper approximation (*B**) are defined (2). A set O is called precise (*crisp*) if $B^*(O) = B_*(O)$, otherwise it is imprecise, rough or approximated.

$$B_*(O) = \{o \in U | U / IND(B) \subseteq O\}; \tag{2}$$

$$B^*(O) = \{o \in U | U / IND(B) \cap O \neq 0\}.$$

A discernibility matrix is defined in (3), whose elements are given in (4).

$$M_D(B) = [m_D(i,j)]_{nxn}, \ i \geq 1, j \leq card(U / IND(B)) \tag{3}$$

$$m_D(i,j) = \{a_k \in B | f(o_i, a_k) \neq f(o_j, a_k)\} \tag{4}$$

A discernibility function is defined in (5), where the set formed by the minimum term of *F(B)* determines the reducts of B, which is defined as a set of minimum attributes necessary to maintain the same properties of an *IS* that utilizes all the original attributes of the system. There may be more than one reduct for the same set of attributes. For a large *IS*, the calculus of minimal reducts can consist a problem of complex computation, which rises with the amount of data of the process. Some approaches are utilized to deal with this kind of problem in reduct processing, for example, through similarity relations (Huang et al., 2007). In information systems with data in numerical values, it usually is not necessary to calculate the reducts, because all the variables of the condition attributes are the reducts themselves.

$$F(B) = \wedge\{\vee \overline{m}_D(i, j)\}; \quad \overline{m}_D(i, j) = \{\overline{a}_k | a_k \in m_D(i, j)\}. \tag{5}$$

To transform a reduct into a decision rule, the values of the conditional attributes from the object class from which the reduct was originated are added to the corresponding attributes, and then the rule is completed with the decision attributes. For a determined reduct, an example of decision rule is illustrated in (6). The use of the rough set theory enables systematically that the decision rules have consice informations concerning the original information system, adequately treating eventual redundant, uncertain, or imprecise information in the data.

$$\text{IF } a_1 = f(o_1,a_1) \text{ AND...AND } a_k = f(o_m,a_k) \text{ THEN}$$
$$d_1 = f(o_1,d_1) \text{ OR...OR } d_i = f(o_i,d_i) \tag{6}$$

2.1 Example 1

As examples of the concepts expressed in this section and the following examples consider Table 2 below, where $U = \{o_1, o_2, o_3, o_4\}$ and $B = \{a_1, a_2\}$. For this information system, we have $U / IND(B) = \{\{o_1\}, \{o_2\}, \{o_3\}, \{o_4\}\}$. The discenibility matrix is illustrated in Table 3. The resulting discernibility function is $F(B) = a_2 \wedge a_1 \wedge (a_1 \vee a_2) \wedge (a_1 \vee a_2) \wedge a_1 \wedge a_2 = a_1 \wedge a_2$. Thus, the reduct obtained is $R = \{a_1, a_2\}$. Therefore, the resulting decision rules are the expressions given in (7).

	a_1	a_2	d
o_1	b	b	δ_1
o_2	b	c	δ_2
o_3	c	b	δ_3
o_4	c	c	δ_4

Table 2. Data referring to Example 1.

	o_1	o_2	o_3	o_4
o_1	-			
o_2	a_2	-		
o_3	a_1	a_1,a_2	-	
o_4	a_1,a_2	a_1	a_2	-

Table 3. Discernibility matrix referring to Example 1.

$$\text{IF } a_1 = b \text{ AND } a_2 = b \text{ THEN } d = \delta_1;$$
$$\text{IF } a_1 = b \text{ AND } a_2 = c \text{ THEN } d = \delta_2;$$
$$\text{IF } a_1 = c \text{ AND } a_2 = b \text{ THEN } d = \delta_3;$$
$$\text{IF } a_1 = c \text{ AND } a_2 = c \text{ THEN } d = \delta_4. \tag{7}$$

3. Methodology

For a more adequate representation of the numerical applications, the illustrated form in Table 4 will be adopted for the information systems employed in this paper. The condition attributes are x_i and their data are $x_N^{(k)}$. The decision attribute is y and their values are $y^{(k)}$.

x_1	x_2	x_3	...	x_N	y
$x_1^{(1)}$	$x_2^{(1)}$	$x_3^{(1)}$	...	$x_N^{(1)}$	$y^{(1)}$
$x_1^{(2)}$	$x_2^{(2)}$	$x_3^{(2)}$	...	$x_N^{(2)}$	$y^{(2)}$
...	...	...	...	...	...
$x_1^{(k)}$	$x_2^{(k)}$	$x_3^{(k)}$	...	$x_N^{(k)}$	$y^{(k)}$
...	...	...	...	...	...
$x_1^{(m)}$	$x_2^{(m)}$	$x_3^{(m)}$	...	$x_N^{(m)}$	$y^{(m)}$
...	...	...	...	...	...
$x_1^{(v)}$	$x_2^{(v)}$	$x_3^{(v)}$	...	$x_N^{(v)}$	$y^{(v)}$

Table 4. Numerical Tabular Representation of an *IS*.

Sentences (8) derive from the *IS* in question. For example, for $x_1 = x_1^{(k)}$, $x_2 = x_2^{(k)}$, $x_3 = x_3^{(k)}$, and $x_N = x_N^{(k)}$ we have $y = y^{(m)}$ expressed by s_k. And for $x_1 = x_1^{(m)}$, $x_2 = x_2^{(m)}$, $x_3 = x_3^{(m)}$,, and $x_N = x_N^{(m)}$ we have $y = y^{(m)}$ defined by s_m.

$$s_1: \text{IF } x_1 = x_1^{(1)} \text{ AND } x_2 = x_2^{(1)} \text{ AND... AND } x_N = x_N^{(1)} \text{ THEN } y = y^{(1)}$$
$$s_2: \text{IF } x_1 = x_1^{(2)} \text{ AND } x_2 = x_2^{(2)} \text{ AND... AND } x_N = x_N^{(2)} \text{ THEN } y = y^{(2)}$$
$$s_k: \text{IF } x_1 = x_1^{(k)} \text{ AND } x_2 = x_2^{(k)} \text{ AND... AND } x_N = x_N^{(k)} \text{ THEN } y = y^{(k)}$$
$$s_m: \text{IF } x_1 = x_1^{(m)} \text{ AND } x_2 = x_2^{(m)} \text{ AND...AND } x_N = x_N^{(m)} \text{ THEN } y = y^{(m)}$$
$$s_v: \text{IF } x_1 = x_1^{(v)} \text{ AND } x_2 = x_1^{(v)} \text{ AND...AND } x_N = x_N^{(v)} \text{ THEN } y = y^{(v)} \tag{8}$$

For numeric values in ranges defined in the table, that is, $x_1^{(k)} \le x_1 \le x_1^{(m)}$, $x_2^{(k)} \le x_2 \le x_2^{(m)}$, $x_3^{(k)} \le x_3 \le x_3^{(m)}$ and $x_N^{(k)} \le x_N \le x_N^{(m)}$, the sentences s_k and s_m defined in (8) may be redefined by generic rule (9), or through the simplified form (10), where $\alpha^{(g)} = [x_1^{(k)}, x_1^{(m)}]$, $\beta^{(g)} = [x_2^{(k)}, x_2^{(m)}]$, $\gamma^{(g)} = [x_N^{(k)}, x_N^{(m)}]$ and $\delta^{(g)} = [y^{(k)}, y^{(m)}]$, considering that $y^{(k)} < y^{(m)}$.

$$r_g: \text{IF } x_1^{(k)} \le x_1 \le x_1^{(m)} \text{ AND } x_2^{(k)} \le x_2 \le x_2^{(m)} \text{ AND ... AND } x_N^{(k)} \le x_N \le x_N^{(m)} \text{ THEN}$$

$$\min\{y^{(k)},..., y^{(m)}\} \le y \le \max\{y^{(k)},..., y^{(m)}\} \tag{9}$$

$$r_g: \text{IF } x_1 = \alpha^{(g)} \text{ AND } x_2 = \beta^{(g)} \text{ AND...AND } x_N = \gamma^{(g)} \text{ THEN } y = \delta^{(g)} \tag{10}$$

To estimate numerical values in ranges of the data obtained in the rules, formula (11) will be used for numerical interpolations (Pinheiro, et al., 2010).

$$y = (x_n, x_n^{(i)}, y^{(i)})_{\substack{i=k,m \\ n=1,N}} = y^{(k)} + \frac{(y^{(m)} - y^{(k)})}{N} \sum_{n=1}^{N} \frac{(x_n - x_n^{(k)})}{(x_n^{(m)} - x_n^{(k)})} \tag{11}$$

3.1 Example 2

In order to illustrate the concepts of this section and of those to follow, Table 5 will illustrate a simple example defined by the function $y = x_1 + x_2$ with x_1 and $x_2 \in [0, 1]$. This table is the same as Table 2 from Example 1. The *IS* associated has two condition attributes (x_1 and x_2) of numerical values. Consequently, the reduct is defined by $\{x_1, x_2\}$, resulting in the same decision rules as those in (7), which can be written as (10), as proposed in the methodology presented in this section, and resulting in (12).

x_1	x_2	y
0	0	0
0	1	1
1	0	1
1	1	2

Table 5. Data referring to Example 2.

$$r_1: \text{IF } x_1 = [0, 1] \text{ AND } x_2 = [0, 1] \text{ THEN } y = [0, 2] \tag{12}$$

Intermediate values in the data range $[0, 1]$ of the general rule in question can be estimated by (13), constituting a specific case of (11) for $n = 2$.

$$y = y^{(k)} + \frac{(y^{(m)} - y^{(k)})}{2}\left(\frac{(x_1 - x_1^{(k)})}{(x_1^{(m)} - x_1^{(k)})} + \frac{(x_2 - x_2^{(k)})}{(x_2^{(m)} - x_2^{(k)})}\right) \tag{13}$$

3.2 Fuzzy models

With the information of decision rules in form (12), it is simple to obtain the parameters of a corresponding fuzzy model. For modeling in linguistic (Mamdani) rules (14), two membership functions (Fig. 1), triangular and equally spaced, can be defined in the interval $[0, 1]$ for the input variables (x_1 and x_2), and another three functions (Fig. 2) defined in interval $[0, 2]$ for the output variable (y). Therefore, the resulting fuzzy rules are expressed by (15).

$$r_n: \text{IF } x_1 = A_n \text{ AND } x_2 = B_n \text{ THEN } y = C_n \tag{14}$$

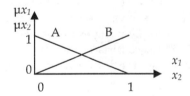

Fig. 1. Membership Functions.

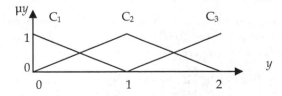

Fig. 2. Membership Functions.

$$r_1: \text{IF } x_1 = \text{ A AND } x_2 = \text{ A THEN } y = C_1;$$
$$r_2: \text{IF } x_1 = \text{ A AND } x_2 = \text{ B THEN } y = C_2;$$
$$r_3: \text{IF } x_1 = \text{ B AND } x_2 = \text{ A THEN } y = C_2;$$
$$r_4: \text{IF } x_1 = \text{ B AND } x_2 = \text{ B THEN } y = C_3. \tag{15}$$

For modeling with functional (Takagi-Sugeno) rules (16), the membership functions can be the same as those in Figure 1 for the input variables. For the polynomial function coefficients of the information from the output variable, the same one can be calculated by (13), resulting in the rules expressed by (17). As an example of the calculation of the polynomial coefficient functions, using the decision rule in the form (12) with $x_1^{(k)} = 0$, $x_1^{(m)} = 1$, $x_2^{(k)} = 0$, $x_2^{(m)} = 1$, $y^{(k)} = 0$ and $y^{(m)} = 2$, where using (13) we have $y = ((2 - 0)/2)((x_1 - 0)/(1 - 0) + (x_2 - 0)/(1 - 0)) = x_1 + x_2$ which defines the coefficients of (16). Other examples of fuzzy models obtained with this methodology are illustrated in Pinheiro et al., 2010.

$$r_n: \text{IF } x_1 = A_n \text{ AND } x_2 = B_n \text{ THEN } y_n = c_{0n} + c_{1n}x_1 + c_{2n}x_2 \tag{16}$$

$$r_1: \text{IF } x_1 = \text{ A AND } x_2 = \text{ A THEN } y_1 = x_1 + x_2;$$
$$r_2: \text{IF } x_1 = \text{ A AND } x_2 = \text{ B THEN } y_2 = x_1 + x_2;$$
$$r_3: \text{IF } x_1 = \text{ B AND } x_2 = \text{ A THEN } y_3 = x_1 + x_2;$$
$$r_4: \text{IF } x_1 = \text{ B AND } x_2 = \text{ B THEN } y_4 = x_1 + x_2. \tag{17}$$

3.3 Rough models

Another simpler modeling option, called rough modeling, directly concerns the representation given in (12), where the data can be interpolated by (13). The advantage of this modeling in relation to the fuzzy models is that it does not require numerical fuzzification and defuzzification procedures, which can be advantageous in real-time applications in control systems, for example. The advantage of fuzzy models is its greater ability to function approximation, which is usually related to the possible intersections between the membership functions of associated fuzzy sets.

In order to illustrate the rough model, we have (12) where $x_1^{(k)} = 0$, $x_1^{(m)} = 1$, $x_2^{(k)} = 0$, $x_2^{(m)} = 1$, $y^{(k)} = 0$ and $y^{(m)} = 2$. For specific values of variables $x_1 = 0.25$ and $x_2 = 0.5$, the corresponding value of y is desired to be estimated. By using expression (13) comes $y = 0+(2-0)/2((0.25-0)/(1-0)+(0.5-0)/(1-0)) = 0.75$, which consists of the same numerical value given by the original function of Example 2, where y is exactly given by $x_1 + x_2$.

3.4 Example 3

With the purpose of illustrating situations where data applications have fractional values, Table 6 illustrates an example defined by the nonlinear function $y = \sin(x_1)$, with $x_1 \in [0, \pi/2]$.

The condition attribute (x_1) has fractional values that will be quantized in this example in three equally-spaced intervals: $a^{(1)} = [0.0000, 0.5236]$; $a^{(2)} = [0.5236, 1.0472]$; $a^{(3)} = [1.0472, 1.5708]$. Therefore, the decision rules are expressed by (18).

$$r_1: \text{IF } x_1 = a^{(1)} \text{ THEN } y = y^{(a)} \text{ OR } y = y^{(b)} \text{ OR } y = y^{(c)};$$
$$r_2: \text{IF } x_1 = a^{(2)} \text{ THEN } y = y^{(c)} \text{ OR } y = y^{(d)} \text{ OR } y = y^{(e)};$$
$$r_3: \text{IF } x_1 = a^{(3)} \text{ THEN } y = y^{(e)} \text{ OR } y = y^{(f)} \text{ OR } y = y^{(g)}. \tag{18}$$

x_1	y
0.0000	$y^{(a)} = 0.0000$
0.2618	$y^{(b)} = 0.2588$
0.5236	$y^{(c)} = 0.5000$
0.7854	$y^{(d)} = 0.7071$
1.0472	$y^{(e)} = 0.8660$
1.3090	$y^{(f)} = 0.9659$
1.5708	$y^{(g)} = 1.0000$

Table 6. Data of Example 3.

Using the proposed form (10), the rough model (19) can be written, where $\delta^{(1)} = [0.0000, 0.5000]$, $\delta^{(2)} = [0.5000, 0.8660]$ and $\delta^{(3)} = [0.8660, 1.0000]$.

$$r_1: \text{IF } x_1 = [0.0000, 0.5236] \text{ THEN } y = [0.0000, 0.5000];$$
$$r_2: \text{IF } x_1 = [0.5236, 1.0472] \text{ THEN } y = [0.5000, 0.8660];$$
$$r_3: \text{IF } x_1 = [1.0472, 1.5708] \text{ THEN } y = [0.8660, 1.0000]. \tag{19}$$

To estimate the intermediate values of this model, the linear interpolation formula (20) can be used, which is the specific case of (11) for $n = 1$.

$$y = y^{(k)} + \left(y^{(m)} - y^{(k)}\right)\left(x_1 - x_1^{(k)}\right) / \left(x_1^{(m)} - x_1^{(k)}\right) \tag{20}$$

For instance, for $x_1 = 0.3927$ we have $y = 0 + (0.5 - 0)(0.3927 - 0)/(0.5236 - 0) = 0.375$, and for $x_1 = 1.1781$, we have $y = 0.866 + (1 - 0.866)(1.1781 - 1.0472)/(1.5708 - 1.0472) = 0.8995$. The average error value in relation to the original function is about 2.3%. A greater degree of quantization relative to the data from the example often leads to better precision in the interpolations, but with an increase in the number of modeling rules.

If eventually more than one rule results in estimated values (for example, for data at the ends of the condition attributes), the resulting value is given by the arithmetic average of the same.

3.5 Software

There are free access computational tools developed specifically for the processing of rough sets, such as RSL (Rough Sets Library), Rough Enough, CI (Column Importance facility), Rosetta, etc. These tools allow the processing of data of generic information systems, providing decision rules in a format similar to (6), for example. Data with fractional numeric values can be properly quantized through some established techniques. The reducts that determine the decision rules can be manually selected or determined by some known methods from the data processing of the *IS* used.

The methodology proposed in this paper allows the use of decision rules derived from processing of information system, aimed at building fuzzy models or rough models in order to design rule-based controllers.

4. Rule-based controllers

Figure 3 illustrates the typical structure of a ruled-based controller with PI action (Proportional plus Integral). The variable "*e*" represents the input error information of the controller, variable "u" symbolizes the output of the same, and "T" denotes the sample time. Equation (21) expresses the discrete mathematical model of a PI controller with the respective proportional (Kp) and integral (Ki) gains. Many articles show the computational accomplishments of rule-based controllers, especially those that employ fuzzy logic. The actions of the fuzzy controllers can be PI, PD (proportional plus derivative), PID or Lead/Lad (Pinheiro & Gomide, 2000), depending on the context of their applications. The gains (proportional, integral, etc.) of fuzzy controllers are generally represented by scale factors that multiply the membership functions of the same, or are already fully incorporated in the expressions of their membership functions. Many control problems can be solved using a PI-controller (Astrom & Wittenmark, 1990) due to their applicability and easy tuning.

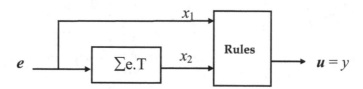

Fig. 3. Typical structure of a rule-based controller with PI action.

$$y = u(t) = K_p e(t) + K_i \sum e(t)T;$$

$$x_1 = K_p e(t); \quad x_2 = K_i \sum e(t)T.$$

(21)

4.1 Example 4

With relation to Figure 3, if the rules are the same as those exemplified in items 3.2 and 3.3 (where the simple data of Example 2 was used), Figure 4 shows the response (u) of the respective fuzzy controllers (linguistic and functional) or of the rough controllers for a step change in the error (e). The sample time (T) used was one tenth of a second. The points on the graph illustrate the discrete values resulting from the rule-based controllers (being practically identical to each other). And for the purpose of exemplification, the solid line represents the response of a conventional controller continuous in time with unit gains (proportional and integral). Comparing the results, it is possible to note that the design of the rule-based controllers was well fit.

The next section of this article will deal with more complex problems and practical contexts. Application examples like those of control systems with adaptive gains, active suspension systems, and speed regulator and current control for electric motors will be shown.

Questions regarding stability analysis resulting from the application of rough controllers can be performed by harmonic balance techniques, for example, in the same way that these techniques are used in stability analysis of fuzzy controls (Pinheiro & Gomide, 1997; Rezek et al., 2010).

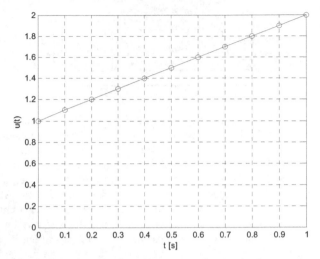

Fig. 4. Responses of rule-based controllers (for a step change in the error).

5. Application examples

This section provides some examples of applications of the methodology proposed to synthesize rule-based controllers, whose objective is to accomplish control loops appropriate for systems with nonlinear behavior, etc.

5.1 Example 5

This example includes a speed control loop of a system that operates in low rotations, which requires a controller with characteristics of adaptive gains due to the nonlinear effects of the controlled process. The block diagram illustrated in Figure 5 represents the controlled process with a transfer function (22) and two nonlinearities. The second nonlinearity, indicated by block (b), defines a dead-zone effect related to gear gaps of the system. The transfer function $P(s)$, shapes an electric motor that drives the system. The poles of the same are related to the electrical part associated with resistance and inductance of the motor. The mechanical part is related to moments of inertia and friction of the machine with its mechanical charge. The nominal values of the parameters are: $K = 2.55$; $c_0 = 0.73$; $c_1 = 1.74$; $d_0 = 0.73$. The saturation levels are ±12, the range of the dead-zone is ±1. Figure 6 illustrates a typical control loop to regulate the speed of the process, which works within a specific rotation range.

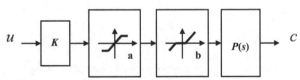

Fig. 5. Non-linear process

$$P(s) = \frac{d_0}{(s^2 + c_1 s + c_0)} \tag{22}$$

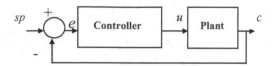

Fig. 6. Control Loop.

Figure 7 shows the responses of the control loop in question for a conventional PI controller with gains K_p = 12 and K_i = 1. The same were adjusted to meet the specifications of overshoot around 20% and settling time around seven seconds for a reference value or set point (sp) at 2.8 [rd/s]. The response values were normalized (c/sp) and are related to the following reference values sp = [1.5; 2; 2.8]. Due to the nonlinear characteristics of the plant, the dynamic responses of the control loop change according to the set-point values. Alterations in the control gains in function with the intensity of the error in the control loop, maintain the system dynamic within the desired specifications. The mapping of these gains by artificial neural networks or by fuzzy logic for example, allows for the accomplishment of controllers with characteristics of adaptive gains. Table 7 illustrates some suitable gain values in function with the intensity (x_1) of the error (e) of the control loop and its integral (x_2), in order to properly compensate the process. The mapping (or scheduling) of the gains can be defined as $u = y = K_p(x_1)x_1 + K_i(x_2)x_2$. Figure 8 illustrates the values of this mapping, where the data relative to the information on the input variables are at the top part of the figure, with x_1 in black and x_2 in gray. The output information (u) of the controller is found below the graphic.

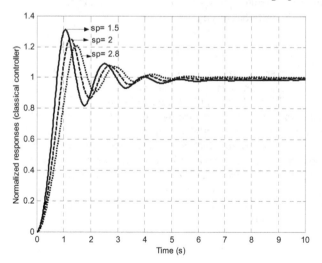

Fig. 7. Responses relative to Example 5 for a classic controller.

The information in Figure 8 represent the table of the information system of the problem in question, where it is desired to design a rule-based controller that incorporates the scaling gains, aiming for an effective compensation of the controlled process. This paper will employ the Rosetta (Øhrn & Komorowski, 1997), a software for processing of data related to information systems in general. This is a simple use freely accessed tool (http://www.idi.ntnu.no/~aleks/rosetta/). The following procedures were performed in

x_1	K_p	x_2	K_i
0.00	20.0	0.00	1.40
0.08	20.0	0.07	1.40
0.16	11.5	0.15	1.00
0.31	6.37	0.30	1.00
0.74	3.23	0.72	1.00
1.19	2.35	1.17	0.89
1.62	2.02	1.60	0.76
2.00	2.00	1.99	0.75
2.50	2.00	2.48	0.75
3.01	2.00	3.00	0.75

Table 7. Adaptive gains in function of the error and its integral.

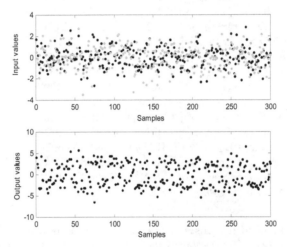

Fig. 8. Mapping of the gains.

the tool: *Import IS; Discretization → Equal frequency binning; → Intervals = 5; Reduction → Exhaustive calculation; Rule generator.* The decision rules (the first three and the last two) resulted from processing the data done by the software are shown below (23). The *"*"* symbol denotes the inferior and superior values of the data of the *IS* correspondent, that in this example are -2.6759 and 2.8149 for x_1 and -3.5027 and 2.7042 for x_2.

x1(0.6875,*) AND x2(0.2942,0.8800) => y(4.0889) OR y(4.2937) ... OR y(2.5230) ...OR y(3.4186)
x1(0.6875,*) AND x2(-0.2123,0.2942) => y(2.4749) OR y(3.6601) OR y(5.4837) ... OR y(1.8793)
x1(0.1744,0.6875) AND x2(-0.9279,-0.2123) => y(1.7301) OR ... OR y(2.0570) OR y(1.2289) ...
...   .
x1(0.1744,0.6875) AND x2(0.2942,0.8800)) => y(2.8625) OR y(3.0640) OR ... OR y(2.2344) ...
x1(*,-0.8340) AND x2(0.2942, 0.8800) => y(-2.4899) OR y(-1.8370) OR ... OR y(-3.2713)... (23)

By using the methodology proposed, the rules above can be written as (24), whose parameter values are $x_1^{(a)}$ = -2.6759; $x_1^{(b)}$ = -0.834; $x_1^{(c)}$ = -0.2338; $x_1^{(d)}$ = 0.1744; $x_1^{(e)}$ = 0.6875; $x_1^{(f)}$ = 2.8149; $x_2^{(a)}$ = -3.5027; $x_2^{(b)}$ = -0.9279; $x_2^{(c)}$ = -0.2123; $x_2^{(d)}$ = 0.2942; $x_2^{(e)}$ = 0.88; $x_2^{(f)}$ = 2.7042.

r_1: IF $x_1 = [x_1^{(e)}, x_1^{(f)}]$ AND $x_2 = [x_2^{(d)}, x_2^{(e)}]$ THEN $y = [2.5230, 4.2937]$;

r_2: IF $x_1 = [x_1^{(e)}, x_1^{(f)}]$ AND $x_2 = [x_2^{(c)}, x_2^{(d)}]$ THEN $y = [1.8793, 5.4837]$;

r_3: IF $x_1 = [x_1^{(d)}, x_1^{(e)}]$ AND $x_2 = [x_2^{(b)}, x_2^{(c)}]$ THEN $y = [1.2289, 2.0570]$;

r_4: IF $x_1 = [x_1^{(b)}, x_1^{(c)}]$ AND $x_2 = [x_2^{(a)}, x_2^{(b)}]$ THEN $y = [-3.4899, -2.8470]$;

r_5: IF $x_1 = [x_1^{(a)}, x_1^{(b)}]$ AND$x_2 = [x_2^{(c)}, x_2^{(d)}]$ THEN $y = [-6.5810, -1.9420]$;

r_6: IF $x_1 = [x_1^{(b)}, x_1^{(c)}]$ AND $x_2 = [x_2^{(e)}, x_2^{(f)}]$ THEN $y = [-1.2319, -0.4610]$;

r_7: IF $x_1 = [x_1^{(a)}, x_1^{(b)}]$ AND $x_2 = [x_2^{(e)}, x_2^{(f)}]$ THEN $y = [-2.7080, 1.1847]$;

r_8: IF $x_1 = [x_1^{(c)}, x_1^{(d)}]$ AND $x_2 = [x_2^{(d)}, x_2^{(e)}]$ THEN $y = [-1.8116, 2.4170]$;

r_9: IF $x_1 = [x_1^{(b)}, x_1^{(c)}]$ AND $x_2 = [x_2^{(c)}, x_2^{(d)}]$ THEN $y = [-2.4210, -1.62330]$;

r_{10}:IF $x_1 = [x_1^{(a)}, x_1^{(b)}]$ AND $x_2 = [x_2^{(b)}, x_2^{(c)}]$ THEN $y = [-4.2604, -2.4360]$;

r_{11}:IF $x_1 = [x_1^{(c)}, x_1^{(d)}]$ AND $x_2 = [x_2^{(e)}, x_2^{(f)}]$ THEN $y = [-1.2340, 2.2624]$;

r_{12}:IF $x_1 = [x_1^{(c)}, x_1^{(d)}]$ AND $x_2 = [x_2^{(b)}, x_2^{(c)}]$ THEN $y = [-3.0277, 1.6000]$;

r_{13}:IF $x_1 = [x_1^{(c)}, x_1^{(d)}]$ AND $x_2 = [x_2^{(a)}, x_2^{(b)}]$ THEN $y = [-4.4430, 4.1896]$; (24)

r_{14}:IF $x_1 = [x_1^{(b)}, x_1^{(c)}]$ AND $x_2 = [x_2^{(b)}, x_2^{(c)}]$ THEN $y = [-3.2030, -2.0760]$.

r_{15}:IF $x_1 = [x_1^{(e)}, x_1^{(f)}]$ AND $x_2 = [x_2^{(b)}, x_2^{(c)}]$ THEN $y = [1.1753, 6.4760]$;

r_{16}:IF $x_1 = [x_1^{(b)}, x_1^{(c)}]$ AND $x_2 = [x_2^{(d)}, x_2^{(e)}]$ THEN $y = [-1.8250, -1.0780]$;

r_{17}:IF $x_1 = [x_1^{(e)}, x_1^{(f)}]$ AND $x_2 = [x_2^{(a)}, x_2^{(b)}]$ THEN $y = [0.6120, 2.7360]$;

r_{18}:IF $x_1 = [x_1^{(c)}, x_1^{(d)}]$ AND $x_2 = [x_2^{(c)}, x_2^{(d)}]$ THEN $y = [-2.0980, 2.1297]$;

r_{19}:IF $x_1 = [x_1^{(d)}, x_1^{(e)}]$ AND $x_2 = [x_2^{(c)}, x_2^{(d)}]$ THEN $y = [1.7996, 2.4580]$;

r_{20}:IF $x_1 = [x_1^{(d)}, x_1^{(e)}]$ AND $x_2 = [x_2^{(e)}, x_2^{(f)}]$ THEN $y = [2.9106, 3.6160]$;

r_{21}:IF $x_1 = [x_1^{(a)}, x_1^{(b)}]$ AND $x_2 = [x_2^{(a)}, x_2^{(b)}]$ THEN $y = [-5.4544, -3.0290]$;

r_{22}:IF $x_1 = [x_1^{(e)}, x_1^{(f)}]$ AND $x_2 = [x_2^{(e)}, x_2^{(f)}]$ THEN $y = [2.8684, 5.6692]$;

r_{23}:IF $x_1 = [x_1^{(d)}, x_1^{(e)}]$ AND $x_2 = [x_2^{(a)}, x_2^{(b}]$ THEN $y = [0.6848, 1.2190]$;

r_{24}:IF $x_1 = [x_1^{(d)}, x_1^{(e)}]$ AND $x_2 = [x_2^{(d)}, x_2^{(e)}]$ THEN $y = [2.2344, 3.0640]$;

r_{25}:IF $x_1 = [x_1^{(a)}, x_1^{(b)}]$ AND $x_2 = [x_2^{(d)}, x_2^{(e)}]$ THEN $y = [-3.2713, -1.8400]$.

Figure 9 has the normalized responses of the control loop now using the rough controller designed by the rules (24). The responses tend to maintain the specified characteristics of overshoot and settling time for different set-point values, different from the conventional PI controller responses (whose responses are shown in Fig. 7). This shows that the rule-based controller incorporated the relationships (nonlinear) of the gains from Table 7 in function of the error and its integration. The performance of the controller has adaptive actions according to the intensity of the error information of the control loop.

The rules for a corresponding functional fuzzy controller are obtained by the form described in item 3.2 from the rules (24). The resulting coefficients of the polynomial functions of the fuzzy model in form (16) are: $c_{01} = 1.79$; $c_{11} = 0.42$; $c_{21} = 1.51$; $c_{02} = 2.05$; $c_{12} = 0.85$; $c_{22} = 3.56$; $c_{03} = 1.62$; $c_{13} = 0.81$; $c_{23} = 0.58$; $c_{04} = -2.60$; $c_{14} = 0.54$; $c_{24} = 0.12$; $c_{05} = -2.24$; $c_{15} = 1.26$; $c_{25} = 4.58$; $c_{06} = -0.88$; $c_{16} = 0.64$; $c_{26} = 0.21$; $c_{07} = -0.82$; $c_{17} = 1.06$; $c_{27} = 1.07$; $c_{08} = -1.66$; $c_{18} = 5.18$; $c_{28} = 3.61$; $c_{09} = -1.70$; $c_{19} = 0.66$; $c_{29} = 0.79$; $c_{010} = -1.75$; $c_{110} = 0.49$; $c_{210} = 1.27$; $c_{011} = -1.08$; $c_{111} = 4.28$; $c_{211} = 0.96$; $c_{012} = 1.30$; $c_{112} = 5.67$; $c_{212} = 3.23$; $c_{013} = 3.90$; $c_{113} = 10.57$; $c_{213} = 1.67$; $c_{014} = 3.89$; $c_{114} = 4.40$; $c_{214} = 3.69$; $c_{015} = 3.75$; $c_{115} = 1.24$; $c_{215} = 3.70$; $c_{016} = -1.49$; $c_{116} = 0.62$; $c_{216} = 0.64$; $c_{017} = 1.71$; $c_{117} = 0.50$; $c_{217} = 0.41$; $c_{018} = 0.00$; $c_{118} = 5.18$; $c_{218} = 4.17$; $c_{019} = 1.82$; $c_{119} = 0.64$; $c_{219} = 0.65$; $c_{020} = 2.62$; $c_{120} = 0.69$; $c_{220} = 0.19$; $c_{021} = -2.04$; $c_{121} = 0.66$; $c_{221} = 0.47$; $c_{022} = 1.74$; $c_{122} = 0.66$; $c_{222} = 0.77$; $c_{023} = 0.96$; $c_{123} = 0.52$; $c_{223} = 0.10$; $c_{024} = 1.88$; $c_{124} = 0.81$; $c_{224} = 0.71$; $c_{025} = -2.59$; $c_{125} = 0.39$; $c_{225} = 1.22$. The modal values for the Gaussian membership functions are obtain by the arithmetic average of the parameter values of the antecedents of the rough rules (24), in other words: $m_{1ab} = (x_1^{(a)} + x_1^{(b)})/2 = -1.755$; $m_{1bc} = (x_1^{(b)} + x_1^{(c)})/2 = -0.5339$; $m_{1cd} = (x_1^{(c)} + x_1^{(d)})/2 = -0.0297$; $m_{1de} = (x_1^{(d)} + x_1^{(e)})/2 = 0.431$; $m_{1ef} = (x_1^{(e)} + x_1^{(f)})/2 = 1.7512$; $m_{2ab} = (x_2^{(a)} + x_2^{(b)})/2 = -2.2153$; $m_{2bc} = (x_2^{(b)} + x_2^{(c)})/2 = -0.5701$; $m_{2cd} = (x_2^{(c)} + x_2^{(d)})/2 = 0.041$; $m_{2de} = (x_2^{(d)} + x_2^{(e)})/2 = 0.5871$; $m_{2ef} = (x_2^{(e)} + x_2^{(f)})/2 = 1.7921$. The dispersion values of the membership functions (0.8 in this example) are chosen in order for the intersection of the same to remain in a membership degree around 0.5. The results obtained with the corresponding fuzzy controller are very similar to the responses illustrated in Figure 9.

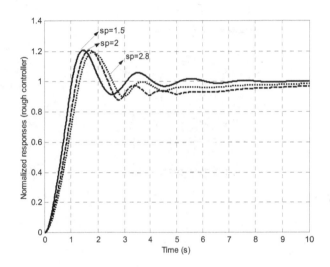

Fig. 9. Responses relative to Example 5 with rough controller.

5.2 Example 6

This example deals with an active suspension model used in automotive systems. Figure 10 illustrates a typical system known as ¼ model. The spring and damper of the structure are represented by coefficients K_f and B, respectively. The parameter M_s corresponds to the sprung mass of the vehicle. The M_r is the mass of the wheel and tire and K_p represents the elasticity of the same. d_p, d_r and d_s are vertical displacement of the tire, wheel and body of the vehicle, respectively. The force F_a represents the action exerted by an active damper aiming the imposition of determined dynamic characteristics in the suspension.

The system can be represented in state variables (25). Variable x_1 represents the vertical displacement of the suspended mass, x_2 represents the speed of the same, and its derivation is the corresponding acceleration. Variable x_3 represents the vertical displacement of the wheel, x_4 represents the speed of the same, and its derivation is the corresponding acceleration. Variable u_1 expresses a disturbance in the suspension, like the vertical displacement of the tire. The magnitude of u_2 represents the compensation force of the damper system.

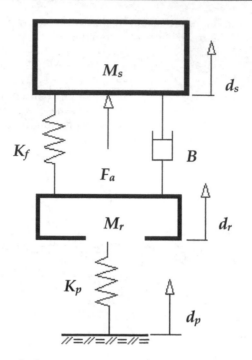

Fig. 10. Model of Example 6.

$$\overset{o}{x_1} = x_2$$

$$\overset{o}{x_2} = -\frac{K_f}{M_s}x_1 - \frac{B_a}{M_s}x_2 + \frac{K_f}{M_s}x_3 + \frac{B_a}{M_s}x_4 + \frac{1}{M_s}u_2$$

$$\overset{o}{x_3} = x_4 \tag{25}$$

$$\overset{o}{x_4} = \frac{K_f}{M_r}x_1 + \frac{B_a}{M_r}x_2 - \frac{K_f + K_p}{M_r}x_3 - \frac{B_a}{M_r}x_4 + \frac{K_p}{M_r}u_1 - \frac{1}{M_r}u_2$$

There are some types of well-known strategies to control active suspension systems. Expression (26) defines a typical strategy. The magnitude of F_a corresponds to the force developed by the active damper in the system. The same depends on values C_{on} and C_{off} defined for the coefficient of the damper system (obtained by controlled leaking of fluid of the damper by an electrically controlled valve) or by variations of magnetic characteristics of the fluid by a current-controlled induction), along with information of the absolute speed (V_{abs}) and relative speed (V_{rel}) of the process. V_{abs} is the absolute speed of the sprung mass and V_{rel} is the relative speed between the sprung mass and the mass of the wheel-tire set.

$$F_a = \begin{cases} C_{on}V_{abs} + C_{off}V_{rel} & \text{if } V_{abs}V_{rel} \geq 0, \\ C_{off}V_{rel} & \text{if } V_{abs}V_{rel} < 0. \end{cases} \tag{26}$$

Some papers (Pinheiro et al., 2007; Dong, et al., 2010) show the application of fuzzy logic to control suspension systems. In the first reference cited, the fuzzy control rules were obtained by qualitative analyses of the logic expressed by (36). The results obtained with the use of fuzzy controller were better than those with the typical control. This explanation is that with the traditional algorithm, the command force of the system is only related to the two values (C_{on} and C_{off}) of the coefficient of the damper selected by the logic. The compensation force for the fuzzy controller can vary in a wider operation range in function of the membership functions adopted. Figure 11 shows the values of the variables of the suspension system under various operating conditions.

Now, the methodology proposed in this paper will be applied to generate a rule-based controller to control the suspension system in question. The data in Figure 11 constitutes the information system of the example, where x_1 is related to V_{abs}, x_2 with V_{rel} and y with F_a. Similar to the previous example, the IS in question was processed by Rosetta, and by using the proposed method the rules (27) were synthesized, where: $x_1^{(a)}$= -2.385; $x_1^{(b)}$= -0.681; $x_1^{(c)}$= -0.184; $x_1^{(d)}$ = 0.383; $x_1^{(e)}$= 0.90; $x_1^{(f)}$= 2.731; $x_2^{(a)}$= -0.3153; $x_2^{(b)}$= -0.078; $x_2^{(c)}$ = -0.008; $x_2^{(d)}$ = 0.04; $x_2^{(e)}$ = 0.1; $x_2^{(f)}$ = 0.368.

r_1: IF $x_1^{(e)} \leq x_1 \leq x_1^{(f)}$ AND $x_2^{(e)} \leq x_2 \leq x_2^{(f)}$ THEN $-3.709 \leq y \leq 1.562$

r_2: IF $x_1^{(e)} \leq x_1 \leq x_1^{(f)}$ AND $x_2^{(d)} \leq x_2 \leq x_2^{(e)}$ THEN $-3.593 \leq y \leq 1.379$

r_3: IF $x_1^{(c)} \leq x_1 \leq x_1^{(d)}$ AND $x_2^{(d)} \leq x_2 \leq x_2^{(e)}$ THEN $0.621 \leq y \leq 0.226$

r_4: IF $x_1^{(e)} \leq x_1 \leq x_1^{(f)}$ AND $x_2^{(b)} \leq x_2 \leq x_2^{(c)}$ THEN $-2.385 \leq y \leq -1.23$

r_5: IF $x_1^{(e)} \leq x_1 \leq x_1^{(f)}$ AND $x_2^{(c)} \leq x_2 \leq x_2^{(d)}$ THEN $-2.279 \leq y \leq -1.218$

r_6: IF $x_1^{(d)} \leq x_1 \leq x_1^{(e)}$ AND $x_2^{(c)} \leq x_2 \leq x_2^{(d)}$ THEN $-1.092 \leq y \leq -0.597$

r_7: IF $x_1^{(a)} \leq x_1 \leq x_1^{(b)}$ AND $x_2^{(a)} \leq x_2 \leq x_2^{(b)}$ THEN $1.513 \leq y \leq 3.387$

r_8: IF $x_1^{(e)} \leq x_1 \leq x_1^{(f)}$ AND $x_2^{(a)} \leq x_2 \leq x_2^{(b)}$ THEN $-2.251 \leq y \leq -1.128$

r_9: IF $x_1^{(a)} \leq x_1 \leq x_1^{(b)}$ AND $x_2^{(d)} \leq x_2 \leq x_2^{(e)}$ THEN $0.967 \leq y \leq 3.443$

r_{10}: IF $x_1^{(d)} \leq x_1 \leq x_1^{(e)}$ AND $x_2^{(b)} \leq x_2 \leq x_2^{(c)}$ THEN $-0.513 \leq y \leq -1.062$

r_{11}: IF $x_1^{(a)} \leq x_1 \leq x_1^{(b)}$ AND $x_2^{(c)} \leq x_2 \leq x_2^{(d)}$ THEN $0.923 \leq y \leq 3.174$

r_{12}: IF $x_1^{(c)} \leq x_1 \leq x_1^{(d)}$ AND $x_2^{(a)} \leq x_2 \leq x_2^{(b)}$ THEN $-0.437 \leq y \leq -0.074$ (27)

r_{13}: IF $x_1^{(b)} \leq x_1 \leq x_1^{(c)}$ AND $x_2^{(a)} \leq x_2 \leq x_2^{(b)}$ THEN $0.783 \leq y \leq 1.547$

r_{14}: IF $x_1^{(c)} \leq x_1 \leq x_1^{(d)}$ AND $x_2^{(c)} \leq x_2 \leq x_2^{(d)}$ THEN $-0.555 \leq y \leq 0.188$

r_{15}: IF $x_1^{(d)} \leq x_1 \leq x_1^{(e)}$ AND $x_2^{(a)} \leq x_2 \leq x_2^{(b)}$ THEN $-1.088 \leq y \leq -0.580$

r_{16}: IF $x_1^{(c)} \leq x_1 \leq x_1^{(d)}$ AND $x_2^{(e)} \leq x_2 \leq x_2^{(f)}$ THEN $-1.048 \leq y \leq 0.116$

r_{17}: IF $x_1^{(d)} \leq x_1 \leq x_1^{(e)}$ AND $x_2^{(d)} \leq x_2 \leq x_2^{(e)}$ THEN $-1.361 \leq y \leq -0.773$

r_{18}: IF $x_1^{(b)} \leq x_1 \leq x_1^{(c)}$ AND $x_2^{(d)} \leq x_2 \leq x_2^{(e)}$ THEN $0.282 \leq y \leq 0.800$

r_{19}: IF $x_1^{(d)} \leq x_1 \leq x_1^{(e)}$ AND $x_2^{(c)} \leq x_2 \leq x_2^{(d)}$ THEN $0.300 \leq y \leq 0.810$

r_{20}: IF $x_1^{(c)} \leq x_1 \leq x_1^{(d)}$ AND $x_2^{(b)} \leq x_2 \leq x_2^{(c)}$ THEN $-0.384 \leq y \leq 0.300$

r_{21}: IF $x_1^{(a)} \leq x_1 \leq x_1^{(b)}$ AND $x_2^{(e)} \leq x_2 \leq x_2^{(f)}$ THEN $0.854 \leq y \leq 2.688$

r_{22}: IF $x_1^{(d)} \leq x_1 \leq x_1^{(e)}$ AND $x_2^{(e)} \leq x_2 \leq x_2^{(f)}$ THEN $-2.169 \leq y \leq -0.992$

r_{23}: IF $x_1^{(b)} \leq x_1 \leq x_1^{(c)}$ AND $x_2^{(e)} \leq x_2 \leq x_2^{(f)}$ THEN $0.235 \leq y \leq 0.848$

r_{24}: IF $x_1^{(a)} \leq x_1 \leq x_1^{(b)}$ AND $x_2^{(b)} \leq x_2 \leq x_2^{(c)}$ THEN $1.073 \leq y \leq 2.998$

r_{25}: IF $x_1^{(b)} \leq x_1 \leq x_1^{(c)}$ AND $x_2^{(b)} \leq x_2 \leq x_2^{(c)}$ THEN $0.408 \leq y \leq 0.991$

A suspension model with the parameters M_s = 400 [Kg], M_r = 50 [Kg], B_a = 500 [Ns/m], K_f = 20000 [N/m], K_p=250000 [N/m], using a classical control with C_{off} = 500 [Ns/m], C_{on} = 1400 [Ns/m], and applying the strategy defined by rules (27), in Figure 12 we have responses of

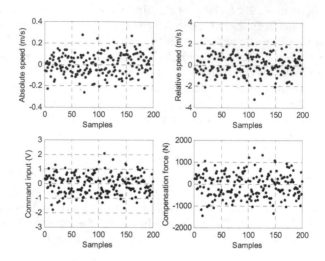

Fig. 11. Values of the variables of the suspension system under various operating conditions.

the acceleration of the sprung mass of the process for a sudden dislocation of 0.05 meters in the tire of the system. The results obtained indicate a better response (smaller acceleration) of the system using a rule-based controller in relation to the classical strategy. Therefore, just as in the fuzzy controller cited, the compensation force commanded by the rough controller can vary in wider operation ranges, since the rules incorporate the various operating conditions of the system (Fig. 11) in its generation procedure.

5.3 Example 7

This example shows a real application of control loops in cascade for speed regulation and current control in a drive system with a DC motor. Figure 13 shows a block diagram of the process in question. The motor is activated by a driver (chopper), which uses power transistor. Electronic circuits generate firing pulses to command the chopper and are controlled by a computer that performs the control algorithms of the system, in other words, two regulation loops in cascaded (Fig. 14) for the variables speed and current. Hall sensors provide information on the stator current (I_a) of the motor and the rotation (W) of the same, whose information are acquired by a data acquisition system coupled with the control computer. A synchronous machine operating as a generator feeds a set of electrical resistors switched by relays, and this set works as variable loads for the DC motor. This system has nonlinearities, mainly due to saturation of the driver used (amplifier and chopper) and the nonlinear characteristics of the series excitation motor. Real results of the tests performed in this system will be shown. The results are derived from experiments that use conventional controllers with PI actions to regulate the speed and current of the system, and rough control algorithms also with proportional and integral actions for the same purposes. Discrete representations equal to (28) were used for the realizations of the control algorithms, where variable "e" represents the control loop error (of the speed and of the current), "u" symbolizes the output variable of the controller in question, and "a_1, b_0 and b_1" are the parameters for the classic PI controllers.

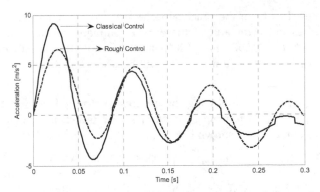

Fig. 12. Responses of the suspension system with classic and rough controls.

$$u(t) = b_o e(t) + b_1 e(t-1) + a_1 u(t-1) \tag{28}$$

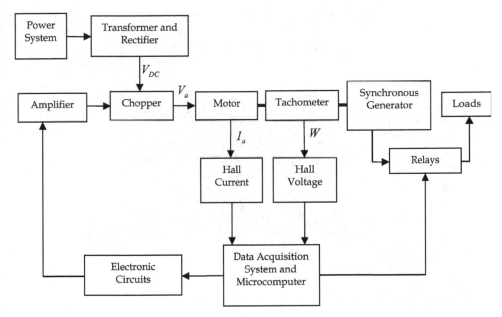

Fig. 13. Block diagram of the system in reference to Example 7.

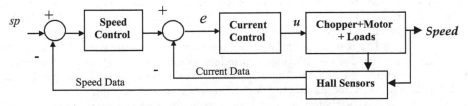

Fig. 14. Control Loops of Example 7

Figure 15 illustrates data from the practical tests with the conventional controllers, where the values of the current error and of the output command are normalized in p.u. The parameters are $a_1 = 1$, $b_0 = 0.5074$, $b_1 = -0.406$, and the sample time is 0.01 [s]. The variables $x_1 = e(t)$, $x_2 = e(t-1)$, $x_3 = u(t-1)$ and $y = u(t)$ will be used to generate the rules of a rough controller for the current loop.

Rosetta was used with the following procedures performed in the tool: *Import IS; Discretization → Equal frequency binning → Intervals = 3; Reduction → Manual Reducer; Rule generator.* The rules obtained are shown below, the first three and the last two.

r_1: x_1 = [0.3283, 1.0000] AND x_2 = [-0.3368, 0.3283] AND x_3 = [-0.0628, 0.3362]
THEN y = [0.1261, 0.9346];

r_2: x_1 = [-0.3434, 0.3283] AND x_2 = [0.3283, 1.0000] AND x_3 = [0.3362, 1.0000]
THEN y = [-0.0640, 0.8150];

r_3: x_1 = [-0.3434, 0.3283] AND x_2 = [-0.3368, 0.3283] AND x_3 = [-0.0628, 0.3362]
THEN y = [-0.2517, 0.4416];

...   .

r_{26}: x_1 = [0.3283, 1.0000] AND x_2 = [-1.0000, -0.3283] AND x_3 = [0.3362, 1.0000]
THEN y = [0.7209, 1.2189];

r_{27}: x_1 = [-1.0000, -0.3434] AND x_2 = [-1.0000, -0.3283] AND x_3 = [0.3362, 1.0000]
THEN y = [0.1696, 0.3973].   (29)

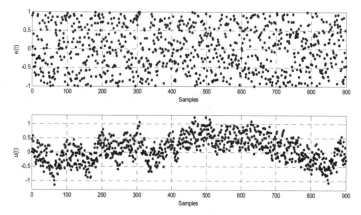

Fig. 15. Values of the variables for the system under various operating conditions.

Now that the rough controller has information on three inputs, numerical values in ranges of the data obtained in the rules can be interpolated by means of (11) with $n = 3$. The acquisition of rules for the rough controller in the speed loop is performed similarly as described for the current loop. Figure 16 shows the real result of a test performed on the described system. The responses of the speed regulation and of the current became better with rough controllers than with classic controllers, as much in the starting of the motor as in the load alterations of the same. There are smaller peaks in the current and speed, both in speed variations (such increasing the input reference in the starting of the motor, for example), and in load variation (in this case a reduction that occurred between 7 and 8 seconds in the test). The explanation for these characteristics is due to the fact that the rule-based controllers incorporate the various operating conditions of the system, generating rules to compensate suitably the nonlinearities of the system.

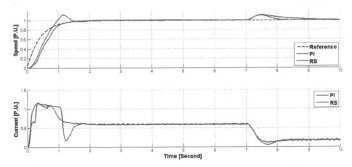

Fig. 16. Real responses of the system with classic and rough controllers.

6. Conclusion

This paper has presented a new approach to design rule-based controllers using concepts about rough sets. The proposed methodology allows obtaining rule parameters in a systematic form and with simple computations, as much for fuzzy controllers as for rough controllers. Example 1 illustrates some basic concepts about rough sets. Using a simple linear function is shown in Example 2 how to apply the approach proposed in this chapter in the modeling of rule-based models. Example 3 shows how a rough model can estimate the values associated with a basic nonlinear function. The results obtained in Example 4 show the same values for a fuzzy model and a rough model, when the approach involves a linear function. In this example the linear function was associated with the function of a proportional-integral controller. These results can also be confronted with those obtained in the work referenced in Pinheiro et al., 2010. In Example 5 a practical context of adaptive gains is synthesized through a rough controller in the control of a nonlinear system. Example 6 deals with an active suspension model used in automotive systems. The methodology proposed in this paper was applied to generate a rule-based controller to control the suspension system in question. The results can be confronted with those obtained in the works referenced in Pinheiro et al., 2007 and Dong et al., 2010. The dynamic responses obtained were similar to the works mentioned. An experimental application was shown in Example 7, an example of control loops in cascade for speed regulation and current control in a drive system with a DC motor. Two rough controllers were synthesized to regulate the speed and current in the system. The results can be compared with those obtained in the work referenced in Rezek et al., 2010. The dynamic responses obtained were similar to the work mentioned, where was used two fuzzy controllers for the same purposes. The results obtained in this work indicate that the methodology proposed is adequate for applications in real control systems. The impact of the rough controllers in relation to the fuzzy controllers is that it does not require fuzzification and defuzzification procedures, which can be advantageous in real-time applications for control systems. The application of LMI (linear matrix inequalities) techniques and Lyapunov functions will also be investigated to design rough controllers and to analyze the stability in control loops, the same way that these methods are applied in control systems that use functional fuzzy controllers (Wang et al., 1996; Tseng & Chen, 2009). Future papers will address issues with rough controllers aiming at applications in control systems with multiple inputs and multiple outputs (MIMO).

7. References

Astrom, K. & Wittenmark, B. (1990). *Computer-Controlled Systems: Theory and Design*, Prentice Hall, ISBN , 0-13-168600-3, Englewood Cliffs, USA

Dong, X.; Yu, M.; Liau, C. & Chen, W. (2010). Comparative research on semi-active control strategies for magneto-rheological suspension, *Nonlinear Dynamics*, Springer, Vol.59, pp. 433-453, Netherlands

Huang, B.; Guo, L. & Zhou, X. (2007). Approximation Reduction Based on Similarity Relation, *IEEE Fourth International Conf. on Fuzzy Systems and Knowledge Discovery*, pp. 124-128

Kusiak, A. & Shah, A. (2006). Data-Mining-Based System for Prediction of Water Chemistry Faults, *IEEE Transactions on Industrial Electronics*, No.2, pp. 593-596

Øhrn, A. & Komorowski, J. (1997). ROSETTA: A Rough Set Toolkit for Analysis of Data. *Third International Joint Conference on Information Sciences*, pp. 403 – 407

Pawlak, Z. (1982). Rough Sets, *International Journal of Computer and Inf. Sciences*, pp. 341-356,

Pawlak, Z. (1991). Rough Sets: Theoretical Aspects of Reasoning about Data. *Kluwer Academic Publishers*, Dordrecht, Holland

Pawlak, Z. & Skowron, A. (2007). Rudiments of rough sets, *Information Sciences*, 177; pp. 3-27

Pedrycz, W. & Gomide, F. (2007). *Fuzzy Systems Engineering: Toward Human Centric Computing*, Wiley Interscience/IEEE, ISBN 978-0-471-78857-7, Hoboken, USA

Pinheiro, C. & Gomide, F. (1997). Frequency Response Design of Fuzzy Controllers, *VII International Fuzzy Systems Association World Congress*, Vol.3, pp. 434-439, Praga

Pinheiro, C. & Gomide, F. (2000). On Tuning Nonlinear Fuzzy Control Systems. In: IEEE International Conference on Fuzzy Systems, *IX IEEE International Conference on Fuzzy Systems* (in CD ROM), San Antonio, USA

Pinheiro, C.; Machado, J.; Bombard, A.; Lima, J. & Dias, J. (2007), Fuzzy Logic Control For Magnetorheological Damper, *Electrorheological Fluids And Magnetorheological Suspensions*, World Scientific, pp. 603-609, Singapore

Pinheiro, C.; Gomide, F.; Carpinteiro, O. & Lima, I. (2010). Granular Synthesis of Rule-Based Models and Function Approximation using Rough Sets, *Novel Developments in Granular Computing*, ed. JingTao Yao, Information Science, ISBN 978-1-60566-324-1, N. York, USA

Rezek, A.; Pinheiro, C.; Darido, T.; Silva, V.; Vicentini, O. & Assis, W. (2010). Comparative Performance Analysis for Digital Regulators in Series DC Motor Controlled Drive, *International Journal of Power & Energy Systems*, Vol.30, No.1, pp. 15-22

Skowron, A. & Son, N. H (1995). Quantization of Real value Attributes: Rough Set and Boolean reasoning approach, *International Joint Conf. on Information Sciences*, pp. 34- 37

Tseng, C. & Chen, B. (2009), Robust Fuzzy Observer-Based Fuzzy Control Design for Nonlinear Discrete-Time Systems with Persistent Bounded Disturbances, *IEEE Transactions on Fuzzy Systems*, Vol.17, No.3, pp. 711-723

Wang, H.; Tanaka, K. & Griffin, M. (1996), An Approach to Fuzzy Control of Nonlinear Systems: Stability and Design Issues, *IEEE Transactions on Fuzzy Systems*, Vol.4, No.1, pp. 14-23

Ziarko, W. & Katzberg, J. (1993). Rough sets approach to system modeling and control algorithm acquisition. *IEEE Conference: Communications, Computers and Power in the Modern Environment*, pp. 154-164

15

A Mamdani Type Fuzzy Logic Controller

Ion Iancu
University of Craiova
Romania

1. Introduction

The database of a rule-based system may contain imprecisions which appear in the description of the rules given by the expert. Because such an inference can not be made by the methods which use classical two valued logic or many valued logic, Zadeh in (Zadeh, 1975) and Mamdani in (Mamdani, 1977) suggested an inference rule called "compositional rule of inference". Using this inference rule, several methods for fuzzy reasoning were proposed. Zadeh (Zadeh, 1979) extends the traditional Modus Ponens rule in order to work with fuzzy sets, obtaining the Generalized Modus Ponens (GMP) rule.

An important part of fuzzy reasoning is represented by Fuzzy Logic Control (FLC), derived from control theory based on mathematical models of the open-loop process to be controlled. Fuzzy Logic Control has been successfully applied to a wide variety of practical problems: control of warm water, robot, heat exchange, traffic junction, cement kiln, automobile speed, automotive engineering, model car parking and turning, power system and nuclear reactor, on-line shopping, washing machines, etc.

It points out that fuzzy control has been effectively used in the context of complex ill-defined processes, especially those that can be controlled by a skilled human operator without the knowledge of their underlying dynamics. In this sense, neural and adaptive fuzzy systems has been compared to classical control methods by B. Kosko in (Kosko, 1992). There, it is remarked that they are model-free estimators, i.e., they estimate a function without requiring a mathematical description of how the output functionally depends on the input; they learn from samples. However, some people criticized fuzzy control because the very fundamental question "Why does a fuzzy rule-based system have such good performance for a wide variety of practical problems?" remained unanswered. A first approach to answer this fundamental question in a quantitative way was presented by Wang in (Wang, 1992) where he proved that a particular class of FLC systems are universal approximators: they are capable of approximating any real continuous function on a compact set to arbitrary accuracy. This class is characterized by:

1) Gaussian membership functions,

2) Product fuzzy conjunction,

3) Product fuzzy implication,

4) Center of area defuzzification.

Other approaches are due to Buckley (Buckley, 1992; 1993). He has proved that a modification of Sugeno type fuzzy controllers gives universal approximators. Although both results are very important, many real fuzzy logic controllers do not belong to these classes, because other membership functions are used, other inference mechanisms are applied or other type of rules are used. The question "What other types of fuzzy logic controllers are universal approximators?" still remained unanswered. This problem were solved by Castro in (Castro, 1995) where he proved that a large number of classes of FLC systems are also universal approximators.

The most popular FLC systems are: Mamdani, Tsukamoto, Sugeno and Larsen which work with crisp data as inputs. An extension of the Mamdani model in order to work with interval inputs is presented in (Liu et al., 2005) , where the fuzzy sets are represented by triangular fuzzy numbers and the firing level of the conclusion is computed as the product of firing levels from the antecedent. Other extensions and applications of the standard FLC systems were proposed in (Iancu, 2009a;b; Iancu, Colhon & Dupac, 2010; Iancu, Constantinescu & Colhon, 2010; Iancu & Popirlan, 2010).

The necessity to extend the fuzzy controllers to work with intervals or linguistic values as inputs is given by many applications where precise values of the input data no interest or are difficult to estimate. For example, in shopping applications the buyer is interested, rather, in a product that is priced within certain limits or does not exceed a given value (Liu et al., 2005). In other cases, the input values are much easier to express in fuzzy manner, for example, in the problem of controlling the washing time using fuzzy logic control the degree of dirt for the object to be washed is easily expressed by a linguistic value (Agarwal, 2007). These examples will be used to show the working of the model proposed in order to expand the Mamdani fuzzy logic controller. In this paper a FLC system with the following characteristics is presented:

- the linguistic terms (or values) are represented by trapezoidal fuzzy numbers
- various implication operators are used to represent the rules
- the crisp control action of a rule is computed using Middle-of-Maxima method
- the overall crisp control action of an implication is computed by discrete Center-of-Gravity
- the overall crisp control action of the system is computed using an OWA (Ordered Weighted Averaging) operator.

2. Preliminaries

Let U be a collection of objects denoted generically by $\{u\}$, which could be discrete or continuous. U is called the universe of discourse and u represents the generic element of U.

Definition 1. *A fuzzy set F in the universe of discourse U is characterized by its membership function* $\mu_F : U \rightarrow [0,1]$. *The fuzzy set may be represented as a set of ordered pairs of a generic element u and its grade of membership function:* $F = \{(u, \mu_F(u))/u \in U\}$.

Definition 2. *A fuzzy number F in a continuous universe U, e. g., a real line, is a fuzzy set F in U which is normal and convex, i. e.,*

$$\max_{u \in U} \mu_F(u) = 1 \qquad (normal)$$

$$\mu_F(\lambda u_1 + (1 - \lambda)u_2) \geq min\{\mu_F(u_1), \mu_F(u_2)\}, \quad u_1, u_2 \in U, \lambda \in [0, 1] \quad (convex)$$

Because the majority of practical applications work with trapezoidal or triangular distributions and these representations are still a subject of various recent papers ((Grzegorzewski & Mrowka, 2007), (Nasseri, 2008), for instance) we will work with membership functions represented by trapezoidal fuzzy numbers. Such a number $N = (\underline{m}, \overline{m}, \alpha, \beta)$ is defined as

$$\mu_N(x) = \begin{cases} 0 & for \ x < \underline{m} - \alpha \\ \frac{x - \underline{m} + \alpha}{\alpha} & for \ x \in [\underline{m} - \alpha, \underline{m}] \\ 1 & for \ x \in [\underline{m}, \overline{m}] \\ \frac{\overline{m} + \beta - x}{\beta} & for \ x \in [\overline{m}, \overline{m} + \beta] \\ 0 & for \ x > \overline{m} + \beta \end{cases}$$

Will be used fuzzy sets to represent linguistic variables. A linguistic variable can be regarded either as a variable whose value is a fuzzy number or as a variable whose values are defined in linguistic terms.

Definition 3. *A linguistic variable V is characterized by: its name x, an universe U, a term set T(x), a syntactic rule G for generating names of values of x, and a set of semantic rule M for associating with each value its meaning.*

For example, if *speed* of a car is interpreted as a linguistic variable, then its term set could be $T(x) = \{slow, moderate, fast, very \ slow, more \ or \ less \ fast\}$ where each term is characterized by a fuzzy set in an universe of discourse $U = [0, 100]$. We might interpret: *slow* as "a speed below about 40 mph", *moderate* as "speed close to 55 mph", *fast* as "a speed about 70 mph".

Definition 4. *A function $T : [0, 1]^2 \rightarrow [0, 1]$ is a t-norm iff it is commutative, associative, non-decreasing and $T(x, 1) = x \ \forall x \in [0, 1]$.*

The most important t-norms are:

- Minimum: $T_m(x, y) = min\{x, y\}$

- Lukasiewicz: $T_L(x, y) = max\{0, x + y - 1\}$

- Probabilistic (or Product): $T_P(x, y) = xy$

- Weak: $T_W(x, y) = \begin{cases} min\{x, y\} \ if & max\{x, y\} = 1 \\ 0 & otherwise. \end{cases}$

Definition 5. *A function $S : [0, 1]^2 \rightarrow [0, 1]$ is a t-conorm iff it is commutative, associative, non-decreasing and $S(x, 0) = x \ \forall x \in [0, 1]$.*

The basic t-conorms are

- Maximum: $S_m(x, y) = max\{x, y\}$

- Lukasiewicz: $S_L(x, y) = min\{1, x + y\}$

- Probabilistic (or Product): $S_P(x, y) = x + y - xy$

- Strong: $S_S(x,y) = \begin{cases} max\{x,y\} \ if & min\{x,y\} = 1 \\ \qquad 1 & otherwise. \end{cases}$

The t-norms are used to compute the firing levels of the rules or as aggregation operators and the t-conorms are used as aggregation operators. The rules are represented by fuzzy implications. Let X and Y be two variables whose domains are U and V, respectively. A causal link from X to Y is represented as a conditional possibility distribution ((Zadeh, 1979), (Zadeh, 1978)) $\pi_{Y/X}$ which restricts the possible values of Y for a given value of X. For the rule

$$IF\ X\ is\ A\ THEN\ Y\ is\ B$$

we have

$$\forall u \in U,\ \forall v \in V,\ \pi_{Y/X}(v,u) = \mu_A(u) \rightarrow \mu_B(v)$$

where $\rightarrow$ is an implication operator and μ_A and μ_B are the membership functions of the fuzzy sets A and B, respectively.

Definition 6. *An implication is a function* $I : [0,1]^2 \rightarrow [0,1]$ *satisfying the following conditions for all* $x,y,z \in [0,1]$:

I1: *If* $x \leq z$ *then* $I(x,y) \geq I(z,y)$

I2: *If* $y \leq z$ *then* $I(x,y) \leq I(x,z)$

I3: $I(0,y) = 1$ *(falsity implies anything)*

I4: $I(x,1) = 1$ *(anything implies tautology)*

I5: $I(1,0) = 0$ *(Booleanity)*.

The following properties could be important in some applications:

I6: $I(1,x) = x$ (tautology cannot justify anything)

I7: $I(x,I(y,z)) = I(y,I(x,z))$ (exchange principle)

I8: $x \leq y$ if and only if $I(x,y) = 1$ (implication defines ordering)

I9: $I(x,0) = N(x)$ is a strong negation

I10: $I(x,y) \geq y$

I11: $I(x,x) = 1$ (identity principle)

I12: $I(x,y) = I(N(y),N(x))$, where N is a strong negation

I13: I is a continuous function.

The most important implications are:
Willmott: $I_W(x,y) = max\{1 - x, min\{x,y\}\}$
Mamdani: $I_M(x,y) = min\{x,y\}$

Rescher-Gaines: $I_{RG}(x,y) = \begin{cases} 1\ if & x \leq y \\ 0\ otherwise \end{cases}$

Kleene-Dienes: $I_{KD}(x,y) = max\{1 - x, y\}$

Brouwer-Gödel: $I_{BG}(x,y) = \begin{cases} 1 \ if & x \leq y \\ y \ otherwise \end{cases}$

Goguen: $I_G(x,y) = \begin{cases} 1 \ if & x \leq y \\ \frac{y}{x} \ otherwise \end{cases}$

Lukasiewicz: $I_L(x,y) = \min\{1 - x + y, 1\}$

Fodor: $I_F(x,y) = \begin{cases} 1 & if \ x \leq y \\ max\{1 - x, y\} & otherwise \end{cases}$

Reichenbach: $I_R(x,y) = 1 - x + xy$.

Definition 7. *An n-ary fuzzy relation is a fuzzy set in $U_1 \times U_2 \times \cdots \times U_n$ expressed as*

$$R_{U_1 \times \cdots \times U_n} = \{((u_1, \cdots, u_n), \mu_R(u_1, \cdots, u_n)) / (u_1, \cdots, u_n) \in U_1 \times \cdots \times U_n\}.$$

Definition 8. *If R and S are fuzzy relations in $U \times V$ and $V \times W$, respectively, then the sup-star composition of R and S is a fuzzy relation denoted by $R \circ S$ and defined by*

$$R \circ S = \{[(u, w), \sup_v (\mu_R(u, v) * \mu_S(v, w))] / u \in U, v \in V, w \in W\}$$

where $*$ can be any operator in the class of t-norms.

Fuzzy implication inference is based on the compositional rule of inference for approximate reasoning suggested by Zadeh in (Zadeh, 1973).

Definition 9. *If R is a fuzzy relation on $U \times V$ and x is a fuzzy set in U then the "sup-star compositional rule of inference" asserts that the fuzzy set y in V induced by x is given by (Zadeh, 1971)*

$$y = x \circ R$$

where $x \circ R$ is the sup-star composition of x and R.

If the star represents the minimum operator then this definition reduces to Zadeh's compositional rule of inference (Zadeh, 1973).

The process of information aggregation appears in many applications related to the development of intelligent systems: fuzzy logic controllers, neural networks, vision systems, expert systems, multi-criteria decision aids. In (Yager, 1988) Yager introduced an aggregation technique based on OWA operators.

Definition 10. *An OWA operator of dimension n is a mapping $F : R^n \to R$ that has an associated n vector $w = (w_1, w_2, ..., w_n)^t$ such as*

$$w_i \in [0,1], 1 \leq i \leq n, \sum_{i=1}^{n} w_i = 1.$$

The aggregation operator of the values $\{a_1, a_2, ..., a_n\}$ is

$$F(a_1, a_2, ..., a_n) = \sum_{j=1}^{n} w_j b_j$$

where b_j is the j-th largest element from $\{a_1, a_2, ..., a_n\}$.

It is sufficiently to work with rules with a single conclusion because a rule with multiple consequent can be treated as a set of such rules.

3. Standard fuzzy logic controllers

3.1 Structure of a fuzzy logic controller

The seminal work by L.A. Zadeh (Zadeh, 1973) on fuzzy algorithms introduced the idea of formulating the control algorithm by logical rules. An FLC consists of a set of rules of the form

$$IF\ (a\ set\ of\ conditions\ are\ satisfied)\ THEN\ (a\ set\ of\ consequences\ can\ be\ inferred).$$

Since the antecedents and the consequents of these IF-THEN rules are associated with fuzzy concepts (linguistic terms), they are often called *fuzzy conditional statements*. In FLC terminology, a *fuzzy control rule* is a fuzzy conditional statement in which the antecedent is a condition in its application domain and the consequent is a control action for the system under control. The inputs of fuzzy rule-based systems should be given by fuzzy sets, and therefore, we have to fuzzify the crisp inputs. Furthermore, the output of a fuzzy system is always a fuzzy set, and therefore to get crisp value we have to defuzzify it. Fuzzy logic control systems usually consist of four major parts: Fuzzification interface, Fuzzy rule base, Fuzzy inference engine and Defuzzification interface, as is presented in the Figure 1.

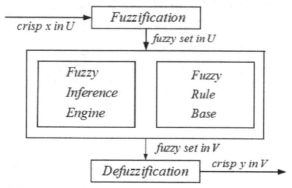

Fig. 1. Fuzzy Logic Controller

The four components of a FLC are explained in the following (Lee, 1990).

The *fuzzification interface* involves the functions:

a) measures the values of inputs variables,

b) performs a scale mappings that transfers the range of values of inputs variables into corresponding universes of discourse,

c) performs the function of fuzzyfication that converts input data into suitable linguistic values which may be viewed as label of fuzzy sets.

The *rule base* comprises a knowledge of the application domain and the attendant control goals. It consists of a "data base" and a "linguistic (fuzzy) control rule base":

a) the data base provides necessary definitions which are used to define linguistic control rules and fuzzy data manipulation in a FLC

b) the rule base characterizes the control goals and the control policy of the domain experts by means of a set of linguistic control rules.

The *fuzzy inference engine* is the kernel of a FLC; it has the capability of simulating human decision-making based of fuzzy concepts and of inferring fuzzy control actions employing fuzzy implication and the rules of inference in fuzzy logic.

The *defuzzification interface* performs the following functions:

a) a scale mapping, which converts the range of values of output variables into corresponding universes of discourse

b) defuzzification, which yields a non fuzzy control action from an inferred fuzzy control action.

A fuzzification operator has the effect of transforming crisp data into fuzzy sets. In most of the cases fuzzy singletons are used as fuzzifiers (according to Figure 2).

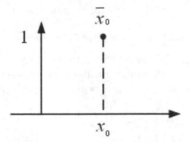

Fig. 2. Fuzzy singleton as fuzzifier

In other words,

$$fuzzifier(x_0) = \bar{x}_0,$$

$$\mu_{\bar{x}_0}(x) = \begin{cases} 1 & for \ x = x_0 \\ 0 & for \ x \neq x_0 \end{cases}$$

where x_0 is a crisp input value from a process.

The procedure used by Fuzzy Inference Engine in order to obtain a fuzzy output consists of the following steps:

1. find the firing level of each rule,

2. find the output of each rule,

3. aggregate the individual rules outputs in order to obtain the overall system output.

The fuzzy control action C inferred from the fuzzy control system is transformed into a crisp control action:

$$z_0 = defuzzifier(C)$$

where *defuzzifier* is a defuzzification operator. The most used defuzzification operators, for a discrete fuzzy set C having the universe of discourse V, are:

- Center-of-Gravity:

$$z_0 = \frac{\sum\limits_{j=1}^{N} z_j \mu_C(z_j)}{\sum\limits_{j=1}^{N} \mu_C(z_j)}$$

- Middle-of-Maxima: the defuzzified value is defined as mean of all values of the universe of discourse, having maximal membership grades

$$z_0 = \frac{1}{N1} \sum_{j=1}^{N1} z_j, \quad N1 \leq N$$

- Max-Criterion: this method chooses an arbitrary value, from the set of maximizing elements of C, i. e.

$$z_0 \in \{z/\mu_C(z) = \max_{v \in V} \mu_C(v)\},$$

where $Z = \{z_1, ..., z_N\}$ is a set of elements from the universe V.

Because several linguistic variables are involved in the antecedents and the conclusions of a rule, the fuzzy system is of the type multi–input–multi–output. Further, the working with a FLC for the case of a two-input-single-output system is explained. Such a system consists of a set of rules

$$R_1 : \textit{IF x is } A_1 \textit{ AND y is } B_1 \textit{ THEN z is } C_1$$
$$R_2 : \textit{IF x is } A_2 \textit{ AND y is } B_2 \textit{ THEN z is } C_2$$

$$\cdots\cdots\cdots\cdots\cdots\cdots\cdots\cdots$$

$$R_n : \textit{IF x is } A_n \textit{ AND y is } B_n \textit{ THEN z is } C_n$$

and a set of inputs

$$\texttt{fact} : \textit{x is } x_0 \textit{ AND y is } y_0$$

where x and y are the process state variables, z is the control variable, A_i, B_i and C_i are linguistic values of the linguistic variables x, y and z in the universes of discourse U, V and W, respectively. Our task is to find a crisp control action z_0 from the fuzzy rule base and from the actual crisp inputs x_0 and y_0. A fuzzy control rule

$$R_i : \textit{IF x is } A_i \textit{ AND y is } B_i \textit{ THEN z is } C_i$$

is implemented by a fuzzy implication I_i and is defined as

$$\mu_{I_i}(u,v,w) = [\mu_{A_i}(u) \textit{ AND } \mu_{B_i}(v)] \rightarrow \mu_{C_i}(w) = T(\mu_{A_i}(u), \mu_{B_i}(v)) \rightarrow \mu_{C_i}(w)$$

where T is a t-norm used to model the logical connective AND. To infer the consequence "z is C" from the set of rules and the facts, usually the compositional rule of inference is applied; it gives

$$consequence = Agg\{fact \circ R_1, ..., fact \circ R_n\}.$$

That is

$$\mu_C = Agg\{T(\mu_{\bar{x}_0}, \mu_{\bar{y}_0}) \circ R_1, ..., T(\mu_{\bar{x}_0}, \mu_{\bar{y}_0}) \circ R_n\}.$$

Taking into account that $\mu_{\bar{x}_0}(u) = 0$ for $u \neq x_0$ and $\mu_{\bar{y}_0}(v) = 0$ for $v \neq y_0$, the membership function of C is given by

$$\mu_C(w) = Agg\{T(\mu_{A_1}(x_0), \mu_{B_1}(y_0)) \rightarrow \mu_{C_1}(w), ..., T(\mu_{A_n}(x_0), \mu_{B_n}(y_0)) \rightarrow \mu_{C_n}(w)\}$$

for all $w \in W$.

The procedure used for obtaining the fuzzy output from a FLC system is

- the firing level of the i-th rule is determined by

$$T(\mu_{A_i}(x_0), \mu_{B_i}(y_0))$$

- the output C'_i of the i-th rule is given by

$$\mu_{C'_i}(w) = T(\mu_{A_i}(x_0), \mu_{B_i}(y_0)) \rightarrow \mu_{C_i}(w)$$

- the overall system output, C, is obtained from the individual rule outputs, by aggregation operation:

$$\mu_C(w) = Agg\{\mu_{C'_1}(w), ..., \mu_{C'_n}(w)\}$$

for all $w \in W$.

3.2 Mamdani fuzzy logic controller

The most commonly used fuzzy inference technique is the so-called Mamdani method (Mamdani & Assilian, 1975) which was proposed, by Mamdani and Assilian, as the very first attempt to control a steam engine and boiler combination by synthesizing a set of linguistic control rules obtained from experienced human operators. Their work was inspired by an equally influential publication by Zadeh (Zadeh, 1973). Interest in fuzzy control has continued ever since, and the literature on the subject has grown rapidly. A survey of the field with fairly extensive references may be found in (Lee, 1990) or, more recently, in (Sala et al., 2005). In Mamdani's model the fuzzy implication is modeled by Mamdani's minimum operator, the conjunction operator is min, the t-norm from compositional rule is min and for the aggregation of the rules the max operator is used. In order to explain the working with this model of FLC will be considered the example from (Rakic, 2010) where a simple two-input one-output problem that includes three rules is examined:

$$Rule1: \quad IF \ x \ is \ A_3 \ OR \ y \ is \ B_1 \ THEN \ z \ is \ C_1$$

$$Rule2: \quad IF \ x \ is \ A_2 \ AND \ y \ is \ B_2 \ THEN \ z \ is \ C_2$$

$$Rule3: \quad IF \ x \ is \ A_1 \ THEN \ z \ is \ C_3.$$

Step 1: Fuzzification

The first step is to take the crisp inputs, x_0 and y_0, and determine the degree to which these inputs belong to each of the appropriate fuzzy sets. According to Fig 3(a) one obtains

$$\mu_{A_1}(x_0) = 0.5, \mu_{A_2}(x_0) = 0.2, \mu_{B_1}(y_0) = 0.1, \mu_{B_2}(y_0) = 0.7$$

Step 2: Rules evaluation

The fuzzified inputs are applied to the antecedents of the fuzzy rules. If a given fuzzy rule has multiple antecedents, the fuzzy operator (AND or OR) is used to obtain a single number that represents the result of the antecedent evaluation. To evaluate the disjunction of the rule antecedents, one uses the OR fuzzy operation. Typically, the classical fuzzy operation union is used :

$$\mu_{A \cup B}(x) = max\{\mu_A(x), \mu_B(x)\}.$$

Similarly, in order to evaluate the conjunction of the rule antecedents, the AND fuzzy operation intersection is applied:

$$\mu_{A \cap B}(x) = min\{\mu_A(x), \mu_B(x)\}.$$

The result is given in the Figure 3(b).

Now the result of the antecedent evaluation can be applied to the membership function of the consequent. The most common method is to cut the consequent membership function at the level of the antecedent truth; this method is called *clipping*. Because top of the membership function is sliced, the clipped fuzzy set loses some information. However, clipping is preferred because it involves less complex and generates an aggregated output surface that is easier to defuzzify. Another method, named *scaling*, offers a better approach for preserving the original shape of the fuzzy set: the original membership function of the rule consequent is adjusted by multiplying all its membership degrees by the truth value of the rule antecedent (see Fig. 3(c)).

Step 3: Aggregation of the rule outputs

The membership functions of all rule consequents previously clipped or scaled are combined into a single fuzzy set (see Fig. 4(a)).

Step 4: Defuzzification

The most popular defuzzification method is the centroid technique. It finds a point representing the center of gravity (COG) of the aggregated fuzzy set A, on the interval $[a, b]$. A reasonable estimate can be obtained by calculating it over a sample of points. According to Fig. 4(b), in our case results

$$COG = \frac{(0 + 10 + 20) \times 0.1 + (30 + 40 + 50 + 60) \times 0.2 + (70 + 80 + 90 + 100) \times 0.5}{0.1 + 0.1 + 0.1 + 0.2 + 0.2 + 0.2 + 0.2 + 0.5 + 0.5 + 0.5 + 0.5} = 67.4$$

3.3 Universal approximators

Using the Stone-Weierstrass theorem, Wang in (Wang, 1992) showed that fuzzy logic control systems of the form

$$R_i : \ IF \ x \ is \ A_i \ AND \ y \ is \ B_i \ THEN \ z \ is \ C_i, \quad i = 1, ..., n$$

with

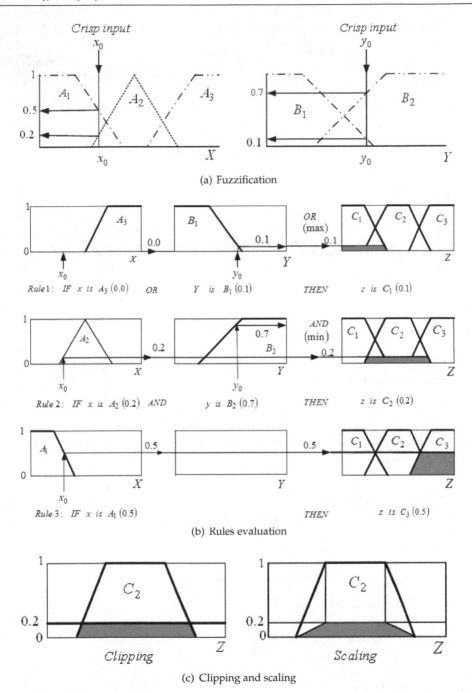

(a) Fuzzification

Rule 1: IF x is A_3 (0.0) OR Y is B_1 (0.1)   THEN z is C_1 (0.1)

Rule 2: IF x is A_2 (0.2) AND y is B_2 (0.7)   THEN z is C_2 (0.2)

Rule 3: IF x is A_1 (0.5)   THEN z is C_3 (0.5)

(b) Rules evaluation

(c) Clipping and scaling

Fig. 3. Mamdani fuzzy logic controller

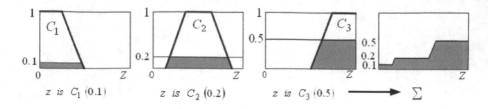

(a) Aggregation of the rule outputs

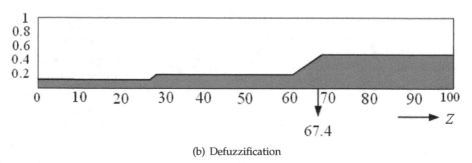

(b) Defuzzification

Fig. 4. Mamdani fuzzy logic controller

- Gaussian membership functions

$$\mu_A(x) = \exp[-\frac{1}{2}(\frac{x - x_0}{\sigma})^2]$$

where x_0 is the position of the peak relative to the universe and σ is the standard deviation

- Singleton fuzzifier

$$fuzzifier(x) = \bar{x}$$

- Fuzzy product conjunction

$$\mu_{A_i}(u) \; AND \; \mu_{B_i}(v) = \mu_{A_i}(u)\mu_{B_i}(v)$$

- Larsen (fuzzy product) implication

$$[\mu_{A_i}(u) \; AND \; \mu_{B_i}(v)] \rightarrow \mu_{C_i}(w) = \mu_{A_i}(u)\mu_{B_i}(v)\mu_{C_i}(w)$$

- Centroid deffuzification method

$$z = \frac{\sum_{i=1}^{n} c_i \mu_{A_i}(x)\mu_{B_i}(y)}{\sum_{i=1}^{n} \mu_{A_i}(x)\mu_{B_i}(y)}$$

where c_i is the center of C_i, are universal approximators, i.e. they can approximate any continuous function on a compact set to an arbitrary accuracy.

More generally, Wang proved the following theorem

Theorem 1. *For a given real-valued continuous function g on the compact set U and arbitrary $\epsilon > 0$, there exists a fuzzy logic control system with output function f such that*

$$\sup_{x \in U} \|g(x) - f(x)\| \leq \epsilon.$$

Castro in (Castro, 1995) showed that Mamdani fuzzy logic controllers

$$R_i : \ IF \ x \ is \ A_i \ AND \ y \ is \ B_i \ THEN \ z \ is \ C_i, i = 1, ..., n$$

with

- Symmetric triangular membership functions

$$\mu_A(x) = \begin{cases} 1 - \dfrac{x-a}{\alpha} & if \quad |x-a| \leq \alpha \\ 0 & otherwise \end{cases}$$

- Singleton fuzzifier

$$fuzzifier(x_0) = \bar{x}_0$$

- Minimum norm fuzzy conjunction

$$\mu_{A_i}(u) \ AND \ \mu_{B_i}(v) = min\{\mu_{A_i}(u), \mu_{B_i}(v)\}$$

- Minimum-norm fuzzy implication

$$[\mu_{A_i}(u) \ AND \ \mu_{B_i}(v)] \rightarrow \mu_{C_i}(w) = min\{\mu_{A_i}(u), \mu_{B_i}(v), \mu_{C_i}(w)\}$$

- Maximum t-conorm rule aggregation

$$Agg\{R_1, R_2, ..., R_n\} = max\{R_1, R_2, ..., R_n\}$$

- Centroid defuzzification method

$$z = \frac{\displaystyle\sum_{i=1}^{n} c_i min\{\mu_{A_i}(x), \mu_{B_i}(y)\}}{\displaystyle\sum_{i=1}^{n} min\{\mu_{A_i}(x), \mu_{B_i}(y)\}}$$

where c_i is the center of C_i, are universal approximators.

More generally, Castro (Castro, 1995) studied the following problem:

Given a type of FLC, (i.e. a fuzzification method, a fuzzy inference method, a defuzzification method, and a class of fuzzy rules, are fixed), an arbitrary continuous real valued function f on a compact $U \subset R^n$, and a certain $\epsilon > 0$, is it possible to find a set of fuzzy rules such that the associated fuzzy controller approximates f to level ϵ?

The main result obtained by Castro is that the approximation is possible for almost any type of fuzzy logic controller.

4. Mamdani FLC with different inputs and implications

Further, the standard Mamdani FLC system will be extended to work as inputs with crisp data, intervals and linguistic terms and with various implications to represent the rules. A rule is characterized by

- a set of linguistic variables A, having as domain an interval $I_A = [a_A, b_A]$
- n_A linguistic values $A_1, A_2, ..., A_{n_A}$ for each linguistic variable A
- the membership function for each value A_i, denoted as $\mu_{A_i}^0(x)$ where $i \in \{1, 2, ..., n_A\}$ and $x \in I_A$.

The fuzzy inference process is performed in the steps presented in the following subsections.

4.1 Fuzzification

A fuzzification operator transforms a crisp data or an interval into a fuzzy set. For instance, $x_0 \in U$ is fuzzified into $\bar{x}_0$ according with the relation:

$$\mu_{\bar{x}_0}(x) = \begin{cases} 1 & if \quad x = x_0 \\ 0 & otherwise \end{cases}$$

and an interval input $[a, b]$ is fuzzified into

$$\mu_{[a,b]}(x) = \begin{cases} 1 & if \quad x \in [a, b] \\ 0 & otherwise \end{cases}$$

4.2 Firing levels

The firing level of a linguistic variable A_i, which appears in the premise of a rule, depends of the input data.

- For a crisp value x_0 it is $\mu_{A_i}^0(x_0)$.

If the input is an interval or a linguistic term then the firing level can be computed in various forms.

A) based on "intersection"

- for an input interval $[a, b]$ it is given by:

$$\mu_{A_i} = \max\{\min\{\mu_{A_i}^0(x), \mu_{[a,b]}(x)\} | x \in [a, b]\}.$$

- for a linguistic input value A_i' it is

$$\mu_{A_i} = \max\{\min\{\mu_{A_i}^0(x), \mu_{A_i'}(x)\} | x \in I_A\}.$$

B) based on "areas ratio"

- for an input interval $[a, b]$ it is given by the area defined by intersection $\mu_{A_i}^0 \cap \mu_{[a,b]}$ divided by area defined by $\mu_{A_i}^0$

$$\mu_{A_i} = \frac{\int_a^b \min\{\mu_{A_i}^0(x), \mu_{[a,b]}(x)\}dx}{\int_a^b \mu_{A_i}^0(x)dx}$$

- for a linguistic input value A_i' it is computed as in the previous case

$$\mu_{A_i} = \frac{\int_a^b \min\{\mu_{A_i}^0(x), \mu_{A_i'}(x)\}dx}{\int_a^b \mu_{A_i}^0(x)dx}$$

It is obvious that, any t-norm T can be used instead of *min* and its dual t-conorm S instead of *max* in the previous formulas.

4.3 Fuzzy inference

The fuzzy control rules are of the form

$$R_i : IF\ X_1\ is\ A_i^1\ AND\ ...\ AND\ X_r\ is\ A_i^r\ THEN\ Y\ is\ C_i$$

where the variables $X_j, j \in \{1, 2, ..., r\}$, and Y have the domains U_j and V, respectively. The firing levels of the rules, denoted by $\{\alpha_i\}$, are computed by

$$\alpha_i = T(\alpha_i^1, ..., \alpha_i^r)$$

where T is a t-norm and α_i^j is the firing level for $A_i^j, j \in \{1, 2, ..., r\}$. The causal link from $X_1, ..., X_r$ to Y is represented using an implication operator I. It results that the conclusion C_i' inferred from the rule R_i is

$$\mu_{C_i'}(v) = I(\alpha_i, \mu_{C_i}(v)), \forall v \in V.$$

The formula

$$\mu_{C'}(v) = I(\alpha, \mu_C(v))$$

gives the following results, depending on the implication I:

Willmott : $\mu_{C'}(v) = I_W(\alpha, \mu_C(v)) = \max\{1 - \alpha, \min(\alpha, \mu_C(v))\}$

Mamdani: $\mu_{C'}(v) = I_M(\alpha, \mu_C(v)) = \min\{\alpha, \mu_C(v)\}$

Rescher-Gaines: $\mu_{C'}(v) = I_{RG}(\alpha, \mu_C(v)) = \begin{cases} 1 & if\ \ \alpha \le \mu_C(v) \\ 0 & otherwise \end{cases}$

Kleene-Dienes: $\mu_{C'}(v) = I_{KD}(\alpha, \mu_C(v)) = \max\{1 - \alpha, \mu_C(v)\}$

Brouwer-Gödel: $\mu_{C'}(v) = I_{BG}(\alpha, \mu_C(v)) = \begin{cases} 1 & if\ \ \alpha \le \mu_C(v) \\ \mu_C(v) & otherwise \end{cases}$

Goguen: $\mu_{C'}(v) = I_G(\alpha, \mu_C(v)) = \begin{cases} 1 & if\ \ \alpha \le \mu_C(v) \\ \frac{\mu_C(v)}{\alpha} & otherwise \end{cases}$

Lukasiewicz: $\mu_{C'}(v) = I_L(\alpha, \mu_C(v)) = \min\{1 - \alpha + \mu_C(v), 1\}$

Fodor: $\mu_{C'}(v) = I_F(\alpha, \mu_C(v)) = \begin{cases} 1 & if\ \ \alpha \le \mu_C(v) \\ \max\{1 - \alpha, \mu_C(v)\} & otherwise \end{cases}$

Reichenbach: $\mu_{C'}(v) = I_R(\alpha, \mu_C(v)) = 1 - \alpha + \alpha\mu_C(v)$

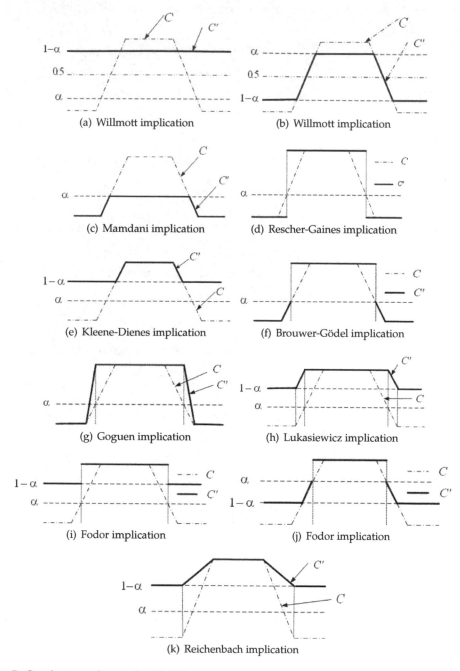

Fig. 5. Conclusions obtained with different implications

4.4 Defuzzification

The fuzzy output C_i' of the rule R_i is transformed into a crisp output z_i using the Middle-of-Maxima operator. The crisp value z_0 associated to a conclusion C' inferred from a rule having the firing level α and the conclusion C represented by the fuzzy number $(\underline{m}_C, \overline{m}_C, \alpha_C, \beta_C)$ is:

- $z_0 = \dfrac{\underline{m}_C + \overline{m}_C}{2}$ for implication $I \in \{I_R, I_{KD}\}$

- $z_0 = \dfrac{\underline{m}_C + \overline{m}_C + (1 - \alpha)(\beta_C - \alpha_C)}{2}$ for $I \in \{I_M, I_{RG}, I_{BG}, I_G, I_L, I_F\}$ or $(I = I_W, \alpha \geq 0.5)$

- $z_0 = \dfrac{a_V + b_V}{2}$ if $I = I_W, \alpha < 0.5$ and $V = [a_V, b_V]$.

In the last case, in order to remain inside the support of C, one can choose a value according to Max-Criterion; for instance

$$z_0 = \frac{\underline{m}_C + \overline{m}_C + \alpha(\beta_C - \alpha_C)}{2}.$$

The overall crisp control action is computed by the discrete Center-of-Gravity method as follows. If the number of fired rules is N then the final control action is:

$$z_0 = (\sum_{i=1}^{N} \alpha_i z_i) / \sum_{i=1}^{N} \alpha_i$$

where α_i is the firing level and z_i is the crisp output of the i-th rule, $i = \overline{1, N}$.

Finally, the results obtained with various implication operators are combined in order to obtain the overall output of the system. For this reason, the "strength" $\lambda(I)$ of an implication I is used:

$$\lambda(I) = N(I)/13$$

where $N(I)$ is the number of properties (from the list $I1$ to $I13$) verified by the implication I (Iancu, 2009a). If the implications are considered in the order presented in the previous section, then according with the Definition 10, one obtains

$$w_1 = \lambda(I_W), w_2 = \lambda(I_M), ..., w_9 = \lambda(I_R)$$

$$a_1 = z_0(I_W), a_2 = z_0(I_M), ..., a_9 = z_0(I_R)$$

and the overall crisp action of the system is computed as

$$\overline{z}_0 = \sum_{j=1}^{9} w_j b_j$$

where b_j is the j-th largest element of $\{z_0(I_W), z_0(I_M), \ldots, z_0(I_F), z_0(I_R)\}$.

5. Applications

In order to show how the proposed system works, two examples will be presented. First example (Iancu, 2009b) is inspired from (Liu et al., 2005). A person is interested to buy a computer using on-line shopping. For this, the customer can make selections on the price and quality of computers. For the price of computers, different intervals are given for customers to choose from, for example, 0-200 EUR, 400-600 EUR, etc. For the quality of computers, five options are offered to the customers, namely Poor, Below Average, Average, Above Average, and Good. After customers make those selections, the satisfaction score for that selected computer is computed based on the fuzzy inference system described in the following. If customers are not satisfied with the satisfaction score, they can go back and make selections again. Therefore, this system will help customers to make decisions. In the next example the system works with two inputs and one output. The input variables are $quality$ (Q) and $price$ (P); the output variable is $satisfaction\ score$ (S). The fuzzy rule base consist of

R_1: IF Q is Poor AND P is Low THEN S is Middle

R_2: IF Q is Poor AND P is Middle THEN S is Low

R_3: IF Q is Poor AND P is High THEN S is Very Low

R_4: IF Q is Average AND P is Low THEN S is High

R_5: IF Q is Average AND P is Middle THEN S is Middle

R_6: IF Q is Average AND P is High THEN S is Low

R_7: IF Q is Good AND P is Low THEN S is Very High

R_8: IF Q is Good AND P is Middle THEN S is High

R_9: IF Q is Good AND P is High THEN S is Middle

There are three linguistic values for the variable $price$:

$$\{Low,\ Middle,\ High\}$$

and five linguistic values for the variable $quality$:

$$\{Poor,\ Below\ Average,\ Average,\ Above\ Average,\ Good\}.$$

The universes of discourse are $[0, 800]$ for $price$ and $[0, 10]$ for $quality$. The membership functions corresponding to the linguistic values are represented by the following trapezoidal fuzzy numbers:

$$Low = (0, 100, 0, 200)$$

$$Middle = (300, 500, 100, 100)$$

$$High = (700, 800, 200, 0)$$

$$Poor = (0, 1, 0, 2)$$

$$Below\ Average = (2,3,1,1)$$

$$Average = (4,6,2,2)$$

$$Above\ Average = (7,8,1,1)$$

$$Good = (9,10,2,0).$$

The *satisfaction score* has following linguistic values:

$$\{Very\ Low,\ Low,\ Middle,\ High,\ Very\ High\}$$

represented, in the universe $[0,10]$, by the following membership functions:

$$Very\ Low = (0,1,0,1)$$

$$Low = (2,3,1,1.5)$$

$$Middle = (4,6,1,1)$$

$$High = (7,8,1,2)$$

$$Very\ High = (9,10,1,0).$$

A person is interested to buy a computer with price = 400-600 EUR and quality = *AboveAverage*. The positive firing levels (based on intersection) corresponding to the linguistic values of the input variable *price* are

$$\mu_{Middle} = 1, \mu_{High} = 0.5$$

and the positive firing levels corresponding to the linguistic values of the input variable *quality* are:

$$\mu_{Average} = 2/3, \mu_{Good} = 2/3.$$

The fired rules and their firing levels, computed with t-norm Product, are:

$$R_5\ \text{with firing level}\ \alpha_5 = 2/3,$$

$$R_6\ \text{with firing level}\ \alpha_6 = 1/3,$$

$$R_8\ \text{with firing level}\ \alpha_8 = 2/3\ \text{and}$$

$$R_9\ \text{with firing level}\ \alpha_9 = 1/3.$$

Working with I_L implication, the fired rules give the following crisp values as output:

$$z_5 = 5,\ z_6 = 8/3,\ z_8 = 23/3,\ z_9 = 5;$$

the overall crisp control action for I_L is

$$z_0(I_L) = 5.5$$

Working with I_R implication, the fired rules give the following crisp values as output:

$$z_5 = 5,\ z_6 = 2.5,\ z_8 = 7.5,\ z_9 = 5;$$

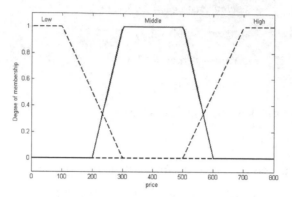

(a) The membership function of the variable *price*

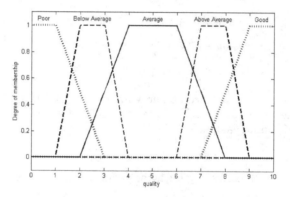

(b) The membership function of the variable *quality*

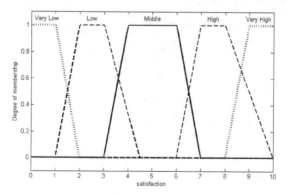

(c) The membership function of the variable *satisfaction score*

Fig. 6. Membership functions for the input and output variables

its overall crisp action is

$$z_0(I_R) = 5.416.$$

Because $\lambda(I_R) = 11/13$ and $\lambda(I_L) = 1$, the overall crisp action given by system is

$$\bar{z}_0 = 5.4615$$

The standard Mamdani model applied for this example gives the following results:

- the firing levels are: $\alpha_5 = 2/3, \alpha_6 = 0.5, \alpha_8 = 2/3, \alpha_9 = 0.5$
- the crisp rules outputs are: $z_5 = 5, z_6 = 5.25/2, z_8 = 23/3, z_9 = 5$
- the overall crisp action is: $z_0 = 23/3 = 7.66$

If the Center-of-Gravity method (instead of maximum operator) is used to compute the overall crisp action then $z_0 = 5.253$

One observes an important difference between these two results and also between these results and those given by our method. An explanation consists in the small value of the "strength" of Mamdani's implication in comparison with the values associated with Reichenbach and Lukasiewicz implications; the strength of an implication is a measure of its quality. From different implications, different results will be obtained if separately implications will be used. The proposed system offers a possibility to avoid this difficulty, by aggregation operation which achieves a "mediation" between the results given by various implications.

Another application that uses this type of controller is presented in (Iancu, 2009b) concerning washing machines (Agarwal, 2007). When one uses a washing machine, the person generally select the length of washing time based on the amount of clothes he/she wish to wash and the type and degree of dirt cloths have. To automate this process, one uses sensors to detect these parameters and the washing time is then determined from this data. Unfortunately, there is no easy way to formulate a precise mathematical relationship between volume of clothes and dirt and the length of washing time required. Because the input/output relationship is not clear, the design of a washing machine controller can be made using fuzzy logic. A fuzzy logic controller gives the correct washing time even though a precise model of the input/output relationship is not available.

The problem analyzed in this example has been simplified by using only two inputs and one output. The input variables are *degree-of-dirt (DD)* and *type-of-dirt (TD)*; the output variable is *washing-time (WT)*. The fuzzy rule-base consist of:

R_1: IF DD is Large AND TD is Greasy THEN WT is VeryLong

R_2: IF DD is Medium AND TD is Greasy THEN WT is Long

R_3: IF DD is Small AND TD is Greasy THEN WT is Long

R_4: IF DD is Large AND TD is Medium THEN WT is Long

R_5: IF DD is Medium AND TD is Medium THEN WT is Medium

R_6: IF DD is Small AND TD is Medium THEN WT is Medium

R_7: IF DD is Large AND TD is NotGreasy THEN WT is Medium

R_8: IF DD is Medium AND TD is NotGreasy THEN WT is Short

R_9: IF DD is Small AND TD is NotGreasy THEN WT is VeryShort

There are three linguistic values for the variable *degree-of-dirt*:

$$\{Small, \ Medium, \ Large\}$$

and five linguistic values for the variable *type-of-dirt*:

$$\{VeryNotGreasy, \ NotGreasy, \ Medium, \ Greasy, \ VeryGreasy\}$$

having the same universe of discourse: $[0, 100]$. The membership functions corresponding to the linguistic values are represented by the following trapezoidal fuzzy numbers:

$$Small = (0, 20, 0, 20)$$

$$Medium = (40, 60, 20, 20)$$

$$Large = (80, 100, 20, 0)$$

$$VeryNotGreasy = (0, 10, 0, 20)$$

$$NotGreasy = (20, 30, 10, 10)$$

$$Medium = (40, 60, 20, 20)$$

$$Greasy = (70, 80, 10, 10)$$

$$VeryGreasy = (90, 100, 20, 0).$$

The *washing-time* has following linguistic values

$$\{VeryShort, \ Short, \ Medium, \ Long, \ VeryLong, \ High\}$$

represented in the universe $[0, 60]$ by the membership functions:

$$VeryShort = (0, 5, 0, 5)$$

$$Short = (10, 15, 10, 5)$$

$$Medium = (20, 30, 5, 5)$$

$$Long = (35, 50, 5, 10)$$

$$VeryLong = (50, 60, 10, 0).$$

A person is interested to wash some clothes with the *degree-of-dirt* between 60 and 70 and *type-of-dirt* is *VeryGreasy*. Working in the same conditions as in the previous example, but using "areas ratio" instead of "intersection" in order to compute the firing levels, one obtains the following results. The positive firing levels corresponding to the linguistic values of the input variable *degree-of-dirt* are

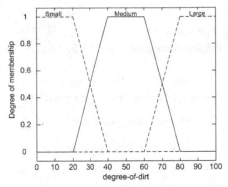

(a) The membership function of the variable *degree-of-dirt*

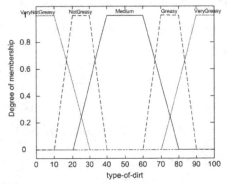

(b) The membership function of the variable *type-of-dirt*

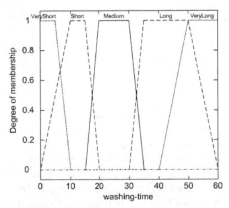

(c) The membership function of the variable *washing-time*

Fig. 7. Membership functions for the input and output variables

$$\mu_{Medium} = 0.1875, \mu_{Large} = 0.0833$$

and the positive firing levels corresponding to the linguistic values of the input variable *type-of-dirt* are:

$$\mu_{Medium} = 0.0312, \mu_{Greasy} = 1/3.$$

The fired rules and their firing levels, computed with t-norm Product, are:

$$R_1 \text{ with firing level } \alpha_1 = 0.0277,$$

$$R_2 \text{ with firing level } \alpha_2 = 0.0625,$$

$$R_4 \text{ with firing level } \alpha_4 = 0.0026 \text{ and}$$

$$R_5 \text{ with firing level } \alpha_5 = 0.0058.$$

Working with I_L implication, the fired rules give the following crisp values as output:

$$z_1 = 50.138, \ z_2 = 44.843, \ z_4 = 44.993, \ z_5 = 25$$

and the overall crisp control action for I_L is

$$z_0(I_L) = 45.152$$

Working with I_R implication, the fired rules give the following crisp values as output:

$$z_1 = 55, \ z_2 = 42.5, \ z_4 = 42.5, \ z_5 = 25$$

and its overall crisp control action is

$$z_0(I_R) = 44.975$$

The overall crisp action given by system is computed using the technique OWA with

$$w_1 = 13/24, w_2 = 11/24, a_1 = 45.152, a_2 = 44.975;$$

it results

$$\bar{z}_0 = 45.079$$

6. Conclusion

This paper presents fuzzy logic controllers of Mamdani type. After the standard Mamdani FLC is explained, an its extension is prezented. Because it can work not only with crisp data as inputs but, also, with intervals and/or linguistic terms its area of applications is very large. As it is mentioned in (Liu et al., 2005), a very important domain of its application is WEB shopping. Web users may use convenient interval inputs for online shopping as in the previous example. The working with various implications in the same time and, moreover, the possibility to aggregate the results given by these implications offer a strong base for more accurate results of our system.

The system can be improved by adding new implications, by using other fuzzy matching techniques or by other aggregate operators in order to obtain a overall crisp action from those given, separately, by every implication.

One of our future preoccupation is to extend this system by incorporating uncertainty about the membership functions of fuzzy sets associated with linguistic terms. For this we intend to work with interval type-2 fuzzy sets in accordance with the results from Mendel (2001; 2003; 2007).

7. References

Agarwal, M. (2007). Fuzzy logic control of washing machines.
　　URL: *http://softcomputing.tripod.com/sample_termpater:pdf*
Buckley, J. J. (1992). Universal fuzzy controller, *Automatica* Vol. 28: 1245–1248.
Buckley, J. J. (1993). Sugeno type controllers are universal controllers, *Fuzzy Sets and Systems* Vol. 53: 299–304.
Castro, J. L. (1995). Fuzzy logic controllers are universal approximators, *IEEE Transactions on Systems, Man, and Cybernetics* Vol. 25(No. 4): 629–635.
Grzegorzewski, P. & Mrowka, E. (2007). Trapezoidal approximations of fuzzy numbers - revisited, *Fuzzy Sets and Systems* 158(7): 757–768.
Iancu, I. (2009a). Extended Mamdani Fuzzy Logic Controller, *The 4th IASTED Int. Conf. on Computational Intelligence*, ACTA Press, Honolulu, USA, pp. 143–149.
Iancu, I. (2009b). Mamdani FLC with various implications, *11th International Symposium on Symbolic and Numeric Algorithms for Scientific Computing - SYNASC 09*, IEEE Computer Society, Los Alamitos, California, Timisoara, Romania, pp. 368–375.
Iancu, I., Colhon, M. & Dupac, M. (2010). A Takagi-Sugeno Type Controller for Mobile Robot Navigation, *Proc. of WSEAS Int. Conf. on Computational Intelligence*, WSEAS Press, Bucharest, Romania, pp. 29–34.
Iancu, I., Constantinescu, N. & Colhon, M. (2010). Fingerprints identification using a fuzzy logic system, *International Journal of Computers Communications & Control* 4(5): 525–531.
Iancu, I. & Popirlan, C.-I. (2010). Mamdani fuzzy logic controller with mobile agents for matching, *Recent Advances in Neural Networks, Fuzzy Systems and Evolutionary Computing*, WSEAS Press, Iasi, Romania, pp. 117–122.
Kosko, B. (1992). *Neural Networks and Fuzzy Systems*, Prentice-Hall, New Jersey.
Lee, C. C. (1990). Fuzzy Logic in Control Systems: Fuzzy Logic Controller - Part I, II, *IEEE Transactions on Systems, Man and Cybernetics* 20(2): 404–418.
Liu, F., Geng, H. & Zhang, Y. Q. (2005). Interactive fuzzy interval reasoning for smart web shopping, *Applied Soft Computing* (5): 433–439.
Mamdani, E. H. (1977). Application of fuzzy logic to approximate reasoning using linguistic synthesis, *IEEE Transactions on Computers* 26(12): 1182–1191.
Mamdani, E. H. & Assilian, S. (1975). An experiment in linguistic synthesis with a fuzzy logic controller, *Int. J. Man-machine Studies* 7: 1–13.
Mendel, J. R. (2001). *Uncertain Rule-Based Fuzzy Logic Systems: Introductions and New Directions*, Prentice-Hall, Prentice-Hall, Upper-Saddle River, NJ.
Mendel, J. R. (2003). Type-2 fuzzy sets: Some questions and answers, *IEEE Connections, Newsletter of the IEEE Neural Networks Society* 1(August): 10–13.
Mendel, J. R. (2007). Type-2 fuzzy sets: Some questions and answers, Ĭ, *IEEE Computational Intelligence Magazine* 2(February): 20–29.
Nasseri, H. (2008). Fuzzy numbers: Positive and nonnegative, *International Mathematical Forum* 36(3): 1777–1789.

Rakic, A. (2010). *Fuzzy Logic. Introduction 3. Fuzzy Inference*, ETF Beograd.
    URL: *http://www.docstoc.com/docs/52570644/Fuzzy-logic-3*

Sala, A., Guerra, T. M. & Babuska, R. (2005). Perspectives of fuzzy systems and control, *Fuzzy Sets and Systems* 156(3): 432–444.

Wang, L. X. (1992). Fuzzy systems are universal approximators, *Proc. of IEEE Inter. Conf. on Fuzzy Systems*, San Diego, USA, pp. 1163–1170.

Yager, R. R. (1988). Ordered weighted averaging aggregation operators in multi-criteria decision making, *IEEE Trans. on Systems, Man and Cybernetics* (18): 183–190.

Zadeh, L. A. (1971). Similarity relations and fuzzy orderings, *Information Sciences* 3: 177–200.

Zadeh, L. A. (1973). Outline of a new approach to the analysis complex systems and decision processes, *IEEE Trans Syst. Man Cibern* SMC(3): 28–44.

Zadeh, L. A. (1975). Calculus of fuzzy restrictions, *in* L. A. Zadeh, K.-S. Fu, K. Tanaka & M. Shimura (eds), *Fuzzy Sets and their Applications to Cognitive and Decision Processes*, Academic Press, New York, pp. 1–39.

Zadeh, L. A. (1978). Fuzzy sets as a basis for a theory of a possibility, *Fuzzy Sets and Systems* (1): 2–28.

Zadeh, L. A. (1979). A theory of approximate reasoning, *Machine Intelligence*, John Wiley & Sons, New York, pp. 149–194.

16

Tuning Fuzzy-Logic Controllers

Trung-Kien Dao[1] and Chih-Keng Chen[2]
[1]*MICA Center, HUST - CNRS/UMI 2954 - Grenoble INP, Hanoi,*
[2]*Dayeh University, Changhua,*
[1]*Vietnam*
[2]*Taiwan*

1. Introduction

The classical proportional-derivative (PD) control is relatively easy to design, but useful for fast response controllers by combining proportional control and derivative control in parallel. However, as PD control is linear, it is not able to be used to deal with non-linear plants. An answer to this problem is fuzzy-logic control, which is also a model-free control scheme and can be applied to systems where mathematical models cannot be obtained. Besides, natural heuristic rules in linguistic expressions that reflect human experiences can be applied in the control design, minimizing the design cost. Fuzzy-logic controllers (FLCs) are the control systems based on a knowledge consisting of the so-called fuzzy IF-THEN rules.

This chapter is a discussion on using genetic algorithms (GAs) to tune the parameters of PD-like FLCs. Genetic algorithms are global search techniques modeled following the natural genetic mechanism to find approximate or exact solutions to optimization and search problems. In a GA, each parameter to be optimized is represented by a gene; moreover, each individual is characterized by a chromosome, which is actually a set of parameters awaiting optimization.

The remainder of this chapter is organized as follows. In Section 2, the optimization technique for PD-like FLCs using GAs is explained. After that, two case studies are presented and discussed in Sections 3 and 4, in which, the introduced technique is applied for a bicycle roll-angle-tracking controller and an ESP controller, respectively. Finally, concluding remarks are given in Section 5.

2. PD-Like fuzzy-logic controller and optimization

In a fuzzy IF-THEN rule, words can be characterized by continuous membership functions (typically taking values from 0 to 1) representing the degree of truth of the statements. For example, to stabilize the bicycle, the following fuzzy rule can be used:

> IF *the bicycle is leaning to the right AND the roll angle is increasing,*
> THEN *apply large steering torque to the right,*

where the words *right, increasing* and *large* are characterized by corresponding membership functions. Similarly, more rules from human knowledge can be defined to make the control system more precise. Combining these rules into a fuzzy system, a rule base is obtained, which is used by the fuzzy inference system (FIS), as shown in Fig. 1. Two common FIS used in the literature are that of Takagi and Sugeno (TS), and that of Mamdani. The difference of the two FIS is in the THEN clause, where TS method uses algebraic linear combination of fuzzy variables, while Mamdani method uses natural-language clauses.

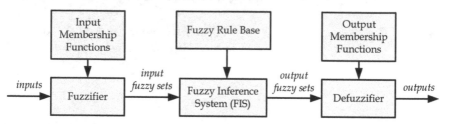

Fig. 1. Basic configuration of fuzzy systems

By using FLC, one major advantage is that there is no need to beware of the exact plant model as when classical control schemes are used. In reality, the plant model is usually non-linear and difficult to specify exactly. Using FLC is a preferable approach to avoid this difficulty. However, in most of cases, the fuzzy membership functions are difficult to be effectively defined manually, and need to be tuned. One usual procedure to design a FLC is to approximately build the fuzzy rules and membership functions heuristically and subsequently use a certain optimization algorithm to tune the parameters.

Mamdani fuzzy inference system (FIS) is preferable in FLC instead of Takagi-Sugeno (TS) because of two reasons. First, since the IF-THEN rules of the Mamdani method are given in natural-language form, it is more intuitive to build the fuzzy rules so that the parameters can be determined later by using genetic algorithms. Secondly, the presentation of output membership functions by the TS method requires much more parameters, e.g. each THEN clause $z = ax + by + c$ of a single rule has three parameters, which make the optimization become more complicated and computationally intensive. The distribution of the membership functions of each fuzzy variable of the FLCs discussed in this study can be determined by two parameters, a scaling factor and a deforming coefficient, using the Mamdani method; or six parameters in total for a two-input, one-output FLC.

To estimate the quality of an individual, a fitness function (objective function, or cost function) must be defined. A genetic algorithm starts by generating an initial population for the first generation; then, the quality of each individual is evaluated by using the fitness function. After one generation, only the advantageous individuals survive and reproduce to generate a new population for the next generation. By this process of selection from generation to generation, the quality of the offspring is improved in comparison with their ancestors.

During the creation of a new generation, a portion of the surviving individuals is recombined randomly via the so-called crossover and mutation operations, being adopted from natural evolution. The advantages of GAs over other searching algorithms are that they do not require any gradient information neither continuity assumption in searching for the best parameters, and that they can explore many characteristics at once, which is necessary when dealing with complex problems. For a complete introduction to GAs, the readers can refer to R.L. Haupt & S.E. Haupt (2004).

The optimization procedure of FLC using GAs is presented in Fig. 2. To reduce the learning efforts for GA computation to optimize the FLC, the scaling factors and deforming coefficients are used. Each fuzzy input or output of the FLC is encoded by two numbers: a scaling factor and a deforming coefficient. This method allows a standard PD-like two-input, one-output FLC to be represented as a six-parameter optimization problem.

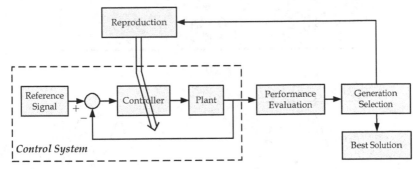

Fig. 2. Optimization of control parameters using GAs

The membership functions of a PD-like FLC are triangular, i.e.,

$$tri_{a,b,c}(x) = \begin{cases} 0, & x < a, \\ (x-a)/(b-a), & a \leq x < b, \\ (c-x)/(c-b), & b \leq x < c, \\ 0, & x > c. \end{cases} \tag{1}$$

The coordinates a, b and c of the membership functions are determined from the optimization process. The effect of the scaling factors is obtained by simply multiplying all points of the universe of discourse of FLCs by the scaling factors. The deforming coefficients, as illustrated in Fig. 3, are introduced to "deform" the membership functions so that they are not equally distributed. Because the membership functions of a PD-like FLC are symmetric with respect to the origin, it is only needed to calculate those on one side, says the positive side, and then to take symmetrization to yield the other side. The membership functions are deformed by multiplying all points of the universe of discourse by the exponent of linearly equally space points within $\left[1, 1/\sqrt{DC} \right]$.

Let the number of points of the universe of discourse on the positive side, excluding the zero origin, be n. The linear space is shown in Fig. 3a. By multiplying all points of the universe of discourse by the exponent of this linear space and then rescaling by dividing to $e^{1/\sqrt{DC}}$, the equally distributed membership functions in Fig. 3b are transmuted into Fig. 3c without changing the maximum limit η_n. With the introduction of the scaling factors and deforming coefficients, six parameters are needed to encode an FLC of two inputs and one output in the form of a chromosome for GAs as follows

$$[SF_1 \quad SF_2 \quad SF_3 \quad DC_1 \quad DC_2 \quad DC_3], \tag{2}$$

where (SF_1, DC_1), (SF_2, DC_2), and (SF_3, DC_3) are used for fuzzy input 1, 2 and output, respectively. Note that all fuzzy inputs and outputs in this study are normalized by scaling factors so that their values are distributed within the range from −1 to 1, the extreme limits of the two outermost triangular membership functions are extended to infinity.

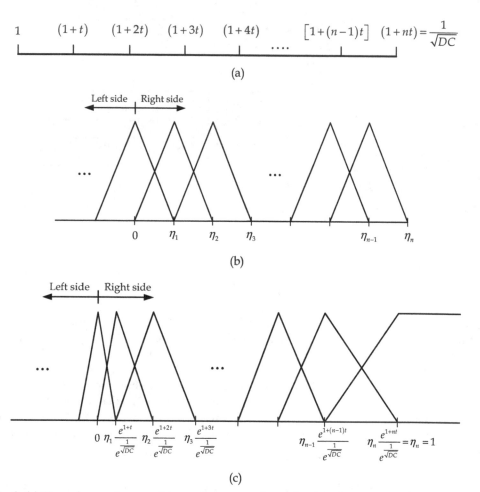

Fig. 3. (a) Linearly equal space, (b) equally arranged membership functions, and (c) deformed membership functions

The learning scheme given in Fig. 2 is in the following. In initial phase, the population consists of randomly generated heterogeneous chromosomes. Then all chromosomes go through three principal parts: evaluation module, selection module and reproduction module. The population will be improved because fitter offspring replace parents. The procedure is repeated until either a maximum number of generations is reached or an optimal solution is obtained, whichever is earlier.

In the following of this chapter, two case studies are introduced to show the application of the PD-like FLCs and the control-parameter optimization technique in reality. In the first case, an FLC is used to establish a controller which helps a bicycle to follow a roll-angle command. In the second one, several FLCs are used in an ESP controller, which is designed to enhance vehicle maneuvers, especially in critical situations.

3. Case study: Bicycle roll-angle-tracking controller

As an unstable and underactuated system, the bicycle is control-challenging and can offer a number of research interests in the area of mechanics and robot control. Control efforts for stabilizing unmanned bicycles have also been addressed in previous studies. Yavin (1999) dealt with the stabilization and control of a riderless bicycle by a pedaling torque, a directional torque and a rotor mounted on the crossbar that generated a tilting torque. Beznos et al. (1988) modeled a bicycle with gyroscopes that enabled the vehicle to stabilize itself in an autonomous motion along a straight line as well as along a curve. In their study, the stabilization unit consisted of two coupled gyroscopes spinning in opposite directions. Han et al. (2001) derived a simple kinematic and dynamic formulation of an unmanned electric bicycle. The controllability of the stabilization problem was also checked and a control algorithm for self-stabilization of the vehicle with bounded wheel speed and steering angle using non-linear control based on the sliding patch and stuck phenomena was proposed.

Among studies relative to two-wheel-vehicle control, Sharp et al. (2004) presented a related work on the roll-angle-tracking of motorcycles. A PID controller was used to generate the steering torque based on the tracking error. In this section, a controller is introduced to control the bicycle to follow a roll-angle command, where an FLC is used in the place of the PID.

3.1 Control structure

Fig. 4 shows the roll-angle-tracking control structure that Sharp et al. (2004) used to control a motorcycle. The steering torque is derived from the roll-angle error using a PID controller, whose gains k_P, k_I and k_D are speed-dependent. Their study has showed good results that the steering torque of a two-wheeled vehicle can be directly controlled from the roll-angle error. In this study, since PID controller is linear, it is replaced by a FLC in order to better deal with the non-linearity of the bicycle. This gives the controller shown in Fig. 5.

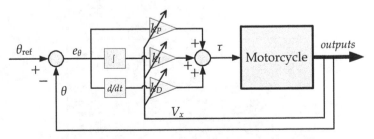

Fig. 4. Roll-angle-tracking controller for motorcycle (Sharp et al., 2005)

The FLC used in this study has two inputs: the roll-angle tracking error $e_\theta = \theta_{ref} - \theta$, which is the difference between the desired roll angle and the actual one; and its change Δe_θ. The controller generates appropriate control output which is the control torque τ to the steering fork. The FLC is PD-like since it requires two inputs, the error need to be minimized, and its variation, which are comparable to the proportional and derivative parts of a PD controller. Compared to the previous studies (Chen & T.S. Dao, 2006, 2007), the controller structure has been simplified so that only one FLC is used to generate the torque τ directly from the roll-angle error e_θ, as shown in Fig. 5. Linguistic quantification used to specify a set of rules for this controller is characterized by the following three typical situations:

1. If e_θ is *negative large* (NL) and Δe_θ is NL, then τ is *positive large* (PL). This rule quantifies the situation wherein the desired roll-angle is much smaller than the actual one and the bicycle is falling to the right at a significant rate. Hence, one should steer the fork to the right more at a large positive angle to make the bicycle lean to the left.
2. If e_θ is *zero* (Z) and Δe_θ is Z, then τ is Z. This rule quantifies the situation wherein the bicycle is already in its proper position. No control effort is needed.
3. If e_θ is PL and Δe_θ is PL, then τ is NL. This rule quantifies the situation wherein the desired roll-angle is much larger than the actual one and the bicycle is falling to the left at a significant rate. Therefore, one should steer the fork to the left at a large angle to make the bicycle lean to the right.

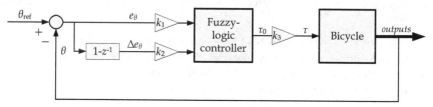

Fig. 5. Roll-angle-tracking controller using FLC

e_θ \ Δe_θ	NL	NM	NS	Z	PS	PM	PL
NL	PL	PL	PL	PM	PM	PS	Z
NM	PL	PL	PM	PM	PS	Z	NS
NS	PL	PM	PM	PS	Z	NS	NM
Z	PM	PM	PS	Z	NS	NM	NM
PS	PM	PS	Z	NS	NM	NM	NL
PM	PS	Z	NS	NM	NM	NL	NL
PL	Z	NS	NM	NM	NL	NL	NL

Table 1. Rule base for roll-angle-tracking FLC

In a similar fashion, the complete rule base is constructed as listed in Table 1, where the membership functions *negative large* (NL), *negative medium* (NM), *negative small* (NS), *zero* (Z), *positive small* (PS), *positive medium* (PM), and *positive large* (PL) are used for the two fuzzy inputs as well as the output. Notice that the body of the table lists the linguistic-numeric consequents of the rules, and the left column and top row of the table contain the linguistic-numeric premise terms. For this controller, with two inputs and seven linguistic values for each of these, there are totally $7^2 = 49$ rules. By using (1), for each input or output of the FLC, the membership functions characterizing seven levels, namely NL, NM, NS, Z, PS, PM and PL, are defined as depicted in Fig. 3c and discussed in the previous section.

3.2 Optimization of control parameters and simulation results

For roll-angle control, the goal is to minimize simultaneously the tracking error and the oscillation of roll angle. Therefore, the fitness function used for optimization is defined as

$$\text{fitness function} = \kappa_e \left(\frac{1}{N} \sum_{i=1}^{N} e_\theta^2(i) \right)^{1/2} + \kappa_{\Delta\theta} \left(\frac{1}{N} \sum_{i=1}^{N} \left(\frac{\Delta\theta(i)}{\Delta t} \right)^2 \right)^{1/2}, \tag{3}$$

where Δt is the simulation time step; N, the number of time steps; $e_\theta(i) = \theta_{\text{ref}}(i) - \theta(i)$ and $\Delta\theta(i) = \theta(i) - \theta(i-1)$, the tracking error and the change in roll angle at time step i, respectively. The fitness function is the aggregation of two terms. The first is the root mean square of the tracking error multiplied by a weighting factor κ_e, and the second is the root mean square of the change in roll angle multiplied by a weighting factor $\kappa_{\Delta\theta}$.

Originally, the normalized membership functions are scaled linearly by the scaling factors and deformed exponentially within the universe of discourse by the deforming coefficients, as presented in Fig. 3. Since the scaling factors of the FLC used in this study are variable, they are explicitly presented on the outside of the FLC. However, it is important to note that, once the scaling factors are presented on the outside of the FLC, their signification is changed, the effect of scaling factors for fuzzy inputs is inversed, since the scaling factors are now applied for signals, not for fuzzy membership functions. These scaling factors are denoted by k_{1-3} in Fig. 5. The controlled bicycle model for simulations in this study is non-linear, non-holonomic, has nine generalized coordinates, and described in detail in (Chen & T.S. Dao, 2006, 2007) with parameters given in (Chen & T.K. Dao, 2010).

The weighting factors of the fitness function used in this study are chosen as $\kappa_e = 0.6$ and $\kappa_{\Delta\theta} = 0.4$. To estimate the performance of PID controller for roll-angle tracking for the developed bicycle model, control simulations were carried out. The PID gains are optimized by using GAs, where the parameters to be optimized are the three PID gains k_P, k_I and k_D. Fig. 6 shows the simulation results of the optimized PID controller at a speed of 12km/h. It appears that the bicycle could not be controlled to follow the command rapidly while minimizing the oscillation.

Fig. 7 shows the control result by the FLC tuned via GA training for a speed of 5km/h (low speed), Fig. 8 for 12km/h (medium speed), and Fig. 9 for 30km/h (high speed). The optimal fitness values of these simulations are presented in Table 2. It can be remarked that when the speed is increased, the optimal fitness value is also increased accordingly. This can be explained by the fact that the tracking error of the roll angle increases for the higher speeds.

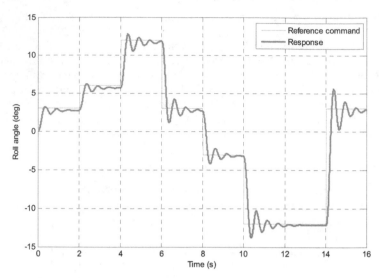

Fig. 6. PID controller performance at normal speed (12km/h)

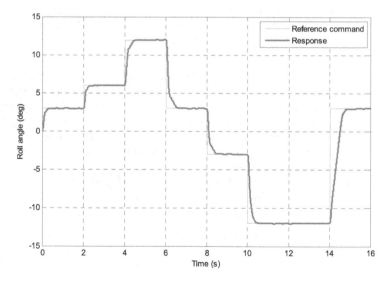

Fig. 7. Roll-angle-tracking performance at low speed (5km/h)

In comparison with the same control simulation but using PID controller in Fig. 6, it appears that the roll-angle tracking error is reduced when the bicycle is controlled by the FLC, as shown in Fig. 8. This is assured by the optimal value of fitness function of 0.0821 from the FLC, and 1.7153 from the PID controller for the same bicycle speed of 12km/h. By applying the optimized control parameters, the FLC can control the bicycle better than the PID controller does, which can be explained by the essential non-linear control properties. The FLC can control non-linear systems with a larger range of parameters.

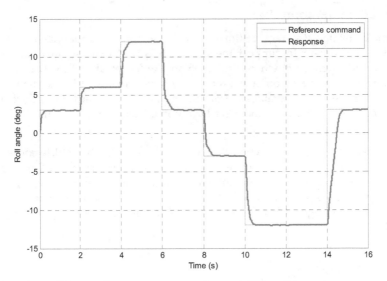

Fig. 8. Roll-angle-tracking performance at normal speed (12km/h)

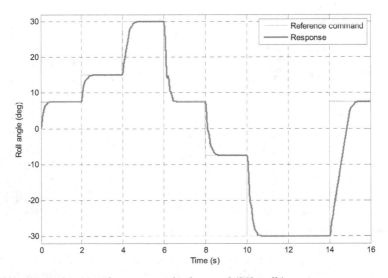

Fig. 9. Roll-angle-tracking performance at high speed (30km/h)

Controller	Speed (km/h)	Optimal fitness value
PID	12	1.7153
FLC	5	0.0430
FLC	12	0.0821
FLC	30	0.1378

Table 2. Optimal fitness values for simulations

4. Case study: ESP controller

The Electronic Stability Program (ESP) is a vehicle dynamics control system that relies on a vehicle's braking system to support the driver in critical driving situations. Since their landmark introduction of Bosch controller (Van Zanten et al., 1995), ESP systems have become popular in the automotive market. The general strategy of ESP systems is to define an indicator for the maneuverability of an automobile, from which the controller aims to enhance handling in extreme maneuvers by automatically controlling the brakes and the engine.

Satisfactory handling behavior is characterized by the fact that the vehicle correctly follows the desire of the driver; i.e., the vehicle yaw rate is accurately maintained according to the steering angle while concurrently remaining stable. The general concept of most ESP systems is primarily based on the sideslip angle, such as those presented by Van Zanten (2000); some systems regard also the vehicle yaw rate, for example the system developed by Kwak and Park (2001).

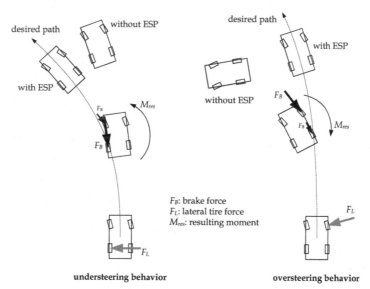

Fig. 10. Understeering/oversteering behaviors

Regarding yaw-moment generation techniques, there are several preferable approaches, namely active yaw moment control (Ikushima & Sawase, 1995), active steering (Ackermann, 1998; Oraby et al., 2004), and direct yaw moment control (DYC) (Esmailzadeh et al., 2003; Tahami et al., 2003). Hybrid yaw-moment generation methods are also used, such as that of Selby et al. (2001) coordinates the two approaches active front steering and direct yaw moment control.

From driving experience, when the vehicle exhibits oversteering behavior, braking the outer wheels will generate compensated yaw moment to depress the oversteering situation; whereas, braking the inner wheels will generate compensated yaw moment in understeering situations. Moreover, Pruckner and Seemann (1997) pointed out that, to stabilize the vehicle while braking, in case of understeering behavior, the main braking intervention should occur on the inner rear wheel. Rear braking force causes a primary yaw moment and a reduction in the rear lateral tire force. In case of oversteering behavior, the main braking force on the outer front wheel helps to stabilize the vehicle. The intervention produces a primary yaw moment and reduces the lateral tire force on the front side. These effects prevent critical oversteering driving situations, as shown in Fig. 10. For a more detailed description of ESP and controller principles, the readers can refer to Bosch (1999).

In this section, an ESP control approach based on an estimation of the desired yaw rate, considered to be the target yaw rate, which the vehicle should follow, is introduced. The fundamental idea regarding the estimated target yaw rate is to generate a compensated yaw moment which corrects the behaviors of the vehicle, thereby improving its handling and stability by using FLCs. When the compensated yaw moment is generated, the system also avoids the vehicle sideslip angle to prevent a counter-effect wherein this angle is increased to the limit. The distribution of braking forces on all wheels instead of two front wheels has two advantages. The first advantage is that the controller can generate larger yaw moment in severe situations. The second one is to make the vehicle more stable when the controller is activated. By distributing braking forces on all wheels, the controller can deal with more situations.

4.1 Control structure

An ESP system is developed to correct the yaw rate of a vehicle, especially in critical situations, so that the vehicle responds normally to the driver's desire. This goal is achieved by estimating a corrective yaw moment, referred to as a compensated yaw moment, and generating the corresponding yaw moment to the vehicle by controlling the braking system, so that the vehicle can dependably respond to the driver's maneuvers in critical situations. This estimation consists of two components, one based on the steering and the other on the sideslip angle.

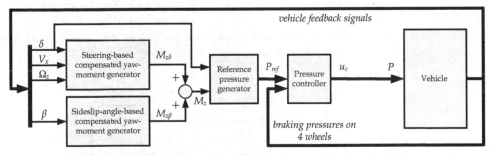

Fig. 11. Overall ESP control structure

The overall control structure is depicted in Fig. 11. As previously mentioned, the compensated yaw moment is combined from two separately estimated components, $M_{z\delta}$ and $M_{z\beta}$. From the estimated compensated yaw moment and the steering orientation, the reference pressure generator determines which wheels to brake and the braking pressures to be applied to each. A closed-loop pressure controller manipulates the EHB (electro-hydraulic brake) hydraulic pressures on the four wheels by following the reference pressures.

4.1.1 Steering-based compensated yaw moment

During operation, the yaw rate of a vehicle should be proportional to the steering angle that the driver makes with the steering wheel so that the time response of the yaw rate has the same shape as that of the steering angle. The goal of the ESP system is to assure that this criterion is achieved, especially in extreme situations.

From the theory of vehicle dynamics, the following equation can be derived:

$$\Omega_z \approx \frac{V_x k_g \delta}{l_2 - \dfrac{m l_1 V_x^2}{2 C_{ar}(l_1 + l_2)}} = \frac{V_x \delta}{\dfrac{l_2}{k_g} - \dfrac{m l_1 V_x^2}{2 k_g C_{ar}(l_1 + l_2)}}. \tag{4}$$

where Ω_z is the vehicle yaw rate, V_x is the longitudinal speed in coordinates fixed to the vehicle, m is the vehicle mass, l_1 and l_2 are the distances from the front and rear axles, respectively, to the center of gravity, C_{ar} is the cornering stiffness of the rear tire, k_g is the gear ratio from the steering wheel to the front wheels, and δ is the angle of the steering wheel. The following two magnitudes are now defined as

$$k_1 = \frac{l_2}{k_g} \text{ and } k_2 = \frac{m l_1}{2 k_g C_{ar}(l_1 + l_2)}; \tag{5}$$

thus, equation (4) can be simply denoted as

$$\Omega_z \approx \frac{V_x \delta}{k_1 - k_2 V_x^2}. \tag{6}$$

It is noticed that every magnitudes involved in equation (5) are constants taken from the configuration of a vehicle; thus, k_1 and k_2 are also constants. In consequence, in equation (6), the steady-state yaw rate Ω_z is a function of the longitudinal speed V_x and the steering angle δ. It should be emphasized that this yaw rate does not depend on the friction coefficient μ. In this ESP system, the objective is to control the vehicle so that its yaw rate follows the reference yaw rate generated by this equation.

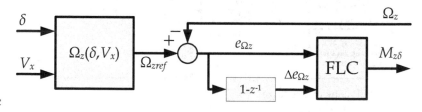

c

Fig. 12. Steering-based compensated yaw moment

Once the reference yaw rate is available, the maneuverability situation, understeering or oversteering, can be determined by comparing the reference yaw rate to the actual one measured from the yaw-rate sensor. When cornering, understeering situation is identified if the absolute value of the real yaw rate is smaller than the desired one, and vice versa.

Oversteering situation is identified if the absolute value of the real yaw rate is larger than the desired one. The yaw-rate error, defined as

$$e_{\Omega z} = \Omega_z - \Omega_{zref},$$

(7)

is used to generate the compensated yaw moment by a PD-like fuzzy logic control (FLC), as shown in Fig. 12. The FLC requires two inputs, namely the yaw-rate error and its variation, and one output, the compensated yaw moment. The ESP controller must generate a moment corresponding to the compensated yaw moment so that the vehicle yaw rate follows the steering angle correctly, thus implying that the vehicle maneuverability is guaranteed.

4.1.2 Sideslip-angle-based compensated yaw moment

Abusing the steering to estimate the compensated yaw moment might make the vehicle go out of control when the sideslip angle β (angle between the vehicle's moving direction and the direction towards which it is pointing) becomes too high. To prevent this situation, when β exceeds a certain predefined value β_0, the system will generate another compensated yaw moment in such a manner that the sideslip angle has the tendency to decrease. This can be achieved by another PD-like FLC as shown in Fig. 13. After Van Zanten (2000), during normal driving, average drivers will not exceed sideslip angles of $\pm 2°$. Beyond this value, the driver has no experience. In this controller, the value of β_0 is chosen to be $1.5°$, which is the value that the sideslip-angle-based compensated yaw moment starts having effect.

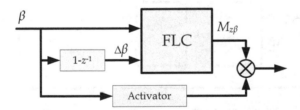

Fig. 13. Sideslip-angle-based compensated yaw moment

Note that for implementing in real cars, there are several methods for estimating the sideslip angle of a vehicle. Two common approaches are the vehicle model observer and the pseudo-integral. The former estimates the sideslip angle based on a vehicle model, which is generally robust against sensor errors, yet sensitive to changes in condition and disturbances; whereas, the latter estimates the sideslip by taking integration of $\dot{\beta} = \left(\ddot{y} - \dot{V}_x \beta \right) / V_x - \Omega_z$, where $\ddot{y}$ is lateral acceleration, V_x is vehicle speed, and Ω_z is vehicle yaw rate, which is robust against changes in road friction and disturbances. However, stabilization should be applied in the latter to minimize the cumulative integral error. Nishio et al. (2001) developed an estimation method using a combination of the vehicle model observer and the pseudo-integral. This method is robust against sensor error as well as changes in road friction and operational disturbances.

The steering-based compensated yaw moment $M_{z\delta}$ and the sideslip-angle-based one $M_{z\beta}$ are later combined as M_z. The activator is a logical block producing 1 or 0, depending on whether β is greater than β_0. Thus, by the multiplication operator, the effect of the activator is to enable or disable the sideslip-angle-based branch regarding whether β exceeds β_0.

4.1.3 Braking-pressure control

As previously discussed, the distribution of the braking pressure aims to generate the yaw moment effectively while keeping the vehicle stable during braking. In understeering situation, the inner rear wheel is braked primarily. If the desired yaw moment is large, the inner front wheel will also be braked secondarily to generate a supplementary yaw moment and stabilize the vehicle. In oversteering situation, the outer front wheel is braked primarily, and the outer rear wheel is braked secondarily if large yaw moment is required. The braking-pressure distribution is summarized in Table 3.

	Understeering				Oversteering			
	Turn left ($\delta > 0$)		Turn right ($\delta < 0$)		Turn left ($\delta > 0$)		Turn right ($\delta < 0$)	
	Small M_z	Large M_z	Small M_z	Large M_z	Small M_z	Large M_z	Small M_z	Large M_z
FL		Secondary					Primary	Primary
FR				Secondary	Primary	Primary		
RL	Primary	Primary						Secondary
RR			Primary	Primary		Secondary		

Table 3. Braking-pressure distribution

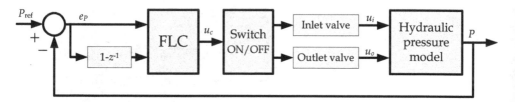

Fig. 14. Structure of pressure controller

The pressure is controlled by a closed-loop control structure using an FLC, as shown in Fig. 14. On the basis of the error between the actual-pressure measurement and the reference pressure, and the variation of the error itself, the FLC generates the control signal u_c. The values of u_c are in the range from -1 to 1, corresponding to the openness of the inlet and outlet valves of the EHB system explicated in the previous section. Regarding the sign and value of u_c, the actuator switch opens or closes the inlet and outlet valves.

4.2 Optimization of control parameters and simulation results

It is clear that the components of this controller, such as the reference yaw-rate estimator, the compensated yaw-moment generators, and the pressure controller, can be optimized separately. Optimizing each component individually reduces the complexity in formulating the problem and avoids unnecessary combinatory operations among unrelated genes caused by the interaction effect between components, thereby saving much computational time. However, it is important to note that the order for optimizing these components is not totally arbitrary, due to their dependence. For example, optimizing the pressure controller requires that the pressure model be built and parameters be tuned *a priori*.

First, the reference yaw-rate generator can be isolated from the whole control model and tuned independently, since their parameters are tuned to fit data measured from experiments. After that, the pressure controller can be optimized. Once these three components are completed, the next step is optimizing the steering-based compensated yaw-moment generator, and finally the sideslip-based compensated yaw-moment generator to complete the optimization procedure. The optimal values of control parameters used in this study are presented in Table 4.

Component	Parameter	Value
Steering-based FLC	Scaling factors	$[0.108 \quad 0.008 \quad 15.106]$
	Deforming coefficients	$[0.704 \quad 0.660 \quad 0.173]$
Sideslip-angle based FLC	Scaling factors	$[1.473 \quad 0.253 \quad 19.593]$
	Deforming coefficients	$[0.193 \quad 0.694 \quad 0.360]$

Table 4. Optimal control parameters for ESP

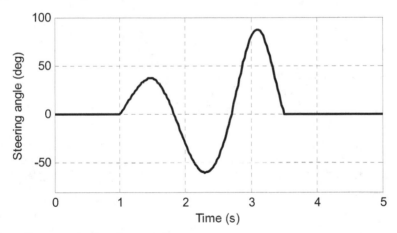

Fig. 15. Open-loop steering angle

Driving maneuvers have been simulated for various driving situations using a full sedan model in CarSim®, which provides the sprung mass, powertrain, suspension model, as well as tire and aerodynamic models with parameters listed in Table 5. In CarSim, from the braking pressure, the tire-road adherence force is obtained via the internal tire model depending on properties of the tire itself and the road surface.

The steering behavior depicted in Fig. 15 was adopted from Pruckner & Seemann (1997) for performance evaluation. The steering input equals three half-sinusoidal waves with increasing amplitude and switching direction; thus, the vehicle response during the change from non-critical to critical behavior can be studied. As has been argued earlier in this paper, the ESP system should drive the vehicle so that its yaw rate follows the shape specified by the steering input. This is assured by the estimator of reference yaw rate.

Description	Value
Sprung mass	800kg
Roll inertia	288kg.m²
Yaw inertia	1152kg.m²
Front axle to C.G.	0.948m
Rear axle to C.G.	1.422m
Height of C.G.	0.480m
Wheel radius	0.281m
Tire width	0.145m
Tire spring rate	0.2N/m

Table 5. Principal simulation parameters of vehicle

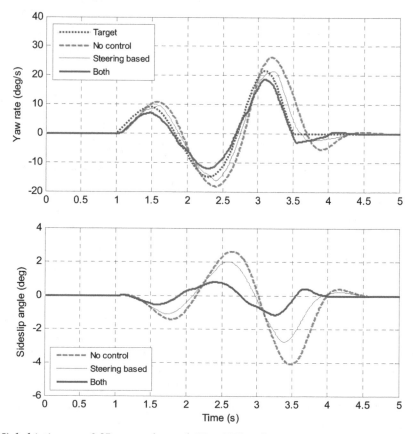

Fig. 16. High friction: $\mu = 0.85$; normal speed: $V_x = 100$km/h

After tuning the controller by using GAs with mutation rate of 0.1, crossover rate of 0.8, population size of 20, maximal number of generations of 50, and randomly generated initial population, simulations for four cases with different road frictions and speeds were conducted. The simulation results of which are shown in figures from 13 to 16. The first simulation (Fig. 16) focused on high-friction and normal-speed conditions to determine how the performance of a vehicle can be improved in non-critical situations. Next, the vehicle behavior and controller performance were examined for three different critical situations, namely high speed on high-friction surfaces (Fig. 17), high speed on normal-friction surfaces (Fig. 18), and normal speed on very low-friction surfaces (Fig. 19). In each case, three trials were considered: the first, without the ESP controller (dashed lines); the second, with only the steering-based compensated yaw moment enabled (thin solid lines); the third, with both steering-based and sideslip-angle-based compensated yaw moments taken into account (thick solid lines). The target yaw rates (dotted lines) are shown in yaw-rate plots for reference.

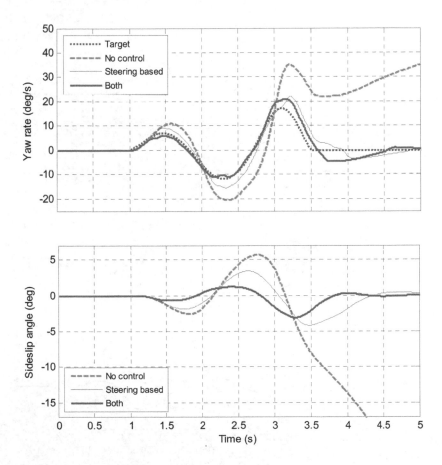

Fig. 17. High friction: μ = 0.85; high speed: V_x = 180km/h

First, a simulation was done for a highly maneuverable case characterized by high friction and normal speed. The first plot in Fig. 16 indicates that without the ESP controller, the vehicle was already following the steering target fairly well. However, a better result can still be obtained with the ESP system enabled. The second plot shows that the sideslip angle was significantly reduced with the use of the compensated yaw moment.

The second simulation was done for conditions characterized by high friction and high speed, the results of which are shown in Fig. 17. Without the ESP controller, the vehicle went out of control when the steering began to become critical (at 3.2 sec). The ESP controller successfully drove the vehicle following the steering target.

The third simulation was done for a case characterized by medium friction and high speed, the results of which are shown in Fig. 18. Without the ESP controller, the vehicle went out of control even when the steering was non-critical (at 2.2 sec). The ESP controller performed quite well in this case while keeping the vehicle yaw rate almost coincidental with the steering target.

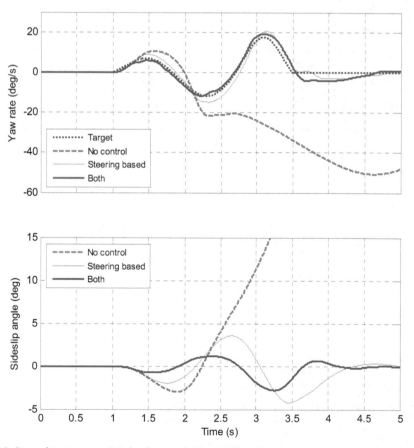

Fig. 18. Medium friction: $\mu = 0.5$; high speed: $V_x = 180$km/h

The last simulation case, the results of which are shown in Fig. 19, was for a very low-friction condition, corresponding to driving on snow-covered or icy surfaces. In this emergency situation, even with the ESP controller, the tracking for critical-steering maneuvering was not really good, the yaw rate drew much closer to the steering target and the sideslip angle being kept under the specified range (two degrees).

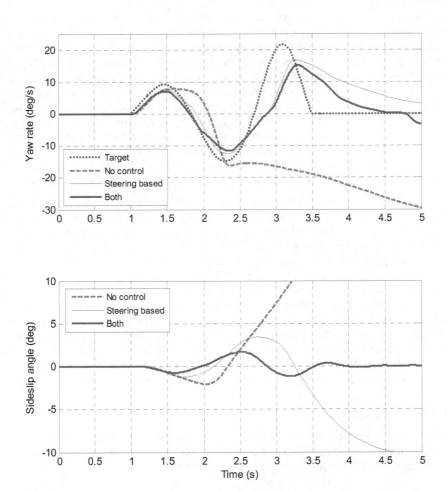

Fig. 19. Low friction: $\mu = 0.2$; normal speed: $V_x = 100 \text{km/h}$

5. Conclusion

In this chapter, an optimization technique was introduced to tune the parameters of PD-like fuzzy-logic controllers. The key point is to parameterize each input and output of a FLC by a scaling factor and a deforming coefficient. In this way, the FLC can be tuned quantitatively by different optimization algorithms, among which the genetic algorithms introduced are a preferable choice. The design of PD-like FLCs is as simple as a PID, as it does not require a mathematic model of the control plant, even a simple one. However, these FLCs gain over PID controllers by the non-linear properties, thus, are widely used in non-linear control problems where plant models are difficult to obtain mathematically.

From the introduced technique, two case studies were presented and discussed. In the first case, a bicycle roll-angle-tracking controller was an attempt to adapt the study of Sharp et al. for motorcycle to control the bicycle, where an FLC was used instead of a PID so that the system non-linearity was better dealt. Simulation results indicated that the bicycle can follow roll-angle commands with small error. In the second case, after the FLCs were optimized, simulations using the ESP system were conducted under different driving conditions. In normal conditions, the controller could still improve the maneuverability to achieve better performance. In high speed conditions, the vehicle was controlled to follow the desired yaw rate with small sideslip angle. In very low friction conditions, although the controller could not control the vehicle back to the normal condition, the yaw rate drew much closer to the steering target and the sideslip angle was kept to be in the specified range. The results indicate that, with the help of proposed ESP control scheme, a vehicle can follow a steering behavior in critical cases while maintaining a small sideslip angle.

The PD-like FLCs can be widely applied in reality due to several advantages. First, the control design is simple, without the need to develop a dynamic model for the control plan. This is because FLC is a model-free control scheme. Second, human experience can be used straightforwardly in the design of the controller. The designer can describe the system behavior with simple IF-THEN rules. All the optimization efforts of control performance are then endorsed by the adjustment process of the fuzzy membership functions. This process has also strengths and weaknesses. While the easily adjustable membership functions give the designers a lot of chance to affect the control performance, there is no general analytical technique. This study is an effort to address this problem by parameterizing the fuzzy membership functions with scaling factors and deforming coefficients, which can be used as control parameters in the optimization. Among many optimization methods, the GA approach introduced in this study is a good choice as it is a general optimization method, which is able to search for the global optimum of knowledge-free problems.

6. Acknowledgement

The work was supported by the National Science Council in Taiwan, Republic of China, under the projects numbered NSC 96-2221-E-212-027 and NSC 97-2221-E-212-007, and by MICA Center, HUST - CNRS/UMI 2954 - Grenoble INP.

7. References

Ackermann, J. (1998). Active steering for better safety, handling and comfort, *Proceedings of Advances in Vehicle Control and Safety*, Amiens, France, pp. 1-10

Beznos, A.V.; Formal'sky, A.M.; Gurfinkel, E.V.; Jicharev, D.N.; Lensky, A.V.; Savitsky, K.V. & Tchesalin, L.S. (1988). Control of autonomous motion of two-wheel bicycle with gyroscopic stabilisation, *Proc. of IEEE Int. Conf. on Robotics and Automation*, Leuven, Belgium, Vol. 3, pp. 2670-2675

Bosch (1999). *Driving-Safety Systems*, 2nd ed., Stuttgart: Robert Bosch GmbH, Society of Automotive Engineers

Chen, C.K. & Dao, T.S. (2006). Fuzzy control for equilibrium and roll-angle tracking of an unmanned bicycle, *Multibody System Dynamics*, Vol. 15, pp. 325-350

Chen, C.K. & Dao, T.S. (2007). Genetic fuzzy control for path-tracking of an autonomous robotic bicycle, *J. of System Design and Dynamics*, vol. 1, pp. 536-547

Chen, C.K. & Dao, T.K. (2010). Speed-adaptive roll-angle-tracking control of an unmanned bicycle using fuzzy logic, *Vehicle System Dynamics (Special Issue: Selected Papers from the 22nd International Congress of Theoretical and Applied Mechanics, Adelaide, 24–29 August 2008)*, Vol. 48, pp. 133-147. DOI: 10.1080/00423110903085872

Esmailzadeh, E.; Goodarzi, A. & Vossoughi, G.R. (2003). Optimal yaw moment control law for improved vehicle handling, *Mechatronics*, Vol. 13, No. 7, pp. 659-675

Han, S.; Han, J. & Ham, W. (2001). Control algorithm for stabilization of tilt angle of unmanned electric bicycle, *Trans. on Control, Automation and Systems Engineering*, Vol. 3, pp. 176-180

Haupt, R.L. & Haupt, S.E. (2004). *Practical Genetic Algorithm*, 2nd ed., John Wiley & Sons, Inc.

Ikushima, Y. & Sawase, K. (1995). A study on the effects of the active yaw moment control, *SAE Technical Paper Series*, No. 950303

Kwak, B. & Park, Y. (2001). Robust vehicle stability controller based on multiple sliding mode control, *SAE Technical Paper Series*, No. 2001-01-1060

Nishio, A.; Tozu, K.; Yamaguchi, H.; Asano, K. & Amano, Y. (2001). Development of vehicle stability control system based on vehicle sideslip angle estimation, *SAE Transactions*, Vol. 110, No. 6, pp. 115-122

Oraby, W.A.H.; El-Demerdash, S.M.; Selim, A.M.; Faizz, A. & Crolla, D.A. (2004). Improvement of vehicle lateral dynamics by active front steering control, *SAE Technical Paper Series*, No. 2004-01-2081

Pruckner, A. & Seemann, M. (1997). Analysis of dynamic driving control systems (DDC) on a full vehicle model in ADAMS, Institut fur Kraftfahrwesen Aachen

Selby, M.; Manning, W.J.; Brown, M.D. & Crolla, D.A. (2001). A coordination approach for DYC and active front steering, *SAE Transactions*, vol. 110, no. 6, pp. 1411-1417

Sharp, R.S.; Evangelou, S. & Limebeer, D.J.N. (2004). Advances in the modelling of motorcycle dynamics, *Multibody System Dynamics*, Vol. 12, pp. 251-283

Tahami, F.; Kazemi, R. & Farhanghi, S. (2003). Direct yaw control of an all-wheel-drive EV based on fuzzy logic and neural networks, *SAE Technical Paper Series*, No. 2003-01-0956

Van Zanten, A.T.; Erhardt, R. & Pfaff, G. (1995). VDC, the vehicle dynamics control system of Bosch, *SAE Technical Paper Series*, No. 950759

Van Zanten, A.T. (2000). Bosch ESP systems: 5 years of experience, *SAE Transactions*, Vol. 109, No. 7, pp. 428-436

Yavin, Y. (1999). Stabilization and control of the motion of an autonomous bicycle by using a rotor for the tilting moment, *Computer Methods in Applied Mechanics and Engineering*, Vol. 178, pp. 233-243

17

Switching Control System Based on Largest of Maximum (LOM) Defuzzification – Theory and Application

Logah Perumal[1] and Farrukh Hafiz Nagi[2]
[1]Multimedia University, Bukit Beruang, Malacca,
[2]Universiti Tenaga Nasional, Kajang, Selangor
Malaysia

1. Introduction

Switching control signals are used to activate and deactivate system actuator periodically based on saturation limits. Switching control system which produces level switching signals (two levels or three levels) are known as level switching control system. Level switching control systems are inexpensive to implement (T.H. Jensen, 2003), but their drawback is that the control systems become non-linear (Slotine et al, 1991; T.H. Jensen, 2003). Two types of level switching control systems are available; bang-bang and bang-off-bang control systems. Bang-bang control system which has two level outputs is used as time optimal control, but it leads to oscillation (Mark Ole Hilstad, 2002). The oscillation can be reduced by using bang-off-bang control system, which has three level outputs, but it requires more time to reach steady state. Sample switching signals are shown in figure 6. As can be seen, figure 6(c) shows two levels switching signals in which the output is either 1 or -1 and figure 6(d) shows three levels switching signals in which the output is 1, 0, or -1.

Example applications utilizing switching control systems are in rocket flight, robots, overhead cranes, satellite attitude control (Parman, S., 2007; Thongchet S. & Kuntanapreeda S., 2001a) and thermal systems. Normally, relays are used to produce switching signals, based on inputs which are supplied by conventional controllers. Later, fuzzy logic is applied to improve robustness of the system. Centroid defuzzification method is the most appealing and popularly used in many applications, including development of switching control signals. Centroid defuzzification method gives a crisp output interpolated between the ranges of the aggregated fuzzy output set. This method does not yield to switching control system requirement and thus additional commands would be used to convert crisp output to level switching control signals (Thongchet S. & Kuntanapreeda S., 2001b). On the other hand, largest (or smallest) of maximum defuzzification method can be used to yield only two or three crisp output levels for all input values.

Initially, fuzzy logic controllers were designed and implemented based on experience-based techniques, due to lack of general design methods for fuzzy logic controllers (FLCs). Thus, performance of resulting design depends entirely on designers' capability and creativity. Since then, systematic design methods for FLCs were investigated and proposed to aid practitioners (K. Michels et al, 2006; J. Jantzen, 2007; L. Mostefai et al, 2009). In this chapter, a systematic design procedure is outlined for development of switching control system using FLC, with largest of maximum (LOM) defuzzification. Matlab-Simulink environment is utilized in development of the controllers. One of optimization techniques, Nelder–Mead simplex search method is later utilized to optimize the FLC. Later, effectiveness of the FLC is demonstrated by controlling angular position of a single axis attitude model. The single axis attitude model is controlled in real time using Matlab-Simulink xPC target environment, without aid of any mathematical models.

2. Defuzzification method for switching control systems

There are numerous defuzzification methods. Each defuzzification method outputs different results (Ajith Abraham, 2005) and thus overall performance of the fuzzy inference system is directly influenced by the selection of defuzzification method. There is no exact rule on selection of defuzzification for certain applications. Suitable defuzzification method for certain application is chosen through trial-and-error by the use of software (Gunadi W. Nurcahyo et al, 2003). Most of defuzzification methods give a crisp output interpolated between the ranges of the aggregated fuzzy output set. These methods do not yield to switching control system requirement, except for largest (or smallest) of maximum defuzzification. The largest (or smallest) of maximum defuzzification method can be used to yield only two or three crisp output levels for all input values. LOM defuzzification is a suitable method to yield switching signals since it selects maximum value of aggregated membership function.

One of the defuzzification methods, which is the centroid method is the most appealing and popularly used in many applications (Timothy J. Ross, 1995). In (Thongchet S. & Kuntanapreeda S., 2001b), centroid defuzzification method is used together with a control output law to yield three level switching signals. The control law outputs the switching signals based on the range of crisp output from the centroid defuzzification process. The switching signals can be directly produced by the LOM defuzzification process, avoiding the use of control law as mentioned above. Maximum defuzzification methods are not commonly used in comparison to centroid method. One of the maximum defuzzification methods - mean of maxima is used in creating Fuzzy State Machines (FuSMs) for computer gaming development. Another example is the use of LOM defuzzification in development of fuzzy monitoring and fault alarm system for the ExoMars Pasteur Payloads drill and fuzzy terrain recognition system performed while drilling (Bruno René Santos et al, 2006). In (T.H. Jensen, 2003), it is pointed out that there are many unexplored ways of making bang-bang control system. In this work, fuzzy logic controller is used to implement bang-bang and bang-off-bang control systems by using LOM defuzzification. LOM defuzzification is proven to be the suitable defuzzification method to yield switching signals.

3. Case study: Satellite single axis attitude control

Response time of a control system complements energy-saving measures especially in embedded control system. Satellite attitude control system is one such example where fuel saving is highly desirable. Likewise, remotely controlled submersibles, deep space exploration probes can also benefit from such measures but to a lesser extent than communication satellites due to their high launching cost. Minimum response time also ensures that satellite orientation error can be efficiently removed without degrading the performance of the satellite. Thus, satellite attitude control has been selected as a case study in this work, due to the need for a suitable controller.

One axis attitude model is used as an example to demonstrate implementation of LOM defuzzification method in both bang-bang and bang-off-bang control systems. The model represents single axis of satellite which can be repeated for other two axes. The model and parameters described here are taken from previous work (Logah P. & Nagi F., 2008). Later in section 9, a practical demonstration based on this model is presented for fuzzy bang-bang control system. Equation of motion describing motion of one axis satellite system (Gulley N., 1991) is given by:

$$M_a = \ddot{\theta}I + \dot{\theta}C \tag{1}$$

where is applied moment due to the thruster, I is moment of inertia of the one axis satellite, C is coefficient of friction, $\dot{\theta}$ is angular rate and $\ddot{\theta}$ is angular acceleration. Matlab - Simulink model of the one axis satellite system is as shown in figure 1.

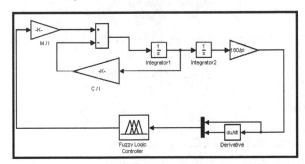

Fig. 1. Simulink model of one axis satellite system

Specifications for the one axis satellite system are taken from (Thongchet S. & Kuntanapreeda S., 2001b) as shown in table 1. Objective of the fuzzy logic controller is to reset attitude of the one axis satellite by producing level switching signals. Reset angle is set to zero degree. Development of the FLCs is described in section 5.

Parameters	Description	Value
M_a	Thruster moment	0.281 Nm
I	Moment of inertia	1.928 kg m^2
C	Coefficient of friction	0.000453 kg m^2/s

Table 1. Satellite parameters

4. Fuzzy system

In fuzzification, an operator transforms crisp data into fuzzy sets, so that data can be processed by the rule-base. Fuzzification process can be described as:

$$A = \text{fuzzifier}(x_0) \tag{2}$$

$x_0 = [x_1, x_2, ... x_n]^T$ is an input vector, $A = [\underset{\sim}{A}_1, \underset{\sim}{A}_2, ... \underset{\sim}{A}_n]^T$ is fuzzy sets, and fuzzifier represents a fuzzification operator. Mamdani implication of max-min fuzzy inference is given by:

$$\mu_{\underset{\sim}{B^k}}(z) = \max[\min[\mu_{\underset{\sim}{A}_1 k}(input(x_1)), \mu_{\underset{\sim}{A}_2 k}(input(x_2))]] \qquad k = 1, 2, ..., r \qquad (3)$$

where $\mu_{\underset{\sim}{B^k}}(z)$ is height of aggregated fuzzy set for r rules. The aggregated fuzzy set is defuzzified to yield crisp output, as represented by:

$$z^* = \text{defuzzifier} (\underset{\sim}{Z}) \qquad (4)$$

$\underset{\sim}{Z}$ where z^* is a crisp output, is fuzzy set resulted from aggregation, and "defuzzifier" represents defuzzification operator. LOM defuzzification is done in two steps. First the largest height in the union is determined:

$$hgt(\underset{\sim}{Z}_k) = \sup_{z \in Z} \mu_{\underset{\sim}{B^k}}(z) \qquad (5)$$

where supremum (sup) is the least upper bound. Then, largest of maximum is calculated:

$$z^* = \sup_{z \in Z} \left\{ z \in Z \middle| \mu_{\underset{\sim}{B^k}}(z) = hgt(\underset{\sim}{Z}_k) \right\} \qquad (6)$$

Where z^* is the crisp output.

5. Development of switching FLCs

Bang–bang and bang-off-bang control of satellite attitude can be accomplished with fuzzy logic controller by using LOM defuzzification method. Triangular membership functions with fifty percent overlap are used. Triangular membership functions are used because they are simple, easy to model mathematically, and recommended by Hill, Horstkptte and Teichrow as reported in (Jan, J, 1998). Triangular membership functions are also proven to perform well even with presence of disturbances/noise in the measured parameters (FLC inputs). Based on the rules of thumb for membership functions reported in (C.W. Taylor et al, 2000), density of the fuzzy sets are made highest around optimal control point of the system and thin out as the distance from that point increases.

Using angle as only input to fuzzy controller would cause the system to become unstable and diverge from reset angle. Thus, angular velocity information is used as an additional input to the fuzzy controller to stabilize the system, as reported in (Gully, N., 1991). Fuzzy logic with Mamdani implication of max-min fuzzy inference is used in development of the fuzzy logic controller. Two level bang-bang controller is formulated first, follwed by three level bang-off-bang controller.

5.1 Bang-bang FLC

Structure of fuzzy logic controller for bang–bang output (fuzzy bang–bang) consists of two inputs and one output. Five fuzzy sets are used in each input as shown in figures 2 and 3, where LN = Large Negative, SN = Small Negative, Z = Zero, SP = Small Positive, and LP = Large Positive. S_a and S_b are spans of the middle fuzzy sets. Output consists of two fuzzy sets as shown in figure 4, where T1 = Thruster 1, and T2 = Thruster 2. The output is either 1 or -1 similar to bang–bang controller output, which activates or deactivates the system actuators. Universe of discourse for the two inputs, $X = \{X_1, X_2\}$ is $-30 \leq X \leq 30$ and universe of discourse for the output, Z is $-1 \leq Z \leq 1$. Relationship between the inputs and output is described in terms of fuzzy rules. Table 2 shows relationship between the inputs and output in tabular linguistic format.

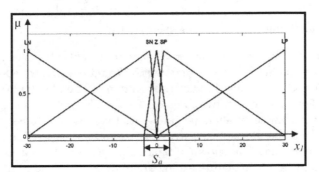

Fig. 2. Membership functions of the input angle

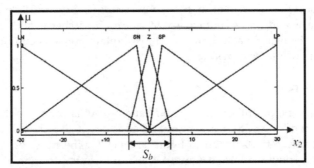

Fig. 3. Membership functions of the input angle rate

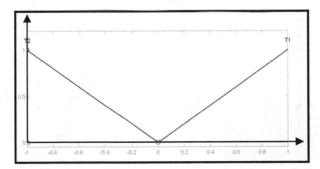

Fig. 4. Membership functions of the output

Angle rate ＼ Angle	LN	SN	Z	SP	LP
LN	T1~	T1~	T1~	T1~	-
SN	T1~	T1~	T1~	-	T2~
Z	T1~	T1~	-	T2~	T2~
SP	T1~	-	T2~	T2~	T2~
LP	-	T2~	T2~	T2~	T2~

Table 2. Inputs and output setting for bang–bang control

Relationship between inputs and output as shown in table 2 are extracted based on observation. T1 and T2 represent thrusters which would eventually cause change in the satellite orientation. Output signal 1 indicates activation of T1 and output signal -1 indicates activation of T2. For a single axis, two thrusters are used to control the attitude; one of the thrusters, T1 for clockwise rotation (angle is positive) and the other thruster, T2 for counterclockwise rotation (angle is negative). The thrusters are placed at the two edges of the single axis satellite model, as shown in figure 17. Once thruster is activated, combusted fuel at high pressure and temperature exiting at nozzle would develop moment M_a which would rotate the satellite and change its attitude. For example if current angle is large positive (tilted clockwise), then in order to reset the attitude, thruster T2 should be activated, so that the system would rotate counterclockwise until it reaches default orientation (reset angle). As for the diagonal in table 2, the system will retain previous output, in which either one of the thrusters would be turned on.

5.2 Bang-Off-bang FLC

Structure of fuzzy logic controller for bang-off-bang output is similar to that of bang-bang, except for addition of one output fuzzy set and addition of five rules. Output consists of three triangular fuzzy sets as shown in figure 5. Span for the fuzzy set *off* is set to zero. Addition of rules is shown in table 3. Output is 1,-1 or 0 similar to bang-off-bang controller output.

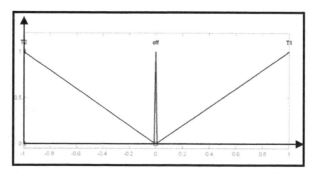

Fig. 5. Membership functions of the output for bang-off-bang controller

Angle rate \ Angle	LN	SN	Z	SP	LP
LN	T1 $\sim$	T1 $\sim$	T1 $\sim$	T1 $\sim$	off
SN	T1 $\sim$	T1 $\sim$	T1 $\sim$	off	T2 $\sim$
Z	T1 $\sim$	T1 $\sim$	off	T2 $\sim$	T2 $\sim$
SP	T1 $\sim$	off	T2 $\sim$	T2 $\sim$	T2 $\sim$
LP	off	T2 $\sim$	T2 $\sim$	T2 $\sim$	T2 $\sim$

Table 3. Relationship between the inputs and outputs for bang-off-bang switching.

Membership function 'off' is used to represent third level in bang-off-bang control system. In case of bang-bang controller, either one of the thrusters is activated at all time; whereas in bang-off-bang controller, either one of the thrusters would be activated or both will be turned off at a given time. As for the diagonal in table 3, both thrusters would be turned off.

For example if current angle is large positive and angle rate is large negative, it indicates that the system is currently tilted clockwise at large angle, but the angle rate is indicating that the system is rotating counterclockwise and approaching the reset angle (default orientation) at a fast phase. Thus in this case the thrusters can be switched off in order to save fuel, since the system is resetting by itself.

6. Simulations using switching FLCs

One axis satellite system described in section 3 is simulated using fuzzy bang-bang and bang-off-bang controllers which were developed in section 5, by using fuzzy system described in section 4. Parameters used for membership functions are: $S_a = 6$, $S_b = 10$. Relationship between inputs and outputs are as shown in table 2 and table 3, where LN = Large Negative, SN = Small Negative, Z = Zero, SP = Small Positive, LP = Large Positive, T1 = Thruster 1, T2 = Thruster 2. Simulation results using above parameters are as shown in figure 6. Initial angle given is 3 degrees.

From figures 6(a) and 6(b), it can be seen that there exists some oscillation in the steady state and system response can be optimized further. Simulation in Matlab-Simulink environment shows that system response is affected by sizes of middle spans S_a and S_b of the inputs (Thongchet S. & Kuntanapreeda S., 2001a), labeled in figures 2 and 3. Oscillation during steady state is affected by span S_a, while overshoot is affected by span S_b. In following sections, simulations are run for various sizes of span S_a and S_b, to determine optimal span sizes to be used. Simulations are run using bang-bang controller. Optimal span sizes selected from the simulations are later applied for both bang-bang and bang-off-bang controllers.

6.1 Manual selection of span size S_a

Simulations are run for various sizes of span S_a while span S_b is kept constant at a value of 10 using fuzzy bang-bang controller. Initial Euler angle given to the system is 10 degrees.

Table 4 summarizes simulation results. Sample results are shown in figures 7 and 8. Based on results in table 4, span size of 0.02 is chosen since it yields smallest oscillation during steady state.

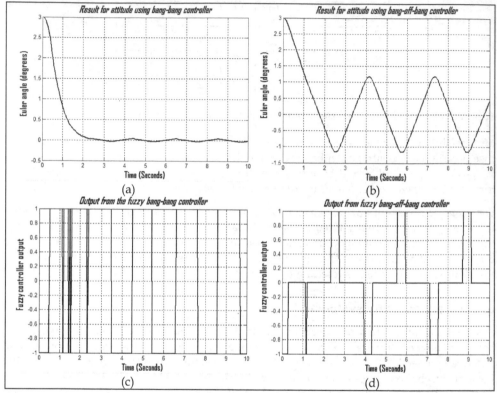

Fig. 6. Simulation results using fuzzy bang-bang and fuzzy bang-off-bang controllers. (a) Results for attitude using fuzzy bang-bang controller (b) Results for attitude using fuzzy bang-off-bang controller (c) Bang-bang output (d) Bang-off-bang output

Span size S_a	Steady state oscillation (degrees)
20	±0.04 (Mean=-1.5×10⁻⁴)
10	±0.04 (Mean=-9×10⁻⁴)
6	±0.04 (Mean=-4.5×10⁻⁴)
2	±0.04 (Mean=-3×10⁻⁴)
1	±0.04 (Mean=-1.6×10⁻³)
0.2	±0.04 (Mean=-1.5×10⁻⁴)
0.02	±7.35×10⁻³ (Mean=-7.35×10⁻³)
0	±8.23×10⁻³ (Mean=1.775×10⁻³)

Table 4. Results obtained for various span sizes S_a.

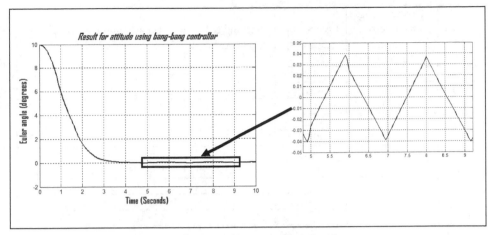

Fig. 7. Results for steady state oscillation using span sizes S_a = 6.

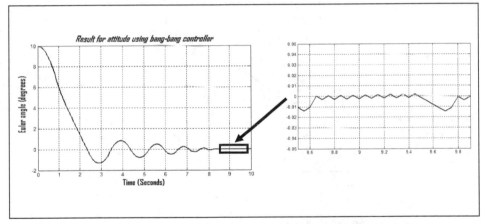

Fig. 8. Results for steady state oscillation using span sizes S_a = 0.02.

Overshoot can be prevented by changing span size S_b as described in next section.

6.2 Manual selection of span size S_b

Simulation is run for various sizes of span S_b while span S_a is kept constant at a value of 0.02 using fuzzy bang-bang con4troller. Initial Euler angle given to the system is 10 degrees. Table 5 summarizes the simulation results. Sample results are shown in figure 9.

Settling time reduces when smaller span S_b is used. Larger span S_b causes larger initial overshoot hence requires larger settling time. Based on results in table 5, span size of 0.2 is chosen since it yields smallest oscillation during steady state without overshoot. Span size of 1 is not chosen despite of its smaller settling time because it causes larger oscillation during gain scheduling, as reported in (Logah P. & Nagi F., 2008).

Span S_b	Time during first zero crossing (seconds)	Overshoot (degrees)	Settling time (seconds)	Steady state oscillation (seconds)
60	1.55	-9.84	44.6	$\pm 7.4 \times 10^{-3}$ (Mean=-7.4×10^{-3})
30	1.60	-6.17	32	$\pm 7.5 \times 10^{-3}$ (Mean=-7.5×10^{-3})
20	1.79	-3.73	21	$\pm 7.25 \times 10^{-3}$ (Mean=-7.25×10^{-3})
10	2.34	-1.32	8.3	$\pm 7.5 \times 10^{-3}$ (Mean=-7.5×10^{-3})
8	2.52	-0.77	6.5	$\pm 7.25 \times 10^{-3}$ (Mean=-7.25×10^{-3})
6	2.73	-0.62	6.6	$\pm 7.25 \times 10^{-3}$ (Mean=-7.25×10^{-3})
2	3.69	-0.06	4.1	$\pm 7.3 \times 10^{-3}$ (Mean=-7.3×10^{-3})
1	4.43	-	4.4	$\pm 7.3 \times 10^{-3}$ (Mean=-7.3×10^{-3})
0.2	5.1	-	5.1	$\pm 7.2 \times 10^{-3}$ (Mean=-7.2×10^{-3})
0.02	5.85	-	4.9	$\pm 7.2 \times 10^{-2}$ (Mean=-2.7×10^{-3})

Table 5. Results obtained for various span sizes S_b.

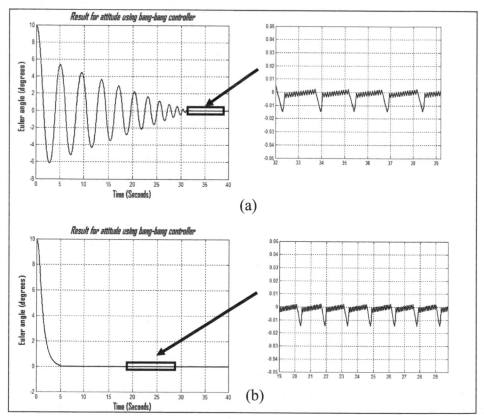

(a)

(b)

Fig. 9. Results for the overshoot and settling time using various span sizes S_b. (a) Result using span size of 30 (b) Result using span size of 0.2

6.3 Simulation results using optimal span sizes

The satellite system is simulated again using optimal span sizes selected from sections 6.1 and 6.2. Initial angles given to the systems are 3 degrees, 15 degrees, and -10 degrees. Simulation results are as shown in figures 10 and 11. Oscillation during the steady state has been reduced and overshoot has been prevented.

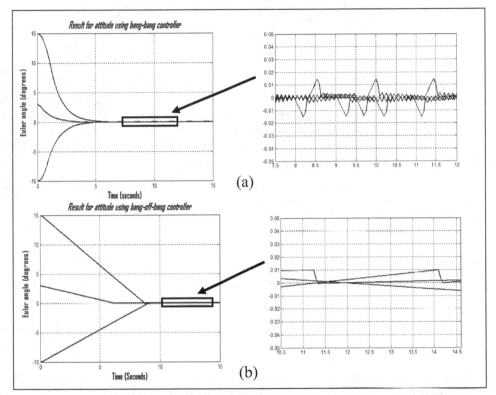

Fig. 10. Results for attitude using the fuzzy controllers (a) fuzzy bang-bang controller (b) fuzzy bang-off-bang controller

From figure 10, it can be seen that the oscillation in the steady state is less when bang-off-bang controller is used compared to the bang-bang controller. The bang-off-bang controller requires more time to settle compared to the bang-bang controller. Based on the figure 11, the bang-bang controller requires rapid switching between the thrusters while the bang-off-bang controller commands only two pulses. First pulse is used to initiate rotation and the second pulse is to terminate it. This causes less fuel to be consumed, but it requires more time to reach the reset angle.

Thus, bang-off-bang controller is an impulse type and can be used as fuel optimal control while bang-bang controller can be used as time optimal control. From figure 11, it can be seen that both controllers continuously activate and deactivate thrusters to maintain the satellite at the reset angle. In (Thongchet S. & Kuntanapreeda S., 2001a), it is stated that the thrusters will be switched off once attitude reaches zero state, thus prevents oscillation.

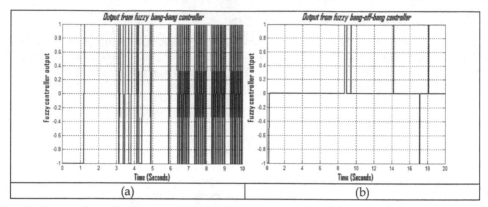

Fig. 11. Output from the fuzzy controllers for initial angle of 15 degrees. (a) Fuzzy bang-bang controller (b) Fuzzy bang-off-bang controller

7. Simulation using centroid defuzzification method

The satellite system in figure 1 is simulated using optimal span size S_a and S_b. Centroid defuzzification method is used. Figures 12 and 13 show the simulation results.

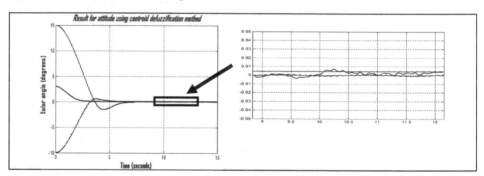

Fig. 12. Result for attitude using centroid defuzzification method

The centroid defuzzification method yields smaller oscillation during steady state compared to when LOM defuzzification is used (for both bang-bang and bang-off-bang controllers). Compared to bang-bang controller (which uses LOM defuzzification method), the centroid defuzzification leads to significant overshoot and longer settling time as seen in figure 12. The longer settling time leads to higher fuel consumption, which significantly reduces the lifespan of the satellite.

From figure 13, it can be seen that the output from the controller is a crisp value interpolated between the ranges of the aggregated fuzzy output set. This type of output requires analog actuators, in order to respond to the signals accordingly. This would lead to more expensive actuators to be installed onto the system. These problems are avoided when bang-bang controller is used, as seen in figures 10(a) and 11(a).

The overshoot is avoided and the settling time is faster compared to when centroid defuzzification method is used. This reduces fuel consumption and increases lifespan of the satellite. The LOM defuzzification yields switching signals in which economical digital actuators would respond to the signals accordingly. This shows that LOM defuzzification method is a suitable method to yield switching signals.

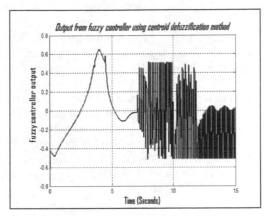

Fig. 13. Output from fuzzy controller using centroid defuzzification method for initial angle of 15 degrees.

8. Optimization

Optimization of fuzzy logic system is of interest to researchers in past and will remain in future as new applications are emerging. In (R. Bicker et al, 2002), the authors have mentioned that implementation of fuzzy logic controller is limited due to the difficultly faced in optimizing the fuzzy logic system. From section 6, it is seen that span sizes S_a and S_b play important roles in performance of FLC controller and optimum span sizes were selected manually. This section shows how the non-linear relation between the initial attitude of satellite and spans of the fuzzy controller membership functions are optimized automatically to achieve minimum response time by using Nelder-Mead simplex search method. Other methods used in optimization of fuzzy controllers are such as genetic algorithms for mobile robot navigation as presented in (R. Martínez et al, 2009), use of linear matrix inequalities and sliding mode control techniques for the Takagi-Sugeno Fuzzy Controllers (FCs) (Y. W. Liang et al, 2009; R.-E. Precup & S. Preitl, 2004), reinforcement ant optimized method (C.-F. Juang & C.-H. Hsu, 2009), combination of online self-aligning clustering with ant and particle swarm cooperative optimization as discussed in (C.-F. Juang & C.-Y. Wang, 2009), use of simulated annealing method (Precup, et al, 2011) and etc.

8.1 Minimum time response

Response time of a control system complements energy-saving measures especially in embedded control system. Satellite attitude control system is one such example where fuel saving is highly desirable. Likewise, remotely controlled submersibles, deep space exploration probes can also benefit from such measures but to a lesser extent than communication satellites due to their high launching cost. Minimum response time also ensures that satellite orientation error can be efficiently removed without degrading performance of the satellite.

The next important factor is the minimum time required to reach the zero states. This can be achieved by tuning the fuzzy logic system. Such controller is known as adaptive FLC controller or self tuning controller (Lhee C-G et al, 2001), which can be further classified as direct or indirect. In direct adaptive FLC controller the parameters are predetermined and selected on criteria of control law. An example of minimum time direct adaptive FLC controller can be found in (Thongchet S. & Kuntanapreeda S., 2001a) where the neural network is trained to output the fuzzy logic membership function parameters required to steer the satellite from initial attitude condition to zero states. Another example can be found in (Logah P. & Nagi F., 2008) where the satellite is brought to the reset angle by switching between two pre-determined fuzzy logic controllers. The switching is accomplished by scheduling the parameter. Indirect adaptive FLC estimates the fuzzy controller parameter online and caters for dynamics changes in the system response. The tuning FLC's parameters which can be altered online are the scaling factors for input and/or output signals (Isomursu P. & Rauma T., 1994; Yazici H. & Guclu R., 2006), the input and/or output membership functions (Isomursu P. & Rauma T., 1994; Jacomet M. et al, 1997) and the fuzzy if-then rules.

8.2 Proposed control system

The proposed control system is shown in figure 14, which optimizes spans (S) of the membership functions. The optimization is an iterative process. First the optimization plant model of the satellite, a mathematical expressions or Neural Network is used for searching the span S in fuzzy controller.

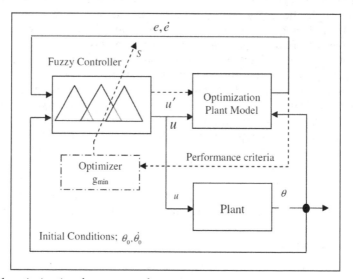

Fig. 14. Model optimization fuzzy control system

Adjustment criterion for minimizing the Euler angle is described in detail below. The lower loop with plant provides initial conditions; $\theta_o, \dot{\theta}_o$ from the plant to the upper optimization loop. The initial angle θ_o, is the set point in absence of desired angle of zero degree. The initial angle rate is set to 0°/sec for all simulations. Initial angle of the plant remains so until optimization process is completed in the upper loop and fuzzy controller injects control signal u into the plant. Control input u' is an intermediate control action for plant model during the iterative search process.

Important factor in optimization of fuzzy logic controller is to determine which parameter is to be tuned. In this work a fuzzy bang-bang control system proposed in figure 13 is optimized for minimum response time by tuning the membership functions of the fuzzy controller. Performance of fuzzy logic system is more dependent on membership function design than rule base design (Dan S., 2002). It is also shown in (Logah P. & Nagi F., 2008; Thongchet S. & Kuntanapreeda S., 2001b) that minimum-time results can be achieved by tuning the span of membership functions.

The optimization method adopted here in this work is based on the Nelder-Mead algorithm. Nelder-Mead simplex search method is selected because it is simple, can be programmed on a computer fairly easily and it is derivative-free (Kim Y-S., 1997). Derivative-free method is desired since they do not use numerical or analytical gradients. Derivative-free method can be applied to a wide range of objective functions and membership function forms (Dan S., 2002). Objective function for the optimization process is the plant model output $y(t, C_j^i(s))$ as shown in equation 7 below

$$f = y(t, C_1^3(s), C_2^3(s)) \tag{7}$$

where $C(s)$ is membership function as a function of span s and $i = 1,2...$ is the index for membership functions; $i = 3$ for optimization of the central membership function. $j = 1,2...$ is the input index for the fuzzy controller; $j = 1$ for input angle and $j = 2$ for input angle rate.

8.3 Performance criteria – Penalty function

The optimization is done by supplying parameters of the membership functions (Sa and Sb) as inputs and Nelder-Mead algorithm searches for optimal values. Initial guess of twelve is used for both Sa and Sb. Points corresponding to peak values of membership functions SN and SP (for both angle and angle rate) are set to be half of spans Sa and Sb in order to maintain 50% overlap and satisfy bezdek's repartition (Jan J., 1994; Demaya B. et al, 1995). The membership function distribution is respected according to bezdek distribution by preventing the modal points (maximum position) of the membership functions from crossing each other (Demaya B. et al, 1995). This is accomplished by assigning wider initial guess values for the span and stopping the optimization process with appropriate f function tolerance.

The performance criteria or also known as penalty function is used in optimization process to measure the deviation from the desired behavior (error). The Nelder-Mead algorithm tends to minimize the penalty function value. An effective penalty function needs to be designed in order to obtain desired response. It can be difficult to find an effective penalty function (Jacomet M. et all, 1997; Smith AE & Coit DW., 1997). In (Jacomet M. et all, 1997) a penalty function is proposed as follows:

$$g = \sum_i^N (f(x_i) - f(p_i))^2 \tag{8}$$

Where g is the sum square of Euler angle, $x(t)$ is the measured value and $p(t)$ is the desired value. Penalty function above is applied to the single axis satellite system. Initial guess in universe of discourse is set to the maximum spans $S_a = S_b = 12$. The desired reset value is zero degree. The simulation results using the penalty function above leads to faster convergence, but causes overshoot as shown in figure 15 below.

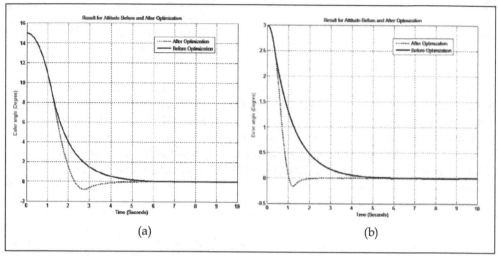

(a)   (b)

Fig. 15. Optimization results using penalty function of equations 3 and 4. (a) Initial angle given is 15 degrees (b) Initial angle given is 3 degrees.

Without squaring the g:

$$g = \sum_{i}^{N} (f(x_i) - f(p_i)) \qquad (9)$$

overshoot again. In equation 8 large penalty function value is nonlinear and the reflection in the simplex algorithm has taken it to negative search angle space. While in equation 9 the simplex search method is unrestricted of angle signs. The overshoot can be prevented by preferable penalty function:

$$g = \sum_{i}^{N} (|f(x_i) - f(p_i)|)^2 \qquad (10)$$

Any other penalty function can be used which yield positive angle and minimum convergence time.

8.4 Simulation results

In this section, the single axis satellite system as shown in section 3 previously is brought to the reset angle in minimum time by optimizing the fuzzy bang-bang controller. The fuzzy bang-bang controller is optimized by utilizing the penalty function described in equation 10. Initial guess values in universe of discourse for the spans $S_a = S_b = 12$. The simulation results are as shown in figures 16 and 17 below. Table 6 summarizes the results for settling time for various initial Euler angles.

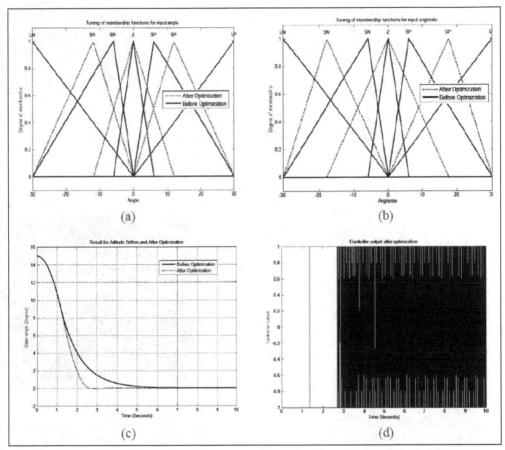

Fig. 16. Simulation results for initial angle of 15 degrees.(a) Optimization of membership functions of input angle (b) Optimization of membership functions of input angle rate (c) Result for attitude before and after optimization (d) Single cycle bang-bang controller output.

From figures 16(d) and 17(d), it can be seen that the fuzzy bang-bang controller yields only one cycle of thruster output before the system reaches the zero state. Once the system reaches the zero state, the thrusters would be switched off (in order to prevent chattering and thruster fuel wastage) (Thongchet S. & Kuntanapreeda S., 2001a) and the control is taken over by other more precise attitude controllers (Cathryn Jacobson, 2002; Hall C. et al, 1998).

Optimized membership functions are shown in figures 16 and 17. The membership functions either shrunk or expanded depending on the initial angle. During optimization, it is observed that the spans S_a shrinks for small initial angles and expands for large initial angles. On the other hand, the span S_b expands for all the initial angles. The span S_b expands more with higher initial angle.

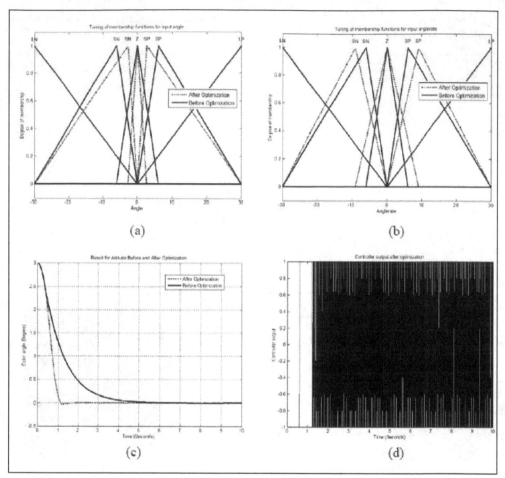

Fig. 17. Simulation results for initial angle of 3 degrees.(a) Optimization of membership functions of input angle (b) Optimization of membership functions of input angle rate (c) Result for attitude before and after optimization (d) Single cycle bang-bang controller output.

Initial Euler angle (degrees)	Settling time (seconds)	
	Using default membership functions	Using optimized membership functions
-2	5.5	1.6
5	6.6	2.2
-91	7.5	3.0
13	8.2	4.1

Table 6. Results for settling time without significant overshoot for various initial Euler angles.

9. Practical application of fuzzy bang-bang control

Fuzzy logic controller has been widely applied in industrial processes due to their simplicity and effectiveness (Garcia-Perez L. et al, 2000). They are proved to be robust and perform well even with disturbances in the input parameters (Logah P. et al, 2007a, 2007b).

Here, a practical application of fuzzy bang-bang control is demonstrated by controlling angular position of a pneumatic rotary actuator which equally represents a single axis satellite system. The pneumatic rotary actuator is controlled in real-time by using Matlab-simulink xPC target environment. There have been some successful applications on xPC Target since its release as a Matlab toolbox (Shangying Z. et al, 2004; Shiakolas PS. & Piyabongkarn D., 2001; Ichinose WE. et al, 2003; Omrc̆en D., 2007).

9.1 Hardware setup

An experiment based on the modal presented earlier in section 3 is presented here to illustrate the fuzzy bang-bang control system. The pneumatic rotary actuator is as shown in figures 18 and 19. Block diagram for experiment setup is shown in figure 20. Angle of the pneumatic rotary actuator is determined with the pulses generated by the inductive proximity encoder. The gear has 18 teeth/rev, giving physical resolution of 20 degrees/teeth.

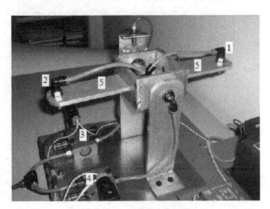

Fig. 18. Pneumatic rotary actuator. i) Nozzle1, ii) Nozzle2, iii) Solenoid valves1, iv) Solenoid valve2 and v) Beam

Resolution of the inductive proximity sensor is coarse, but it provides latency for fuzzy controller so that outputs T1 and T2 are available to solenoids within their response time (FESTO, 2007). The latency time is also necessary to build necessary pressure at nozzles.

Solver step size is kept at 0.01sec (figure 20), determines sampling rate of 100 KHz, which is necessary for interrupt driven scheduler of xPC Target kernel. The inlet pressure used is 3bars. Airflow rate at the nozzle outlet is determined based on characteristic graph provided by FESTO (FESTO, 2007). The air is treated as incompressible since air density changes only slightly at velocities much less than speed of sound. Force produced by the nozzle is calculated to be 2.2 Newton based on general thrust equation:

Fig. 19. Close-up view of the inductive proximity sensor and gear assembly. i) Inductive proximity sensor and ii) 18 teeth gear

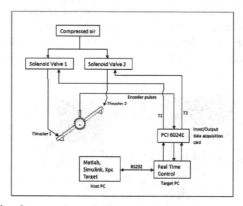

Fig. 20. Block diagram for the experiment setup

$$F = \dot{m}_2(V_2 - V_1) + (P_2 - P_1)A_2 \qquad (11)$$

where F = nozzle force, $\dot{m}_2$ = mass flow rate, V_1 = nozzle inlet velocity, V_2 = nozzle exit velocity, P_1 = nozzle inlet pressure, P_2 = nozzle exit pressure and A_2 = nozzle exit area.

The moment, M_a (Equation 1) produced by the nozzle force at half beam length is calculated to be 0.314 Nm. Coefficient of friction, C due to bearing contact, misalignment and unbalance is considered to be 0.4kgm2/s. Moment of inertia of the beam in figure 17 is evaluated using parallel axis theorem and found to be 0.00244 kgm2. Parameters of the pneumatic rotary actuator are summarized in Table 7:

Parameters	Description	Value
Ma	Thruster moment	0.314 Nm
I	Moment of Inertia	0.00244 kgm2
C	Coefficient of Friction	0.4 kgm2s

Table 7. Specification of the pneumatic rotary actuator

9.2 Real-time xPC controller

Simulink real time control program is as shown in figure 21. State flow is used to calculate angle, direction and angle rate of the pneumatic rotary actuator based on pulse input from the inductive proximity sensor. The signals are then supplied to the fuzzy logic controller, which in turn determines which valve to be activated.

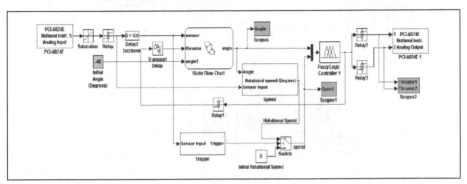

Fig. 21. Simulink real time control program

Structure of the fuzzy logic controller used is as described in section 5. The universe of discourse for the input angle is $-90 \leq x_1 \leq 90$, for the input angle rate is $-6.5 \leq x_2 \leq 6.5$ and for the output is $-1 \leq z \leq 1$.

9.3 Rotary actuator control

Optimization of the real-time xPC controller (Figure 21) requires optimal span S_a and S_b. The optimization process is accomplished by repeating the simulation described earlier in section 8.4 and by using the absolute penalty function (Equation 10). Parameters for real time application are given in Table 7. The optimized S_a and S_b values evaluated by simulation is later used in real-time xPC controller. Initial angle of 30 degrees is given to the system and the system resets to zero degree as shown in figure 22.

A curve fitting is added to discrete output pulses of the encoder in figure 21 to approximate continous angle convergence to 0 degree. The encoder output has resolution of 20 degree/teeth, which is obvious in figure 22 and is not a limitation for continuous time simulation. Thruster firing cycle to reset the beam angle is shown in figure 23.

Half cycle is required as seen in figure 23. Time required to reach 0 degree is 0.6 seconds. The bang-bang switching then causes oscillation about the reset angle 0 degree, at which the controller should be switched off, as described in section 8.4.

10. Conclusions

Fuzzy logic controllers which produce switching signals have been developed using LOM defuzzification method. The fuzzy bang-bang and bang-off-bang controllers are then successfully implemented on one axis satellite attitude control system (through simulations). The bang-bang controller can be used as time optimal control while the bang-off-bang can be used as a fuel optimal control. The optimization of the fuzzy controller's membership function can be easily achieved by using Nelder-Mead algorithm. Two different penalty functions are compared in this paper. Simulation results show that the absolute penalty function yields better results by yielding minimum time convergence and without significant overshoot.

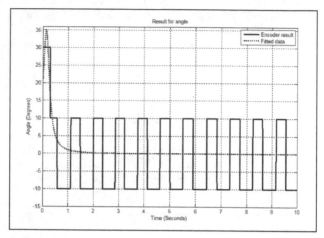

Fig. 22. Encoder output of rotary actuator system; resetting the angle to 0^0 with 20^0/teeth resolution

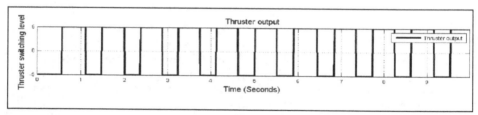

Fig. 23. Thruster switching voltage level for solenoid valves 3 and 4.

During optimization process, it is observed that spans of the central membership functions change proportionally to the initial angle. The work described here successfully demonstrated the optimization scheme proposed in figure 13, by implementing it to a pneumatic rotary actuator which equally represents a single axis satellite system. The real-time control is achieved by using Matlab-simulink xPC target environment. For real time control the optimized fuzzy membership function parameters were determined on off-line model. On-line optimization is possible by using embedded Cmex S-function for C coded simplex search optimization and C coded fuzzy controller programs in the host computer.

11. References

Ajith Abraham. (2005), *Rule-Based Expert Systems*, Handbook of Measuring System Design,John Wiley & Sons, LTD., 2005.
Bruno René Santos, Pedro Tiago Fonseca, Nuno Ávila & Rita Ribeiro (2006), *MODI-Simulation of knowledge enabled monitoring and diagnosis tool for ExoMars Pasteur Payloads*, Executive Summary Report, Document Ref: MODI_ESR_300, Edition 1-0.

C.-F. Juang & C.-H. Hsu (2009), Reinforcement ant optimized fuzzy controller for mobile-robot wall-following control, *IEEE Trans. Ind. Electron.*, vol. 56, pp. 3931–3940, Oct.

C.-F. Juang & C.-Y. Wang (2009), "A self-generating fuzzy system with ant and particle swarm cooperative optimization," *Expert Syst. Appl.*, vol. 36, pp. 5362–5370, April.

C.W. Taylor, V. Venkatasubramanian & Y. Chen (2000), Wide-Area Stability and Voltage Control, *Proc. VII Symposium on Specialists in Electric Operational and Expansion Planning*, VII SEPOPE, Curitiba, Brazil.

Cathryn Jacobson. (2002), Flywheel-based attitude control system article, In: Spinofftechnology #535, Quoin International, Inc. dated 3/11/2002. Available from:<http://www.mdatechnology.net/techsearch/spin.aspx?articleid=535>

Dan S. (2002), Sum normal optimization of fuzzy membership functions. *Int J Uncertain Fuzziness Knowledge-Based Syst* 2002 Vol.10(4), pp. 363–84.

Demaya B, Palm R, Boverie S, & Titli A. (1995), Multilevel qualitative and numerical optimization of fuzzy controller, *IEEE international conference on fuzzy systems*, Yokohama, Japan, 1995. p. 1149–54.

FESTO online catalogue. Products 2007. Available from: <http://catalog.festo.com/>

Garcia-Perez L, Canas JM, Garcia-Alegre MC, Yanez P, & Guinea D. (2000), Fuzzy control of an electropneumatic actuator, *STYLF2000*, Sevilla, September 2000, p. 133–8.

Gulley N. (1991), *Simulink application note.*, Aerodynamic division, NASA Ames Research Center.

Gunadi W. Nurcahyo, Siti Mariyam Shamsuddin, Rose Alinda Alias, & Mohd. Noor Md. Sap. (2003), Selection of Defuzzification Method to Obtain Crisp Value for Representing Uncertain Data in a Modified Sweep Algorithm, *Journal of Computer Science & Technology*, Vol.3, No.2, October 2003, pp. 22-28.

Hall C, Tsiotras P, & Shen H. (1998), Tracking rigid body motion using thrusters and momentum wheels. In: *Astrodynamics specialists conference AIAA*, Paper 98-4471, Boston, MA, August 10–12, 1998.

Ichinose WE, Reinkensmeyer DJ, Aoyagi D, Lin JT, Ngai K, Reggie Edgerton V & et al. (2003), A robotic device for measuring and controlling pelvic motion during locomotor rehabilitation. In: *Proceedings of the 25th annual international conference of the IEEE EMBS*, Cancun, Mexico, September 17–21, 2003. p.1690–3.

Isomursu P & Rauma T. (1994), A self-tuning fuzzy logic controller for temperature control of superheated steam, *Proceedings of the 3rd IEEE international conference on fuzzy systems*, vol. 3. 1994. p. 1560–3.

J. Jantzen (2007), *Foundations of Fuzzy Control*. Chichester: Wiley, 2007.

Jacomet M, Stahel A, & Walti R. (1997), *On-line optimization of fuzzy systems*, Infor Sci 98, Elsevier Sciences Inc.

Jan, J. (1998), *Design of fuzzy controllers*, Technical report no 98-E 864 (design)

K. Michels, F. Klawonn, R. Kruse, & A. Nürnberger (2006), *Fuzzy Control: Fundamentals, Stability and Design of Fuzzy Controllers*. Berlin, Heidelberg, New York: Springer-Verlag.

Kim Y-S. (1997), Refined simplex method for data fitting. In: Astronomical data analysis software and systems VI. *ASP conference series*, vol. 125, 1997.

L. Mostefai, M. Denai, S. Oh, & Y. Hori. (2009), Optimal control design for robust fuzzy friction compensation in a robot joint, *IEEE Trans. Ind. Electron.*, vol. 56, pp. 3832–3839, Oct. 2009.

Lhee C-G, Park J-S, Ahn H-S, & Kim D-H (2001), Sliding mode – like logic control with self-tuning the deadband zone parameters. *IEEE Trans Fuzzy Syst*, Vol. 9(2). April.

Logah P, Nagi F. (2008) Fuzzy control system based on largest of maximum (LOM) defuzzification. AJEEE, 2008; Vol. 4(2), pp.167–78.

Logah P, Nagi FH, & Yusoff MZ, (2007b), Fuzzy logic gain scheduler for a missile autopilot. In: *Proceedings of AEROTECH II – 2007*, Putrajaya, Malaysia, 20th and 21st June, 2007. p. 84–9.

Logah P., Nagi FH, & Yusoff MZ. (2007a), Altitude control of an aircraft using fuzzy logic control system. In: *Student's conference on research and development (SCORED)*, vol. 1, 14–15th May 2007. p. 65–74.

Mark Ole Hilstad (2002). *A Multi-Vehicle Testbed and Interface Framework for the Development and Verification of Separated Spacecraft Control Algorithms*, Master Thesis, Massachusetts Institute of Technology.

Omrc̆en D. (2007), Developing Matlab–Simulink and xPC target real-time controlenvironment for humanoid jumping robot. In: *Proceedings of 16th international workshop on robotics in Alpe–Adria–Danube region-RAAD*, Ljubljana, Slovenia, June.

Parman, S. (2007). Attitude Maneuvers of a Flexible Satellite by Using Improved Time-Optimal Inputs for Linear System, *Proceedings of AEROTECH II – 2007*, Putrajaya, Malaysia, 20th and 21st June 2007, pp. 90-94.

Precup, R.-E., David, R.-C., Petriu, E. M., Preitl, St. & Rădac, M.-B. (2011), Fuzzy control systems with reduced parametric sensitivity based on simulated annealing. *IEEE Transactions on Industrial Electronics*, vol. PP, no. 99, pp. 1-15

R. Bicker, Z. Hu, & K. Burn (2002), A Self-tuning Fuzzy Robotic Force Controller, *Proceedings of the 14th CISM-IFToMM Symposium on the Theory and Practice of Robots and Manipulators, RoManSy 2002*, Udine, Italy,.

R. Martínez, O. Castillo, & L. T. Aguilar (2009), Optimization of interval type-2 fuzzy logic controllers for a perturbed autonomous wheeled mobile robot using genetic algorithms," *Inf. Sci.*, vol. 179, pp. 2158–2174, June.

R.-E. Precup & S. Preitl (2004), Optimisation criteria in development of fuzzy controllers with dynamics, *Eng. Appl. Artif. Intell.*, vol. 17, pp. 661–674, Sept. 2004.

Shangying Z, Junwei H & Hui Z. (2004), RCP and RT control of 6-DOF parallel robot. In: *Forth international workshop on robot motion and control*, 2004. p. 133–7.

Shiakolas PS & Piyabongkarn D. (2001), On the development of a real-time controlsystem using xPC-target and a magnetic levitation device. In: *Proceedings of the 40th IEEE conference on decision and control*, 2001. p. 1348–53.

Slotine, J.J.E. & Li, W. (1991). *Applied Nonlinear Control*, Prentice-Hall, Englewood Cliffs, N.J.

Smith AE & Coit DW. (1997), *Penalty functions*. In: Baeck T, Fogel DB, Michalewicz Z, editors. Handbook on evolutionary computation. Oxford University Press; 1997. C5.2:1–6.

T.H. Jensen (2003). *Modeling A Resistive Wall Mode Control System Of The Bang-Bang Type*, General Atomics Project Report.

Thongchet S. & Kuntanapreeda S (2001b) Minimum-time Control of Satellite Attitude using a Fuzzy Logic Controller", *2001 WSES International Conference on Fuzzy Sets & Fuzzy Systems (FSFS'01)*, Puerto De La Cruz, Spain, February 11-15, 2001b.

Thongchet S. & Kuntanapreeda S. (2001a) A Fuzzy Neural Bang-Bang Controller for Satellite Attitude Control, Proceedings of SPIE-Volume 4390, *Applications and Science of Computational Intelligence IV*, March 2001, pp. 97-104.

Timothy J. Ross (1995), *Fuzzy Logic With Engineering Applications*, New York, McGraw-Hill Inc.

Y.-W. Liang, S.-D. Xu, & L.-W. Ting (2009), T-S model-based SMC reliable design for a class of nonlinear control systems, *IEEE Trans. Ind. Electron.*, vol. 56, pp. 3286–3295, Sept.

Yazici H, & Guclu R. (2006), Self-tuning fuzzy logic controller of vibrations of multidegree-of-freedom structural systems, *Proceedings of 5th international symposium on intelligent manufacturing systems*, May 29–31, 2006. p. 462–74.

18

Fuzzy Control: An Adaptive Approach Using Fuzzy Estimators and Feedback Linearization

Luiz H. S. Torres and Leizer Schnitman
Centro de Capacitação Tecnológica em Automação Industrial (CTAI),
Universidade Federal da Bahia, Rua Aristides Novis, nº 02, Escola Politécnica, 2ºandar,
Salvador, Bahia
Brazil

1. Introduction

In recent years the area of control for nonlinear systems has been the subject of many studies (Ghaebi et al., 2011; Toha & Tokhi, 2009; Yang & M., 2001). Computational advances have enabled more complex applications to provide solutions to nonlinear problems (Islam & Liu, 2011; Kaloust et al., 2004). This chapter will present an application of fuzzy estimators in the context of adaptive control theory using computational intelligence (Pan et al., 2009). The method is applicable to a class of nonlinear system governed by state equations of the form $\dot{x} = f(x) + g(x)u$, where $f(x)$ and $g(x)$ represent the nonlinearities of the states. Some classic control applications can be described by this specific class of nonlinear systems, for example, inverted pendulum, conic vessel, Continuously Stirred Tank Reactor (CSTR), and magnetic levitation system. The direct application of linear control techniques (*e.g.*: PID) may not be efficient for this class of systems. On the other hand, classical linearization methods may lead an adequate performance when the model is accurate, even though normally limited around the point in which the linearization took place (Nauck et al., 2009). However, when model uncertainties are considerable the implementation of the control law becomes difficult or unpractical. In order to deal with model uncertainties an adaptive controller is used (Han, 2005; Tong et al., 2011; 2000; Wang, 1994). The controller implements two basic ideas. First, the technique of exact feedback linearization is used to handle the nonlinearities of the system (Torres et al., 2010). Second, the control law formulation in presence of model uncertainties is made with the estimates of the nonlinear functions $f(x)$ and $g(x)$ (Cavalcante et al., 2008; Ying, 1998). The adaptation mechanism is used to adjust the vector of parameters θ_f and θ_g in a singleton fuzzyfier zero-order Takagi-Sugeno-Kang (TSK) structure that provides estimates in the form $f(x|\hat{\theta}_f)$ and $g(x|\hat{\theta}_g)$. The fuzzy logic system is built with a product-inference rule, center average defuzzyfier, and Gaussian membership functions. One of the most important contributions of the adaptive scheme used here is the real convergence of the estimates $f(x|\hat{\theta}_f)$ and $g(x|\hat{\theta}_g)$ to their optimal values $f(x|\theta_f^*)$ and $g(x|\theta_g^*)$ while keeping the tracking error with respect to a reference signal within a compact set (Schnitman, 2001). Convergence properties are investigated using Lyapunov candidate functions. In order to illustrate the methodology, a nonlinear and open-loop unstable magnetic levitation system is used as an example. Experimental tests in a real plant were conducted to check the reliability and robustness of the proposed algorithm.

2. A specific structure

The proposed method is applicable to a specific class of nonlinear system that can be described by state equations of form:

$$\begin{cases} \dot{x} = Ax + B\left[f(x) + g(x)u\right] \\ y = Cx \end{cases} \tag{1}$$

where,

$$A = \begin{bmatrix} 0 & 1 & 0 & \cdots & 0 \\ 0 & 0 & 1 & \cdots & 0 \\ \vdots & \vdots & \vdots & \ddots & \vdots \\ 0 & 0 & 0 & 0 & 1 \\ 0 & 0 & 0 & 0 & 0 \end{bmatrix}_{n \times n}$$

$$B = \begin{bmatrix} 0 & \cdots & 0 & 1 \end{bmatrix}^{T}_{1 \times n}$$

$$C = \begin{bmatrix} 1 & 0 & \cdots & 0 \end{bmatrix}_{1 \times n} \tag{2}$$

n is the dimension of the system

$x \in X \subset \Re^{n}$, are the states of the system

$f(x) : \Re^{n} \rightarrow \Re$ s.t. $f(x)$ is continuous and $f(x) \in U_f \subset \Re, \forall x \in X$

$|f(x)| \leq f^{U}, \forall x \in X$

$g(x) : \Re^{n} \rightarrow \Re$ s.t. $g(x)$ is continuous and $g(x) \in U_g \subset \Re, \forall x \in X$

$0 < \zeta < |g^{L}| \leq |g(x)| \leq |g^{U}|, \forall x \in X$, for a constant $\zeta > 0$

u is the control signal

y is the output signal

or, in an equivalent form:

$$\begin{cases} \dot{x}_1 = x_2 \\ \dot{x}_2 = x_3 \\ \vdots \\ \dot{x}_n = f(x) + g(x)u \\ y = Cx = x_1 \end{cases} \tag{3}$$

where X, U_f and U_g are compact sets, $sign(g(x)) = sign(g^{L}) = sign(g^{U})$ and $x = 0$ is an interior point of X.

2.1 Examples of nonlinear systems

Once the class of nonlinear systems is defined, it is important to select a plant to highlight the controller properties. As this structure is very common in control applications, some classic systems can be written using Equation (1) format (see below Figure (1)):

3. Control law

Consider a nonlinear system described by state equations in the form of Equation (1). Let the control objective be to track a reference signal $r(t) \in S \subset \Re$, where S is a compact set of possible references which can be supplied to the nonlinear plant.

Exact feedback linearization technique can be used here for exacting cancellation of the nonlinear functions $f(x)$ and $g(x)$ (Isidori, 1995; Slotine & Li, 1991; Sontag, 1998). If one

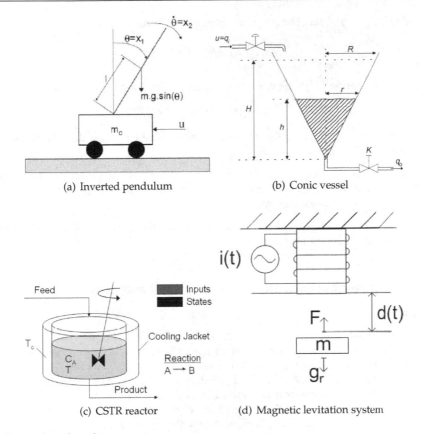

(a) Inverted pendulum (b) Conic vessel

(c) CSTR reactor (d) Magnetic levitation system

Fig. 1. Examples of nonlinear systems

assumes that the functions $f(x)$ and $g(x)$ are known, then an interesting structure for the control law would be

$$u = \frac{1}{g(x)} \left[-f(x) + D(x) \right] \tag{4}$$

where D is to be selected in the design phase.

By substituting Equation (4) in the nonlinear system Equation(1) one gets

$$\dot{x} = Ax + BD(x) \tag{5}$$

so that $\dot{x}_n = D(x)$, which can be chosen as the desired dynamics for the controlled system.

3.1 Example

Let a gain vector K be

$$K = [K_1, ..., K_n] \in R^n \tag{6}$$

and consider $D(x) = r - Kx$. The proposed control law becomes

$$u = \frac{1}{g(x)} [-f(x) + r - Kx] \tag{7}$$

By substituting Equation (7) in the nonlinear system in Equation (1), one gets

$$\dot{x} = (A - BK) x + B r \tag{8}$$

which yields a linear dynamic. In this case, the stability can be verified directly by computing the eingevalues of the matrix $(A - BK)$.

Conclusion 1. *Based on Equation (4), a large number of control laws can be suggested. For instance, the control laws used in (Wang, 1994) and (Wang, 1993), as well as the control law proposed in Equation (7) are particular cases of Equation (4).*

Remark 2. *Without loss of generality, $r = 0$ is considered for stability analysis and the nominal system is considered to be of the form*

$$\dot{x} = (A - BK) x \tag{9}$$

4. Mathematical requirements for fuzzy logic control application

4.1 Fuzzy structure

Since the fuzzy logic was proposed by L.A. Zadeh (Zadeh, 1965), a lot of different fuzzy inference engines have been suggested. Other researchers have also been used with success in a variety of applications for control of nonlinear systems (e.g.: Han, 2005; Jang et al., 1997; Lin & Lee, 1995; Nauck et al., 1997; Pan et al., 2009; Predrycz & Gomide, 1999; Tong et al., 2011; Tsoukalas & Uhrig, 1997; Yoneyama & Júnior, 2000)). Based on previous researches (Sugeno & Kang, 1988; Takagi & Sugeno, 1985), which propose the Takagi-Sugeno-Kang fuzzy structure (TSK), this work makes use of a fuzzy logic system with product-inference rule, center average defuzzyfier, and Gaussian membership functions.

Consider singleton fuzzifier and let a fuzzy system be composed by R rules, each one of them of the form

$$\text{IF } x_1 \text{ is } A_1^j \text{ and } x_n \text{ is } A_n^j \text{ THEN } y \text{ is } B_j \tag{10}$$

where $x = [x_1, \ldots, x_n] \in \Re^n$ is the input vector, $\left\{ A_1^j, \ldots, A_n^j \right\} / B_j$ are the input/output fuzzy sets related to the jth rule ($j = 1, \ldots, R$), and y is the fuzzy output.

Consider y_j as the point in which B_j is maximum ($\mu_{B_j}(y_j) = 1$) and define θ as the vector of parameters of the form

$$\theta^T = [y_1, \ldots, y_R] \tag{11}$$

Therefore, the fuzzy output can be expressed as

$$y = \theta^T.W(x) \tag{12}$$

where

$$W(x) = [W_1(x), \ldots, W_R(x)]^T$$
$$W_j(x) = \frac{\prod_{k=1}^{n} \mu_{A_k^j}(x_k)}{\sum_{j=1}^{R} \left(\prod_{k=1}^{n} \mu_{A_k^j}(x_k) \right)}, \quad j = 1 \ldots R \tag{13}$$

and

$$W_j(x) \in [0,1] \tag{14}$$

is usually called the *weight* of the jth rule. The scheme is shown in Figure (2).

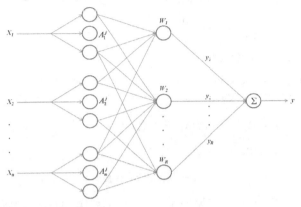

Fig. 2. Zero-order TSK fuzzy structure

4.2 Fuzzy as universal approximators

For any given real continuous function $f(x)$ on a compact set $x \in X \subset \Re^n$ and arbitrary $\varepsilon > 0$, there exists a fuzzy logic system $f(x|\theta^*)$ in the form of Equation (12) such that

$$\max_{x \in X} |f(x) - f(x|\theta^*)| < \varepsilon \ , \ \forall x \tag{15}$$

Remark 3. *Proof of this theorem is available in (Wang, 1994).*

This work follows the classical work by Wang Wang (1993), Wang (1994) and some of related papers (e.g.: Fischle & Schroder (1999); Gazi & Passino (2000); Lee & Tomizuka (2000); Tong et al. (2000)). Most of these works involve fuzzy estimators in order to approximate nonlinear functions which appear in the model describing the plant. The fuzzy estimates are then used in the control law which may, for instance, be based on the exact feedback linearization techniques. However, it is shown by an example that the convergence of the estimates may not be achieved, even though the system exhibits good reference tracking properties. The new approach proposed in this work is thus aimed at obtaining convergence of the estimates of the nonlinear functions which are modelled by fuzzy structures.

Notice that the control law in Equation (7) can not be implemented because the functions $f(x)$ and $g(x)$ are unknown and must be estimated. The idea is to construct fuzzy structures to generate the estimates $f(x|\hat{\theta}_f)$ and $g(x|\hat{\theta}_g)$, where $\hat{\theta}_f$ and $\hat{\theta}_g$ are the respective vector of parameters.

In this work, Equation (1) uses the fuzzy structures of form

$$\begin{aligned} f(x|\hat{\theta}_f) &= \hat{\theta}_f^T W(x) \\ g(x|\hat{\theta}_g) &= \hat{\theta}_g^T W(x) \end{aligned} \tag{16}$$

where $W(x)$ is associated with the antecedent part of the rules (see 13). Moreover, the parameters $\hat{\theta}_f$ and $\hat{\theta}_g$ are (see 12) obtained using an adaptation scheme. Thus, the implementable version of the control law in Equation (7) becomes

$$u = \frac{1}{g(x|\hat{\theta}_g)} \left[-f(x|\hat{\theta}_f) + r - Kx \right] \qquad (17)$$

5. The proposed control structure

A control method is proposed here by introducing equations that are analogous to those of state observers but with $f(x)$ and $g(x)$ replaced by corresponding fuzzy approximations

$$\dot{x}_f = Ax_f + B\left(f(x|\hat{\theta}_f) + g(x|\hat{\theta}_g)u \right) + k^T C \left(x - x_f \right) \qquad (18)$$

where k is a gain vector of the form

$$k = [k_1, ..., k_n] \in R^n \qquad (19)$$

Remark 4. *From Equation (2), it can be noticed that the pair (A, C) is observable.*

5.1 Target Parameters

Fuzzy approximators possess universal approximation properties (see, for instance, (Wang, 1994; Ying, 1998; Ying et al., 1997)). Thus, given $\varepsilon_f, \varepsilon_g > 0$ there exist target parameters θ_f^* and θ_g^* such that

$$\begin{aligned} \left| f(x|\theta_f^*) - f(x) \right| &< \varepsilon_f \qquad \forall x \in X \\ \left| g(x|\theta_g^*) - g(x) \right| &< \varepsilon_g \qquad \forall x \in X \end{aligned} \qquad (20)$$

where X is the input universe of discourse and $\varepsilon_f, \varepsilon_g > 0$ are arbitrary positive constants. Hence, the real system (1) can be approximated by a model based on fuzzy structures up to the required precision by choosing ε_f and ε_g. Let the target fuzzy system be described by

$$\dot{x}_f^* = Ax_f^* + B\left(f(x|\theta_f^*) + g(x|\theta_g^*)u \right) + k^T C \left(x - x_f^* \right) \qquad (21)$$

If the parameters of the target model were available, then Equation (17) could be used to produce an approximating control law of the form

$$u = \frac{1}{g(x|\theta_g^*)} \left[-f(x|\theta_f^*) + r - Kx \right] \qquad (22)$$

In the present approach, θ_f^* and θ_g^* are replaced by estimates $\hat{\theta}_f$ and $\hat{\theta}_g$ obtained by an adaptive scheme. Later, it will be shown that, under appropriate conditions, $\hat{\theta}_f \to \theta_f^*$, $\hat{\theta}_g \to \theta_g^*$.

In order to establish, initially, the stability properties of the control based on the target model, consider $r = 0$ without loss of generality. Inserting Equation (22) into Equation (1) one obtains that

$$\dot{x} = Ax + B\left[f(x) - g(x)\frac{1}{g(x|\theta_g^*)} \left[f(x|\theta_f^*) + Kx \right] \right] \qquad (23)$$

which can be rewritten as

$$\dot{x} = (A - BK)x + \lambda\left(x, \theta_f^*, \theta_g^*\right) \tag{24}$$

where $\lambda\left(x, \theta_f^*, \theta_g^*\right)$ is given by

$$B\left[f(x) - g(x)\frac{1}{g(x|\theta_g^*)}\left[f(x|\theta_f^*) + Kx\right] + Kx\right] \tag{25}$$

Now, given a $\delta > 0$, it is possible to choose ε_f and ε_g in Equation (20) so that for fixed target values θ_f^* and θ_g^* one has

$$\left\|\lambda\left(x, \theta_f^*, \theta_g^*\right)\right\| < \delta \quad \forall x \in X \tag{26}$$

If θ_f^* and θ_g^* corresponded to the situation of exact matching, then $\lambda\left(0, \theta_f^*, \theta_g^*\right) = 0$ and $\lambda\left(x, \theta_f^*, \theta_g^*\right)$ would be a vanishing perturbation so that Lemma 5.1 in Chapter 5 of (Khalil, 2001) could be applied to estabilish exponential stability. In general, the universal approximation properties of fuzzy structures only guarantees Equation (20) with $\varepsilon_f, \varepsilon_g > 0$. Therefore, one requires Theorem 5.1 in Chapter 5 of (Khalil, 2001) which ensures that $x(t)$ does not escape a region

$$\|x(t)\| \leq \beta\left(x(t_0), t - t_0\right) \tag{27}$$

where $\beta\left(\cdot, \cdot\right)$ is a class of *KL* function.

5.2 Estimation errors

Define the estimation error vector by

$$e = x_f^* - x_f = \left[e_1 \, e_2 \, \cdots \, e_n\right]^T \tag{28}$$

Subtracting Equation (18) from Equation (21) one gets

$$\begin{aligned}\dot{e} = &\left(A - k^T C\right)e + \\ &+ B\left[f(x|\theta_f^*) - f(x|\hat{\theta}_f) + \left(g(x|\theta_g^*) - g(x|\hat{\theta}_g)\right)u\right]\end{aligned} \tag{29}$$

For the sake of simplicity, introduce the notation

$$\dot{e} = \Lambda e + \rho \tag{30}$$

where

$$\begin{aligned}\Lambda &= \left(A - k^T C\right) \\ \rho &= B\left[f(x|\theta_f^*) - f(x|\hat{\theta}_f) + \left(g(x|\theta_g^*) - g(x|\hat{\theta}_g)\right)u\right]\end{aligned} \tag{31}$$

Because Λ is a stable matrix, there exists an unique positive definite and symmetric matrix $P_{n\times n}$, which satisfies the Lyapunov equation

$$\Lambda^T P + P\Lambda = -Q \tag{32}$$

where $Q_{n\times n}$ is an arbitrary positive definite matrix.

5.3 Adaptation law and convergence analysis

The target estimates θ_f^* and θ_g^* are not known a priori. Therefore, adaptation laws must be provided in order to force $\hat{\theta}_f \to \theta_f^*$, $\hat{\theta}_g \to \theta_g^*$ and $e \to 0$.

Following (Wang, 1997), adopt as a candidate function in the sense of Lyapunov

$$V = \frac{1}{2}e^T Pe + \frac{1}{2\gamma_f}\phi_f^T\phi_f + \frac{1}{2\gamma_g}\phi_g^T\phi_g \tag{33}$$

where

$$\begin{aligned} \phi_f = \theta_f^* - \hat{\theta}_f \quad \text{and} \quad \dot{\phi}_f = -\dot{\hat{\theta}}_f \\ \phi_g = \theta_g^* - \hat{\theta}_g \quad \text{and} \quad \dot{\phi}_g = -\dot{\hat{\theta}}_g \end{aligned} \tag{34}$$

and γ_f, γ_g are positive constants.

The time-derivative is of the form

$$\dot{V} = \frac{1}{2}\left(\dot{e}^T Pe + e^T P\dot{e}\right) - \frac{1}{\gamma_f}\phi_f^T\dot{\hat{\theta}}_f - \frac{1}{\gamma_g}\phi_g^T\dot{\hat{\theta}}_g \tag{35}$$

and an interesting choice for the adaptation laws are

$$\begin{aligned} \dot{\hat{\theta}}_f &= -\gamma_f\, e^T PBW(x) \\ \dot{\hat{\theta}}_g &= -\gamma_g\, e^T PBW(x)u \end{aligned} \tag{36}$$

In fact, using the adaptation laws 36 each term of Equation (35) can be rewritten as

$$\begin{cases} \frac{1}{2}\left(\dot{e}^T Pe + e^T P\dot{e}\right) = -\frac{1}{2}e^T Qe + e^T P\rho \\ \frac{1}{\gamma_f}\phi_f^T\dot{\hat{\theta}}_f = e^T PB\left(f(x|\theta_f^*) - f(x|\hat{\theta}_f)\right) \\ \frac{1}{\gamma_g}\phi_g^T\dot{\hat{\theta}}_g = e^T PB\left(g(x|\theta_g^*) - g(x|\hat{\theta}_g)\right)u \end{cases} \tag{37}$$

and Equation (35) becomes

$$\dot{V} = -\frac{1}{2}e^T Qe \tag{38}$$

which is negative semi-definite.

Conclusion 5. *A semi-negative definition of Equation (38) guarantees that the error e is bounded. The application of the Barbalat's Lemma yields that $e \to 0$ when $t \to \infty$. From Equation (28), $e \to 0$ implies that $x_f \to x_f^*$ and the convergence of the parameter estimates to their respective target values is obtained.*

6. Simulation results

Considering that a magnetic levitation system is available at the Control Lab of CTAI, it may represent future opportunities for continued researches with hands on experimentation. Hence it is selected as the system which will be used here as an example to illustrate the method. The scheme is presented in Figure (3) and the aim in this problem is to suspend an

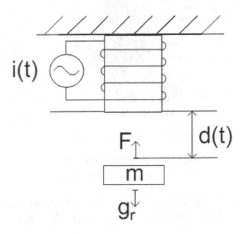

Fig. 3. Magnetic levitation system

iron mass by adjusting the current in a coil. It is nonlinear and open-loop unstable. Also note that the magnetic field is not uniform and the attraction force is nonlinear.

A model for this system is

$$\ddot{d} = g_r - \frac{F}{m} \tag{39}$$

where m is the mass of the disc, g_r is the gravitational acceleration and F is the electromagnet force produced by a coil fed with current i

$$F = c\frac{i^2}{d^2} \tag{40}$$

with c a positive constant, and d the position of the disc.

Denoting by $x_1 = d$ and $x_2 = \dot{d}$ the components of the state vector and combining Equations (39) and (40) one may write

$$\begin{cases} \dot{x}_1 = x_2 \\ \dot{x}_2 = g_r - c\frac{i^2}{m.x_1^2} \end{cases} \tag{41}$$

Hence, comparison with Equation (1) yields the following association

$$\begin{aligned} f(x) &= g_r \\ g(x) &= -c\frac{1}{m.x_1^2} \\ u &= i^2 \end{aligned} \tag{42}$$

For simulation results, this work adopted the following values for the model parameters

$$\begin{aligned} c &= 0.15 \left[Nm/A^2\right] \\ m &= 0.12 \left[kg\right] \\ g_r &= 9.81 \left[m/s^2\right] \end{aligned} \tag{43}$$

The free parameters are chosen as follows:

$$K = \begin{bmatrix} 1 & 1 \end{bmatrix}$$
$$k = \begin{bmatrix} 50 & 100 \end{bmatrix} \tag{44}$$
$$\gamma_g = 10^4$$

For the initial condition of the nonlinear system let $d(0) = x_1(0) = 1.2$ and $x_2(0) = 0$. The initial conditions for the fuzzy estimates are zero.

Choosing Q as the identity matrix, Equation (32) leads to

$$P = \begin{bmatrix} 1.2550 & 0.0100 \\ 0.0100 & 0.0051 \end{bmatrix} \tag{45}$$

From practical inspection of the actual experimental setup, let the range of $d(t)$ be $Rx_1 = [0.6, 3.4]$, which represents the fuzzy input universe of discourse. Also define

$$g^L(x) = -\frac{c}{m \left[\max(Rx_1) \right]^2} \tag{46}$$

as the lower bound of $|g(x|\hat{\theta}_g)|$, which also guarantees that $|g(x|\hat{\theta}_g)| \neq 0$.

Choosing the vector Xc of the centers of the membership functions as given by

$$Xc = \begin{bmatrix} 0.6 & 0.8 & 1.0 & 1.2 & 1.4 & 1.8 & 2.2 & 2.6 & 3.0 & 3.4 \end{bmatrix}^T \tag{47}$$

one gets membership functions for the sets A^j as shown in Figure (4).

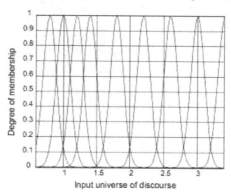

Fig. 4. Membership functions

Remark 6. *This fuzzy input universe of discourse is desired in this application since the magnetic force increases with second power of d (situation that may put in risk the controller in experimental tests).*

For each $t \in \Re$ and fuzzy set A^j, define a single rule of the form

$$\text{IF } d(t) \text{ is } A^j \text{ THEN } y \text{ is } y_j \qquad j = 1 \ldots R \tag{48}$$

where $R = \text{length}(Xc)$.

In order to compute the target values of θ_g^*, not available in practical situation, but useful in simulation purposes to evaluate the method, note that rules can be generated simply by computing the real value of the function $g(x|\hat{\theta}_g)$ as

$$y_j = -\frac{c}{m(Xc_j)^2}, \quad j = 1 \dots R \tag{49}$$

As for the actual initialization of the vector $\hat{\theta}_g$ one can use randomly generated values such as

$$
\theta_g^* = \begin{bmatrix} -55.5556 \\ -31.2500 \\ -20.0000 \\ -13.8889 \\ -10.2041 \\ -6.1728 \\ -4.1322 \\ -2.9586 \\ -2.2222 \\ -1.7301 \end{bmatrix}, \quad
\theta_g = \begin{bmatrix} 9.7945 \\ -2.6561 \\ -5.4837 \\ -0.9627 \\ -13.8067 \\ -7.2837 \\ 18.8600 \\ -29.4139 \\ 9.8002 \\ -11.9175 \end{bmatrix} \tag{50}
$$

Remark 7. *The randomized initialization of θ_g must satisfy the constraint $|g^L(x)| \leq |g(x|\hat{\theta}_g)|$ and the sign of $g(x|\hat{\theta}_g)$ must be equal to the sign of $g(x)$.*

Let the reference signal $r(t)$ be a square wave in the range 1.2 to 2.8 . Figures from (5) to (8) present the obtained simulation results. The nominal case corresponds to the situation with real $f(x)$ and $g(x)$.

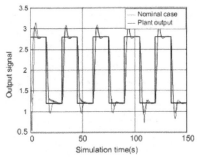

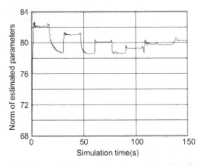

(a) Plant output compared with the case optimal parameters.

(b) Norm of the parameter vector (in the estimator blocks).

Fig. 5. Simulation Results

It could be observed in Figure (5(a)) that the reference signal $r(t)$ was tracked by the plant output. The magnetic disc position (process variable) could be observed in Figure (5(a)) with some oscillations but bounded and stable in steady state. The adaptive scheme used here provides the real convergence of the estimates $f(x|\hat{\theta}_f)$ and $g(x|\hat{\theta}_g)$ to their optimal values $f(x|\theta_f^*)$ and $g(x|\theta_g^*)$ while keeping the estimation errors with respect to a reference signal within a compact set (according to Figures (8(a)) and (8(b))). The control effort u associated with the electrical current is bounded as shown in Figure (6(a)).

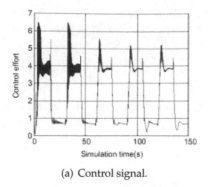

(a) Control signal.

(b) Function estimates of the nonlinear function $g(x)$ in the model.

Fig. 6. Simulation Results

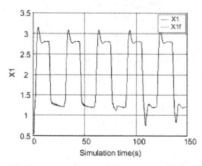

(a) Component x_1 of the state and fuzzy state estimation (X1f).

(b) Component x_2 of the state and fuzzy state estimation (X2f).

Fig. 7. Simulation Results

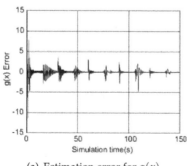

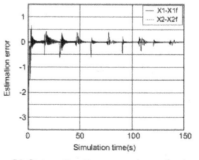

(a) Estimation error for $g(x)$.

(b) State estimation errors (x_1 and x_2)

Fig. 8. Simulation Results

It is worth noticing in Figures (6(b)), (7(a)) and (7(b)) that the function estimates converge to their real values and, in turn, they force the system to reproduce the nominal case as proposed in Equation (4) where the knowledge of $f(x)$ and $g(x)$ are considered.

7. Experimental tests

7.1 Magnetic levitation

The magnetic levitation test bed supplied by ECP Model 730 (see (ECP, 1999)) which is used for these experiment tests is shown in Figure (9).

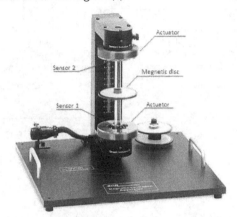

Fig. 9. Practical setup of magnetic levitation system ECP Model 730 ECP (1999)

The plant shown in Figure (10), consists of upper and lower coils that produce a magnetic field in response to a DC current. One or two magnets travel along a precision ground glass guide rod. By energizing the lower coil, a single magnet is levitated through a repulsive magnetic force. As the current in the coil increases, the field strength increases and the levitated magnet height is increased. For the upper coil, the levitating force is attractive. Two magnets may be controlled simultaneously by stacking them on the glass rod. The magnets are of an ultra-high field strength rare earth (NeBFe) type and are designed to provide large levitated displacements to clearly demonstrate the principle of levitation and motion control. Two laser-based sensors measure the magnet positions. The lower sensor is typically used to measure a given position of the magnet in proximity to the lower coil, and the upper one for proximity to the upper coil. This proprietary ECP sensor design utilizes light amplitude measurement and includes special circuitry to desensitize the signal to stray ambient light and thermal fluctuations.

The Magnetic Levitation setup apparatus dramatically demonstrates closed loop levitation of permanent and ferro-magnetic elements. The apparatus includes laser feedback and high flux magnetics to affect large displacements and provide visually stimulating tracking and regulation demonstrations. The system is quickly set up in the open loop stable and unstable (repulsive and attractive fields) configurations as shown in Figures (9) and (10). By adding a second magnet, two SIMO plants may be created, and by driving both actuators with both magnets, MIMO control is studied. The field interaction between the two magnets causes strong cross coupling and thus produces a true multi-variable system. The inherent magnetic field nonlinearities may be inverted via provided real-time algorithms for linear control implementation or the full system dynamics may be studied.

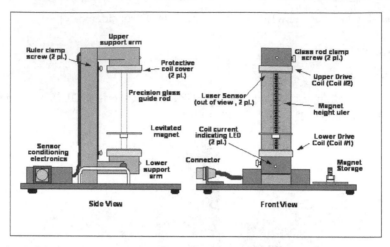

Fig. 10. Side and front view of magnetic levitation system ECP (1999)

The complete experimental setup is comprised of the three subsystems as shown in Figure (11) (from right to left):

Fig. 11. Block diagram of experimental control system

1. The first subsystem is the Magnetic Levitation system itself (described above) which consists of the electromagnetic coils, magnets, high resolution encoders.

2. The next subsystem is the real-time controller unit that contains the Digital Signal Processor (DSP) based real-time controller, servo/actuator interfaces, servo amplifiers, and auxiliary power supplies. The DSP is capable of executing control laws at high sampling rates allowing the implementation to be modeled as continuous or discrete time systems. The controller also interprets trajectory commands and supports such functions as data acquisition, trajectory generation, and system health and safety checks.

3. The third subsystem is the executive program which runs on a PC under the Windows operating system. This menu-driven program is the user's interface to the system and supports controller specification, trajectory definition, data acquisition, plotting, system execution commands, and more. Controllers may assume a broad range of selectable block diagram topologies and dynamic order. The interface supports an assortment of features which provide a friendly yet powerful experimental environment. Real-time implementation of the controllers is also possible using the Real Time Windows Target (RTWT).

7.2 Experimental method

Following some related works with using the ECP Model 730 (Nataraj & Mukesh, 2008; 2010), the steps followed to carry out the experiment are as follows:

1. Linearization of the sensor (see (ECP, 1999, p. 81)) with the following values:

$$e = 115720000;$$
$$f = 7208826;$$
$$g = 30540;$$
$$h = 0.2411.$$

(51)

2. Nonlinear compensation of the actuator (see (ECP, 1999, p. 81)) with the following values:

$$a = 1.0510^{-4};$$
$$b = 6.2.$$

(52)

3. Construct the design control system in Simulink environment as shown in Figure (12) along with reference command signal. Figure (13) shows the inside view of "Adaptive Fuzzy Controller" block;

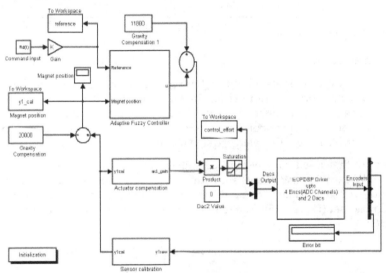

Fig. 12. The simulation block diagram used for RTWT

4. Build and execute the real time model using Real Time Windows Target(RTWT), to convert the control algorithm in C++ code. Download this code onto the DSP via RTWT;

5. Start the real-time implementation from within RTWT environment for desired length of time;

6. After the experiment is over, make the appropriate conversions and plot the data.

For experimental tests, this work adopted the following values for the plant parameters (see (ECP, 1999)):

$$c = 0.15 \left[Nm/A^2 \right]$$
$$m = 0.12 \left[kg \right]$$
$$g_r = 9.81 \left[m/s^2 \right]$$

(53)

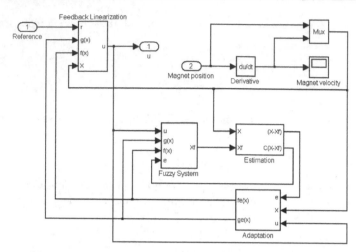

Fig. 13. Adaptive fuzzy controller

7.3 Experimental results

The adaptive fuzzy control system proposed in Section 5 is now implemented real time and experimentally tested for its performance. Initially, the magnet is brought to equilibrium position of $2cm$ as plant is linearized to $2cm$. The upper coil (attractive force) was used with one magnet. Therefore, an open-loop unstable SISO system was implemented and tested with the designed controller. Now the reference signal is applied.

The response of the closed loop system for a given reference command signal is shown in Figure (14). The experimental results show that a reference input signal was tracked by the controller output signal while keeping the tracking error with respect to a reference signal within a compact set (Figure (15). The required control effort is low, with a peak of 6.5 volts (see Figure (16)).

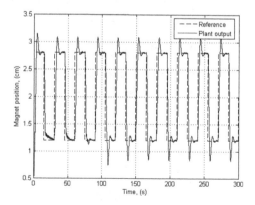

Fig. 14. Step response of closed loop system

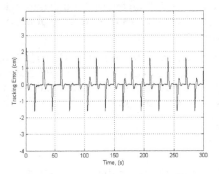

Fig. 15. Tracking Error

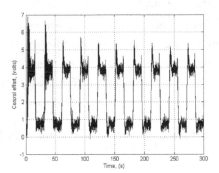

Fig. 16. Control effort required to levitate the magnet

8. Conclusions

The adaptive control scheme presented in this work considers the difference between the nonlinear system and an associated dynamic system using fuzzy estimates. The model of the associated dynamics is analogous to that of state observers but using fuzzy structures to estimate the nonlinear functions. If optimal parameters are considered, then the stability may be investigated using a classical method of perturbed system. Thus, since adequate fuzzy structures are used stability is assured when optimal parameters are considered. A Lyapunov function is then used in order to show the convergence of the estimates to their respective optimal values. Hence, when the fuzzy structures are carefully chosen, the estimates approach optimal values which may be arbitrarily close to the true values.

In some previous work, successful results have been attributed to nonlinear approximators such as fuzzy or neural blocks. However, the proof of the estimates convergence had not been presented. Moreover, the adaptation law does not force the convergence of the estimates. In these previous results, the robustness of the tracking error is reached as a consequence of the application of the tracking control theory. It keeps the error in a compact set without requiring the convergence of the estimates to their real values. It is important to mention that the real convergence of the estimates represents the most significant contribution of this work. The error analysis is analogous to the previous work, but a new scheme for the adaptive fuzzy control was proposed. Differently from previous research, the adaptation laws force the convergence of the function estimates. Moreover, although the tracking error is not considered to be of primary concern, it is obtained as a consequence of the proposed control law when the convergence of the estimates is attained.

The proposed adaptive controller is tested on ECP Model 730 Magnetic Levitation setup through Real Time Windows Target (RTWT). It has been successfully applied to experimental Magnetic Levitation setup and desired reference tracking properties are also achieved. Therefore, the experimental tests show the reliability and robustness of the proposed algorithm.

9. Future contributions

One of the most important contributions of this work is a new approach for designing of adaptive control techniques based on intelligent estimators which may be either fuzzy or neural. The continuation of this research may lead to:

a. The analysis of the proposed method in other nonlinear systems;

b. The application of the proposed method with artificial neural networks as estimators;

c. The generalization of the obtained results for a larger class of nonlinear systems;

d. Analysis of the proposed method in other practical applications.

10. Acknowledgement

The authors wish to acknowledge the support with facilities and infrastructure from CTAI at Universidade Federal da Bahia and CAPES for the financial support.

11. References

Cavalcante, M. D., Costa, A. C. P. L. d. & Schnitman, L. (2008). An intelligent adaptive controller, *Proceedings of 5th Latin American Robotics Symposium*.

ECP (1999). *Educational Control Products - Manual for Model 730*, California, USA.

Fischle, K. & Schroder, D. (1999). An improved stable adaptive fuzzy control method, *IEEE Trans. on Fuzzy Systems* 7: 27–40.

Gazi, V. & Passino, K. M. (2000). Direct adaptive control using dynamic structure fuzzy systems, *Proceedings of American Control Conference*, Vol. 3, pp. 1954–1958.

Ghaebi, P. P., Ataei, M. & Shafiei, A. (2011). An adaptive fuzzy sliding mode control of a permanent magnet linear synchronous motor for an inimical command velocity profile, *Proceedings of IEEE International Conference on System Engineering and Technology, ICSET*, pp. 41–46.

Han, H. (2005). Adaptive fuzzy controller for a class of nonlinear systems, *International Journal of Innovative Computing, Information and Control* 1(2): 727–742.

Isidori, A. (1995). *Nonlinear Control Systems*, 3rd edn, Springerl. ISBN-13: 978-1852331887.

Islam, S. & Liu, P. X. (2011). Robust adaptive fuzzy output feedback control system for robot manipulators, *IEEE/ASME Transactions on Mechatronics* 16(2): 288–296.

Jang, J.-S. R., Sun, C.-T. & Mizutani, E. (1997). Neuro-fuzzy and soft computing, âĂć, Prentice Hall.

Kaloust, J., Ham, C., Siehling, J., Jongekryg, E. & Han, Q. (2004). Nonlinear robust control design for levitation and propulsion of a maglev system, *IEE Proc.-Control Theory Appl.* 151(4). doi: 10.1049/ip-cta:20040547.

Khalil, H. K. (2001). *Nonlinear Systems*, 3rd edn, Prentice Hall.

Lee, H. & Tomizuka, T. (2000). Robust adaptive control using a universal approximator for siso nonlinear systems, *IEEE Trans. on Fuzzy Systems* 8: 95âĂŞ106.

Lin, C.-T. & Lee, C. S. G. (1995). *Neural Fuzzy Systems: A Neuro-Fuzzy Synergism to Intelligent Systems*, Prentice Hall.

Nataraj, P. S. V. & Mukesh, D. P. (2008). Robust control design for nonlinear magnetic levitation system using quantitative feedback theory (qft), *Proceedings of Annual IEEE India Conference, INDICON 2008*, Bombay, India, pp. 365–370.   d.o.i: 10.1109/INDCON.2008.4768751.

Nataraj, P. S. V. & Mukesh, D. P. (2010). Nonlinear control of a magnetic levitation system using quantitative feedback theory (qft), *Proceedings of 2nd International Conference on Reliability, Safety and Hazard - ICRESH-2010*, Mumbai, India, pp. 542–547. d.o.i: 10.1109/ICRESH.2010.5779608.

Nauck, D., Klawonn, F. & Kruse, R. (1997). *Foundations of Neuro-Fuzzy Systems*, John Wiley.

Nauck, D., Klawonn, F. & Kruse, R. (2009). *Modern Control Engineering*, 5th edn, Prentice Hall. ISBN-13: 978-0136156734.

Pan, Y., Huang, D. & Sun, Z. (2009). Indirect adaptive fuzzy control with approximation error estimator for nonlinear systems, *Proceedings of 2nd International Conference on Intelligent Computing Technology and Automation, ICICTA 2009*, pp. 748–751.

Predrycz, W. & Gomide, F. A. C. (1999). *An Introduction to Fuzzy Sets Analysis and Design*, MIT Press.

Schnitman, L. (2001). *Intelligente controller for dynamic sustems with state and input constraints and subjected to model uncertainties*, PhD thesis, ITA - Instituto Tecnológico da Aeronáutica.

Slotine, J.-J. E. & Li, W. (1991). *Applied Nonlinear Control*, Prentice Hall.

Sontag, E. D. (1998). *Mathematical Control Theory: Deterministic Finite Dimensional Systems*, 2nd edn, Springer. ISBN 0-387-984895.

Sugeno, M. & Kang, G. (1988). Structure identification of fuzzy model, *Fuzzy Sets and Systems* 28: 15–33.

Takagi, T. & Sugeno, M. (1985). Fuzzy identification on systems and its applications to modeling and control, *IEEE Trans. on Systems, Man, and Cybern.* 15(2): 116–132.

Toha, S. F. & Tokhi, M. O. (2009). Dynamic nonlinear inverse-model based control of a twin rotor system using adaptive neuro-fuzzy inference system, *Proceedings of EMS 2009 UKSim 3rd European Modelling Symposium on Computer Modelling and Simulation*, pp. 107–111.

Tong, S., Liu, C. & Li, Y. (2011). Adaptive fuzzy backstepping output feedback control for strict feedback nonlinear systems with unknown sign of high-frequency gain, *Neurocomputing*. ISSN: 09252312.

Tong, S., Wang, T. & Tang, J. T. (2000). Fuzzy adaptive output tracking control of nonlinear systems, *Fuzzy Sets and Systems* 15(3): 674–692. doi: 10.1109/TNN.2004.826130.

Torres, L. H. S., Vasconcelos Júnior, C. A. V., Schnitman, L. & Felippe de Souza, J. A. M. (2010). Feedback linearization and model reference adaptive control of a magnetic levitation system, *Proceedings of Latin American Control Conference, LACC 2010*.

Tsoukalas, L. H. & Uhrig, R. E. (1997). *Fuzzy and Neural Approaches in Engineering*, John Wiley.

Wang, L.-X. (1993). Stable adaptive fuzzy control of nonlinear systems, *IEEE Trans. on Fuzzy Systems* 1(2): 146–155.

Wang, L.-X. (1994). *Adaptive Fuzzy Systems and Control*, Prentice Hall.

Wang, L.-X. (1997). *A Course in Fuzzy Systems and Control*, Prentice Hall.

Yang, Z. J. & M., T. (2001). Adaptive robust nonlinear control of a magnetic levitation system, *Automatica* (37): 1125–1131.

Ying, H. (1998). General SISO takagi-sugeno fuzzy systems with linear rule consequent are universal approximators, *Proceedings of IEEE Int. Conf. on Systems, Man and Cybern*, pp. 582–587.

Ying, H., Ding, Y. & Shao, S. (1997). Necessary conditions for general MISO fuzzy systems as universal approximators, *Proceedings of IEEE Int. Conf. on Systems, Man and Cybern*.

Yoneyama, T. & Júnior, C. L. N. (2000). *Inteligência Artificial Em Automação e Controle*, Edgard Blucher.

Zadeh, L. A. (1965). Fuzzy sets, *Information and Control* 8: 338–353.

19

Survey on Design of Truss Structures by Using Fuzzy Optimization Methods

Aykut Kentli
Marmara University Engineering Faculty,
Mechanical Engineering Department,
Turkey

1. Introduction

This study aims to reveal the studies on design optimization of trusses using fuzzy logic. In literature there are many surveys on truss optimization or on fuzzy logic, but, none of them is focused on fuzzy design optimization of truss. We believe that this study will help the researcher willing to study on this area by drawing a framework of the studies and by showing the lack of the area.

Firstly, a brief information fuzzy logic and optimization will be given. Then, studies will be classified under the topics related with the type of optimization problem and used method. In each topic, application area of fuzzy logic and main difference of the study will be explained. Classifications will also be shown as tables to show the overall picture. Lack of the area will be given in conclusion.

2. Fuzzy logic

Fuzzy sets are generalized sets introduced by Professor Zadeh as a mathematical way to represent and deal with vagueness in everyday life (Zadeh, 1965). Indeed, Zadeh informally states what he calls the principle of incompatibility: "As the complexity of a system increases, our ability to make precise and yet significant statements about its behavior diminishes until a threshold is reached beyond which precision and significance (or relevance) become almost mutually exclusive characteristics".

Fuzzy logic is a superset of conventional (Boolean) logic that has been extended to handle the concept of partial truth – the truth values between "completely true" and "completely false". A type of logic that recognizes more than simple true and false values. With fuzzy logic, propositions can be represented with degrees of the truthfulness and falsehood. For example, the statement, today is sunny, might be 100% true if there are no clouds, 80% true if there are a few clouds, 50% true if it's hazy and 0% true if it rains all day.

Even though fuzzy sets were introduced in their modern form by Zadeh (1965), the idea of a multi-valued logic in order to deal with vagueness has been around from the beginning of the century. Peirce was one of the first thinkers to seriously consider vagueness; he did not believe in the separation between true and false and believed everything in life is a continuum. In 1905 he stated: "I have worked out the logic vagueness with something like completeness" (Peirce, 1935). Other famous scientists and philosophers probed this topic further. Russell (1923) claimed, "All language is vague" and went further saying; "vagueness is a matter of degree" (e.g., a blurred photo is vaguer than a crisp one, etc.). Einstein said that "as far as the laws of mathematics refer to reality, they are not certain, and as far as they are certain, they do not refer to reality" (Black, 1937). Lukasiewicz took the first step towards a formal model of vagueness, introducing in 1920 a three-valued logic based on true, false, and possible (Lukasiewicz, 1970). In doing this he realized that the laws of the classical two-valued logic might be misleading because they address only a fragment of the domain. A year later Post outlined his own three-valued logic, and soon after many other multi-valued logics proliferated (Godel, von Neumann, Kleene etc.) (McNeill & Freiberger, 1993). A few years later, Black (1937) outlined his precursor of fuzzy sets. He agreed with Peirce in terms of the continuum of vagueness and with Russell in terms of the degrees of vagueness. Therefore, he outlined a logic based on degrees of usage, based on probability that a certain object will be considered belonging to a certain class. Finally, Zadeh (1965) elaborated a multi-valued logic where degrees of truth (rather than usage) are possible.

Fuzzy set theory generalizes classical set theory in that the membership degree of an object to a set is not restricted to the integers 0 and 1, but may take on any value in [0,1]. By elaborating on the notion of fuzzy sets and fuzzy relations we can define fuzzy logic systems (FLS). FLSs are rule-based systems in which an input is first fuzzified (i.e. converted from a crisp number to a fuzzy set) and subsequently processed by an influence engine that retrieves knowledge in the form of fuzzy rules contained in a rule-base. The fuzzy sets computed by the fuzzy inference as the output of each rule are then composed and defuzzified (i.e., converted from a fuzzy set to a crisp number). A fuzzy logic system is a nonlinear mapping from the input to the output space.

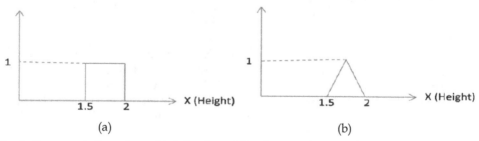

(a)   (b)

Fig. 1. Representation of set of heights from 1.5 to 2 meter for crisp (a) and fuzzy (b)

As Figure 1 shows, crisp set is defined by membership of element X of set A . Fuzzy set contain objects that satisfy imprecise properties of membership .

3. Optimization problem types

An optimization or a mathematical programming problem can be stated as follows:

$$\text{Find which minimizes } f(X) \tag{1}$$

Subject to the constraints:

$$g_j(X) \leq 0, j=1,2,\ldots,m \quad \text{and} \quad l_j(X)=0, j=1,2,\ldots,p \qquad (2)$$

where X is an n-dimensional vector called the design vector, $f(X)$ is called the objective function and $g_j(X)$ and $l_j(X)$ are, respectively, the inequality and the equality constraints. The number of variables n and the number of constraints m and/or p need not be related in any way.

Design vector. Any engineering system or component is described by a set of quantities some of which are viewed as variables during the design process. In general certain quantities are usually fixed at the outset and these are called preassigned parameters. All the other quantities are treated as variables in the design process and are called design or decision variables x_i, $i=1,2,\ldots,n$.

Design constraints. In many practical problems, the design variables cannot be chosen arbitrarily; rather they have to satisfy certain specified functional and other requirements. The restrictions that must be satisfied in order to produce an acceptable design are collectively called design constraints.

Objective functions. The conventional design procedure aim at finding an acceptable or adequate design, which merely satisfies the functional and other requirements of the problem. In general, there will be more than one acceptable designs and the purpose of optimization is to choose the best one out of the many acceptable design available. Thus a criterion has to be chosen for comparing the different alternate acceptable designs and for selecting the best one. The criterion with respect to which design is optimized, when expressed as a function of the design variables is known as criterion or merit or objective function.

Optimization problems can be classified in several ways as described below. This classification is extremely useful from the computational point of view since there are many methods developed solely for the efficient solution of a particular class of problems. This will, in many cases, dictate the types of solution procedures to be adopted in solving the problem.

3.1 Classification based on the existence of constraints

As indicated earlier, any optimization problem can be classified as a constrained or an unconstrained one depending upon whether the constraints exist or not in the problem. Previously defined problem is called a constrained optimization problem. Used methods will differ according to problem type and at each following topic, appropriate methods will be given. Some optimization problems do not involve any constraints and can be stated as:

$$\text{Find which minimizes } f(X) \qquad (3)$$

Such problems are called unconstrained optimization problems. Mostly known methods are Hooke-Jeeves Pattern Search Method and Powell's Conjugate Gradient Method. Some methods (Penalty Function etc.) transform the constrained problem into unconstrained problem and then use mentioned methods (Rao, 1984).

3.2 Classification based on the nature of equations involved

Another important classification of optimization problems is based on the nature of expressions for the objective function and the constraints. According to this classification, optimization problems can be classified as linear, nonlinear and dynamic programming problems.

Nonlinear Programming Problem: If any functions among objective and constraints functions are nonlinear, the problem is called a nonlinear programming (NLP) problem. This is the most general programming problem and all other problems can be considered as special cases of the NLP problem. There are several type methods. Complex method is using only the function value to find optimum. On the other hand, feasible direction algorithm uses the derivative of the objective and constraints.

Linear Programming Problem: If the objective function and all the constraints are linear functions of the design variables, the mathematical programming problem is called a linear programming (LP) problem. A linear programming problem is often stated in the following standard form:

$$\text{Find which minimizes} \tag{4}$$

$$\text{subject to the constraints} \qquad , j=1,2,\ldots,m \tag{5}$$

and $\qquad x_i \geq 0, i=1,2,\ldots,n$ where c, a_{jk} and b_j are constants.

Although allocating resources to activities is the most common type of application, linear programming has numerous other important applications as well. Furthermore, a remarkably efficient solution procedure called the Simplex method, is available for solving linear programming problems of even enormous size.

The Simplex method is a general procedure for solving linear programming problems and developed by George Dantzig in 1947 (Dantzig, 1963). It has proved to be a remarkably efficient method that is used routinely to solve huge problems on today's computers.

Dynamic Programming: In most practical problems, decisions have to be made sequentially at different points in time, at different points in space, and at different levels, say, for a component, for a subsystem, and/or for a system. The problems in which the decisions are to be made sequentially are called sequential decision problems. Since these decisions are to be made at a number of stages, they are also referred to as multistage decision problems. Dynamic programming is a mathematical technique well suited for the optimization of multistage decision problems. This technique was developed by Richard Bellman in the early 1950s.

3.3 Classification based on the permissible values of the design variables

Depending on the values permitted for the design variables, optimization problem is called a real-valued programming problem.

Integer Programming Problem: If some or all of the design variables $x_1, x_2, \ldots x_n$ of an optimization problem are restricted to take on only integer (or discrete) values, the problem is called an integer programming problem. Branch-and-Bound methods are widely used in this area. Local Search methods (GA etc.) are also used for this problem type. Moreover, there are hybrid applications like GA+ANN. The genetic algorithm (GA) is an optimization and search technique based on the principles of genetics and natural selection. The method was developed by John Holland over the course of the 1960s and 1970s and finally popularized by one of his students, David Goldberg, who was able to solve a difficult problem involving the control of gas-pipeline transmission for his dissertation. Holland's original work was summarized in his book (Holland, 1995).

3.4 Classification based on the number of objective functions

Depending on the number of objective functions to be minimized, optimization problem can be classified as single and multi-objective programming problem.

Multiobjective Programming Problem: Multiobjective optimization in last two decades has been acknowledged as an advanced design technique in structural optimization (Eschenawer et.al., 1990). The reason is that most of the real-world problems are multidisciplinary and complex, as there is always more than one important objective in each problem. To accommodate many conflicting design goals, one needs to formulate the optimization problem with multiple objectives. One important reason for the success of the multiobjective optimization approach is its natural property of allowing the designer to participate in the design selection process even after the formulation of the mathematical optimization model. The main task in structural optimization is determining the choice of the design variables, objectives, and constraints. Sometimes only one dominating criterion may be a sufficient objective for minimization, especially if the other requirements can be presented by equality and inequality constraints. But generally the choice of the constraint limits may be a difficult task in a practical design problem. These allowable values can be rather fuzzy, even for common quantities such as displacements, stresses, and natural frequencies. If the limit cannot be determined, it seems reasonable to treat that quantity as an objective. In addition, usually several competing objectives appear in a real-life application, and thus the designer is faced with a decision-making problem in which the task is to find the best compromise solution between the conflicting requirements.

A multiobjective optimization problem can be formulated as follow:

$$\text{Min } [f1(x), f2(x),..., fn(x)] \qquad (6)$$

subject to

$$gj(x) \geq 0j = 1,2,...,m \qquad (7)$$

$$hj(x) = 0j = 1,2,...,p< n \qquad (8)$$

where x is n-dimensional design variable vector, fi(x) is objective function.

A variety of techniques and applications of multiobjective optimization have been developed over the past few years. The progress in the field of multicriteria optimization was summarized by Hwang and Masud (1979) and later by Stadler (1984). Stadler inferred from his survey that if one has decided that an optimal design is to be based on the consideration of several criteria, then the multicriteria theory (Pareto theory) provides the necessary framework. In addition, if the minimization or maximization is the objective for each criterion, then an optimal solution should be a member of the corresponding Pareto set. Only then does any further improvement in one criterion require a clear tradeoff with at least one other criterion. Radfors, et al (1985) in their study has explored the role of Pareto optimization in computer-aided design. They used the weighting method, noninferior set estimation (NISE) method, and constraint method for generating the Pareto optimal. The authors discussed the control and derivation of meaning from the Pareto sets.

Pareto optimality serves as the basic multicriteria optimization concept in virtually all of the previous literature (Grandhi & Bharatram, 1993). A general multiobjective optimization problem is to find the vector of design variables $X = (x_1, x_2, ..., x_n)T$ that minimize a vector objective function $F(X)$ over the feasible design space X. It is the determination of a set of nondominated solutions (Pareto optimum solutions or noninferior solutions) that achieves a compromise among several different, usually conflicting, objective functions. The Pareto optimal is stated in simple words as follows: A vector X^* is Pareto optimal if there exists no feasible vector X which would increase some objective function without causing a simultaneous decrease in at least one objective function. This definition can be explained graphically. An arbitrary collection of feasible solutions for a two-objective maximization problem is shown in Figure 2. The area inside of the shape and its boundaries are feasible. The axes of this graph are the objectives F1 and F2. It can be seen from the graph that the noninferior solutions are found in the portion of the boundary between points A and B. Thus, here arises the decision-making problem from which a partial or complete ordering of the set of nondominated objectives is accomplished by considering the preferences of the decision maker. Most of the multiobjective optimization techniques are based on how to elicit the preferences and determine the best compromise solution.

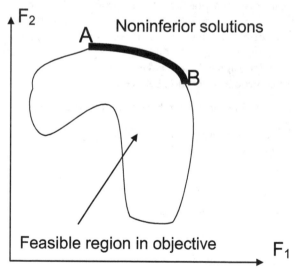

Fig. 2. Graphical Interpretation of Pareto Optimum

Nearly all of the solution schemes used in multiobjective optimization involve some sort of scalarization of the vector optimization problem. The vector problem is replaced by some equivalent scalar minimization problem. Because the Pareto set is generally infinite, an additional use of scalarization is the selection of a unique member of the Pareto set as the optimum for the vector optimization problem. Usually, a problem is scalarized either by defining an additional supercriterion function or by considering the criteria sequentially. There are various techniques for generating noninferior solutions (Stadler, 1984;Radford et.al., 1985; Grandhi & Bharatram, 1993),

Weighting Method: This technique is based on the preference techniques of the weights' prior assessment for each objective function. It transforms the multicriteria function to a single criterion function through a parameterization of the relative weighting of the criteria. With the variation of the weights, the entire Pareto set can be generated. Because the results of solving an optimization problem can vary significantly as the weighting coefficients change, and very little is usually known about how to choose these coefficients, a necessary approach is to solve the same problem for many different values of weighting factors. However, because the shape and distribution characteristics of the Pareto set are unknown, it is difficult to determine beforehand the nature of the variations required in the weights so as to produce a new solution at each pass. The second important disadvantage of the method is that it will not identify the Pareto solutions in a nonconvex part of the set.

The idea of this technique consists in adding all the objective functions together using different coefficients for each. It means that we change our multicriteria optimization problem to a scalar optimization problem by creating one function of the form

$$f(x) = \sum_{i=1}^{k} w_i f_i(x) \tag{9}$$

where $w_i \geq 0$ are the weighting coefficients representing the relative importance of the criteria. It is usually assumed that

$$\sum_{i=1}^{k} w_i = 1 \tag{10}$$

Since the results of solving an optimization model using Eq. (9) can vary significantly as the weighting coefficients change and since very little is usually known about how to choose these coefficients, a necessary approach is to solve the same problem for many different values of w_i.

Note that the weighting coefficients do not reflect proportionally the relative importance of the objectives but are only factors which when varied locate points in the domain. For the numerical methods of seeking the minimum of Eq. (10) this location depends not only on values of w_i but also on units in which the functions are expressed.

The best results are usually obtained if objective functions are normalized. In this case the vector function is normalized to the following form

$$\tilde{f}(x) = [\tilde{f}_1(x), \tilde{f}_2(x), \ldots, \tilde{f}_k(x)]^T \tag{11}$$

where $\tilde{f}_i(x) = \dfrac{f_i(x)}{f_i^o}$

Here, fio is generally the maximum value of ith objective function. A condition fio$\neq$0 is assumed and if it is not satisfied which rarely happens; another value of normalizing function must be chosen by the decision maker.

Game Theory: Game theory deals with decision situations in which two intelligent opponents with conflicting objectives are trying to outdo one another. It is a mathematical theory that deals with the general features of competitive situations like these in a formal, abstract way. It places particular emphasis on the decision-making processes of the adversaries. Typical examples include launching advertising campaigns for competing products and planning strategies for warring armies.

In a game conflict, two opponents, known as players, will each have a (finite or infinite) number of alternatives or strategies. Associated with each pair of strategies is a payoff that one player receives from the other. Such games are known as two-person zero-sum games because a gain by one player signifies an equal loss to the other. It suffices, then, to summarize the game in terms of the payoff to one player.

Because games are rooted in conflict of interest, the optimal solution selects one or more strategies for each player such that any change in the chosen strategies does not improve the payoff to either player. These solutions can be in the form of a single pure strategy or several strategies mixed according to specific probabilities (Frederick & Gerald, 2001).

Goal Programming: Goal programming was proposed by Charnes & Cooper (1961) for a linear model. It has been further developed by others (Ijiri, 1965; Charnes & Cooper, 1977). This method requires the decision maker (DM) to set goals for each objective that he wishes to attain. A preferred solution is then defined as the one, which minimizes the deviations from the set goals. Thus a simple GP formulation of the multiobjective optimization problem is given by

$$\text{Min}\left\{\sum_{j=1}^{k}(d_j^- +d_j^+)^p\right\}^{1/p} \quad , p\geq 1 \tag{12}$$

Subject to:

$$G_i(x) \leq 0, \ i=1,2,...,m$$

$$F_j(x)+d_j^- +d_j^+ = b_j \quad , j=1,2,...,k$$

$$d_j^-,d_j^+ \geq 0 \text{ and } d_j^- \cdot d_j^+ = 0 \quad \text{for all } j \tag{13}$$

where bj's are the goals set by the DM for the objectives, and are respectively the under-achievement and over-achievement of the jth goal. The value of p is based on the utility function of the DM. Other than p = 1 results in a nonlinear goal programming problem.

The most common form of GP requires that the DM, in addition to setting the goals for objectives, also be able to give an ordinal ranking of the objectives. This may result in a nonlinear goal-programming problem if objectives or constraints are nonlinear.

Goal Attainment Method, Global Criterion Method and Utility Function Method are also used to solve multiobjective optimization problems.

4. Fuzzy optimization

The available general model of a programming with fuzzy resources can be formulated as:

$$\min f(X) \tag{14}$$

$$\text{subject to}, \ i=1,2,\ldots,n \tag{15}$$

$$XL \leq X \leq XU \tag{16}$$

where the objective function and the ith in-equality constrained function are indicated as f (X) and $g_i(X)$, respectively. The fuzzy number ,$\forall i$ are in the fuzzy region of [b_i , b_i + p_i] with given fuzzy tolerance pi. Assume the fuzzy tolerance pi for each fuzzy constraint is known, then, , will be equivalent to (b_i + θ p_i) ,$\forall i$ where θ is in [0 , 1]. Several methods are described in the following section. All methods, except the first one (R.E. Bellman and L.A. Zadeh's approach), are derivatives of the level cuts method and generally using ordinary crisp optimization methods by converting problem into crisp optimization problem.

4.1 R.E. Bellman and L.A. Zadeh's approach

In Bellman and Zadeh (1970) approach, the problem in fuzzy environment can be stated as,

$$\text{Find X which minimizes } f(X) \tag{17}$$

$$\text{subject to } g_j(X) \in G_j \quad j=1,2,\ldots,n \tag{18}$$

where ordinary subset Gj denotes the allowable interval for the constraint function gj, Gj =[gj(l) , gj(u)] the bold face symbols indicate that the operations or variables contain fuzzy information. The constraint $g_j(X) \in G_j$ means that gj is a member of a fuzzy subset Gj in the sense of $\mu G_j(g_j) > 0$. The fuzzy feasible region is defined by considering all the constraints as

$$S = \bigcap_{j=1}^{m} G_j \tag{19}$$

And the membership degree of any design vector X to fuzzy feasible region S is given by

$$\mu_S(X) = \min_{j=1,2,\ldots,m} \left\{ \mu_{G_j}[g_j(X)] \right\} \tag{20}$$

i.e., the minimum degree of satisfaction of the design vector X to all of the constraints.

A design of vector X is considered feasible provided $\mu S(X) > 0$ and the differences in the membership degrees of two design vectors X1 and X2 imply nothing but variations in the minimum degrees of satisfaction of X1 and X2 to the constraints. Thus the optimum solution will be a fuzzy domain D in S with f(X). The fuzzy domain D is defined by

$$D \qquad {}_f(X) \qquad {}_{j \ 1,2,\ldots,m} \quad {}_{G_j}(g_j(X)) \tag{21}$$

that is

$$\mu_D(X) = \min\left\{\mu_f(X), \min_{j=1,2,\ldots,m} \mu_{Gj}[g_j X]\right\}$$
(22)

If the membership function of D is unimodal and has a unique maximum, then the maximum solution X^* is one for which the membership function is maximum:

$$\mu_D(X^*) = \max \mu_D(X), X \in D$$
(23)

4.2 Verdegay's approach: α-cuts method

Verdegay (1982) considered that if the membership function of the fuzzy constraints has the following form:

$$\mu_{g_i}(X) \begin{cases} 1 & \text{if } g_i(X) < b_i \\ 1 - \dfrac{g_i(X) - b_i}{p_i} & \text{if } b_i + p_i \leq g_i(X) \leq b_i \\ 0 & \text{if } g_i(X) > b_i + p_i \end{cases}$$
(24)

Simultaneously, the membership functions of $\mu g_i(X)$, $\forall I$, are continuous and monotonic functions, and trade-off between those fuzzy constraints are allowed; then problem is equivalent to the following formulation:

$$\text{Min } f(X)$$
(25)

$$\text{Subject to } X \varepsilon X\alpha$$
(26)

where $X\alpha = \{x \mid \mu g_i(X) \geq \alpha, \forall i X \geq 0\}$, for each $\alpha\varepsilon [0, 1]$. This is the fundamental concepts of α-level cuts method of fuzzy mathematical programming. The membership function indicates that if $g_i(X) \varepsilon(b_i, b_i + p_i)$; then the memberships functions are monotonically decreasing. That also can means, the more resource consumed, the less satisfaction the decision maker thinks. One can then obtain the following formulation:

$$\text{Min } f(X)$$
(27)

$$\text{subject to } g_i(X) \leq b_i + (1-\alpha) p_i, \forall i$$
(28)

where $XL \leq X \leq XU$ and $\alpha\varepsilon[0, 1]$. Thus, the problem is equivalent to a crisp parametric programming formulation while $\alpha = 1-\theta$. For each α, one will have an optimal solution; therefore, the solution with αgrade of membership function is fuzzy. This model was applied by Wang & Wang (1985) and Rao (1987a) in structural design problems.

4.3 Werner's approach: Max-α method

Werner's (1987) proposed the objective function should be fuzzy due to the fuzziness existing in fuzzy inequality constraints. For solving equations, one needs to define f_{max} and f_{min} as follows:

$$f_{max} = \text{Min } f(X), \text{ s.t. } g_i(X) \leq b_i \forall i \text{ , and } XL \leq X \leq XU$$
(29)

$$f_{min} = \text{Min } f(X), \text{ s.t } g_i(X) \leq b_i + p_i, \forall i, \text{ and } XL \leq X \leq XU \tag{30}$$

The membership function mf(X) of the objective function is stated as:

$$\mu_f(X) \begin{cases} 1 & \text{if } f(X) < f_{min} \\ 1 - \dfrac{f(X) - f_{min}}{f_{max} - f_{min}} & \text{if } f_{min} \leq f(X) \leq f_{max} \\ 0 & \text{if } f(X) > f_{max} \end{cases} \tag{31}$$

One can consequently apply the max-min operator to obtain the optimal decision. Then, equations can be solved by the strategy of max-α, where

$\alpha = \min[\mu f(X), \mu g_1(X), \mu g_2(X), \dots, \mu g_m(X)]$. That is:

$$\text{Max } \alpha$$

$$\text{Subject to } \alpha \leq \mu f(X) \tag{32}$$

$$\alpha \leq \mu g_i(X), \forall i$$

where $\alpha \, \varepsilon \, 0, 1]$ and $XL \leq X \leq XU$. This model is similar to the model proposed by Zimmermann (1978) and applied in structural design by Rao (1987b) and Rao et.al. (1992).

4.4 Xu's approach: Bound search method

Suppose there are a fuzzy goal function f and a fuzzy constraint C in a decision space X, which are characterized by their membership functions $\mu f(X)$ and $\mu C(X)$, respectively. The combined effect of those two can be represented by the intersection of the membership functions and the following formulation.

$$\begin{aligned} \mu_D(X) = \mu_{f \cap C}(X) &= \mu_f(X) \wedge \mu_C(X) \\ &= \min\{\mu_f(X), \mu_C(X)\} \end{aligned} \tag{33}$$

Then Bellman & Zadeh (1970) proposed that a maximum decision could be defined as:

$$\mu_D(X^M) = \max \mu_D(X) \tag{34}$$

If $\mu D(X)$ has a unique maximum at XM, then the maximizing decision is a uniquely defined crisp decision. From equations and following the procedure given, one can obtain the particular optimum level α^* corresponding to the optimum point XM such that:

$$\mu_D(X) = \max_{X \in C_{\alpha^*}} \mu_f(X) \tag{35}$$

where $C\alpha^*$ is the fuzzy constraint set C of α^*-level cut.

Xu (1989) used a goal membership function of f(X) as following:

$$\mu_f(X) = \frac{f_{min}}{f(X)} \tag{36}$$

where fmin has been defined as before. It is apparent that the upper and lower bound of this goal membership function is between 1 and fmin /fmax. As a result, the optimum α^* can be achieved through an iteration computation. This method has been called the 2nd phase of α-cuts method in his paper(Xu, 1989).

4.5 Single level cuts method

It is observed in Xu's approach where maximizing $\mu f(X)$ is similar to maximizing α in Werner's approach; therefore, it is predicted the final result of those two approaches have the similar tendency, even though the form of their membership function is not the same, in which Werner's approach uses the linear function and Xu's approach uses the nonlinear function.

For obtaining the unique solution of the original α-level cuts approach in nonlinear programming problem with fuzzy resources, another alternative single level-cut approach called the single level-cut approach of the second kind is proposed (Shih et.al., 2003). This approach contains both linear membership function and nonlinear membership function of objective function.

$$\mu_f(X) = \frac{f_{max} - f(X)}{f_{max} - f_{min}} = 1 - \frac{f(X) - f_{min}}{f_{max} - f_{min}} \tag{37}$$

The mathematical formulation of the fuzzy problem with unique α–cut level can be written in the following:

$$Find [X, \alpha]T$$

$$min\ f(X)$$

$$subject\ to\ f(X)-[f_{max}-\alpha(f_{max}-f_{min})]=0\ (for\ linear\ \alpha f(X))$$

$$f(X)-(f_{min}/\alpha)=0\ (for\ nonlinear\ \alpha f(X)) \tag{38}$$

$$g_i(X) \le b_i+(1-\alpha p_i),\ \forall i$$

$$\alpha \in [0,1]\ (for\ linear\ \alpha f(X))$$

$$\alpha \in [f_{min}/f_{max}]\ (for\ linear\ \alpha f(X))$$

where $XL \le X \le XU$ and f(X) can be nonlinear or linear membership functions.

There are also new approaches in literature, based on fuzzy set theory like Evidence Theory. Evidence theory is based on the Belief (Bel) and Plausibility (Pl) fuzzy measures. Fuzzy measures provide the foundation of fuzzy set theory.

5. Fuzzy design optimization applications

This section will classify the applications using previously mentioned methods. As mentioned earlier, optimization can be classified according to how many objectives problem have. Investigated literature studies are shown in Table 1 from objective perspective.

OBJECTIVES	
Single	Multi
(Jensen, 2001; Yeh & Hsu, 1990; Mohandas et.al., 1990; Maglaraset.al., 1997; Fang et.al., 1998; Hsu et.al., 1995; Tonona & Bernardini, 1998; Liu, 2006; Shih, 1997; Arakawa et.al., 1999; Sarma & Adeli, 2000b; Yang & Soh, 2000; Joghataie & Ghasemi, 2001; Sarma, 2001; Xiong, 2002; Shih et.al., 2003; Marler et.al., 2004; Shih & Lee, 2004; Xiong & Rao, 2005; Shih & Lee, 2006; Khorsand & Akbarzadeh, 2007)	(Rao, 1987b; Chen & Wang, 1989; Rao et.al., 1992; Yu & Xu, 1994; Shih & Lai, 1994; Forouraghi et.al., 1994; Shih & Wangsawidjaja, 1995; Shih & Chang, 1995; Shih & Wangsawidjaja, 1996; Cheng & Li, 1997; Shih, 1997; Shih et.al., 1997; Yoo, 2000; Sarma & Adeli, 2000a; Yoo & Hajela, 2001; Kiyotaet.al., 2001; Sarma, 2001; Xiong, 2002; Kiyotaet.al., 2003; Wang et.al., 2005; Kelesoglu & Ulker, 2005a; Rao & Xiong, 2005a; Rao & Xiong, 2005b; Kelesoglu & Ülker, 2005b; Kelesoglu, 2007)

Table 1. Investigated Literature

Shih et.al. (2003) developed and proposed three alternative α-level-cuts approaches: single-cut, double-cuts, and multiple-cuts, for solving nonlinear programming design problems of structuring engineering with fuzzy resources. The approaches have performed better than that of conventional α-level-cuts method.

Hsu et.al. (1995) considered the optimization process as a closed-loop control system. Traditional "controllers", the numerical optimization algorithms, are usually "crisply" designed for well defined mathematical models. However, when applied to engineering design optimization problems in which function evaluations can be expensive and imprecise, very often the crisp algorithms will become impractical or will not converge. They presented how the heuristics of this human supervision can be modeled into the optimization algorithms using fuzzy control concept.

Shih (1997) employed three fuzzy models to combine with an improved imposed-on penalty approach for attacking a nonlinear multiobjective in the mixed-discrete optimization problem. He presented a penalty method, including the forms of penalty function and the values of each parameter. The presented strategy is suggested as appropriate for solving a generalized mixed-discrete optimization problem.

Arakawa et.al. (1999) showed the effectiveness of the use of fuzzy members as design variables, by comparing with the other robust design methods. They proposed a way to raise certainties in estimating robustness by using approximation concepts in operation of fuzzy function.

Fang et.al. (1998) considered an approach to the optimum design of structures, in which uncertainties with a fuzzy nature in the magnitude of the loads. The optimization process under fuzzy loads is transformed into a fuzzy optimization problem based on the notion of Werners' maximizing set by defining membership functions of the objective function and constraints. An example of a ten-bar truss is used to illustrate the present optimization process. The results are compared with those yielded by other optimization methods.

Mohandas et.al. (1990) has combined Zadeh's approach in Eq. (20) with goal programming. They implemented this approach to single objective optimization problems. As example problems, optimization of four bar and ten bar truss are selected. No comparison is made in this work.

Yang and Soh (2000) proposed a fuzzy logic integrated genetic programming (GP) based methodology to increase the performance of the GP based approach for structural optimization and design. Fuzzy set theory is employed to deal with the imprecise and vague information, especially the design constraints, during the structural design process.

Joghataie and Ghasemi (2001) implemented fuzzy membership functions in the multistage optimization technique to improve its performance for the minimum weight design of truss structures of fixed topology. It has been found that this technique has significantly improved the convergence speed at the expense of increasing the minimum weight by a negligible amount.

Shih et.al. (2004) presented new method (Two single level cut approach). Also, new method is implemented on three bar, ten bar and 25 bar truss optimization problems and objective function values are compared with Verdegay's approach in section IV.2, Werner's approach in section IV.3 and Xu's approach in section IV.4.

Shih and Lee (2006) presented the modified double-cuts approach for large-scale fuzzy optimization, typically in 25-bar and 72-bar truss design problems. The proposed approach is better than the single-cut approach and easy programming for use to instead of multiple-cuts approach.

Maglaras et.al. (1997) compared probabilistic and fuzzy set based approaches in designing a damped truss structure.

Sarma (2001) developed a fuzzy discrete multicriteria cost optimization model by considering three criteria 1) minimum cost 2) minimum weight and 3) minimum number of section types. In the design, the uncertainty of fuzziness of the AISC code based design constraints is considered.

Sarma and Adeli (2000a, 2000b) presented a fuzzy augmented Lagrangian GA for optimization of steel structures subjected to the constraints of the AISC allowable stress design specifications taking into account the fuzziness in the constraints. The algorithm is applied to two space axial-load structures including a large 37-story structure with 1310 members.

Rao and Xiong (2005) presented a new method in which the fuzzy lambda-formulation and game theory techniques are combined with a mixed-discrete hybrid genetic algorithm for solving mixed-discrete fuzzy multiobjective programming problems. They dealt with three example problems: the optimal designs of a two-bar truss, a conical convective spine and a twenty-five bar truss.

Wang et.al. (2005) studied the principle of solving multiobjective optimization problems with fuzzy sets theory. Membership functions based on functional-link net have been used in multiobjective optimization.

Yoo and Hajela (2001) have dealt with a genetic algorithm based optimization procedure for solving multicriterion design problems where the objective or constraint functions may not be crisply defined.

Forouraghi et.al. (1994) introduced a new methodology in which multiobjective optimization is formulated as unsupervised learning through induction of multivariate regression trees. In particular, they showed that learning of Pareto-optimal solutions can be eficiently accomplished by using a number of fuzzy tree-partitioning criteria. The widely used problem of design of a three-bar truss is presented.

Shih et.al. (1997) introduced a design method using fuzzy logic to find the best stochastic design by maximizing Hasofer-Lind's (H-L's) reliability and simultaneously optimizing design goals. The objective weighting strategy in multiobjective fuzzy formulation is adopted to represent the importance among the design goals.

Rao (1987b) has used Werner's approach in section IV.3. This approach is presented to solve multiobjective optimization problems. Sample problems are three bar and 25 bar truss optimization problems. No comparison is made in this work.

Shih & Chang (1995) has combined Werner's approach in section IV.3 with Global Criterion method and implemented on multiobjective optimization problems. As sample cases, three bar truss and 11 bar truss are solved and results (objective function values) are compared.

Chen and Wang (1989) proposed a general fuzzy programming with wide generality in order to consider the overall fuzzy factors and fuzzy information in optimum design of engineering structures.

Shih & Lai (1994) has used two weighting strategies to get Pareto optimum values: objective weighting and membership weighting strategies. Three bar truss optimization problem is selected as sample multiobjective optimization problem. Objective function values are presented as comparison criteria.

Rao et.al. (1992) have used two methods: Verdegay's approach in section IV.2 and Werner's approach in section IV.3 for multiobjective optimization problems. As sample cases, optimization of three bar and 25 bar truss systems are selected. Objective function values are used to compare methods.

Kiyota et.al. (2001, 2003) described a fuzzy satisficing method for multiobjective optimization problems using Genetic Algorithm (GA). A multiobjective design problem with constraints is expressed as a satisficing problem of constraints by introducing an aspiration level for each objective.

Kelesoglu & Ulker (2005a) optimized space truss systems by using fuzzy sets. The algorithm of multi-objective fuzzy optimization was formed using the macros of Ms-Excel.

Cheng and Li (1997) presented a constrained multiobjective optimization methodology by integrating Pareto Genetic algorithm with fuzzy penalty function method. A 72-bar space truss with two criteria and a 4-bar truss with three criteria were investigated.

Kelesoglu & Ulker (2005b) presented a general algorithm for nonlinear space truss system optimization with fuzzy constraints and fuzzy parameters. The analysis of the space truss system is performed with the ANSYS program.

Kelesoglu (2007) proposed a genetic algorithm to solve fuzzy multiobjective optimization of space truss. This method enables a flexible method for optimal system design by applying fuzzy objectives and fuzzy constraints. An algorithm was developed by using MATLAB programming. The algorithm is illustrated on 56-bar space truss system design problem.

At following pages, these studies will be classified according to used methods and application area.

5.1 Single objective applications

Table 2 shows the objectives in literature. It is seen that minimizing weight is the most common objective for single objective optimization studies. Minimizing failure possibility and natural frequency are also used even though found rarely.

SINGLE OBJECTIVE	
Minimize Weight	(Yeh & Hsu, 1990; Mohandas et.al., 1990; Hsu et.al., 1995; Shih, 1997; Fang et.al., 1998; Tonona & Bernardini, 1998; Arakawa et.al., 1999; Sarma & Adeli, 2000b; Yang & Soh, 2000; Joghataie & Ghasemi, 2001; Jensen, 2001; Sarma, 2001; Xiong, 2002; Shih et.al., 2003; Marler et.al., 2004; Shih & Lee, 2004; Xiong & Rao, 2005; Shih & Lee, 2006; Liu, 2006)
Minimize the system failure possibility	(Maglaraset.al., 1997)
Maximize the fundamental natural frequency	(Khorsand & Akbarzadeh, 2007)

Table 2. Objectives in single objective problems

Used methods differ at each study. But, generally there are two different applications: Direct methods and Hybrid Methods. Also, hybrid methods differ according to at where fuzzy logic is applied. Sometimes, fuzzy logic assists to another optimization method and sometimes vises versa. Table 3 shows the studies in literature according to used method type. Table 4 shows the hybrid methods.

Direct	Hybrid
(Maglaraset.al., 1997; Fang et.al., 1998; Arakawa et.al., 1999; Jensen, 2001; Shih et.al., 2003; Shih & Lee, 2004; Marler et.al., 2004; Shih & Lee, 2006)	(Yeh & Hsu, 1990; Mohandas et.al., 1990; Hsu et.al., 1995; Shih, 1997; Tonona & Bernardini, 1998; Sarma & Adeli, 2000b; Yang & Soh, 2000; Joghataie & Ghasemi, 2001; Sarma, 2001; Xiong, 2002; Xiong & Rao, 2005; Liu, 2006; Khorsand & Akbarzadeh, 2007)

Table 3. Used methods in single objective problems

HYBRID TECHNIQUES	
Unconstrained	(Yeh & Hsu, 1990)
Penalty Function	(Joghataie & Ghasemi, 2001; Shih, 1997)
PD Controller	(Liu, 2006)
Goal Programming	(Mohandas et.al., 1990)
Evidence Theory	(Tonona & Bernardini, 1998)
Linear Programming	(Hsu et.al., 1995)
GA	(Sarma & Adeli, 2000b; Yang & Soh, 2000; Sarma, 2001; Xiong, 2002)
ANN+GA	(Khorsand & Akbarzadeh, 2007)
Dynamic Programming	(Xiong & Rao, 2005)

Table 4. Hybrid methods in single objective problems

Mentioned methods are applied to different truss structures. These structures are listed in Table 5.

	PLANAR (2D)	SPACE(3D)
2 bar:	(Khorsand & Akbarzadeh, 2007)	
3 bar:	(Yeh & Hsu, 1990; Hsu et.al., 1995; Shih, 1997; Arakawa et.al., 1999; Shih et.al., 2003; Shih & Lee, 2004; Liu, 2006)	
4 bar:	(Mohandas et.al., 1990; Fang et.al., 1998; Xiong, 2002; Xiong & Rao, 2005)	
10 bar:	(Mohandas et.al., 1990; Tonona & Bernardini, 1998; Yang & Soh, 2000; Joghataie & Ghasemi, 2001; Shih & Lee, 2004)	
25 bar:		(Jensen, 2001; Shih & Lee, 2004; Marler et.al., 2004; Shih & Lee, 2006)
30 bar:		(Maglaraset.al., 1997)
46 bar:	(Joghataie & Ghasemi, 2001)	
72 bar:		(Sarma & Adeli, 2000b; Sarma, 2001; Shih & Lee, 2006)
135 bar:	(Joghataie & Ghasemi, 2001)	
1310 bar:		(Sarma & Adeli, 2000b; Sarma, 2001)

Table 5. Truss structures in single objective problems

5.2 Multi objectives applications

Table 6 shows the objectives in literature. It is seen that minimizing weight is still the most common objective for single objective optimization studies. Minimizing deflection and natural frequency are also used.

MULTIOBJECTIVE	
Minimize weight	(Rao, 1987b; Chen & Wang, 1989; Rao et.al., 1992; Yu & Xu, 1994; Shih & Lai, 1994; Forouraghi et.al., 1994; Shih & Chang, 1995; Shih & Wangsawidjaja, 1995; Shih & Wangsawidjaja, 1996; Cheng & Li, 1997; Shih et.al., 1997; Shih, 1997; Yoo, 2000; Sarma & Adeli, 2000a; Sarma, 2001; Kiyotaet.al., 2001; Yoo & Hajela, 2001; Xiong, 2002; Kiyotaet.al., 2003; Wang et.al., 2005; Kelesoglu & Ulker, 2005a; Rao & Xiong, 2005a; Rao & Xiong, 2005b; Kelesoglu & Ülker, 2005b; Kelesoglu, 2007)
Minimize deflection	(Rao, 1987b; Chen & Wang, 1989; Rao et.al., 1992; Forouraghi et.al., 1994; Yu & Xu, 1994; Shih & Lai, 1994; Shih & Chang, 1995; Shih & Wangsawidjaja, 1995; Shih & Wangsawidjaja, 1996; Shih, 1997; Yoo, 2000; Kiyotaet.al., 2001; Yoo & Hajela, 2001; Xiong, 2002; Kiyotaet.al., 2003; Kelesoglu & Ulker, 2005a; Wang et.al., 2005; Rao & Xiong, 2005a; Rao & Xiong, 2005b; Kelesoglu & Ülker, 2005b; Kelesoglu, 2007)
Minimize number of cross-sections	(Sarma & Adeli, 2000a; Sarma, 2001)
Minimize cost	(Sarma & Adeli, 2000a; Sarma, 2001)
Minimize Hasofer's and Lind's reliability	(Shih et.al., 1997)
Minimize strain energy	(Cheng & Li, 1997)
Minimize control effort	(Cheng & Li, 1997)
Maximize the fundamental natural frequency	(Rao, 1987b; Rao et.al., 1992; Xiong, 2002; Rao & Xiong, 2005a; Rao & Xiong, 2005b)

Table 6. Objectives in multi objective problems

Table 7 shows the studies in literature according to used method type. Table 8 shows the hybrid methods.

Direct	Hybrid
(Rao, 1987b; Chen & Wang, 1989; Rao et.al., 1992; Yu & Xu, 1994; Forouraghi et.al., 1994; Shih & Chang, 1995; Shih & Wangsawidjaja, 1995; Shih & Wangsawidjaja, 1996; Shih et.al., 1997; Yoo, 2000; Kelesoglu & Ulker, 2005a; Kelesoglu & Ülker, 2005b)	(Shih & Lai, 1994; Cheng & Li, 1997; Sarma & Adeli, 2000a; Sarma, 2001; Kiyotaet.al., 2001; Yoo & Hajela, 2001; Xiong, 2002; Kiyotaet.al., 2003; Wang et.al., 2005; Rao & Xiong, 2005a; Rao & Xiong, 2005b; Kelesoglu, 2007)

Table 7. Used methods in multiobjective problems

HYBRID TECHNIQUES	
ANN	(Wang et.al., 2005)
Weighting	(Shih & Lai, 1994)
Game Theory	(Rao & Xiong, 2005a; Rao & Xiong, 2005b)
GA	(Cheng & Li, 1997; Sarma & Adeli, 2000a; Sarma, 2001; Kiyotaet.al., 2001; Yoo & Hajela, 2001; Xiong, 2002; Kiyotaet.al., 2003; Kelesoglu, 2007)

Table 8. Hybrid methods in multi objective problems

Mentioned methods are applied to different truss structures. These structures are shown in Table 9.

	PLANAR (2D)	SPACE (3D)
2 bar:	(Xiong, 2002; Rao & Xiong, 2005a; Rao & Xiong, 2005b)	
3 bar:	(Rao, 1987b; Chen & Wang, 1989; Rao et.al., 1992; Yu & Xu, 1994; Shih & Lai, 1994; Forouraghi et.al., 1994; Shih & Chang, 1995; Shih & Wangsawidjaja, 1995; Shih & Wangsawidjaja, 1996; Shih et.al., 1997; Yoo, 2000; Yoo & Hajela, 2001; Wang et.al., 2005)	
4 bar:	(Kiyota et.al., 2001; Kiyota et.al., 2003)	(Cheng & Li, 1997; Kelesoglu & Ülker, 2005b)
9 bar:		(Kelesoglu & Ulker, 2005a)
10 bar:	(Shih, 1997)	
11 bar:	(Yoo & Hajela, 2001)	
25 bar:		(Rao, 1987b; Rao et.al., 1992; Xiong, 2002; Rao & Xiong, 2005a; Rao & Xiong, 2005b; Kelesoglu & Ülker, 2005b)
56 bar:		(Kelesoglu, 2007)
72 bar:		(Cheng & Li, 1997)
120 bar:		(Kelesoglu & Ulker, 2005a)
244 bar:		(Kelesoglu & Ulker, 2005a)
1310 bar:		(Sarma & Adeli, 2000a; Sarma, 2001)

Table 9. Truss structures in multi objective problems

6. Conclusions

Design of structural systems has always been one of the most important topics to study. But, over the years, optimization of structural system has gained popularity. Today, there are a few conferences and journals concerning only the optimization of structural systems. This study aimed to summarize the studies on using fuzzy logic in optimization of structural systems. Following results has been found as remarkable to notice:

*Fuzzy logic is applied to different variety of structural design problems (single and multiobjective problems, simple and complex problems etc.)

*Most important objectives in designing optimal structures are minimizing weight and deflection.

*Both direct and hybrid methods are used. Especially using GA together with fuzzy logic has given better performance. It is recommended to the researchers to use also other evolutionary algorithms (Simulated Annealing, Particle Swarm Optimization etc.)

*Mostly used case examples are 3 bar and 25 bar truss systems.

7. References

Arakawa, M.; Yamakawa, H.; Ishikawa, H. (1999). Robust Design Using Fuzzy Numbers with Intermediate Variables. *Proceedings of 3rd ISSMO/UBCAD/UB/AIAA World Congress on Structural and Multidisciplinary Optimization*, NewYork, USA.

Bellman, R.E.; Zadeh, L.A. (1970). Decision-making in a Fuzzy Environment. *Management Science*, Vol. 17, pp. B141-B164.

Black, M. (1937). Vagueness: An Exercise in Logical Analysis. *Philosophy of Science*, Vol. 4, pp. 427-455.

Borkowski, L. (1970). *Selected works of J. Lukasiewicz*. North Holland, London.

Charnes, A.; Cooper, W.W. (1961). *Management Models and Industrial Applications of Linear Programming*, John Wiley & Sons, New York.

Charnes, A.; Cooper, W.W. (1977) Goal programming and multiple objective optimizations. *European Journal of Operational Research*, Vol. 1, pp. 39-54.

Chen, S.-X.; Wang, G.-Y. (1989). Theory and solution of general fuzzy optimization for structures. *Acta Mechanica Solida Sinica*, Vol. 2, No 3, pp. 271-283.

Cheng, F.Y.; Li, D. (1997). Multiobjective optimization design with pareto genetic algorithm. *Journal of Structural Engineering*, Vol.123, No 9, pp. 1252-1261.

Dantzig, G.B. (1963). *Linear programming and extensions*, Princeton University Press.

Holland, J.H. (1995). *Hidden order: how adaptation builds complexity*. Addison-Wesley, Reading, Mass.

Eschenawer, H.; Koski, J.; Osyczka, A. (1990). *Multicriteria Design Optimization-Procedures and Applications*, Springer, Berlin.

Fang, J.; Smith, S.M.; Elishakoff, I. (1998). Combination of Anti-Optimization and Fuzzy-Set-Based Analyses for Structural Optimization under Uncertainty. *Mathematical Problems in Engineering*, Vol. 4, pp. 187-200.

Forouraghi, B.; Schmerr, L.W.; Prabhu, G.M. (1994). Fuzzy multiobjective optimization with multivariate regression trees. *Proceedings of IEEE World Congress on Computational Intelligence*, Orlando, USA.

Grandhi, R.V.; Bharatram, G. (1993). Multiobjective Optimization of Large-Scale Structures. *AIAA Journal*, Vol. 31, pp. 1329-1337.

Hartshorne, C.; Weiss,P. (1935). *Collected Papers of Charles Sanders Peirce*. Harvard University Press, Cambridge, MA.

Hillier, F.S.; Lieberman, G.J. (2001). *Introduction to Operations Research* (7th Ed), McGraw-Hill.

Hsu, Y.L.; Lin, Y.F.; Sun, T.L. (1995). Engineering Design Optimization as a Fuzzy control process. *Proceedings of International Joint Conference of the Fourth IEEE International Conference on Fuzzy Systems and The Second International Fuzzy Engineering Symposium*,Yokohoma, Japan.

Hwang, C.L.; Masud, A.S.M. (1979). *Multiple Objective Decision Making Methods and Applications*, Springer, Berlin.

Ijiri, Y. (1965). *Management Goals and Accounting for Control*, North-Holland.

Jensen, H.A. (2001). Structural Optimal Design of Systems with Imprecise Properties: a Possibilistic Approach. *Advances in Engineering Software*, Vol. 32, pp. 937-948.

Joghataie, A.; Ghasemi, M. (2001). Fuzzy Multistage Optimization of Large-Scale Trusses. *Journal of Structural Engineering*, Vol. 127, pp. 1338–1347.

Kelesoglu, O.; Ulker, M. (2005a). Fuzzy optimization of geometrical nonlinear space truss design. *Turkish Journal of Engineering & Environmental Sciences*, Vol. 29, pp. 321-329.

Kelesoglu, O.; Ulker, M. (2005b). Multi-objective fuzzy optimization of space trusses by MS-Excel. *Advances in Engineering Software*, Vol. 36, pp. 549-553.

Kelesoglu, O. (2007). Fuzzy multiobjective optimization of truss-structures using genetic algorithm. *Advances in Engineering Software*, Vol. 38, pp. 717-721.

Khorsand, A.R.; Akbarzadeh, M.R. (2007). Multi-objective meta level soft computing-based evolutionary structural design. *Journal of the Franklin Institute*, Vol. 9, No 5, pp. 595-612.

Kiyota, T.; Tsuji, Y. Y.; Kondo, E. (2001). An interactive fuzzy satisficing approach using genetic algorithm for multi objective problems. *Proceedings of Joint 9th IFSA World Congress and 20th NAFIPS International Conference*, Vancouver, Canada.

Kiyota, T.; Tsuji, Y.; Kondo, E. (2003). Unsatisfying Functions and Multiobjective Fuzzy Satisficing Design Using Genetic Algorithms. *IEEE Transactions on Systems, Man and Cybernetics – PART B: Cybernetics*, Vol. 33, No 6, pp. 889-897.

Liu, T.C. (2006). *Developing a fuzzy proportional-derivative controller optimization engine for engineering design optimization problems*. PhD Thesis, Yuan-Ze University.

Maglaras, G.G.; Nikolaidis, E.; Haftka, R.T.; Cudney, H.H. (1997). Analytical-experimental comparison of probabilistic methods and fuzzy set based methods for designing under uncertainity. *Structural Optimization*, Vol. 13, pp. 69-80.

Marler, R.T.; Yang, J.; Rao, S.S. (2004). A Fuzzy Approach for Determining a Feasible Point in a Constrained Problem. *Proceedings of ASME/JSME Pressure Vessels and Piping Division Conference*, San Diego, USA.

McNeill, D.; Freiberger, P. (1993). *Fuzzy Logic/the Discovery of a Revolutionary Computer Technology and How It Is Changing Our World*, Simon & Schuster, New York.

Mohandas, S.U.; Phelps, T.A.; Ragsdell, K.M. (1990) Structural optimization using a fuzzy goal programming approach. *Computers & Structures*, Vol. 37, pp. 1-8.

Radford, A.D.; Gero, J.S.; Roseman, M.A.; Balachandran, M. (1985). Pareto Optimization as a Computer Aided Design Tool. In: *Optimization in Computer-Aided Design*, J.S. Gero, Springer, Berlin.

Rao, S.S. (1984). *Optimization, Theory and Applications*, John Wiley & Sons.

Rao, S.S. (1987a). Description and Optimum Design of Fuzzy Mechanical Systems. *ASME Journal of Mechanisms, Transmissions, and Automation in Design*, Vol. 109, pp. 126-132.

Rao, S.S. (1987b). Multiobjective Optimization of Fuzzy Structural Systems. *International Journal for Numerical Methods in Engineering*, Vol. 24, pp. 1157-1171.

Rao, S.S.; Sundararaju, K.; Prakash, B.G.; Balakrishna, C. (1992). Multiobjective Fuzzy Optimization Techniques for Engineering Design. *Computers & Structures*, Vol. 42, pp. 37-44.

Rao, S.S.; Xiong, Y. (2005a). Mixed-discrete fuzzy multiobjective programming for engineering optimization using hybrid genetic algorithm. *AIAA Journal*, Vol. 43, No 7, pp. 1580-1590.

Rao, S.S.; Xiong, Y. (2005b). Mixed-discrete fuzzy multiobjective optimization of structures using a hybrid genetic algorithm. *Proceedings of 6th World Congress on Structural and Multidisciplinary Optimization*, Rio de Janeiro, Brazil.

Russell, B. (1923). Vagueness. *Australian Journal of Psychology and Philosophy*, Vol. 1, pp. 84-92.

Sarma, K.C.; Adeli, H. (2000a). Fuzzy Discrete Multicriteria Cost Optimization of Steel Structures. *Journal of Structural Engineering*, Vol.126, pp. 1339–1347.

Sarma, K.C.; Adeli, H. (2000b). Fuzzy Genetic Algorithm for Optimization of Steel Structures. *Journal of Structural Engineering*, Vol. 126, pp. 596–604.

Sarma, K.C. (2001). *Fuzzy discrete multicrteria cost optimization of steel structures using genetic algorithm*. PhD Thesis, Ohio State Univeristy.

Shih, C.J.; Lai T.K. (1994). Fuzzy weighting optimization with several objective functions in structural design. *Computers & Structures*, Vol. 52, pp. 917-924

Shih, C.J.; Wangsawidjaja, R.A.S. (1995). Multiobjective fuzzy optimization with random variables in a mix of fuzzy and probabilistic environment. *Proceedings of International Joint Conference of the Fourth IEEE International Conference on Fuzzy Systems and The Second International Fuzzy Engineering Symposium*, Yokohoma, Japan.

Shih, C.J.; Chang, C.J. (1995). Pareto Optimization of Alternative Global Criterion Method for Fuzzy Structural Design. *Computers & Structures*, Vol. 54, pp. 455–460.

Shih, C.J.; Wangsawidjaja, R.A.S. (1996). Mixed fuzzy-probabilistic programming approach for multiobjective engineering optimization with random variables. *Computers & Structures*, Vol. 59, pp. 283-290.

Shih, C. J. (1997). Fuzzy and Improved Penalty Approaches for Multiobjective Mixed-Discrete Optimization in Structural Systems. *Computers & Structures*, Vol. 63, pp. 559-565.

Shih, C.J.; Wang, C.S.; Lin, Y.Y. (1997). Hasofer-Lind's Reliability Based Optimization for Multiobjective Fuzzy and Stochastic Design Problem. 6nd IEEE International Conference on Fuzzy Systems, (1997) 1191- 1196.

Shih, C.J.; Chi, C.C.; Hsiao, J.H. (2003). Alternative α-level-cuts Methods for Optimum Structural Design with Fuzzy Resources. *Computers & Structures*, Vol. 81, pp. 2579–2587.

Shih, C.J.; Lee, H. W. (2004). Level-Cut Approaches of First and Second Kind for Unique Solution Design in Fuzzy Engineering Optimization Problems. *Tamkang Journal of Science and Engineering - An International Journal*, Vol. 7, pp. 189-198.

Shih, C.J.; Lee, H.W. (2006). Modified double-cuts approach in 25-bar and 72-bar fuzzy truss optimization. *Computers and Structures*, Vol. 84, pp. 2100-2104.

Stadler, W. (1984). Multicriteria Optimization in Mechanics (A Survey). *Applied Mechanics Reviews*, Vol. 37, pp. 277-286.

Tonona, F.; Bernardini, A. (1998). A Random Set Approach to the Optimization of Uncertain Structures. *Computers & Structures*, Vol. 68, pp. 583-600.

Verdegay, J. L. (1982). Fuzzy Mathematical Programming. In: *Approximate reasoning in decision analysis*, M.M. Gupta, E. Sanchez, pp. (231-236), North-Holland Pub. Co.

Wang, G.Y.; Wang W.Q. (1985). Fuzzy Optimum Design of Structures. *Engineering Optimization*, Vol. 8, pp. 291-300.

Wang, P.; Huang, H.; Zuo, M.J.; Wu, W.; Liu, C. (2005). Functional-link net based multiobjective fuzzy optimization. In: *Advances in Neural Networks – Lecture Notes in Computer Science*, J. Wang et.al., pp. (800-804), Springer, Berlin .

Werner, B. (1987). Interactive Fuzzy Programming Systems. *Fuzzy Sets and Systems*, Vol. 23, pp. 131-147.

Xiong, Y. (2002). *Mixed Discrete Fuzzy Nonlinear Programming for Engineering Design Optimization*. Ph.D. thesis, University of Miami.

Xiong, Y.; Rao, S.S. (2005). A fuzzy dynamic approach for the mixed-discrete design optimization of mechanical systems. *ASME Journal of Mechanical Design*, Vol. 127, pp. 1088-1099.

Xu, C. (1989). Fuzzy Optimization of Structures by the Two-phase Method. *Computers & Structures*, Vol. 31, pp. 575-580.

Yang, Y.; Soh, C.K. (2000). Fuzzy logic integrated genetic programming for optimization and design. *Journal of Computing in Civil Engineering*, Vol. 14, pp. 249-254.

Yeh, Y.C.; Hsu, D.S. (1990). Structural optimization with fuzzy parameters. *Computers & Structures*, Vol. 37, pp. 917-924.

Yoo, J.S. (2000). *Adaptation of soft computing methods in multidisciplinary and structural optimization*. PhD Thesis, Rensselaer Polytechnic Institute.

Yoo, J.; Hajela, P. (2001). Fuzzy Multicriterion design using immune network simulation. *Structural and Multidisciplinary Optimization*, Vol. 22, pp. 188-197.

Yu, M.; Xu, C. (1994) Multi-objective Fuzzy Optimization of Structures Based on Generalized Fuzzy Decision-Making. *Computer & Structures*, Vol. 53, pp. 411-417.

Zadeh, L.A. (1965). Fuzzy Sets. *Information and Control*, Vol. 8, pp. 338-352.

Zimmermann, H.J. (1978). Fuzzy Programming and Linear Programming with Several Objective Functions. *Fuzzy Sets and Systems*, Vol. 1, pp. 45-55.

Permissions

The contributors of this book come from diverse backgrounds, making this book a truly international effort. This book will bring forth new frontiers with its revolutionizing research information and detailed analysis of the nascent developments around the world.

We would like to thank Elmer P. Dadios, for lending his expertise to make the book truly unique. He has played a crucial role in the development of this book. Without his invaluable contribution this book wouldn't have been possible. He has made vital efforts to compile up to date information on the varied aspects of this subject to make this book a valuable addition to the collection of many professionals and students.

This book was conceptualized with the vision of imparting up-to-date information and advanced data in this field. To ensure the same, a matchless editorial board was set up. Every individual on the board went through rigorous rounds of assessment to prove their worth. After which they invested a large part of their time researching and compiling the most relevant data for our readers. Conferences and sessions were held from time to time between the editorial board and the contributing authors to present the data in the most comprehensible form. The editorial team has worked tirelessly to provide valuable and valid information to help people across the globe.

Every chapter published in this book has been scrutinized by our experts. Their significance has been extensively debated. The topics covered herein carry significant findings which will fuel the growth of the discipline. They may even be implemented as practical applications or may be referred to as a beginning point for another development. Chapters in this book were first published by InTech; hereby published with permission under the Creative Commons Attribution License or equivalent.

The editorial board has been involved in producing this book since its inception. They have spent rigorous hours researching and exploring the diverse topics which have resulted in the successful publishing of this book. They have passed on their knowledge of decades through this book. To expedite this challenging task, the publisher supported the team at every step. A small team of assistant editors was also appointed to further simplify the editing procedure and attain best results for the readers.

Our editorial team has been hand-picked from every corner of the world. Their multi-ethnicity adds dynamic inputs to the discussions which result in innovative outcomes. These outcomes are then further discussed with the researchers and contributors who give their valuable feedback and opinion regarding the same. The feedback is then collaborated with the researches and they are edited in a comprehensive manner to aid the understanding of the subject.

Apart from the editorial board, the designing team has also invested a significant amount of their time in understanding the subject and creating the most relevant covers. They scrutinized every image to scout for the most suitable representation of the subject and create an appropriate cover for the book.

The publishing team has been involved in this book since its early stages. They were actively engaged in every process, be it collecting the data, connecting with the contributors or procuring relevant information. The team has been an ardent support to the editorial, designing and production team. Their endless efforts to recruit the best for this project, has resulted in the accomplishment of this book. They are a veteran in the field of academics and their pool of knowledge is as vast as their experience in printing. Their expertise and guidance has proved useful at every step. Their uncompromising quality standards have made this book an exceptional effort. Their encouragement from time to time has been an inspiration for everyone.

The publisher and the editorial board hope that this book will prove to be a valuable piece of knowledge for researchers, students, practitioners and scholars across the globe.

List of Contributors

Bin Zi
School of Mechanical and Electrical Engineering, China University of Mining and Technology, Xuzhou, Jiangsu, China
The State Key Laboratory of Fluid Power and Mechatronic Systems, Zhejiang University, Hangzhou, Zhejiang China

José Antonio Cortajarena, Julián De Marcos, Fco. Javier Vicandi, Pedro Alvarez and Patxi Alkorta
University of the Basque Country (EUITI Eibar), Spain

Elmer P. Dadios, Jazper Jan C. Biliran, Ron-Ron G. Garcia, D. Johnson and Adranne Rachel B. Valencia
De La Salle University, Manila, Philippines

Tang Sai Hong, Danial Nakhaeinia and Babak Karasfi
Universiti Putra Malaysia, Malaysia

Salmiah Ahmad
International Islamic University Malaysia, Malaysia

N. H. Siddique
Ulster University, United Kingdom

M. O. Tokhi
The University of Sheffield, United Kingdom

Abdel Ghani Aissaoui
Faculty of Science & Technology, University of Bechar, Bechar, Algeria

Ahmed Tahour
Faculty of Science & Technology, University of Mascara, Mascara, Algeria

Harold R. Chamorro and Gustavo A. Ramos
Universidad de los Andes, Bogotá, Colombia

Hamid Reza Pourshaghaghi, Juan Diego Echeverri Escobar and José Pineda de Gyvez
Electronic Systems Group, Eindhoven University of Technology, Eindhoven, The Netherlands

Rosa Maria Alsina-Pages, Claudia Mateo Segura, Joan Claudi Socoró Carrié and Pau Bergada
La Salle - Universitat Ramon Llull, Spain

Jong Shik Kim, Han Me Kim and Seong Ik Han
School of Mechanical Engineering, Pusan National University, Republic of Korea

Seiyed Hamid Zareh, Atabak Sarrafan, Meisam Abbasi and Amir Ali Akbar Khayyat
Sharif University of Technology, School of Science and Engineering, Iran

Orhan Ekren
Southern Illinois University, Mechanical Engineering Department, Edwardsville, USA

Savas Sahin
Ege University, Ege Technical College, Department of Control and Automation, Bornova, Izmir, Turkey

Yalcin Isler
Zonguldak Karaelmas University, Department of Electrical and Electronics Engineering, Incivez, Zonguldak, Turkey

Vanilson G. Pereira, Roberto C.L. De Oliveira and Fábio M. Soares
Federal University of Pará, Brazil

Carlos Pinheiro, Ulisses Camatta and Angelo Rezek
Federal University of Itajuba, Brazil

Ion Iancu
University of Craiova, Romania

Trung-Kien Dao
MICA Center, HUST - CNRS/UMI 2954 - Grenoble INP, Hanoi, Vietnam

Chih-Keng Chen
Dayeh University, Changhua, Taiwan

Logah Perumal
Multimedia University, Bukit Beruang, Malacca, Malaysia

Farrukh Hafiz Nagi
Universiti Tenaga Nasional, Kajang, Selangor, Malaysia

Luiz H. S. Torres and Leizer Schnitman
Centro de Capacitação Tecnológica em Automação Industrial (CTAI), Universidade Federal da Bahia, Rua Aristides Novis, no 02, Escola Politécnica, 2oandar, Salvador, Bahia, Brazil

Aykut Kentli
Marmara University Engineering Faculty, Mechanical Engineering Department, Turkey